Afrika
Dispatches from
the Outside Edge

Kingsley Holgate

An epic journey to save and improve lives

MASHOZI
WIFE, FRIEND AND
FELLOW ADVENTURER

Mozambique – muddy routes

Afrika

Dispatches from the Outside Edge

Kingsley Holgate

An epic journey to save and improve lives

S STRUIK TRAVEL & HERITAGE

Mediterranean Sea
Red Sea
ATLANTIC OCEAN
INDIAN OCEAN
Gulf of Guinea
Mozambique Channel
Day 1
Day 8
Day 40
Day 65
Day 67
Day 73
Day 105
Day 110
Day 121
Day 126
Day 127
Day 145
Day 152
Day 161
Day 164
Day 189
Day 193
Day 194
Day 209
Day 224
Day 225
Day 289
Day 301
Day 307
Day 314
Day 341
Day 349
Day 355
Day 364
Day 377
Day 388
Day 425
MOROCCO
Atlas Mountains
J. Toubkal 4164m
Tangier
Rabat
Casablanca
Algiers
Constantine
Tunis
TUNISIA
Tripoli
Banghazi
Alexandria
Cairo
El Gîza
Luxor
Aswan
Lake Nasser
Nile
Islas Canarias (Spain)
El Aai'n
WESTERN SAHARA (Occupied by Morocco)
Ad Dakhla
Kediat Idjil 915m
ALGERIA
Hoggar
Tahat 2917m
Taoudenni
Sahara
LIBYA
Libyan Desert
Bette 2266m
EGYPT
Tibesti
Emi Koussi 3414m
Mont Greboun 1943m
Nubian Desert
Port Sudan
MAURITANIA
Nouakchott
MALI
Timbuktu
Hombori Tondo 1155m
NIGER
Agadez
Niamey
CHAD
Ennedi
Abéché
Lake Chad
N'Djaména
Chari
SUDAN
Omdurman
Khartoum
White Nile
Wau
Juba
ERITREA
Asmara
Ras Dashen 4619m
DJIBOUTI
Djibouti
Shimbiris 2415m
Addis Ababa
ETHIOPIA
Lake Tana
SOMALIA
Mogadishu
Kismaayo
Elemi Triangle
Lake Turkana
SENEGAL
Dakar
THE GAMBIA
Banjul
Bissau
GUINEA-BISSAU
GUINEA
Conakry
Freetown
SIERRA LEONE
Monrovia
LIBERIA
Bamako
Niger
BURKINA FASO
Ouagadougou
Yamoussoukro
CÔTE D'IVOIRE
GHANA
Accra
TOGO
Lomé
BENIN
Porto-Novo
Lagos
Kano
NIGERIA
Abuja
Mont Karre 1420m
CENTRAL AFRICAN REPUBLIC
CAMEROON
Yaoundé
Malabo
EQUATORIAL GUINEA
Bangui
Congo
São Tomé
SÃO TOMÉ & PRÍNCIPE
Libreville
GABON
CONGO
Brazzaville
Kinshasa
DEMOCRATIC REPUBLIC OF CONGO
Ruwenzori Mt Stanley 5109m
UGANDA
Kampala
Lake Victoria
Kigali
RWANDA
Bujumbura
BURUNDI
Kananga
Lake Tanganyika
Kinyeti 3186m
KENYA
Mt Kenya 5198m
Nairobi
Mt Kilimanjaro 5895m
Mombasa
Pemba
Zanzibar
Dar es Salaam
TANZANIA
Dodoma
Mbeya
Lake Malawi
Nyika Plateau 2147m
MALAWI
Victoria
Platte Islands
SEYCHELLES
Aldabra Islands
COMOROS
Moroni
Antsirahana
Maromokotro 2875m
Mayotte (Fr.)
CABINDA (Angola)
Luanda
ANGOLA
Benguela
Morro de Môco 2609m
Huambo
Menongue
Namibe
Cunene
Etosha Pan
Okavango
Lubumbashi
Ndola
ZAMBIA
Lusaka
Zambezi
Lilongwe
Tete
Mulanje 3001m
Pemba
Nampula
MOZAMBIQUE
Harare
Lake Kariba
Inyangani 2591m
ZIMBABWE
Bulawayo
Quelimane
Beira
1375m
Okavango Delta
Limpopo
Brandberg 2572m
Grootfontein
Windhoek
Walvis Bay
Namib Desert
NAMIBIA
Francistown
BOTSWANA
Serowe
Gaborone
Kalahari Desert
Pretoria
Johannesburg
Maputo
SWAZILAND
Mbabane
Inhambane
Lüderitz
Upington
Bloemfontein
Orange
Kimberley
Springbok
SOUTH AFRICA
Maseru
LESOTHO
Durban
Langebaan
Ceres
Paarl
Worcester
Cape Town
George
Knysna
Port Elizabeth
East London
Table Mountain 1085m
MADAGASCAR
Antananarivo
Fianarantsoa
Toliara
Ambovombe
MAURITIUS
Port Louis
St-Denis
Réunion (Fr.)
N
Capital city
City/Town
International boundary
State boundary
Disputed boundary

Contents

How It All Began	6
South Africa	26
Namibia	32
Angola	42
Democratic Republic of Congo	54
Congo	58
Gabon	63
Cameroon	75
Nigeria	81
Benin	86
Togo	92
Ghana	95
Côte d'Ivoire	101
Liberia	106
Sierra Leone	114
Guinea	119
Guinea-Bissau	127
Senegal	131
The Gambia	134
Mauritania	145
Western Sahara	152
Morocco	156
Algeria	168
Tunisia	176
Libya	182
Egypt	188
Sudan	197
Eritrea	203
Djibouti and Somalia	209
Kenya	214
Tanzania	219
Mozambique	226
South Africa – The Return	234
Glossary	246
Bibliography	248

JUBILANT MUMS WITH THEIR MOZZIE NETS —

The long road ahead ...

How It All Began

My Childhood

The youngest of three boys, I was South Africa-born in the tropical city of Durban in the KwaZulu-Natal province, on 28 February 1946. I suppose Africa beckoned from an early age when as a small boy my father – the tall, somewhat serious Reverend Arthur, a missionary teacher – held me on his lap and enthralled me with stories of the great Victorian explorers. Dad's favourites were the exploits of the Scottish explorer Dr David Livingstone. I loved the bit when he got attacked by a Kalahari lion. There was even an old black-and-white etching to prove it, coupled with Livingstone's words from his journal that read:

> *The Lion caught my shoulder as he sprang, and we both came to the ground below together. Growling horribly close to my ear, he shook me as a terrier dog does a rat.*

I was a mischievous young lad, and the Reverend Arthur was strict. I remember a stinging hiding with a fly swatter for digging into the hot homemade sausage-roll snacks before they'd found their way into the prayer meeting next door.

On the other hand, I think I might have been mom's favourite. Ivy May, with her ample bosoms and blue rinse hair, was delightful. She loved adventure and we'd all be piled into an old Chevy to camp in the bush as we made our way on long missionary journeys into the interior. I loved the fire at night; the old canvas bell tent flapping in the wind and the sounds of the wild. Some of you who have been around long enough will still remember the sisal guy ropes, the wooden pegs and mallets and the hissing of the old paraffin pressure lamp. The seed of travel and adventure was planted.

Off to See the World

Once out of school I went off to do the typical freedom, rucksack-on-the-back, grow-a-beard thing. It was the sixties, with long-haired hippies shacked up with cheap drugs at the Pudding Shop in Istanbul, where you could sell your blood to stay alive. I taught English in Tehran in the old Persia; worked in kibbutzim and put up machine-gun bunkers in Israel; lost all my bucks at the *Oktoberfest* in Germany; sold insipid, pink hotdogs with soggy onions from a wheeled cart to drunks outside a pub in England; and even got a job with a bunch of gypsies erecting kiddies fairground rides. I hated the dishwashing jobs and proved way too thirsty to make a 'good barman'. When I met lovely Yorkshire lass Gill Adams I was 23, a beach photographer on Paignton Pier in Devon in the beautiful south of England, and missing Africa. We fell in love and, after an on-and-off stormy romance, Gill joined me back in Africa where I belonged.

Early Days in Zululand

Despite her Yorkshire accent, the Zulus loved Gill at first sight and, in return, she fell in love with Africa. They nicknamed her *Mashozi*, meaning 'she who wears shorts', and that name has stuck to this day. We travelled South Africa in an old Kombi and survived by buying arts and crafts out in the bush and selling them to curio shops and collectors. We got married at a small stone-built mission church called Mandawe Cross, situated high up on Mandawe Hill close to where KwaBulawayo, King Shaka Zulu's great military kraal, once stood. The church only holds about 25 people and the steeple is designed to look like an *ithunga*, or milking pail. Old Father Herald, the Catholic priest who built the church, claimed that it had been erected there in the face of 'great Zulu superstition'.

Local folklore has it that Shaka would force the sangomas, or diviners, to sleep out here under the stars in order for them to prove their immortality. It wasn't only the spirits of the many dead bodies slaughtered by the king's men that made the place dangerous, but also the huge local hyenas that had become 'man-eaters'.

Out of respect for the Reverend Arthur there was no booze at the wedding, but this didn't stop John Prescott from slipping a silver hip flask into his sports-jacket pocket. It was his job to announce the arrival of the bride's vehicle, which was the cue for a little visiting Swedish girl to strike up the wedding march on the pump-up organ. But, aided by the hip flask, things went wrong and John started vigorously ringing the bell at the first sighting of the vehicle's dust, still miles and many hills away. Too early came the signal for the Swedish girl to furiously pump away at the foot pedals, breathing enough air into the organ to get the wedding march going, with the congregation all looking for the bride. I was in an ill-fitting suit, sweating nervously in the unbearable heat, the organist's face was getting redder and redder, and the wedding march slower and more funereal, whilst the bell outside was still ringing away stridently to each sip of the hip flask. Eventually Mashozi arrived some 15 minutes later, cool and collected in a white wedding dress, after we'd had to revive the poor Swedish girl with some water. Somewhat drunk and jolly, a group of Zulus pitched up outside the church to be part of what the *Zululand Observer*, in the typical journalism of the time, called 'the first white wedding at Mandawe Cross'. Our honeymoon suite was a double mattress in the back of the Kombi as we travelled Zululand buying arts and crafts.

KINGSLEY- REFERRED TO AS 'THE BEARD'

Our son Ross was born at the old Pobane trading store on 17 December 1972 and in no time at all he was running around half naked with the Zulus. Mashozi and I had set up a Zulu handcraft cooperative and had been running a trading store; we were having a great time but only just surviving financially. Then, because of our Zulu interest, we were able to play a major role in building sets and hiring and organising thousands of Zulu extras for the filming of a movie called *Zulu Dawn*, along with good friend Barry Leitch, who really is a white Zulu. We got to hobnob with stars like Burt Lancaster and Peter O'Toole, learnt about the movie industry and later became seriously involved in the international TV series *Shaka Zulu*. After the filming, a group of us bought the principal film set and with the local Zulus turned it into a historic lodge and living museum to the old Zulu order. Today South Africans and visitors from all over the world visit Shakaland, which has become South Africa's best-known Zulu cultural attraction.

Calabash Journeys

Throughout this time we did our best to keep adventuring, but it was becoming increasingly difficult as the poor politics of apartheid steadily closed us off from the world. The miracle of Mandela's release changed things and soon we were cooking up our first expedition in 1993. It was called Afrika Odyssey, a waterway journey in open boats from Cape Town to Cairo, Alexandria and the mouth of the Nile. It will always be our greatest adventure, like a first love. After the wasted years of apartheid the journey opened Africa up to us as a family. Later we wrote a book called *Cape to Cairo* and told the story of how, in gale-force winds, we rounded the Cape of Storms and filled a Zulu calabash with Cape Point seawater before tracking the coastlines, rivers and lakes of Africa to arrive in Alexandria a year later, where we emptied it again at the mouth of the Nile. It was a journey that changed our lives forever and made us feel true citizens of greater Mama Afrika.

And so the adventures unfolded, including running several commercial expeditions in East Africa; climbing Kilimanjaro, the tallest free-standing mountain in the world; and following in the footsteps of famous Victorian explorers, men like Livingstone, Stanley, Speke, Grant and Teleki, which we did on and off for more than a decade. We circumnavigated Lake Turkana, the world's largest desert lake, and travelled the Zambezi and Congo rivers, east to west across Africa. That proved to be tough and two of us nearly died from malaria.

We even used Livingstone's Kalahari journeys as an excuse to circumnavigate the 12 000-square-kilometre

> To the expedition.
> Good luck for your endeavours to save life around the African Continent. We wish you well in your worthy fight against malaria.
>
> Mandela
> 4.4.07

> Ndlela nhle – 'Bon Voyage'
> Tsela tswewu. Safari njema
> Mag God u elmed seen
> What a fantastic project. Thank you so very much for your commitment to fight the scourge of malaria. We can defeat malaria – one net, one life.
> God bless you
> †Desmond
> 8.3.07
> Cape Town
>
> = A message of peace & goodwill from Archbishop Desmond Tutu – 8/3/2007

Makgadikgadi saltpans using land yachts. It was a sensational challenge – a small six-wheel-drive Polaris all-terrain motorbike as backup, a green Dragonfly microlight for navigation from the air and five three-wheeled, two-seater land yachts, each with a Bushman painting on the sail. We sped along with goggles, gloves and sunburnt noses and our backsides just 6 inches off the ground, at up to 80 kilometres per hour, overtaking ostrich and springbok, with our bedrolls, firewood, GPSs, Captain Morgan and supplies stashed in the carriers behind. In laying the land yachts down at night, using the sails as groundsheets, and listening to the crackling mopane campfire, the cry of jackal and hyena and the roar of a distant lion, indeed we were experiencing that there is no place quite like Africa.

But the calabash needed to be filled again, this time in a father-and-son journey, at the source of the Tugela, high up on *Izinthaba zo Khahlamba*, the Barrier of Spears, in the mighty Drakensberg. It was the first *National Geographic* documentary that Ross ever produced, called *Zulu River Odyssey*. I fell on the mountain, dislocating my shoulder and getting it stuck behind the shoulder blade. In absolute agony, I remember having to jump from a high rock into a deep Tugela Gorge pool, with Ross waiting at the bottom to rescue me if I passed out from the pain. It's a special bond between father and son; ours strengthened by the sharing of countless adventures.

In a journey called Rio Rovuma, Lake of Stars, we used an old field notebook of Dr Livingstone to follow the Rovuma River and then continued by land on to Lake Nyasa, which Livingstone had dubbed the Lake of Stars. We survived banditry, unexploded landmines, dangerous wild animals and countless attacks of malaria. East Africa's great Rufiji River beckoned us next and, with the symbolic calabash still on board, we tracked her course in a journey of tribute to that great outdoorsman, Frederick Courtney Selous. At Beho Beho, in the game reserve that bears his name, we emptied a little calabash water onto his grave; wrapped in an old army blanket, he was buried where he fell after he was shot through the mouth by a German sniper. The remaining calabash water was emptied into the Indian Ocean off the massive Rufiji Delta.

Then we found a map in London that I'd been searching for for years. It showed Livingstone's final journey where, bleeding to death, he was carried by his two loyal African companions, Chuma and Susi, and their team of porters. They had been in search of the source of the Nile and we followed their journey across the Bangweulu Swamps in northern Zambia to Chief Chitambo's village, where Dr Livingstone had died in May 1873. It was at this village that they had cut open Livingstone's chest, removed his heart and buried it in an old biscuit tin under a giant mapundu tree. They had then carried the preserved corpse more than a thousand miles to get it shipped back to England for burial. And so it was not surprising that when we filled the calabash again, this time to circumnavigate the globe by land along the Tropic of Capricorn, we named our two Landies 'Chuma' and 'Susi' after the two true unsung heroes of African exploration.

We learnt to love East Africa: the Mountains of the Moon, the migration of more than a million wildebeest across the Serengeti plains, looking into the soft brown eyes of a silverback gorilla and quickly learning, whilst living with the Maasai, that when drinking blood from the dewlap of a slaughtered beast, you need to get in first before it coagulates, especially if, like me, you've got a great, big beard.

Amongst the milkwoods of KwaZulu-Natal's (KZN) coast is our Swahili-styled house. It is aptly called 'Afrika House' and on the wall in the upstairs Captain's Bar is a massive hand-painted map of Africa marking the journeys already undertaken. But there were still too many blank spaces that needed filling in.

So filling the symbolic Zulu calabash once again, we launched the next journey of discovery, this time in the footsteps of the man who immortalised the words 'Dr Livingstone, I presume.' Travelling in a boat that, like his, was called the *Lady Alice*, we circumnavigated Africa's largest lake, Lake Victoria, following the notes from the expedition journal of Henry Morton Stanley. Mohammed the Brave, a dhow captain from Mafia Island just south of Zanzibar, sailed with Mashozi and me. At night, we'd sit around the fire and talk about the possibilities of one day getting hold of a jahazi, a big Swahili sailing dhow, so that we could relive the experience of exploring the East African coast, blown by the trade winds under a lateen sail. What an adventure that would be.

Saving and Improving Lives through Adventure
As always, malaria continued to plague us as we travelled, and we were the lucky ones. It was always a thud to the heart when, miles from the nearest clinic or hospital, we'd come across villages with babies screaming from a malarial fever and the mothers not knowing what to do. The shocking statistic is that for every minute of every day and night two African babies die from the bloodsucking bite of the *Anopheles* mosquito – in many areas it's far worse than HIV and Aids. We had for some time been distributing mosquito nets to pregnant mums and those with infants, but I vowed that on the next expedition we'd try even harder to make a difference in fighting this silent killer.

African Rainbow Expedition
By this time, the expedition family nucleus of Mashozi, Ross and myself had been added to by young farm boy, Bruce Leslie. He'd survived being the backup person for the Rufiji and Lake Victoria expeditions and now volunteered to travel up the Swahili Coast in search of a traditional dhow. Two months later, on Chole Island just south of Mafia on the coast of Tanzania, he and Mohammed the Brave found the 35-tonne jahazi called *Amina*. We changed her name to *Amina Spirit of Adventure* and spent a year living out the dream. We travelled from Durban to the Somali border and back – barefoot on her creaking decks, with the groans and scrapes of the rigging and the massive hand-stitched lateen sail pregnant with the trade winds. Life was an adventure of sailing rough with a Swahili crew, sleeping on the deck under the stars and living off fish and *ugali*, the East African version of *mieliepap*.

It was traditional sailing dhows such as this one that had raped Africa of her people for slavery – human flesh that had been driven to the coast like chained oxen. Now, in a sort of humanist turnabout, we were able to use such a vessel to carry tens of thousands of life-saving mosquito nets to mothers and babies. It wasn't easy. Bruce was knifed by a pirate and had to be casevaced out, and near Somalia the crew mutinied and we had to proceed with our own little armed militia. A bit gung ho I suppose, but we'd always had this notion of travelling from Durban to the Somali border and back. Having reached this end point, we retreated to Lamu where we refitted and refurbished our dhow. The Kas Kazi, the northeast trade wind that blows from India and Arabia, blew us back south to end our sailing odyssey at historic Ilha de Mozambique. Then, as part of our homeward journey, coinciding with Africa Malaria Day, we launched a 600-kilometre malaria prevention journey down the Zambezi from below Cahora Bassa Gorge to the 8 000-square-kilometre delta on the Indian Ocean, then down the Pungwe River to Beira, south to ancient Sofala at the mouth of the Rio Save, and finally back to a welcome-home party at Shakaland.

Sure, we were a bit worn out and still running on adrenalin, but, friends, we could not have had a better homecoming. 'Would you do it again?' came a question from across the fire. I thought for a while: would we as a family be crazy enough to repeat it all – another year-long safari, barefoot on the creaking deck of a hand-built Swahili dhow, with the smell of fish, the lack of privacy, our movements dependent on the winds and the tides? Roger Gaisford, our eccentric local historian, threw another piece of acacia thorn onto the fire and the sparks drifted up into the night sky. 'No,' came my hesitant answer, 'I don't think I could. But what this crazy dhow journey has taught me is that we have one of the most fascinating coastlines on earth. Just imagine how wonderful it would be to track the entire coastline of Africa – but more by land, with inflatable boats just for the rivers and lakes. Now wouldn't that be a fantastic adventure?'

A Window of Opportunity

We're so privileged to have Mama Afrika as our home. It's quiet times like these when I think back and realise just how fortunate we've been to have adventured as a family and returned safely home together. But as always we are itching for the next trip, and the dream of circumnavigating Africa has been with me for some time now. Having crossed Africa from south to north and east to west, and now to have explored the east coast Sea of Zinj under sail, surely in our lifetimes we need to complete the entire rim of Africa – do the full circle? Start from the Cape of Good Hope, the most southwesterly point, and then take it clockwise, 33 countries around the outside edge of Africa, sticking as close as possible to the coast. I can smell a window of opportunity. Angola has peace, there are UN Peacekeepers in Liberia and the blood-diamond war is over in Sierra Leone. We can cross Mauritania, Western Sahara and risk Algeria. Gaddafi will hopefully allow us into Libya, we have some experience of the Sudan already, and now there's a lull in the war between Ethiopia and Eritrea. Djibouti's okay, and surely we can make a plan to get around the dangerous Horn of Africa? Then it's back following our dhow journey down the east coast back to the Cape of Good Hope. Can we do it? Is it achievable? If it's going to be done, we must get on it before it's too late ...

The Seven Pebbles of Life

Some time ago I was with Don Pinnock of *Getaway* magazine. We were talking about our views on life and how time gets more precious the older you get. To demonstrate my philosophy I took seven pebbles and placed them on the bar counter. 'Think of it this way Don, each of these pebbles represents 10 summers, totalling 70 summers and a fortunate man's life span.' To Don's surprise I then reached over and tossed five of the seven pebbles out of the window. 'Gone forever!' I said. 'Great experiences, wonderful times, but they're over and there's no use gazing in the rear-view mirror. The seventh pebble? Sorry, but there's no bloody guarantee that you'll still be in good enough shape to enjoy that one. If you are, it's a gift, but it certainly can't be relied upon.' So out the window it also went. Both of us put down our drinks to study the one lonely remaining pebble. 'Don, this might be all I've got left: the remains of the 10 summers that this pebble represents, and cheers to that!'

So I put the remaining pebble in my pocket, knowing full well it would get caught up in the car keys and my wallet and become a bloody nuisance. On the bedside table at night it would go, and back in the pocket again the next morning. I knew I'd rub it between my fingers like a worry bead and that it would become smooth and shiny with patina. Yes, the moral of the pebble story is all about getting out and doing it! And so the Africa Outside Edge expedition was born. It's going to be a *safari kubwa sana* – a big journey – and, to make it even more of a logistical challenge, not only is it going to be a tough geographic expedition but also a deeply humanitarian one. Like all adventures, this one starts with selecting a team and making a bunch of hand-scribbled notes that somehow, if there's enough passion, become a reality.

Pilgrims of Adventure – An Introduction to the Expedition Team

My wife Gill, or Mashozi, is in charge of expedition finance, paperwork and supplies and she's also the mama of the expedition. I truly admire her tough spirit and the dedication she puts into the humanitarian side of things. She has a wonderful way with African people and after a long day still knocks up a great bean stew.

Annelie Muller, Ross's girlfriend, with her quiet purposeful way, is joining us for her first expedition. It's going to be a huge challenge for her, this year-long adventure in the Landies. Anna also has the added responsibility of media liaison, including sending out oddball dispatches.

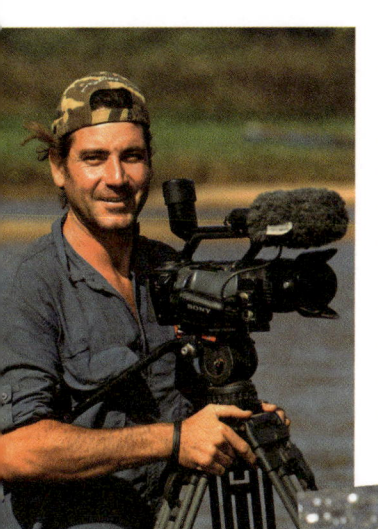

My son Ross will run the technical side of the expedition, including the important tasks of navigation and logistics. He will also be filming a documentary about life on the Edge. We have had many adventures together already and he is 100% dependable – my right-hand man.

Young Bruce Leslie, a veteran of Holgate family expeditions, has been bitten by the adventure bug since his first journey with us five years ago. He is to be our expedition stills photographer, taking the images to go with our story, and is also a good logistics man.

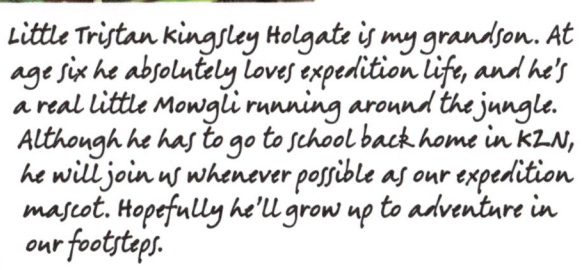

Little Tristan Kingsley Holgate is my grandson. At age six he absolutely loves expedition life, and he's a real little Mowgli running around the jungle. Although he has to go to school back home in KZN, he will join us whenever possible as our expedition mascot. Hopefully he'll grow up to adventure in our footsteps.

Scribbles That Become an Adventure

OUTSIDE EDGE ROUGH KIT LIST —

- MEDICAL KIT TO INCLUDE: BLOOD GROUP DETAILS, A DRIP SET, SYRINGES, TOURNIQUET, ANTIBIOTICS, DIARRHOEA MUTHI, PAIN KILLER, ANTISEPTIC CREAM, COUGH MIXTURES, MALARIA TREATMENT, BANDAGES, SURGICAL PLASTER. EVACUATION INSURANCE.

- MASHOZI'S CONDIMENTS BOX, WITH ALL THOSE FAVOURITES LIKE, MARMITE, MRS BALL'S CHUTNEY, NANDO'S SAUCES, ROOIBOS ROOT BOS TEA.

- VEHICLE RECOVERY KIT, HIGH LIFT JACK, TOOLS, BASIC SPARES, TYRE REPAIR KITS, SOME CHAIN, THREAD BAR, WIRE, CABLE TIES, GAFFER TAPE, STEEL PUTTY, GLUE, FUSES, SPARE ELECTRICAL WIRE, TAPE, ASSORTED BOLTS/NUTS, FIRE EXTINGUISHERS, ENGEL FRIDGE TIE DOWNS, ROPE, RATCHET STRAPS.

- SAT PHONE AND EMERGENCY NUMBERS, LAP TOP, CAMERAS, VHS RADIOS.

- SOUND SYSTEM, PULL DOWN INFORMATION SCREENS, PAMPHLETS / FOR ONE NET ONE LIFE MALARIA PREVENTION CAMPAIGN

- BE EXTRA TENT, BEDROLLS, POTS, PANS, CUTLERY, BRAAI GRIDS, KETTLE, CAMP CHAIRS, TABLES, BATTERY LIGHTS, HEAD TORCHES, BATTERIES.

- PERSONAL MOZZIE NETS, TABARD SPRAY AND LOTION, SUNBLOCK, PERSONAL TOILETRIES, PERSONAL SUPPLY MALARIA TREATMENT.

- LEATHERMANS, HEADTORCHES, MAGLITES, SPARE BATTERIES, PANGAS, SILKY SAWS, SPARE BLADES.

- 6 SPARE COOPER TIRES, GARMIN GPS, PAPER MAPS.

- GUIDE BOOKS, REFERENCE BOOKS, RESEARCH INFORMATION / ALL MALARIA PREVENTION CONTACTS, EXPEDITION STAMPS, LETTERS OF INTRODUCTION IN FRENCH, ENGLISH, PORTUGUESE, ARABIC & SWAHILI

- PASSPORTS, INTERNATIONAL DRIVERS LICENCES, INSURANCE, COPIES OF PASSPORTS, VEHICLE CARNETS, EXTRA PASSPORT PICS, EXPEDITION STAMPS AND PENS FOR 'DOCTORING' PAPER WORK / CASH IN RAND, US DOLLARS, EUROS, CARDS.

- EXPEDITION JOURNALS, THE CALABASH, SCROLL OF PEACE AND GOODWILL IN SUPPORT OF MALARIA PREVENTION, A GREAT BIG SENSE OF HUMOUR & OPTIMISM

GEMINI
ONE NET ONE LIFE MALARIA PREVENTION

2 x 6m HIGH FLOTATION GEMINI INFLATABLE BOATS — WE'LL CALL THEM 'LIVINGSTONE' AND 'STANLEY' —

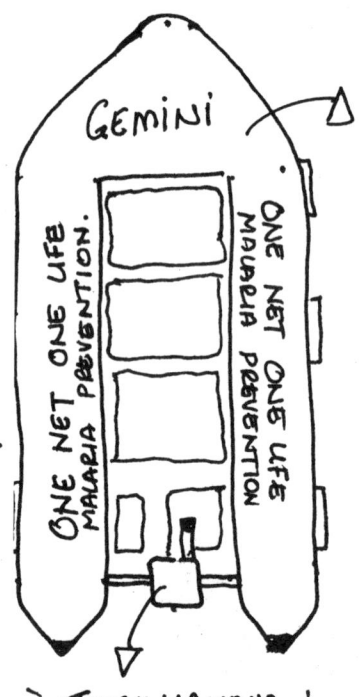

TOUGH YAMAHA 30 HP ENDURO OUTBOARD.

PEBBLE
THE ZULU CALABASH OF CAPE OF GOOD HOPE SEAWATER
SCROLL OF PEACE AND GOODWILL MALARIA PREVENTION

PREPARING THE EXPEDITION KIT —
3 LANDIES CONSISTING OF TWO
TDI'S AND A 130 TD5 DEFENDER

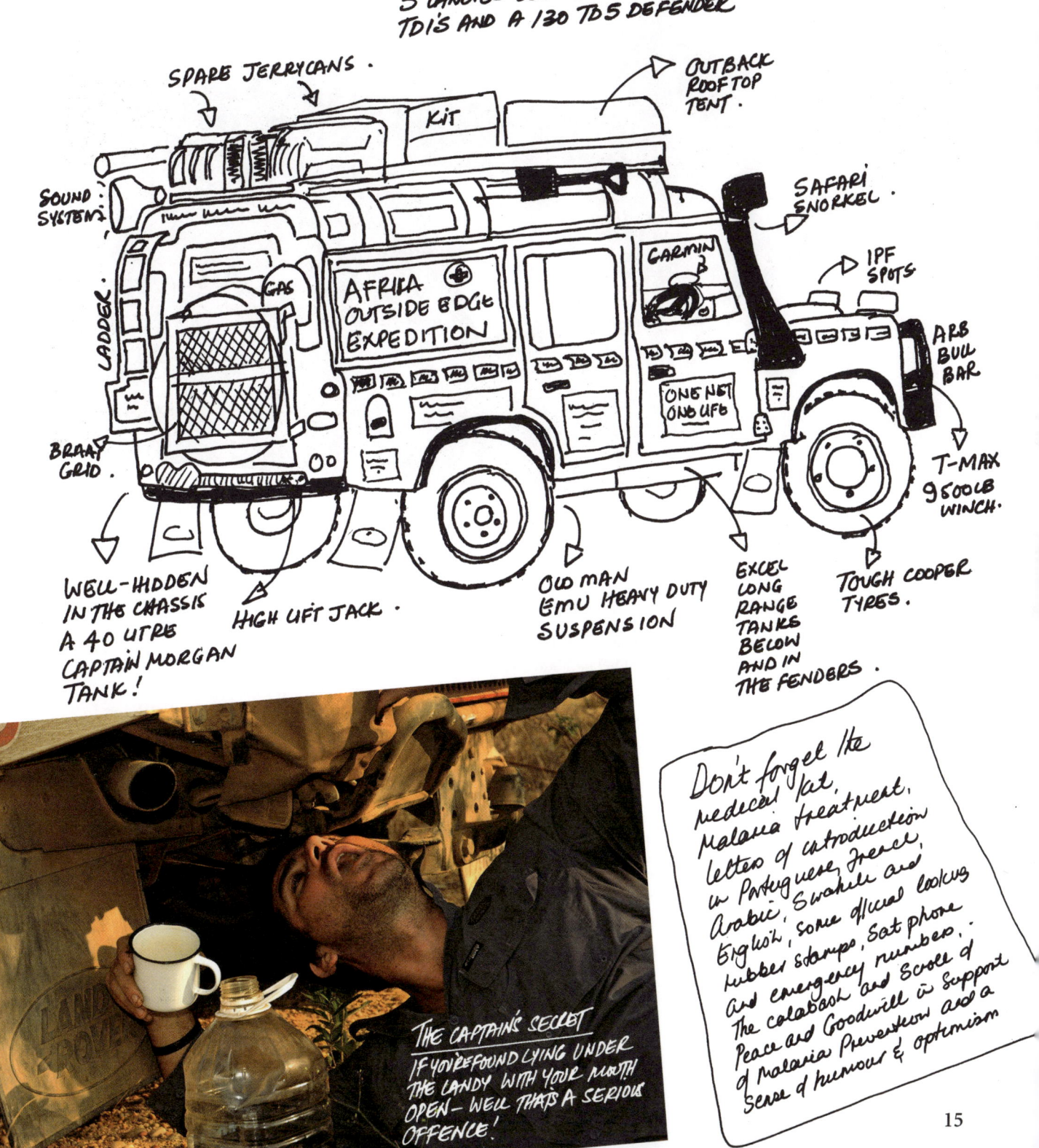

- SPARE JERRYCANS
- KIT
- OUTBACK ROOFTOP TENT
- SOUND SYSTEM
- SAFARI SNORKEL
- LADDER
- GAS
- AFRICA OUTSIDE EDGE EXPEDITION
- GARMIN
- IPF SPOTS
- ONE NET ONE LIFE
- ARB BULL BAR
- BRAAI GRID
- T-MAX 9500LB WINCH
- WELL-HIDDEN IN THE CHASSIS A 40 LITRE CAPTAIN MORGAN TANK!
- HIGH LIFT JACK
- OLD MAN EMU HEAVY DUTY SUSPENSION
- EXCEL LONG RANGE TANKS BELOW AND IN THE FENDERS
- TOUGH COOPER TYRES

THE CAPTAIN'S SECRET
IF YOU'RE FOUND LYING UNDER THE LANDY WITH YOUR MOUTH OPEN — WELL THAT'S A SERIOUS OFFENCE!

Don't forget the medical kit, Malaria treatment, letters of introduction in Portuguese, French, Arabic, Swahili and English, some official looking rubber stamps, Sat phone and emergency numbers, The calabash and Scroll of Peace and Goodwill in support of Malaria Prevention and a sense of humour & optimism.

We'll keep a journal and send you dispatches from the Outside Edge.

Dispatches from the Outside Edge

Thanks to the internet there seems to be a demand for immediacy, and blogs and Facebook are all the rage. Gone, it appears, are the days of the old scribbled notebook when we could send a handwritten note on a piece torn off from an old soap-box carton or a postcard from a remote trading station, or just give a message to a fellow traveller to pass on when he got to South Africa in a few months' time. Now it's all Dictaphones and laptops. This was a big expedition and we were under pressure from magazines and sponsors to send out regular updates. *Die Burger* and several other newspapers wanted weekly columns and *Getaway*, *SA 4x4* and *Wildside* magazines needed regular features. And so I kept scribbling them as we travelled, and it was Anna's task as the expedition communications person to set up a satellite dish linked to a laptop and, from wherever we were, be it lonely beach, river mouth, jungle clearing or Sahara dunes, somehow to transfer my scribbles to cyberspace. Come what may, she succeeded, sometimes against impossible odds with only minutes to spare before deadlines. We sent stories from each country and called them Dispatches from the Outside Edge – I hope you enjoy them.

Siyabonga and *asante sana*,

Kingsley Holgate

Angola – broken roads

Benin — Hotel Ganvié on stilts

Gabon – road to Mayumba

AREMU BABATUNDE AKIOLU I

Nigeria – king of Lagos

Ghana – lady vendor

Mali – Djenné streets

Mauritania – Cap Blanc

Egypt – the mouth of the Nile

MALARIA PREVENTION REPORT – ONE NET • ONE LIFE

COUNTRY	Côte d'Ivoire
PROVINCE	BAS sasandra
VILLAGE OR COMMUNITY CENTRE	District sanitarie de Sassandra
GPS CO-ORDINATES	N 04°58'018" W 006°06'357"
NAME OF COMMUNITY LEADER	Dr ABBET ABBET
POPULATION SIZE	348 687 habitants
NUMBER OF NETS DISTRIBUTED TO MOTHERS WITH BABIES	200
MALARIA RISK	HIGH X MEDIUM LOW
NEAREST HOSPITAL OR CLINIC	Maternité HG et maternité des Centres de santé ruraux
COMMENTS	Merci jump tout. Ce don contribuera à la réduction de la mortalité infantile

STAMP: AFRICA OUTSIDE EDGE EXPEDITION — OFICIAL

During our Outside Edge exhibition we distributed over 240 000 mosquito nets to Africa's poorest. The donations to villages, schools and clinics along the way were recorded on forms like this one.

we begin ...

South Africa

Day 1, Country 1 on the Edge

Land of our birth, cradle of all humankind. We depart on this epic odyssey just after Africa Malaria Day. We've invited Land Rover owners to meet us at the Cape of Good Hope for the filling of the calabash ceremony and then to escort us out of Cape Town, although the weather report is shitty. The challenge of 33 countries around the edge makes me nervous as all hell – let's see what happens...

IN THE DISTANCE – THE DOTS OF THE 347-STRONG LANDY CONVOY

YOU CAN SEE THE BEARD POPPING OUT FROM UNDER THE GORILLA MASK

Dispatch #1 – Longest Land Rover Expedition Send-off Ever!

It's bloody unbelievable; 347 Landies pitch up in the rain to see us off. What an incredible act of solidarity in the fight against malaria and a wonderful send-off for a humble expedition now hell bent on following Africa's outside edge.

There's a brief lull in the weather – just enough blue in the sky to make an elephant a pair of pyjamas – when a journalist shouts, 'Quickly, all of you please, the whole team for a photo behind the Cape of Good Hope sign!' 'Just a moment,' I say, 'my boot's come off'. With that I duck down behind the sign, pull on a hideous gorilla mask and leap up roaring, arms in the air. Poor bloke falls backwards and nearly drops his camera. After all the intense preparation, the huge effort to gather sponsor support for this geographic and humanitarian challenge and getting the kit together, we all get the giggles. I look around at the core team members who are going on this outrageous journey with me: Mashozi, Ross, Anna and Bruce – at last we have an expedition.

Dispatch #2 – Dancing in the Mud

The Cape Peninsula winter rains have come early but the miserable conditions fail to dampen the spirits of hundreds of Land Rover owners who, dressed in an array of bush jackets, balaclavas and gumboots, dance in the mud in a vast paddock at De Grendel wine estate in the northern suburbs. Adventurers have travelled from a variety of destinations such as Namibia, Gauteng, the Eastern Cape and KwaZulu-Natal. Some have even pitched tents and the braais are blazing. Earlier I'd sent out an email that read:

Dear friends in adventure. We're expecting lousy weather but Land Rover owners aren't wussies – see you as planned.

AFRICA
OUTSIDE EDGE
EXPEDITION

OFFICIAL

FILLING THE
SYMBOLIC
ZULU CALABASH
— CAPE OF GOOD
HOPE.

NOTES — S'AFRICA:

- AFTER APARTHEID'S BAD YEARS IT'S GOOD TO BE PART OF THE EXCITEMENT OF MADIBA'S 'RAINBOW NATION' — TO BE PART OF THE GREATER 'MAMA AFRIKA' & 'THE EDGE'

- IT'S OUR HOME COUNTRY, 11 OFFICIAL LANGUAGES AND AROUND 50 MILLION RAINBOW PEOPLE — WE'RE NERVOUS AND EXCITED / AFRICA MALARIA DAY / MEDIA RELEASE

- THE S'ATLANTIC AND INDIAN OCEAN COASTLINES STRETCH OVER MORE THAN 2500 KM, INCREDIBLE BEAUTY — NEED TO GET GOING.

- IN 1488 KING JOHN II OF PORTUGAL CALLED IT CABO DA BOA ESPERANÇA — THE CAPE OF GOOD HOPE, TOMORROW WE FILL THE CALABASH WITH COLD S'ATLANTIC SEAWATER

Now enamel mugs of the Captain's rum are raised in a victory salute. It's been an incredible day as, bumper to bumper, a record-breaking 347 Landies of every shape, colour and vintage braved the weather to join the longest humanitarian Land Rover convoy ever to leave from the Cape of Good Hope. With Africa Malaria Day just two days behind us, this was a massive act of support in the fight against the disease. Nobel Prize laureates Archbishop Desmond Tutu and Madiba himself, together with hundreds of well-wishers, have endorsed a Scroll of Peace and Goodwill in support of malaria prevention, which the expedition will carry around the outside edge of Africa.

Dispatch #3 – The Dutchman and the Devil

'It's fantastic,' I laugh. It's the friendliness of the people that makes it all worthwhile. Some of the convoy members have stayed on with their Land Rovers to escort us up the West Coast. The weather is still shitty and the clouds droop over Table Mountain. There's a Cape Town story about the Dutchman and the Devil that's been doing the rounds since the early 1700s. There was a *Nederlander* called Van Hunks who was said to live on the slopes of Table Mountain with his wife and daughters. Van Hunks had the habit of smoking his great big pipe at the kitchen table, but one evening, needing a bit of solitude, he decided to go for a walk up the mountain and have a quiet smoke alone. As he sat there, a tall man in a long cloak approached him and they began to talk about their mutual love of tobacco. The talk got competitive, the two men loaded up their pipes and the challenge was on. Some say that Van Hunks won. Others say he glimpsed a cloven hoof and ran for his life. Most people, when they look up and see the clouds dropping like a tablecloth over the mountain, say the battle is still on. Out to sea, we get occasional glimpses through the mist of Robben Island, now famous as Nelson Mandela's island of imprisonment. Thank God that's all over.

Dispatch #4 – 'They only started shitting on the cars when the new government came in'

At Langebaan we sit on the lawn and share our giant portions of fish and chips with Brian, the ruddy-faced car guard. 'Used to work on the whalers,' he says, 'but those days are over now.' Seagulls shriek and swoop for titbits, and one of them shits on the windscreen of my Land Rover. 'They only started shitting on the cars when the new government came in,' says Brian, who looks like a man in need of a drink. We laugh. We're up the West Coast; it's not a malaria area so here we'll concentrate on our Teaching on the Edge programme and have enlisted some enthusiastic volunteers with extra Land Rovers. We've got Hugh and Tessa Roe and Shaun and Yolanda Rudiger. They'd love to do the entire expedition, but are hampered by children and jobs. Marc and Brigid Lurie are past volunteers who've joined us for the South African bit, and then there's Alwyn van Wyk. What a character – full of humour, knows the West Coast backwards and is travelling in a battered 32-year-old Land Rover forward control nicknamed 'Mafunyane', with his boots and some small, dried fish known as *bokkoms* tied to the

MEDIA RELEASE
APRIL 2007
HOLGATES HIT THE ROAD TO HUMANITARIAN ADVENTURE

A MEDIA RELEASE THANKS THE EXPEDITION SPONSORS

At the Cape of Good Hope, media cameras flashed as Kingsley Holgate, one of Africa's best known adventurers, with his trousers rolled up to his knees and his characteristic grey beard blowing sideways, filled a decorated Zulu calabash with cold seawater from the South Atlantic Ocean. 'It's fitting that we launch our yearlong clockwise circumnavigation of the African continent from this, the most southwesterly point,' explained the Greybeard of African Adventure, as he held up the calabash for all to see.

By Land Rover and Yamaha-powered Gemini inflatable boats, Kingsley and his family team are off again on what he calls 'their greatest humanitarian adventure ever'. Linked to a One Net One Life campaign in support of malaria prevention, this Africa Outside Edge expedition will distribute tens of thousands of life-saving mosquito nets to pregnant women and young mothers with children under the age of five. The shocking statistic is that for every minute of every day and night two babies die from the bloodsucking bite of the female *Anopheles* mosquito. It's a deadly disease that affects 3,5 million Africans annually, killing more people than HIV and Aids. 'Thanks for helping make a difference and showing that you care for Africa,' shouted Kingsley through a megaphone.

Other humanitarian efforts linked to the expedition are a Rite to Sight programme in which 'spectacles' are distributed to the poor-sighted in remote villages and there's an innovative Centurus Colleges/Rotary initiative, Teaching on the Edge, in which hundreds of mobile libraries will be distributed to needy schools.

South African National Parks officials Gavin Bell and Christa Stringer handed over three symbolic Cape Agulhas stones and a conservation scroll tied with a thin piece of kelp. A stone will be dropped and another picked up at the most westerly, northerly and easterly points of the continent, and these new stones will be returned to the southernmost point at Cape Agulhas, provided the expedition survives. After having almost completed the full circle at Cape Agulhas, the Zulu calabash of seawater will be brought back to the Cape of Good Hope in a year's time, hopefully to coincide with Africa Malaria Day, 25 April 2008.

The Land Rover revellers continued to dance into the night. Nando's, one of the supporters of the expedition, provided a peri-peri feast and Kingsley did his traditional Captain Morgan flambéed steak-on-the-spade – a tradition that started years ago on the Holgates' Tropic of Capricorn expedition. 'Sure, we're nervous,' said Kingsley, standing next to his 4x4MegaWorld-prepared Land Rover with the colourful flags of 33 African countries decaled on the side. 'Tomorrow we're on our own – three Landies and two big inflatable boats ready to circumnavigate Africa. We know it will be tough, but with all this incredible goodwill behind us and great sponsor partners, how can we possibly fail?

'British Airways and Grindrod, the Durban-based shipping and logistics company, are assisting with logistics and funding, and after a campfire gathering with the Nedbank vehicle-and-asset finance team they are putting up the bucks for diesel. We've got tough wheels sponsored by Cooper Tires, Melvill and Moon seat covers to soak up the sweat and the farts and Central African Gold is supporting a massive malaria prevention campaign in Ghana and Mali. Thanks to Evolution Communications in Cape Town, we are larnies and will be able to communicate with you through state-of-the-art satellite equipment. In Nigeria Protea Hotels and Nando's are collecting life-saving mosquito nets ahead of our arrival.

'Following the edge won't be easy and where there are no roads or tracks we will use the ducks and proven Garmin navigational equipment. There are some wonderful challenges ahead … it all promises to be a wonderfully exciting odyssey, using adventure to improve and save lives.'

'TEACHING ON THE EDGE'

THE BEARD WITH OOM HANNES AND TANNIE MAGDA ENGELBRECHT ON VANPUTTENSVLEI STOEP.

ladder at the back. Dedicated adventurer and humanitarian Eugene le Roux and his sidekick Max Methi will be travelling all the way to Angola with us in a Nando's-sponsored Land Rover Discovery. Then there's old friend Babu Cossa from Mozambique who'll be with us until Gabon. We've travelled together before and, amongst his other skills, we've come to rely on his Portuguese. We're a jolly gang in an easy-to-travel country with loads of support for what we are doing.

We survive a noisy gang of well-wishers at the Panty Bar in Paternoster which is adorned with hundreds of women's panties and bras. In the cold and the wind we camp on the edge of the South Atlantic's pebbled shoreline at Tietiesbaai.

The next day the children sing and chant at St Augustine's school where the mobile libraries, which include learning materials, pencils, exercise books, erasers and rulers, are a hit for these underprivileged kids. Teachers and pupils endorse the Madiba Scroll of Peace and Goodwill. Then it's on to the little mission school at Leipoldtville where we do the same and have a competition to see who's best at reading out the 33 flags on the expedition Land Rovers.

Dispatch #5 – *Bokkoms* and *Moskonfyt*

People have been reading about us in the newspapers and my ugly beard is plastered all over the cover of *Getaway* magazine. Are you the crazy blokes going around Africa? And so the word spreads. Berg River fishermen offer us *bokkoms* to chew on, something new for us Banana Boys from KZN. *Oom* Hannes and *Tannie* Magda Engelbrecht from Vanputtensvlei not only share their home with us but also catch-of-the-day snoek on the coals, cooked West-Coast style and served with fresh home-baked bread and hanepoot-grape-made *moskonfyt*. We add *Renosterkoffie*; that's a heaped spoon of coffee with boiling water, condensed milk and Captain Morgan rum. This brew of 'rhinoceros coffee' has the kick of its namesake and is a favourite on expedition. For dessert we enjoy *ingelegde elandsvye*, tinned sour figs, around the fire.

We leave loaded with gifts of bottled pickled onions and sweet gherkins. Land Rovers in the dust, chirps on the radios, and it's on to Donkinsbaai where we find the great Springbok rugby player Jannie Engelbrecht sitting outside on his stoep with his Dalmatians. We share a glass of wine, from his own vineyards *nogal,* and he endorses the scroll. Here the coast is wild, beautiful and unspoilt. For the first time since leaving Cape Town we feel the excitement of the adventure ahead as, by the light of the full moon, we open and close the 17 farm gates that take us across Namaqualand's strandveld down to Hondeklipbaai and the diamond coast.

Dispatch #6 – Noup Cottages

Freezing cold, we're in jackets and beanies and there's red-faced Dudley Wessels just in his shirtsleeves. He and Aletta are wonderfully hospitable Namaqualanders who run the old diamond divers' camp at Noup. They've heard about our goodwill journey and out come the lamb chops and booze, or *tjops* and *dop* as we South Africans call them. The wind continues to blow cold and the mist swirls – no tents tonight as we crawl under the blankets in the little hobgoblin rooms. What characters these diamond divers must have been. When the Atlantic was too rough to dive they would spend their time collecting wood from the shipwrecks for bar counters, doors and window frames. Smooth pebbles and stones were used to build fireplaces and extend the walls of their shacks.

With the tyres of our Land Rovers down to 1 bar and with special permission from De Beers mine, we follow Dudley along the Diamond Coast shoreline. The torn, rusty hulls of wrecks appear like ghosts through the mist. 'This one,' says Dudley, 'is a Brazilian vessel, the *Piratinia*. She ran aground in 1943 whilst carrying bales of cloth and they reckon that by the next *Nagmaal* the children in the area were all dressed in matching clothes looking as if they had all been fitted by the same tailor.' Standing out in the wind, Dudley draws a rough map of his world in the canvas-bound expedition journal. Over the years, the stormy Atlantic prevented many ships from completing their voyages, sending them to a final resting place along the coast between Kleinsee and Koningnas. There's so much to see and so few pebbles of life. I rub my sixth pebble in my pocket, feeling glad that we're going on this incredible adventure. Covering the South African coast alone could be a yearlong expedition. This is the West Coast at its best – the colourful characters, the food and the music, the solitude and the shipwrecks and the good-hearted *boeregasvryheid*, ideals of share and share alike.

Dispatch #7 – Port Nolloth

'I remember the days when the "carat money" from the diamond sales was paid on the fifteenth of every month. It was like the Wild West,' says Anne Allan, curator of the Port Nolloth Museum, which is housed in the late-19th-century clubhouse of the Cape Copper Company. 'There was always some lucky boat whose crew had hit the jackpot and the entire town would party. Easy come, easy go. Work hard and party hard. Those tough characters lived for the day, adrenalin junkies waiting for their next diamond fix.' The faded pictures on the museum walls tell the story of the shipwrecks and those who risked their lives – as some still do – diving for diamonds in the cold South Atlantic. Down at the harbour the diamond boats are all anchored in the wind and mist. The divers are in town; it's another non-sea day, no 'carat money' to be earned in this weather. 'That's the problem,' says an old seadog, 'no diving, no cash.' I see some of the divers loaded up with bags, walking purposefully out of the Queen's liquor store. Then the wind clears a pocket of light and we see a ghost ship trailing lengths of dive pipes like spilt intestines.

Dispatch #8 – 'Jesus is Lord in Alexander Bay'

Next is Alexander Bay, another diamond-mining town where every visitor needs a pass. There's a sign that reads *Geen smouse* – 'no hawkers' – and another that tells us that 'Jesus is Lord in Alexander Bay'. There's a big red concrete Aids ribbon, a crime-line 0800 telephone number and a sign to the right that reads 'Alexander Bottle Store'. The mist still hangs thick over the sea. A golf course shines bright green amidst the dry, windswept gravel. There's a rugby field, Frikkie Snyman's guesthouse, some speed humps, a Dutch Reformed church, a hospital, a school and a road down to the sea where the greater flamingos look like mirages in the mist and the twisted pieces of driftwood that have washed down in the last floods look like ghosts. Down on the beach we see the remains of a lone office chair, a security hut on stilts and a diamond-area sign that reads 'No entry between sunset and sunrise'. We've reached the mouth of the Orange River. Across lies Namibia.

Already the 'outside edge' is littered with wrecks.

Namibia

Day 8, Country 2 on the Edge

Across the Orange River lies the Sperrgebiet, Namibia's forbidden diamond coast. This will take us on to the great sand ocean of the world's oldest desert, the Namib, followed by the Skeleton Coast, one of the wildest and most inhospitable coastlines on earth. No wonder the early mariners called it the 'Coast of Death'. Fortunately God favours the Brave, or is it the Crazy? But we still don't know how we will cross the Kunene River into Angola.

THE FORBIDDEN COAST

CHRIS SIVERTSEN AND THE DESERT WANDERERS

Dispatch #9 – Into the Sperrgebiet

Seven days after leaving the Cape of Good Hope and the volunteers having returned home, the four Land Rovers leave South Africa to cross the bridge over the Orange River into Namibia and the Sperrgebiet. Oryx graze on the banks of the river, the border post is easy and Chris Sivertsen, the friendly general manager of Namdeb diamond mines, is there to escort us into this restricted area. Weeks before, we'd sent in all our details for security clearance. Now we're X-rayed and through we go. It's a special privilege for the expedition; we're being allowed to follow a stretch of protected diamond coast normally closed to travellers. Chris, over a welcome dinner party, explains that it all began in 1908 when August Stauch, who was supervising the maintenance work on the railway line from Lüderitz to Aus, told his workers to keep an eye open for 'pretty stones'. One of the labourers, Zacharias Lewala, found a diamond and handed it over to Stauch, who staked a claim to the region on behalf of the German government. And so the diamond rush began. In 1911 a section of land demarcated by the Atlantic on the west and extending 137 kilometres inland, and reaching from the Orange River in the south to 26° north, was declared the *Sperrgebiet*, meaning 'restricted area', which has since become known as the 'Forbidden Coast'.

Dispatch #10 – Ghost Towns and Diamonds

Chris and his wife Jenny put a team together. JJ and Iana are the geologists who will accompany us and with them is their little daughter Emilia. At six months old it's her first outing. Then there's Trygve Cooper, who still remembers the days when the Forbidden Coast was patrolled by men on camels from three police posts. Trygve is setting up the 26 000-square-kilometre Sperrgebiet National Park. He's a man of the wild who knows this area like the back of his hand. From the northern mouth of the Orange our Landies follow the Namdeb convoy along the

NOTES – NAMIBIA:

- SMALL POPULATION – ABOUT 2 PEOPLE/SQ KM. WILD OPEN COASTLINE, MOSTLY UNDEVELOPED – JUST HOW WE LIKE IT
- NAMIBIA'S SKELETON COAST HAS LONG BEEN A GRAVEYARD FOR SHIPS, CREWS. EARLY PORTUGUESE SAILORS CALLED IT 'AREIAS DO INFERNO' OR 'SANDS OF HELL'
- THE CHALLENGE OF THE ANCIENT NAMIB / GOING TO BE TOUGH.
- STILL AWAITING FINAL PERMISSION FOR SKELETON COAST.
- ABOUT 1500 KM, ON THE SAND, FOLLOWING THE VERY EDGE
- LET'S GET THE SPERRGEBIET OVER FIRST, THEN WORRY ABOUT THE REST ——

WE'RE SANDWICHED BETWEEN THE DESERT DUNES AND THE COLD SOUTH ATLANTIC — INTERESTING.

OUT ON THE SPERRGEBIET IT WAS A TOUGH LIFE FOR THE OLD GERMAN PIONEERS.

OLD GERMAN COLONIAL CHURCH IN SWAKOP –

in a deep, booming voice. It's a song about Namibia being a land as hard as camel-thorn wood, the stones burnt by the sun. Babu Cossa from Mozambique sings in Shangaan and we add Zulu from KZN as well as English and Afrikaans. These diamond-mining lads have both a great thirst and insatiable appetite and more meat is thrown on the coals. Tonight their general manager is partying with them and they feel proud. Early next morning we're still singing around a hardwood fire outside the 'pink house'. The ghosts of the departed German miners have been quiet.

Dispatch #11 – Diamond Thieves

Interesting – they've caught them shooting diamonds over the security fence with crossbows. They try all sorts of things; 'stones' are cut into the heels of work boots and sewn into clothes, a Rasta man's hair lit up like a Christmas tree when they X-rayed him, and even carrier pigeons were used. Two little feathered friends were found with 144 rough diamonds attached to parcels on their legs. 'But don't get any ideas,' chuckles Chris. 'You'll be X-rayed before you leave for Lüderitz – we'll leave no stone unturned (no pun intended).' Don't forget to search the calabash …

Dispatch #12 – Lüderitz and Beyond

In Lüderitz we meet Robbie Brozin, the chairman of Nando's, who's flown in from South Africa with a team to experience a few days of desert life.

The geographic challenge remains the same – to follow Africa's outside edge – as from Lüderitz we continue to grind slowly up the coast. Volker Jahnke's big Strandwolf Land Cruiser with its massive sand tyres leads the way. He's a famed desert expert and in order to get a permit we must travel with him. We're all on the same radio frequency and this delightful big man of the desert feeds us colourful snippets of information over the air as we drive. It's all good stuff but sometimes difficult to comprehend when your heart's in your mouth, the Landy sliding sideways into a mousehole, or as you race the guts out of your overloaded Tdi trying to get over the ridge of an impossibly high dune. '*Did you know a cubic metre of fog contains 27 litres of water?*' comes Volker's dry Teutonic commentary over the air. 'Watch the ridge!' screams Mashozi as we fly through the air. Then again over the air from Volker: '*Did you know brown hyena*

outside edge to Chameisbucht, Baker's Bay and Bogenfels. The wind whistles through the old sun-bleached remains of the German diamond-mining settlements, with their old graves, tumbledown homesteads, schools, hospitals, mining equipment and railway lines through the desert. These were some of the richest diamond deposits in the world. Men would lie on their stomachs on a moonlit night and pick up 'sparkles' in the gravel. 'Careful the ghosts, it's supposedly haunted,' says Chris, handing us over the keys to the old 'pink house' at Bogenfels.

That night at the nearby mining camp, out comes the gorilla mask, and Sakkie Oberholzer sings *Das Südwester Lied*

kill up to 60 seal pups in a single orgy of feeding? Sadly they just crush their skulls and eat only one or two.' Jeez! Bruce slides sideways down a dune, hits the bottom and nearly rolls the big long-wheel-base TD5. We're simply carrying too much weight, loaded up with everything for a yearlong adventure, and the roof tents make us top-heavy. Volker had warned us; generally he wouldn't allow vehicles with roof tents. It's too dangerous with too much weight on top, but he understands we've got a long way to go. Eugene's Discovery, lighter, more powerful and with better weight distribution, has an easier time over the dunes. '*And by the way, did you know that jackals turn seal pups inside out for a better meal? It's called a jackal's sleeping bag.*' Thinking about that, not concentrating, I miss a gear and have to reverse all the way back down the dune and give it another run. '*Did you know,*' comes Volker's voice over the air again, '*most of the early German miners who lived out here on the Skeleton Coast were over 50? The youngsters couldn't take it and no wives would ever live out here. But it's rumoured,*' says the big German with a chuckle, '*that when the odd "ladies of the night" were rowed ashore, it was always under the cover of darkness. Not so much for discretion but rather that the girls wouldn't see the barren coastline – that would have frightened them off whatever the stakes!*'

The high tide's starting to push. I get *klapped* by a wave and seawater pours over the bonnet and comes in through the open air vents. Poor Landies, and this is only the beginning. '*Brown hyena territory,*' says Volker. '*There were two regulars, we named them John Travolta and Silly Sarah, but when researchers darted them they found that John was female and Silly Sarah the male! Careful, there's a dangerous ridge ahead with a bad fall away to the right, so take it flat out and once over swing immediately sharp left.*'

'Copy that Volker, thanks,' I say. The adrenalin pumps and we drive barefoot for better clutch and brake control. It's hell on the vehicles. '*See those shabby-looking life rafts of old planks, fishing buoys and plastic barrel?*' asks Volker. I look up to the right and there they are, half covered by the dunes. '*It's not uncommon to have stowaways put overboard. Many a cruel sea captain would rather do that than have to repatriate them from the next port. I've come across the poor unfortunates three times. It's like sending them to a certain death … Whoa, careful ahead. Don't follow, I'll radio you when I've found a way around.*'

We stop on a high ridge with not a human being in sight, just the endless dunes sweeping down to the Atlantic. This is the outside edge at its most desolate – it is magnificent in its wild beauty. A lone oryx walks slowly over a dune and at the water's edge a black-backed jackal feeds off a dead seal.

Dispatch #13 – The Tropic of Capricorn
'*Ross, do you copy me?*' '*Come in Volker.*' '*Okay. Keep inland a little and follow my tracks – it's a difficult piece, be careful.*' An hour later we're still battling. Forward and then reverse, compacting the sand and building a track. Finally the light fails and we camp in a big hole. Ross checks the Garmin – he's the navigator. Only then do we realise that we are camped just a hundred metres or so off 23° 26' 22" S, the Tropic of Capricorn. We all walk off onto the line and, in a little ceremony that involves a bottle, we hand over one of my Capricorn books to Volker. Inside the cover I'd written:

LITTLE TRISTAN CAN'T BELIEVE THE WHALE BONES

Thursday 10 May 2007
Thanks Volker for sharing the great sand ocean with us – and for your towrope.

It was here on this very line, three years ago, that we'd slid our Landies down a dune slip face, having crossed the continent from east to west as part of a journey to circumnavigate the globe along Capricorn.

Dispatch #14 – Hit by a Sandstorm

It hits us in the early morning. Still dark. The wind threatens to tear the rooftop tent off the Landy. My head throbs. Babu was the barman last night – he pours stiff three-finger Captains. Mind you, Volker and his sidekick Volkanjan (alias *The Strandwolf*, or beach wolf) gave it a full tonk and we heard them growling well into the night.

'The wind's changed to an easterly, let's get out of here,' roars Volker in the dark. 'There are big dunes ahead. With the sandstorm on us it could bury vehicles and then we'd really shit it off.' Volker's a master of understatement. He's done the Lüderitz to Walvis Bay journey over 50 times and is an expert Namib Desert man.

There's no time for breakfast, not even coffee and rusks. It's back to the madness of sliding the overloaded expedition Landies down the slip faces of some of the highest dunes in the world, then clawing, digging, pushing and winching our way to the summit of the next one, always with engines screaming. Then it's sliding down to the cold South Atlantic again, hugging the dunes, the waves washing against the deflated tyres, and to help things along we've got this east wind sandstorm.

What a great adventure: black-backed jackal around the fire at night, brown hyena feeding on Cape fur seal pups, more whale bones and shipwrecks, oryx in the desert and finally the 1915 lighthouse at Pelican Point. We say *Auf Wiedersehen* to Volker, that fine character who brought us safely through his great sand ocean, and I'm sure one of the most challenging sections of Africa's outside edge.

Dispatch #15 – Anxious Moments

Dave and Drieka Wylie, managers at the Protea Hotel in Walvis Bay, are there to meet us with soft beds and hot showers sponsored by the hotel chain. After the freezing desert nights it's all so warm and cosy. But I have an uneasy

△ DAVE WYLIE AND THE BEARD AT THE PELICAN POINT LIGHTHOUSE NEAR WALVIS.

feeling – we still don't have final permission from the Ministry of Environment and Tourism to complete the Skeleton Coast all the way through to the Kunene River and the border with Angola. There's been lots of correspondence and fortunately Ben Beytel, head of the ministry, is the same man who gave us permission to do the Capricorn crossing of the Namib in 2003. Surely the Scroll of Peace and Goodwill and our letters from the South African Department of Foreign Affairs will help? There's also the humanitarian nature of our journey. If we don't get permission, what then? The credibility of our outside edge odyssey will be lost. It is, after all, all about following the coast.

Dispatch #16 – Good News

And then we get the unbelievably good news. Just a police clearance and then we're off. The ministry has issued the permit. We leave in 24 hours. Skeleton Coast expert Eric Reinhardt, who heads up Wilderness Safaris, is in Namibia and he and his girlfriend Tanja will escort us up the coast to the Skeleton Coast Park's headquarters at Möwe Bay. There a warden will join us for our Skeleton Coast dash to the Kunene River. Isn't it wonderful when a plan comes together? Dave takes us for a celebratory dinner at the Raft Restaurant in Walvis Bay – fishermen, diamond miners, local businessmen, Bratwurst, Eisbein, Sauerkraut and good German beer.

Before we go, the Walvis Bay Rotary Club assists with the distribution of mobile libraries, which have been flown in by Centurus Colleges from Pretoria. Ross and Anna have now been joined by Tristan. Aged six, he's a delightful long-haired little Mowgli character straight out of Rudyard Kipling's *Jungle Book,* dances like Johnny Clegg and loves expedition life. He's been flown in – pity we've only got him for the school holidays as already he's become the expedition mascot.

The familiar growl of the Landies has become a way of life. Ross and Anna's Landy is nicknamed 'John Ross', after the young Scottish guy who walked up the coast to the then Delagoa Bay, escorted by Shaka's impis. Then there's Mashozi and me in the other Tdi Defender nicknamed 'Mary Kingsley', after that great Victorian lady explorer who travelled the waterways of West Africa. Bruce and Babu are in the long-wheel-base TD5 crew cab called 'Lady Baker', wife of Sir Samuel Baker who was rescued from slavery to become the first woman to travel the length of the Nile.

IRON CAMELS OF THE DESERT ON THEIR WAY TO FOZ DU CUNENE —

△ WE DRIVE BAREFOOT TO BETTER JUGGLE THE PEDALS —

A BLACK-BACKED JACKAL AND CAPE FUR SEALS

REMAINS OF THE VENTURA BOMBER'S RADIAL ENGINES.

This section of the outside edge would be incomplete without stopping for a German pint at Grünies, the tugboat bar in Swakopmund. 'This place is great,' says Eric, 'it even has its own German-like annual *Karnival* – it's practically more German than Germany.' Swakop, as it's fondly known, has, much like Victoria Falls, reinvented itself as an adventure sports capital. Here you can race through the sand sea on a quad bike, sandboard some of the highest dunes in the world, take a hot-air balloon ride over the desert, go on a 4x4, camel or horse safari, take an adrenalin-pumping desert skydive or go sports fishing and watch the sun set over the Atlantic. After the desert quiet of the Namib and the Sperrgebiet it's a bit of a culture shock and we immediately head north along the outside edge.

Dispatch #17 – North up the Coast

'*How about fish 'n chips?*' comes Ross's voice over the radio. I flash my lights at Eric and we stop at Hentiesbaai's Fishy Corner, with faded pictures of great fish and fishermen on the walls. Kabeljou is the favourite and you can have a *dop* whilst you wait. It's a grey day, moody and somewhat bleak. The fishing spots are marked off in miles. 'They're all great,' says Eric, 'especially Mile 108.' The only other traffic on the coastal road is the odd rusty Namibian-registered 4x4 with front-bumper rod holders carrying long fishing rods – they look like long-whiskered prehistoric insects in the mist. The red-faced occupants, helped on no doubt by the odd Jägermeister, are constantly in search of 'The Big One'. Across the bleak, black basalt plains, interspersed with pink granite and Namib dunes, Eric points out the remains of a massive oil rig. It appears that the whole thing was a scam, the brainwave of Ben du Preez and a certain Jack Scott. There was never a drop of oil – they took the bank for millions.

Torra Bay is windswept and deserted. 'Hey, but it's not always like this,' says Eric. 'Over the Christmas season it's crazy, you won't believe it. Farmers from the interior send cattle trucks ahead with drivers and labourers, tents and camping equipment, supplies of firewood and deep-freezers full of meat. One bloke even has a mobile bar complete with optics, and every year a Torra Bay mayor is elected amongst the festive fishermen. Farmers and friends have been coming here for generations.'

We push on to Terrace Bay. The general public aren't allowed beyond this point. It's our last chance for diesel and we fill all the jerry cans and long-range tanks from a single, lonely diesel pump. The wind howls and it's freezing cold. We push on through the dark, 70 kilometres to Möwe Bay, headquarters of the 16 000 km² Skeleton Coast Park. John Patterson points us down to the beach. Tents up, we huddle around the stew pot. Waves crash onto the rocks and the southwesterly howls; it's no wonder that early Afrikaners called it *Seekus van die Dood*, or 'Coast of Death'. Sounds ominous. Tomorrow we'll tackle it.

Dispatch #18 – Shipwrecks, Seal, Jackal and Hyena

Maybe we should have started with the east coast instead of the west – this Skeleton Coast is not for the faint-hearted. Anyway, here we are, four Landies overloaded with inflatable boats and supplies, tyres down to 1 bar for the sand. We're nine expedition members plus Skeleton Coast game warden Alwyn Engelbrecht and the delightful characters Eric and Tanja. It's bloody freezing, the cold South Atlantic is upside down, the southwesterly is howling and we're sitting huddled around a fire waiting for low tide so that we can push north up the beach to the Kunene River mouth.

The 2 400-kilometre coast of Namibia is proving an incredible challenge, extremely tough on Landies and crew; sliding the overloaded Landies down hundred-metre-dune slip faces, then foot flat, clawing our way up the crest of the next dune, Atlantic on the left, desert on the right. It's a land of shipwrecks, seal, jackal and brown hyena and the *Soo-oop-wa*, the constant southwesterly wind that blows sand into your eyes, nose and food and in a moment covers your tracks. But if you think we've got it tough, how about the castaways from the *Dunedin Star*, wrecked on 30 November 1942 close to where we're now camped?

As if being a passenger on an unescorted merchantman sailing U-boat-infested seas were not enough, the ship hit an underwater obstacle and rapidly started taking on water. After grounding the ship 500 metres offshore, the captain started sending passengers to shore via a motorised lifeboat. Several trips later, the motor failed, but not before 42 passengers were delivered to the relative safety of this desolate beach. As many as 43 people were left marooned on the wreck of the *Dunedin Star*, that was slowly but surely being battered to pieces by the Atlantic. Fortunately the captain had sent out an SOS, and several ships came to assist. Between them they managed to rescue those stranded on the *Dunedin Star*, but the surf was just too rough to rescue the castaways, who had to endure nearly a month of Skeleton Coast hell.

En route back to Walvis Bay, one of the saviours, a rescue tug called the *Sir Charles Elliott*, ran into trouble of its own. For the second time, the survivors of the *Dunedin Star* on board found themselves shipwrecked.

Meanwhile, Captain Naudé, a dapper David Niven look-alike flying a 1942 twin-engined Ventura bomber, was sent to drop car tubes of water and supplies for the original castaways from the sky. In an attempt to rescue the women and children, the brave pilot landed on a nearby saltpan, but then broke through the crust, so adding a stranded bomber and crew to the calamity. The unrelenting captain and his team managed to repair the plane and fly off again after a few days, only to crash into the surf about 40 minutes later. Amazingly, they all survived and swam to shore, and the saga continued.

The situation was dire. The eyes of the youngest castaway, 13-month-old Sidney, became so gummed up with sand that they feared he might lose his sight.

Luckily, a police convoy of 18 men in two-wheel-drive 1940s Chevrolet trucks was busy pushing, pulling and digging its way from Outjo to reach the survivors. By some miracle, the relief convoy of trucks came upon the stranded survivors of the *Sir Charles Elliot* tug boat at the dry Khumib River, loaded them up and pushed north to finally rescue both the *Dunedin Star* castaways and the airmen. They all made it safely back to safety some 26 days after the original disaster.

On our way here we had come across the mast of the wrecked *Sir Charles Elliott* tug sticking out of the sea, and the lonely grave of Mathias Koraseb on the shore nearby, who, along with Angus McIntyre, drowned whilst attempting to swim to shore.

Here on the beach we find pieces of scattered fuselage, a tyre, some rusted landing gear and one of the 18-cylinder radial engines from brave Captain Naudé's Ventura bomber, and at the castaway's camp we find bits of canvas and rope, old nails and planks, sand-blasted bottles and rusty cans. How they

We find old sand-blasted bottles in the desert.

It's still a coast of wrecks –

must have struggled. Sixty-five years later we too struggle, despite our modern Landies fitted with Old Man Emu suspensions, winches and built-in tyre compressors. Imagine how it was for them, with narrow tyres peeling off the rims and only one hand pump for 36 tyres. We know the only way to get through the sand is to let our Cooper tyres down and then pump them up again to get over the razor-sharp rocks of the basalt sections.

The tide has turned; we must go.

Dispatch #19 – Kunene or Bust

It's foot flat to avoid getting stuck, and zigzagging around rocks and incoming waves. Albatross swoop and dive in front of the Landies, seals wobble and flap into the ocean, whilst ghost crabs gawk in amazement at our passing convoy. This is the nature of the outside edge.

Closer to Angola the dunes sweep down to touch the rocky plains above the ocean. The *Soo-oop-wa* howls like never before and then in a moment we are there. Our Garmin GPS records the coordinates as 17° 15' 20" S and 11° 45' 81" E.

Mission accomplished – we've arrived at the end of Namibia's Skeleton Coast. We jump out of the Landies. It's bitterly cold. Up goes our Africa Outside Edge flag, and attached to the same piece of driftwood is also a simple hand-drawn sign with the words 'Kunene Mouth'.

To stay true to our mission to circumnavigate Africa around the outside edge, the expedition must follow the coast wherever possible. Now the north bank of the Kunene and Angola are only a kilometre away, but there's no way of getting the Landies across the fast-flowing river mouth. The authorities won't allow us to cross by rubber duck, so it's a 12-day detour through Kaokoland to get back to the river at Ruacana, cross into Angola and then work our way back to the north bank of the Kunene. With Eric and Tanja leading us we use dry riverbeds to detour out of the Skeleton Coast.

Fresh water, makalani palms and ancient *omborombonga*, or leadwood trees, are a change from the desert coast. Traditional Himba girls endorse the expedition Scroll of Peace and Goodwill with simple red-ochred handprints and we spend hours with the desert elephants of the Hoarusib.

Himba tribespeople dance in the dust and we distribute mosquito nets to mums with babies. Near Swartbooisdrift, where the Dorslandtrek settlers crossed the river in their search for better lives, we roll out our bedrolls under a giant *omborombonga*. Little Tristan finds some Himba mates who now share his tent. It's so delightfully peaceful: the moon, the leadwood trees, the sound of the rapids. We've survived 2 400 kilometres of one of the wildest and most inhospitable coastlines on earth, a journey made possible by Chris Sivertsen of Namdeb, the Namibian Ministry of Environment and Tourism, Volker Jahnke, as well as Eric and Tanja of Wilderness Safaris. We couldn't have done it without them. I look across the fire at one of the Landies, at the flags of the 31 countries still to come. Wouldn't it be wonderful if they all could be as tranquil as northern Namibia's Koakoland? Now it's over and we're at the Kunene River, ready to cross into Angola above the Ruacana Falls – or is it?

Dispatch #20 – Help Nando's Fight Malaria

Next day we get an email on our BGAN system, our Broadband Global Area Network that we use for internet and telephony via satellite. I'm booked to fly from Ondangwa in northern Namibia all the way to Malaysia to talk about our One Net One Life malaria campaign at the Nando's 20th birthday celebration. Three days later I'm back at Ondangwa with a pledge from Nando's UK for an extra £50 000 to fight malaria. The money will be deposited directly with Vestergaard Frandsen, producers of PermaNets. These life-saving, long-lasting mosquito nets will be delivered to key high-risk malaria points on the outside edge of Africa, and we'll distribute them to mums with babies. We'll call the campaign 'Help Nando's Fight Malaria'. Wow!

A traditional Himba girl endorses the scroll with a simple red-ochre handprint. It's Anna's first expedition – she's doing just great.

NEAR SWARTBOOISDRIFT WE MEET PROSPECTOR & POET CHARLES ZANDBERG

Ag- Kingsley he says 'Visitors think I'm you and I score loads of free Captain Morgan'.

Angola

BATTLE SCARRED AND EXCITING.

Day 40, Country 3 on the Edge

We're battling to get good info, but so far following Angola's edge promises to be a tough challenge. It's got an undiscovered sort of 'out of bounds' feeling; believe it's beautiful but scarred painfully by years of tragic warfare. We'll need to be aware of unexploded landmines in the north. I don't want to die for this adventure. It's good to have Babu Cossa with us – we're expecting some post-war bureaucratic snarl-ups so we'll need his Portuguese.

THE POLICE CHIEF AT FOZ DO CUNENE ENDORSES THE SCROLL – (HELPED BY A LITTLE CAPTAIN FROM THE TANK)

Dispatch #21 – They Come Barefoot in the Dark

'They will make you unload everything,' said the pessimists, but the expedition Scroll of Peace and Goodwill signed by Madiba does the trick and even gets endorsed by customs and immigration. Smiles, handshakes, buckets of patience and some hours later our humanitarian convoy rolls into Chitado, where the administrator adds his goodwill message to the scroll and, right there in the dusty street outside his office, we distribute mosquito nets and learning materials under the Angolan flag.

That night they come barefoot in the dark, shouting the whooping cries of hyena to call the others to where we'd pitched camp, in the middle of nowhere, shielded from the wind by a rocky outcrop. With them they bring a goat to be slaughtered. The Himba have arrived. Through Babu, we speak to their chief in Portuguese. A dear little man with a twinkle in his eye, his prized possession is his snuff container with its silver spoon. Around the fire, Molisani Mohomba tells us of the war days when the South Africans interrogated them to see if they were hiding members of SWAPO, the South West Africa People's Organisation, who were fighting for Namibian liberation from South African rule, and even if they weren't, they were beaten. 'But that is life,' he says. 'Now things are better. We are free and can even cross into Namibia.'

Molisani throws a twisted piece of hardwood onto the fire whilst the near-naked Himba girls take it in turns to admire Mashozi's Zulu bangle. One of the girls leans forward to touch my beard and the others giggle with glee. They are beautiful in their naivety. Fresh goat meat sizzles on the fire.

'We are Himba,' says Molisani, 'and this is our life. Our girls must never wash; this is how it is from birth to death. Their bodies stay covered in red ochre and butterfat. They cleanse themselves with aromatic smoke. But for the men it is different because they take the herds to water and there they bathe. The missionaries tried to change our ways, but we are Himba, and our women are beautiful. When we die we

The Ruacana Falls on the Cunene are spectacular

ANGOLA-NOTES:

- A massive 1 246 700 km² with 2800 km of coastline
- About 14 million people
- Ravaged by war / landmines still a problem!
- One of Africa's richest countries in iron ore, copper, diamonds and oil
- Bordered by the Congo, DRC, Zambia and Namibia
- BIG QUESTION: How the hell do we get the 3 Landies across the 26-kilometre-wide mouth of the Congo river to the DRC on the other side? There's no bridge or ferry!
- Going to be interesting! / Be careful —

THE POLICE POST AT FOZ

THE BEAUTIFUL PLAINS OF IONA

↙ DISTRIBUTING LEARNING MATERIALS AT A BUSH SCHOOL IN SOUTHERN ANGOLA —

go to meet our ancestors. Sacred cattle are slaughtered and their skulls and horns adorn our graves.'

Molisani goes into a guttural funeral chant and teaches us how to join in. We share snuff tobacco. I ask him what the greatest thing is he could wish for. 'Rain,' comes the answer. 'With rain anything is possible. There will be plenty of grass and the herds will grow fat. I wish for nothing more.'

Dispatch #22 – The Plains of Iona

And so we roll up our bedrolls and cross the beautiful grass plains of Iona, dotted with stunted acacia trees, occasional pronking springbok and ancient welwitschia plants, the whole lot surrounded by far pavilions of rough-hewn mountains. We're five Landies now, having been joined by Eugene's friends *Senhor* Paulo Fernandes and Anthony Walley, and William Gwebu has taken over from Max Methi as Eugene's travelling companion. Also with us is *Getaway* magazine's senior journalist, author and traveller Don Pinnock, who's come in for a taste of outside edge expedition life. *Getaway* will be covering the entire adventure and, what's more, is running a competition in which a reader can win my Land Rover. The magazine's also included a pledge for mosquito nets – it's all good stuff. Don's travelling with Babu and Bruce, who drives the big long-wheel-base Landy that Don has now nicknamed 'the Stomach' because it carries all the grub.

We're all overcome by the beauty of southern Angola and Don scribbles these words in the expedition journal:

> *The peaks around us now – the vast plains and the green welwitschia spiders that seem to scuttle across them. This is straight out of Lord of the Rings. We're half expecting the elven armies of Galadriel to appear, the banners of Rivendell undulating in the cool morning breeze.*

Dispatch #23 – Foz du Cunene

Senhor Pedro, the police chief at Foz du Cunene, greets us warmly. He's been expecting us. Last week, at our request, diamond miners from the south bank, using a fishing rod and sinker, had cast a package across the river. In it was a *Getaway* magazine with me, the Greybeard, on the cover and a Portuguese note written by Babu informing them of our journey. We are asked to wait, however, whilst he and his men get into uniform so as to receive us correctly. Shortly after, in his war-torn office, his rough-and-ready (and uniformed) men all gathered around, *Senhor* Pedro takes great pride in writing carefully in Portuguese in the scroll, but, oh my gosh, halfway through he makes a spelling mistake. I hope it's not because of the celebratory Captain we've decanted from the tank and are now all sharing. *Senhor* Pedro takes off his beret and shakes his head. He's upset. Imagine if his commanding officer up the coast at the Namibe garrison were to see his page with the error. Fortunately he's on a clean one, so to avert any embarrassment I tear the page out of the scroll, give it to him to throw away and, much relieved, he starts afresh.

We camp under the Angolan flag and eat kabeljou caught at the river mouth. We decant more Captain from the tank and one of the Angolan troops plays Portuguese songs on a homemade guitar. The next day, using the megaphone that we use for malaria prevention education, we shout to the diamond miners across the river: 'Coming over by boat, see you tomorrow!' 'Careful of the diamond police,' floats a voice back on the wind. 'Don't worry!' I shout, 'we'll bring them with us.' And so with *Senhor* Pedro on board as proof that we aren't smugglers, we cross the Kunene in one of our inflatables, thus remaining true to our outside edge journey. The river is running swiftly. We go upstream to the first rapids, passing some big crocs. On the Namibian side, the high desert dunes fall steeply into the river. For the first time the men from opposite sides of the river shake hands, now joined somehow by our expedition.

Dispatch #24 – The Baía dos Tigres Gap

The words of Rico Sakko of Angolan Adventure Safaris echo in my mind. 'You've got only one chance at it,' he said when I phoned ahead for directions. 'You can only do it at low spring tide. Break down or get stuck and you'll lose your vehicle.' Springbok fisherman Neil Gouws is leading the convoy. Fortunately he was headed our way, en route to Rico's fishing camp at Flamingo Bay, and knows the terrain. He'd found us at first light where we'd been camping in the cold and the wind, awaiting the tide like Strandlopers on the beach, feeding ourselves on giant black-shelled mussels.

Adrenalin pumping, 0,8 of a bar in the Cooper tyres, foot flat in the Landies and with a pebble in the pocket, we ride the Baía dos Tigres gap. If we peal a tyre off the rim as we

THE RUGGED OUTSIDE EDGE AT FLAMINGO BAY.

duck and weave at crazy angles between dune slope and the Atlantic, we will roll. All that will be left to do will be to scramble with money, passports and drinking water to the top of the dune. Bruce stops to take a photograph and Ross would like to do some filming, but Neil is edgy. 'C'mon guys,' he says, 'we must keep moving, the tide's pushing. If we get stuck or have to winch, we'll have waves breaking over the vehicles. Believe me, I've seen it happen.'

And so, with engines screaming, we push on. '*I've got a bloody flat!*' comes Eugene's voice over the radio. '*No time,*' we hear Neil's reply. '*Quickly use the compressor to pump in some air and keep moving. There are only eight kilometres to go and then the beach will widen out and we'll be safe.*' We make it through the Baía dos Tigres gap and then down the beach past the yapping dogs and the fishermen of Tombua, who use colourful, handheld, plastic plates to propel their small rafts to and from the fishing grounds. Tombua, the old Porto Alexandre, has been hammered by war and neglect. Cops and immigration give us a going over, which pisses Neil off to no end. 'How the hell are they going to grow tourism? You've got a visa and an entry stamp, so why do you have to be hassled?' 'Don't worry,' I respond, 'it will change eventually, and they've got a black mark against them in the meantime.'

I've started a scorecard you see – any shit experience from bureaucrats, roadblocks and the like and the country gets a black mark next to its name on the inside of the Landy sun visor. It's become a fun thing for the team, with much radio banter after the event. Any sign of trouble and the felt-tipped pen is out. 'I say sir, would you like a mark?'

As we leave town, there's a mob beating a dog to death with a pipe. Maybe it's got rabies.

Dispatch #25 – Flamingo Bay

Hangovers all round. Last night Mashozi unearthed a bottle of Captain Morgan Special Reserve from its hiding place in the back of the Landy. It was a farewell to the two Landy Discovery teams of Eugene and Willy, and *Senhor* Paulo and Anthony, who headed back to Johannesburg early this morning. Anthony had entertained us with his guitar, everything from *Puff the Magic Dragon* to *Streets of London* – a song that Mashozi says reminds her of her dad. His ashes are still in a bottle in the Land Rover, hoping one day to reach the Niger River and Timbuktu. Last night, putting his arm around his mother's shoulders, Ross had said, 'We should move the jar out of the grub box and hide it somewhere away from customs officers. Imagine if someone thought it was curry powder or Aromat.'

We say cheers to the hospitable team at Flamingo Bay, including Rico's blonde girlfriend and co-manager Ursula de la Guerra and their dog called Strooitjie. 'Be careful of the cliff edges,' says Neil. 'Some of the lips have been eroded by the waves from underneath – it can be dangerous. But go carefully and you can make it all the way to Namibe.' We were back to just the three expedition Land Rovers, but now newcomers Paulito and Romano have asked to tag along with us as far as Lobito in their Cape Town-registered Land Rover. They are two laid-back characters, and together we hug the edge of high, dramatic sandstone cliffs, heading slowly north.

Dispatch #26 – Namibe, Old Moçâmedes

We follow the edge, direction Namibe City. Neil was right – it's an adventurous 4x4 challenge of beach and rugged sandstone cliffs falling steeply into the Atlantic. Ross in the leading Land Rover comes over the radio, warning us to put our cameras away. The southern outskirts of Namibe, formerly the port of Moçâmedes, are all rocket batteries and military barracks, but once into town, what a beautiful city. Friendly people and no hassles from cops. There are avenues of tall palm trees with white-washed lower trunks, clean streets, painted buildings and a municipal market with everything, including fresh *pão*. There's a bank that's happy to change rands into Angolan kwanzas and, best of all, diesel at R2,90 per litre. The poor live in shacks and holes dug into the cliffs. High and dry on the beach is the wreck of the *Spirit of Independence,* registered in the Cape Verde Islands.

Dispatch #27 – The Tricks of Travel

'What are you doing here? Who are you?' floats a Portuguese voice from across the dark in a dry river canyon in remote Angola. 'We are poisonous snake collectors,' comes the instant reply from Ross via Babu's Portuguese as we sit huddled around a hardwood fire. 'Please, for your own safety, don't come near the vehicles. The snakes are in boxes, but they're very dangerous. *Muito perigosa*.' 'We hear you,' they say, and the voices drift off into the night.

When travelling, I believe it's most important not to take oneself too seriously. Since first shocking a photographer with my gorilla mask at Cape Point, I had recently used it for a laugh in an encounter with an immigration official. Thinking about our supposed cargo, Don Pinnock gets the giggles and we start chatting around the fire about the tricks of travel.

In the old days we had a sound machine under the bonnet, which, with the click of a switch, would moo like a herd of cattle. The sound, complete with a cow's tail sticking out from the side of the bonnet, would delight nomadic Maasai and Samburu cattle herders who would point with their spears in wide-eyed amazement. And so they would gather, and we would talk and all become part of the same journey.

Too many curious onlookers on the other hand, or gawkers as we call them around camp, sometimes wear you down. And so out comes the Zulu calabash with a few incantations, the sprinkling of a little water and the dancing of a jig. Finally, the words 'powerful medicine to protect', stage-whispered by our interpreter, usually give us a bit of privacy.

Fake traffic fines can be interesting if the greedy cops are in pairs, which is generally the case. 'I can deal with only one of you if we are passing money,' you whisper, and so, smiling in anticipation, one of them comes to the door where, with engine running, you slip him the bundle of one million whats-its. As you roar off waving, you shout to his mate: 'he's got the five million'. In the rear-view mirror you see them arguing like hell – just desserts I always think.

PROVIDED THE SEAS ON OUR LEFT WERE O.K.—

There you are, caught with a case of Captain Morgan, a cool box full of fresh meat and three cartons of cigarettes under the seat. This is not allowed, definitely not allowed, so that's when, as expedition leader, you start jumping up and down, roundly abusing the expedition team for their stupidity. 'I told you, you bloody fools, no fresh meat through this border. And then, you idiots, you sneak in tobacco and booze too!' That's the cue for Ross to duck from a mock slap and Gill to start sobbing uncontrollably. The customs man is bound to shake his head, embarrassed that the old Greybeard can get so red-faced and angry with his own family. 'Leave them be sir,' he'll say, 'it was obviously a mistake. You can go.' Travelling is all about drama, and laughter is always the best medicine. Being arrogant and uptight doesn't work with officials in Africa.

The conversation turns from travel tricks to the need not to march into Africa like boys with their toys from the south. I always suggest that you immerse yourself in the culture of local communities instead – don't let the bureaucrats spoil it for you, that's part of travel. Give your journey a specific purpose and a name, have the right paperwork and, where possible, put something back into Africa. I remember once meeting Lorenzo Ricciardi, who travelled across Africa from the mouth of the Rufiji to the mouth of the Congo in open boats. His advice was to smile and wave a lot, especially when you're in shit. And, oh yes, the stuttering trick can be a good one too. Red-faced, beard twitching, eyes bulging and ba… baa…battling to get a word out generally has you ushered out of the man's office at record speed.

Dispatch #28 – Boulder Hopping

Outside Bentiaba, we photograph an old 1824 fort, but then the vultures arrive – uniformed men on mopeds – and we're carted off to be interrogated at the administrator's office. It's a bit ugly at first, but then it's all smiles and backslapping thanks to Babu's Portuguese. Now it's on to Lucira, a gem of a fishing village with a row of pastel-coloured waterfront houses, brightly coloured fishing boats in the bay and fish for Luanda drying on racks in the sun. Then the road turns into a back-breaking, boulder-hopping 4x4 track that has the occupants lurching from side to side and the driver hanging on for dear life. We use first and second gear only, in low ratio with difflock. Our diesel dogs, with their specially adapted Old Man Emu suspensions, are made for this sort of work, but if they're getting this heavily punished so early in the journey, how will they possibly make it? There were the valve-bouncing, engine-screaming dunes of the Namib and now there are roads that are like goat tracks – at times it's quicker to get out of the vehicles and walk.

We camp in a dry riverbed, still with Paulito and Romano. There's not another vehicle to be seen, but then later that day, whilst stopping for bully beef and baked beans sarmies, two big, yellow 6x6 overland trucks, the ones that you see on TV doing the Dakar Rally, come thundering along. It's a safari outfit travelling from Windhoek to Cameroon, where clients pay big bucks to fly in and do sunburnt sections. It's always fun when two expeditions meet. There's a little grey-haired lady on board who's doing a pilgrimage. Her husband died in southern Angola on a previous trucking safari, when the lorry jack collapsed and he got crushed to death. I give her a big hug.

Dispatch #29 – The Journey to Lobito

Africa's broken dreams. On past the old Portuguese colonial houses, compounds, administrative buildings and old mango trees of the one-time sugar mill at Dombe Grande. It's

Whilst their mums dry fish for the market, we entertain the local kids with some learning materials.

Annelie's birthday; she's a *boeremeisie* from an Eastern Cape farm on her first expedition. She's doing great, learning to drive the Landies and live in the bush. It's not always easy – pitch camp, strike camp, move, move, move, forever up the coast. It seems timeless and endless. The sun is up, *Renosterkoffie* is on the boil and for breakfast we've got pawpaw and big, yellow bananas – our first fresh fruit in weeks. We sing *Happy Birthday*. Hunting dogs bark hysterically. There are small figures in the distance, and *chop!* A panga comes down. The hunter lifts a dark shape into the air – probably a little grey duiker or maybe an antbear. Down from our hilltop camp we dodge the *wag-'n-bietjie* bushes. Our bodies are alert and tense; hopefully there are no unexploded landmines about.

I can't believe it, we're in Lobito at last and straight into the arms of a Shoprite supermarket where Mashozi has the chance to stock up on those South African favourites like Marmite, boxed wine, Aromat, Nando's sauces and Mrs Ball's chutney. The car guards have AKs – we've hit 'civilisation'. Oil and diamond revenues are trickling south but there's still a great divide between rich and poor – mud shacks on the hills, mansions on the beach. A dude in a blue Porsche Boxter wheelspins into the car park. The hood goes up electronically – not the ideal car for dodging the serious potholes, but great, I am sure, for keeping the ego intact. Lobito, established by the Portuguese in 1843, is still a grand place. There's a silver-coloured mermaid statue in the bay, a roundabout centred with a high-and-dry fishing boat called *Zaire* and a thatched restaurant aptly called Zulu – great for us gang from KZN. We have a peri-peri flat-chicken birthday lunch for Annelie and give her a homemade birthday card decorated with pressed flowers and the words: 'Anna, what better way of celebrating your birthday than living on the edge.' The bash continues into the dark. 'Camp here next to the restaurant,' says Mario, owner of the Restaurant Zulu. 'How's the crime?' I ask. 'Was terrible, but then the chief of police decided to close the jails and open the graveyards, and now things are quiet,' he assures, and so we camp on the beach.

Dispatch #30 – Loadworks and Lovesick

Up early after not much sleep, as the restaurant security guards were pissed and noisy, determined to show they were looking after us. The needy are picking up cigarette butts from between the beach tables. We shampoo our hair in the Atlantic; it's a lot warmer here, not like the cold water we know from the Cape of Good Hope and the Skeleton Coast. Driving through the traffic out of Lobito, we see markets, mopeds, stray dogs dodging overloaded trucks and blue-and-white minibus taxis racing to overtake us and wave. The people are friendly. After 30 years of war there is hope.

The road north is broken and potholed, the worst of its kind. Chinese road gangs are at work redoing it. We stop for a brunch of fat chunks of pawpaw, bananas, fresh *pão* and coffee, served on the bonnet of a Landy. The road builders come to chat and, intrigued, they photograph the 33 flags running along the sides of the Landies. 'Ah,' says Chinese John with a toothy grin, 'it's a velly long load all the way lound Aflika. Load ahead velly good.' Later Loss comes on the ladio '*Loadworks ahead*,' he says with a giggle and so we sit for hours in a long snake of a line, heading for Luanda. The loadworks tluck behind us plays loud Chinese music – *Sukiyaki amongst the baobabs* – and then it's north up the coastal road to Sumbe, Cabo das Tres Pontas and the white cliffs of Porto Amboim, not unlike those of Dover on the English Channel. From Calamba to the bridge over the mangroved banks

Flat chicken or prawns peri-peri? Difficult!

of the Cuanza River is open, park-like country, green with scattered palm trees and baobabs. I've been worried about Bruce. He's been very down lately – seems he's lovesick. He'd met little Sam shortly before departure – she'd then joined us in Cape Town, desperately in love – and now the separation is getting to him. 'Hey boss,' he says to me that night, 'feels like my heart's in a blender. It's never been like this before.' And so I agree that she should fly in to join us for a while, come to Pointe Noire in the Congo with big Deon Schürmann, who's coming to join us as French interpreter.

The next day Bruce's spirits have picked up no end, we even catch him whistling. We need to care for one another, it's a long way to go.

NAMIBE

Relics of war

Dispatch #31 – Foz do Cuanza

Just south of Luanda we set up an expedition base camp at Cuanza River Lodge. It's the best place to stay if you don't want to get caught up in the mayhem of Luanda City.

Assisted by Bruce Bennett, the lodge manager, and using our Yamaha-powered Gemini inflatables, we distribute mosquito nets to isolated communities living upriver in the mangrove swamps. Across the river is the Quiçama National Park, where, according to Bruce, everything got eaten during the war. 'Elephant, buffalo, hippo – the lot were gunned down and transported in military helicopters to a fishing trawler offshore where the carcasses were blast frozen and then sold as bushmeat up the coast.'

Every week or two, together with these dispatches, we send out a short Africa Outside Edge geography lesson and a few expedition visuals to the pupils at Centurus Colleges in the Pretoria area. It's these students and teachers who have supplied one of the Land Rovers and are assisting with the expedition's Teaching on the Edge campaign, including malaria education, learning materials and the mobile libraries that we've been giving out. It's wonderful for these youngsters; now they can name and are learning about the 33 countries that make up the outside edge of Africa. Different classes have adopted different outside edge countries as projects. It's exciting and possibly the first time in history that more than a thousand schoolchildren along with their teachers have adopted an expedition. Now the directors and some of the staff are flying in to Luanda for a field visit, and Bruce Bennett offers to send his driver and a vehicle to fetch them so that we can avoid Luanda's traffic. Obviously we include a large cool box of sustenance. It's dark by the time they arrive, somewhat inebriated, at the mouth of the Cuanza. The entire expedition team is hiding within earshot – even the generator is off. '*Boa noite,*' says the lone security guard to the visitors. 'Where's Kingsley and expedition? Big man, beard, *mafuta*?' they ask, using hand movements to show a beard and tummy. 'No Eenglish,' says the security man, handing over a note that reads: 'Take a rubber duck and go about 15 kilometres up the Cuanza – you'll see our lights in the forest on the left. Be careful of the crocs.' 'Jeez!' says one of them, putting down his rucksack, 'it's pitch-black.' 'Have you got any beer?' another asks the security guard who continues to mumble 'No Eenglish' and points to the river. And so the huffing, puffing and cursing continues as our visitors launch the expedition duck. 'Which way is upstream?' 'No Eenglish!' shouts back the security guard. We're all in stitches as they start to paddle over a mud bank. I nudge Ross. On goes the switch and they're blinded by a searchlight. I shout in a disguised British accent: 'Who the fuck's stealing the boat?' We all rush into the river, scaring the shit out of them, but just pulling them ashore. It's great to have visitors and news from home.

The next day they assist with the distribution of more mosquito nets and learning materials to local rural schools. They're a jolly bunch and we really value their support.

Dispatch #32 – The Chaos of Luanda

As we're driving into Luanda, Mashozi reads from the *Lonely Planet Africa* guide that correctly refers to the city as 'hot, heaving, oil-rich and cash-poor'. Words can't explain the gridlocked, bumper to bumper traffic. The city, designed to house 750 000, is now home to some five million, most of whom have run here seeking sanctuary from the war. There's litter and poverty alongside the incredible wealth from diamonds and oil. Shiny black Hummers, overloaded with chrome and spotlights, pretty girls in jeans and jewellery, night clubs and bars and the buzz of the city are juxtaposed with ragtag kids digging in the rubbish for titbits, the old boiled-cabbage smell of sewerage and street vendors selling everything from illegal DVDs and Barbie dolls to toothbrushes and dog collars. It all brings Rio de Janeiro to mind, Brazil being linked to Angola by the slave trade.

We visit a clinic in downtown Luanda. The mums and babies are lovely as they patiently await their mosquito nets. British Airways and the United States Agency for International Development (USAID) have helped to arrange the day. The local media love the story of the scroll and the adventures of a South African family who are helping in the fight against malaria. Local actors do a colourful malaria prevention skit. We have a great day.

That night, back at the Cuanza River mouth, I pick up *Another Day of Life* by war correspondent Ryszard Kapuściński and read a few pages on wartime Luanda:

> *The dogs were still alive, they were pets abandoned by owners fleeing in panic. You could see dogs of the most expensive breeds, without masters – boxers, bulldogs, greyhounds, Dobermans, dachshunds, Airedales, spaniels, even Scottish terriers and Great Danes, pugs and poodles. Deserted, stray, they roamed in a great pack looking for food. As long as the Portuguese army was there, the dogs gathered every morning on the square in front of the general headquarters and sentries fed them canned NATO rations. It was like*

Gridlocked in downtown Luanda

watching an international pedigreed dog show ...When the army left, the dogs began to go hungry and slim down. For a while they drifted around in the city in a desultory mob, looking for a handout. One day they disappeared. I think they followed the human example and left Luanda, since I never came across a dead dog afterward, though hundreds of them had been loitering in front of the general headquarters and frolicking in front of the palace. One could suppose that an energetic leader emerged from the ranks to take the pack out of the dying city ... Perhaps they're still roaming, but I don't know in what direction and in what country. After the exodus of the dogs, the city fell into rigor mortis. (2001, pp. 25–26)

Dispatch #33 – The Bay of Wrecks

North of Luanda we hear the booming sound of waves breaking against the empty, rust-red hulls – a graveyard of over 40 ships. It's incredible. There are fishing boats, cargo ships and oil tankers, the broken bones of vessels with great names like *Karl Marx* and *Antonio*. It's as if an angry giant had picked them up and thrown them down all together in the bay. We're so close to Luanda and yet there's not a person in sight other than a small Renault van with the back doors open and a Portuguese lad and a local girl caught with their pants down, so to speak. Armed with their cameras, Bruce and Don climb into the bowels of a ship. Ross shakes his head from behind the lens of his video camera. 'I can't believe it,' he says. 'What could possibly have happened to have brought all these ships together in one bay?'

We camp beneath the red-and-white hull of the ship *Lundoge* – her rusted derricks sticking into the starlit sky, the panga, cog and star of the Angolan flag on her funnel and a rope ladder hanging from her side. The south wind brings the sounds of a Saturday night disco from outside Luanda – it's difficult to sleep in this place of seafaring ghosts. The next morning Don looks a bit haggard. He'd camped down on the beach and had been hassled all night by giant rats.

Dispatch #34 – The Road to Soyo

It's a road to hell, wrecked trucks and potholes so deep that sometimes you need low range to tackle them, catching your tow hitch as you accelerate out the other side. For fear of landmines, we camp, shit and eat on narrow tracks or in deserted quarries. At Ambriz we're interrogated by the navy, the administrator and the police. Three black marks on the sun visor later, we're finally allowed to camp on the beach on an old, unused Portuguese tennis court. Three love to the expedition. At Soyo we are looked after by a South African de-mining outfit. Pieter Kok and Braam Rossouw head up the unit – great guys whose teams have risked their lives in Mozambique, the Sudan, Eritrea, Ethiopia, Bosnia and now Angola – and they invite us for a *ware Suid-Afrikaanse braai*. We eat huge chunks of Brazilian beef from an open fire, and we tap some Captain Morgan from where it lives in the Land Rover water tank. 'How the hell are you going to get over the Congo River?' they ask. There's no bridge and it's 26 kilometres across to Banana in the DRC. 'You'll have to be careful,' they say. 'This place is bristling with military security because of the oil wells.' I look across the fire, feel the pebble in my pocket and give Ross a wink. Somehow we will have to make a plan. That's the nature of following the outside edge.

Dispatch #35 – Ponta de Padrão

In 1482 the Portuguese naval Captain Diogo Cão erected a stone cross at Ponta de Padrão at the mouth of the Congo. In time, this claiming of the land led to great suffering as hundreds of thousands of slaves were exported down the Congo River along with ivory and rubber. Before reaching the cross we have to make libations to the souls of the dead. There's singing and the beating of drums and, more importantly, the supply of red wine, which we had to bring along to appease the spirits. We pour just a little at the foot of a tree and the rest we enjoy in small glasses with the Congo rivermen. In the late afternoon we sit at the base of the cross, or, more correctly, its replica, whilst Eduardo, the community leader, endorses the scroll. Ross and Bruce bodysurf in the long line of waves that break onto the beach, while I take a stick and write 'Mouth of the Congo' in the sand. As the sun sets, mums and babies gather around the Gemini inflatable for a malaria education session and life-saving mosquito nets. We feel good about helping people in places where previously there has been so much pain and suffering.

Dispatch #36 – Crossing the Congo

The next day, 83 men manhandle our three Landies onto a leaking wooden barge called the *Tumi Mi Tangwa*. She trades barrels of fuel from Angola for hardwood planks from the forests of the Congo. 'Quickly, the winch cable!' screams Ross as one of the boarding planks snaps with a crack like a rifle shot. It's only this quick intervention that saves the Landy, the one that's been sponsored by the schoolchildren from Centurus Colleges, from ending up in the drink. The humidity of the Congo River stifles us as the third Land Rover Defender, amidst shouting, screaming and organised chaos, is finally loaded. The barge lists badly, and empty drums are moved into the back corner. Once filled with Congo riverwater, they form ballast and she slowly rights herself. Two rusty, antique 40HP Yamaha outboards, one without a tiller arm, the other with new spark plugs from our toolkit, push us slowly out from the south bank of the Congo. We've taken the precaution of tying one of our Gemini inflatables alongside the barge, and bolted to the transom is our 30HP expedition Yamaha, ready and running. In our top pockets we have money and passports. If a storm comes up the overloaded barge will roll and the Land Rovers will drown. Second only to the Amazon, this outpouring of the river into the sea is the largest in Africa and has formed a 160-kilometre-long canyon that is more than a kilometre deep. We're shitting ourselves.

53

Democratic Republic of Congo

Day 65, Country 4 on the Edge

I think of Joseph Conrad's 'Heart of Darkness' and the atrocities that happened here during and after King Leopold's time, but we're not over the river yet. The country's potential is breathtaking, as there is said to be massive mineral wealth still waiting to be tapped, but our experience of the DRC is that it'll be wise to get across the narrow stretch of coastline as soon as possible. Just 110 km – happy to keep it short.

PISSED ON PALM WINE – IT'S A JOLLY GANG THAT DRAGS THE LANDIES TO SHORE.

Dispatch #37 – On the Raw Edge of Africa

Jeez! She rolls like a cork in a bathtub each time a swell comes in from the Atlantic. It seems to be made worse by the Landies' independent suspensions as they rock with the motion. 'Who's got the bloody knife?' I ask. 'C'mon guys, we chatted about it last night. Okay Ross, you've got it. If this thing rolls cut the inflatable free and jump for the tiller bar. Anna, Mashozi, you've got life jackets. If she goes down, jump for the duck, don't worry about anything else other than your lives. You've all got bucks and passports and emergency kit.' Shit! There she goes again.

The skipper *Senhor* José chugs towards calmer water near a mangrove island. Still more than 20 kilometres to go. In 1842 the experienced naval captain Diogo Cão was astounded by this enormous river mouth, larger than any a European had ever seen. In his book *King Leopold's Ghost: A Story of Greed, Terror, and Heroism in Colonial Africa*, Adam Hochschild quotes him as saying:

> *For the space of 20 leagues [the river] preserves its fresh water unbroken by the briny billows which encompass it on every side; as if this noble river had determined to try its strength in pitched battle with the ocean itself …* (1999)

And this is what we have to cross.

The sweat trickles down our backs. Amidst the tension Mashozi smears cheese squares and bully beef onto Portuguese bread and we eat, sitting on top of the Landies. The skipper battles the current. Binoculars show the Port of Banana all *bliksemed* by war. We drop anchor. Such a historic river mouth, it's seen so much pain and suffering. Tens of thousands of slaves were exported from here, human flesh chained and yoked like cattle. The famous Victorian explorer Henry Morton Stanley ended his 100-day east-to-west journey across Africa near here. Later King Leopold's men chopped the hands off forest dwellers if they didn't collect enough wild rubber – such a heart of darkness he had. Finally there was the tragic civil war that followed independence from Belgium, with President Mobutu stealing billions of US dollars, even hiring a Concorde to take him and his family on shopping trips to the Champs Elysées. But today on the river there's peace.

Immigration officer *Monsieur* Paul sits in a blue-painted, palm-frond hut. Behind him hangs a picture of *Le Général Major* Joseph Kabila, *Président de la République Democratique du Congo*. Fortunately Paul speaks Swahili, so we can communicate. We show our visas and the passports are stamped with a flourish. It's Independence Day and the Primus beer is flowing like water. Everybody is jolly as now, in reverse, in low ratio and difflock, and with the help of 87 laughing, joking, singing and somewhat pissed Congolese, the three Landies roll onto terra firma over thick hardwood planks supported underneath by 210-litre drums. Don Pinnock shakes his head with relief. 'It's the Zen of Travel,' he laughs, referring to the make-or-break hands that fate deals one when travelling. 'It's on our side.' I'm delighted; at least we've remained true to the edge of Africa. 'It's been my best day,' says Ross with a grin. 'I love that we got the Landies across the Congo when everybody said it would be impossible – the sheer adventure of it.' That's what we came for.

Dispatch #38 – Pygmy Roadblock

Thick, green equatorial forest, fan palms, tree ferns and palmnut vultures. Commotion on the red dust road. There

---

DEMOCRATIC REPUBLIC OF CONGO – NOTES:
- FORMERLY ZAIRE | WILD AND WOOLLY!
- UNTAMED WILDERNESS, RAINFOREST AND VOLCANOES.
- ONLY FOR 'THE BRAVEST OF TRAVELLERS' READS THE GUIDEBOOK —
- TRAGIC HISTORY, GRAVE MISCONDUCT BY KING LEOPOLD FOLLOWED BY THE CORRUPTION OF MEGALOMANIAC MOBUTU SESE SEKO —
- NOW IT'S JOSEPH KABILA
- MASSIVE 2.3-MILLION-SQUARE-KILOMETRE COUNTRY, DRAINED BY THE MIGHTY CONGO RIVER INTO THE SOUTH ATLANTIC.

WE MAKE IT TO BANANA.

A PYGMY ROADBLOCK

MUTI FROM THE TANK.

are pygmies in masks, their entire bodies covered in layers of dry banana leaves. With no arms, legs or heads, these creatures make little grunting noises. People at the roadside are singing and *jolling*. We must pay ten dollars to pass; it's the custom we're told. There are plastic chairs and tables under palm thatch, and Primus beer in thick brown bottles. We shake hands with the secretary of the village, and Captain Morgan is tapped from our secret 48-litre tank under the Landy into two big plastic mugs. We dance and sing – we've survived the river.

Dispatch #39 – No-Man's-Land

Our stint in the DRC nearly over already, we're trying to reach Cabinda. The boom is down, however. Surely we should know, it's their national day. Everything is closed, and the somewhat-drunk DRC immigration officials are having a shouting match. We're surrounded by litter, crows and humidity. We give out mosquito nets to smiling mums with babies on their backs who are climbing onto an old military truck. The men stop their arguing – now they want nets. They're only for mothers with little children, we explain.

The sun sinks in an orange ball over the Atlantic, and distant flames from oil wells light up the sky. The decayed buildings, filth and litter fade into darkness and all we have is a circle of sweating faces around the fire, white eyes and teeth, and the soft glow of the moon. We've been joined by slurring military border officials, with camouflage and guns and keen glances eyeing up our kit. 'Don't eat too much of that,' says Ross in Swahili to our 'guests' as they hungrily eye a single coil of inferior wors, bought in Angola and now sizzling on the coals. 'It's snake,' says Ross quite seriously, 'a South African delicacy, but it can give you bad guts. It's okay for us – we're used to it – but for you guys, careful, it could make you *mgonjwa*.' So the wors gets left largely to us. Mashozi adds baked beans and bread. Bruce finds a few big bottles of warm Primus beer and there's Captain from the tank. We crank up the music. What a laugh, all of us dancing. The soldiers put their AKs to one side and join in. Don's hat falls off and his bald head shines in the moonlight as he moves to a jerky chicken dance.

The next morning, as we're breaking camp, a gong goes. 'Quick!' I shout. 'Everybody off with your hats, stand to attention, don't move!' We've learnt from the past that when the national flag goes up at any government or military post you'd better jump to attention and not move until the flag's up and you get the okay. Another tip is always to remove your hat when walking into an immigration or customs post – it shows respect and buys you points. Then, as we are preparing to enter Cabinda, the vultures say they want money or they will search the Landies piece by piece, keeping us here all day. Ross is outraged and blows his top in Swahili. 'Last night we were *rafikis*, friends. We shared our fire and food with you. You saw us unpacking the vehicles, taking out our equipment. You shared our rum and we gave your people mosquito nets and now you want to SEARCH us? We don't pay bribes. You know we are on a humanitarian expedition.' The border guards break into smiles, lift the boom and shout '*Kwaheri, safari njema*,' goodbye and a good journey.

Border crossings are all drama, each one like a game of chess. If you ever get to this spot you'll know it's the backside of the world. All heat and humidity. We sit with the flies and the litter, having passed through the DRC boom, we are now awaiting entry at the Cabinda side. Six local piss cats watch a French soap opera at full volume, the speakers distorting like hell. 'Go back to Moanda, back to the DRC, get a visa from the Cabinda consul,' says an arrogant little bloke in a red T-shirt. 'But,' we stutter, 'immigration in Soyo told us we would be okay with our existing Angolan visas.' The finger comes out. 'You go back to Moanda.'

So we're in bloody no-man's-land, stamped out of the DRC, but *no entrada* into Angola's Cabinda. Soldiers with AKs are everywhere, protecting the oil riches. Finally we are able to buy visas at $78 each – American – and 19 hours and 100 metres later the boom at the *Poste Frontière* at Yema, gateway to Cabinda, is lifted. It's no bloody wonder that not too many people are doing what we do. Fortunately, the ordinary people we come across are absolutely delightful, but oh my God, when border officials are bad, they're fucking bad.

Back to Angola

Dispatch #40 – Reflection

We enter Cabinda, the small Angolan-owned, oil-rich enclave that hugs the Atlantic coast between the DRC and Congo-Brazzaville. It's all part of the outside edge. We're feeling upbeat about having got this far and having made it across the mouth of the Congo and along the short coastline of the DRC. At night, with the already battle-worn Landies parked, roof tents up, camp chairs pulled close to the fire and soot-blackened kettle bubbling away, we talk about the route and sticking as close as possible to the outline of Africa. That's what makes this humanitarian expedition such a geographic challenge – it's all about tracking the outside edge of the continent. When we get back home I want to be able to stand on the beach at Zinkwazi, look north up towards the mouth of the Tugela and south down to that of the Nonoti and know that, as best we could, we've gone the full circle.

Dispatch #41 – Oil-Rich Cabinda

'*Quickly, put all cameras away, masses of military ahead,*' comes Ross's voice over the radio. Ahead of us, as we enter Cabinda City, are lines of tanks, military equipment and heavily-armed troops. Some 80% of Angola's military is stationed here to ensure that Cabinda's oil riches stay in Angolan hands. So here we are in oil-rich Cabinda City and amazingly enough we have to queue for ages for fuel, but at least the diesel is cheap. Cabinda is hilly, with big trees, plenty of oil wells, cinnamon-brown surf washed north from the mouth of the Congo, small wooden houses with rust-coloured, corrugated-iron verandas, music booming from bars, and lots of military. It's a Sunday, and the black Hummers are out in full force. North of Cabinda City we drive past the beach bar at Cacongo where the forest lines a long, crumbling hardwood jetty and big dugout canoes wait for the surf to flatten. Two American oil workers with big beers in their hands shout, 'Hey, we love you man!'

Dispatch #42 – *Gindungu* and Polygamy

We meet immigration official Donna Vanda, plump and smiling in a bright-yellow blouse, black pants and gold handbag. Donna joins us for a peri-peri feast at the bar-restaurant Barracão. Meeting her, I am once again reminded of the people of distant Brazil – the music, the dancing and the culture that the slaves took across the Atlantic. The chilli is hot, and we call for water and beer to accompany our steak and chicken served with thin slices of green tomato and chips spread with peri-peri. Donna laughs and sweats. 'This is the best peri-peri in Angola,' she says, 'you have to find the tiny *gindungu pequeño* chillies, the small ones. You buy them for 50 kwanzas a bunch. We grind them in a mortar and pestle, then add garlic and onion, salt, lemon and olive oil.'

Early missionaries to the Congo region were horrified by the polygamy they found here. They thought it was the spices in the African food that provoked this dreadful practice, but we find our peri-peri feast a great way to celebrate our crossing into Cabinda. Donna allows us to camp in a mangrove clearing behind the gutted customs and immigration building. The wind blows and the sea roars – it's another night on the edge.

The birdsong in the morning is wonderful; little Cabinda, we're told, has the highest recorded variety of birds anywhere in Africa. Back in the Landies we stop at the Centro da Saúde, the small clinic in Massabi. Malaria is bad here – there's a mama on a quinine drip and a seriously ill baby. At least they now have nets and, thanks to the expedition's Rite to Sight campaign, seven poor-sighted people in Massabi now have spectacles. Congo-Brazzaville here we come.

Congo

Day 67, Country 5 on the Edge

Officially the country is known as the Republic of Congo, sometimes Congo-Brazzaville, not to be confused with the Democratic Republic of Congo, the old Zaire, on the opposite bank of the Congo River. Confusing, isn't it? The country is noted for its lowland gorillas and wild chimpanzees, and contains more than 80% of the world's population of these primates. We would be thrilled to see these creatures along the way.

◁ TYPICAL CONGO 'HIGHWAY'

Dispatch #43 – The Greybeard is the Cook

The equatorial heat beats down as we cross into the Congo at the Tchiamba–Nzassi border post. What a buzz – street vendors, moneychangers and banana, groundnut and sweet-potato sellers; transborder vehicles being offloaded and checked, with mumbled words and telling hand signs as the poor travellers get fleeced by customs; and a lorry full of big, very black, tough-looking soldiers in tight camouflage gear and red berets taking a smoke break. It's all so French – no English or Portuguese here. And what are your professions? It's always such an important question at immigration and so, to relieve the tension of it all, Don Pinnock instantly becomes a priest, Anna a teacher and Ross jumps from documentary filmmaker to engineer. Bruce, the expedition photographer, becomes an architect and Babu, who's been battling to get his Mozambican driver's license, suddenly qualifies as a chauffeur. Mashozi becomes a medical doctor and before I can even think of something distinguished, she drops my status from expedition leader to that of simple cook.

There are a few youngsters locked up in the police post, grandly called *Commissariat Spécial de Police Nationale*. They whisper through the bars, asking us for food and water, or better still, if we can nick the keys from the chief's pocket and spring them. Outside the blue-and-white taxis dart about as if they were in Paris.

Dispatch #44 – A Call to the Ambassador

It's like a French movie at the first roadblock. A round man in blue uniform, clipped moustache and round French police hat blows his whistle furiously and jumps out into the road, ordering us to stop. He grabs my beard and shouts to his mates: 'Look! We've got Karl Marx!' 'Now that's a black mark,' I mumble. 'He probably doesn't know I've just become a famous chef!' Passports, carnets, papers? He then gets a bit threatening, demanding a bribe. Ross puts up the satellite phone and makes a great pretence of phoning the ambassador in Brazzaville. 'There seems to be a problem, would you like to speak to the ambassador yourself?' he asks Inspector Clouseau. 'Vamoose!' he snaps back, hastily waving us on. His whistle blows again. I look in the rear-view mirror to see a taxi driver laden with transborder goods paying over his daily bribe – sadly this is the way of Africa. Mashozi hands me the felt-tipped pen as I flip down the sun visor.

'Bruce, come in!' Mashozi then calls over the radio. '*Go,*' says Bruce. '*Are you going to put on some clean clothes and shave?*' she asks. Bruce chuckles. He's a bundle of excitement – girlfriend Sam, aged 20, flies in tomorrow on the Johannesburg–Brazzaville–Pointe-Noire flight. With her is big Deon Schürmann. He's an old mate; built like a brick shithouse, he used to play professional rugby in France and is now coming in as our French interpreter. I hope he remembers the biltong.

Dispatch #45 – Pointe-Noire and Beyond

Bustling Pointe-Noire, the Republic of Congo's major seaport, is choked with traffic and diesel fumes. I sense that the team is a bit worn out and now's not the time to sweat it out in a city looking for an expedition camp and safe parking for the Landies. I consider carrying on a bit towards a quieter spot. It's the sort of decision I always bounce off Ross. '*I'm keen,*' he says over the radio. '*There's a place called Pointe Indienne, it's about 15 kilometres to the north. The French expats used to hang out there, so maybe there's a decent beach.*'

After another bad roadblock and a black mark on the sun visor, we turn off on a dirt track across grassy plains and a few small rivers, through a friendly village and down to a beautiful coastline of palm-fronded beach and quaint, somewhat unkempt, expatriate beach cottages dating back to

BASE CAMP AT POINTE INDIENNE

CONGO - NOTES:
- CAPITAL IS BRAZZAVILLE
- AREA 342 000 KM2
- BORDERS ANGOLA, CAMEROON, THE CENTRAL AFRICAN REPUBLIC, THE DRC AND GABON
- OFFICIAL LANGUAGE – FRENCH. OTHER LANGUAGES ARE LINGALA, MUNUKUTUBA, AND LARI
- POPULATION IS ABOUT 4 MILLION
- CURRENCY IS THE CFA FRANC
- THE CONGO IS CHARACTERISED BY DENSE RAINFOREST AND IMPENETRABLE JUNGLE JUXTAPOSED AGAINST A NARROW 169-KILOMETRE COASTAL STRIP.

DON'T LET HER TIP – BAD ANGLE AHEAD

BIG DEON – EXPEDITION MUSCLE POWER AND FRENCH INTERPRETER

DON PINNOCK ENDORSING THE SCROLL – HE LEAVES IN THE MORNING.

before the civil war and now mostly empty. For just a few dollars, the caretaker of a French-owned cottage allows us to rent the place and we quickly turn it into our expedition base camp, with two security guards to look after the Landies at night. Soon there's a fish on the coals outside and a few cold Primuses from the nearby village. Bruce shaves off his red beard and scrubs up. We get the chance to unwind after the stressful crossing of the Congo. The next day Don Pinnock leaves with Bruce for the airport. He's been great company and through his colourful and regular blogs and dispatches has kept the story alive for *Getaway* readers. He'd come for three weeks and stayed for six; now the good news is that when he gets back to Cape Town he'll be editor-in-chief. 'Just shows you, Don,' I joke, 'stick around for the whole expedition and they'll make you a director.' Before he leaves, Don scribbles these words in the expedition scroll:

> It's been wonderful travelling with you guys … I've never met anyone who travels with such great heart. May the Zen of Travel continue to ride on your shoulder. Best wishes, Mr P.

Dispatch #46 – 'You're lucky it's dry'

It's incredible how there's always a friendly South African on Africa's outside edge. We find them, or sometimes they find us, in the strangest of places, and tonight we meet Johan Coetze and a couple of mates. Johan runs a shipping and logistics company in Pointe-Noire, speaks perfect French and has facilitated Don's flight out and now Sam and Big Deon's flight in. It's time for celebration – chicken peri-peri on the fire. Johan brought a big blue-and-white cool box of snacks, French champagne and some South African wine. He spreads out a detailed map of the Congo coast. 'You're lucky it's dry now. You'd never have made it in the wet,' he says. 'Some hunters have also just confirmed that the Conkouati Ferry is running – they were up north a couple of weeks ago.' 'Oh yes,' he continues, pointing to a big patch of green on the map, 'you should try and get to Tchimpounga, the Jane Goodall chimp sanctuary – but it's a hell of a road.'

Dispatch #47 – The Chimps of Tchimpounga

The day starts with a Teaching on the Edge distribution of learning materials to children from the village. Then it's out from Pointe Indienne, Land Rover side mirrors pulled in, branches being brushed aside by the windscreen deflectors, and, with the tearing sound of thorn branches against aluminium, we follow a narrow track through thick forest.

At Tchimpounga we meet John Maboto, who loves chimps and has worked with them for 15 years. 'Every chimpanzee you see here,' he tells us, 'is an orphan – their mothers killed in tragic circumstances with cruelty. Fifty years ago there were approximately two million chimpanzees living in 25 African countries – today there are less than two hundred thousand living in the wild in just 21 African countries. It is estimated that five thousand chimpanzees are killed every year by the bushmeat trade, along with three thousand gorillas.'

The 136 chimps of Tchimpounga welcome us with whooping screams of excitement. In the nursery pen we meet mothers with babies and in the fenced forest a group of 25 swings from the trees. Big Bob and eight delinquents have to be permanently caged. 'They are just too intelligent,' says John. 'They've learnt to short-circuit the electric fence and even take a length of bamboo and pole-vault to freedom. The plan is to reintroduce them into the wild.'

Dispatch #48 – Grégoire's Story

We are introduced to the oldest chimp in the sanctuary, 63-year-old *Monsieur* Grégoire. Tall and thin, the old ape's story is best told in the words of Dr Jane Goodall, taken from a nearby plaque:

> *How, I am continually asked, can we justify providing food for nonhuman beings in a zoo when human beings are starving? The answer, I think, is simple. Humans put those animals into cages. They cannot get out to search for their food. They rely on us. If we are not to feed them, they must either be freed or killed.*
>
> *During my first visit to the Brazzaville zoo I met Grégoire. It was a while ago, but I can still recall my sense of disbelief and outrage as I gazed at the strange being, alone in his bleak cement-floored cage. His pale, almost hairless skin was stretched tightly over his emaciated body so that every bone could be seen. His eyes were dull as he reached out with a thin, bony hand for a proffered morsel of food. Was this really a chimpanzee? Apparently so: 'Shimpanse', announced a notice over the cage, with the added information 'Grégoire – 1944'. 1944! It was hard to believe. In that dim, unfriendly cage Grégoire had endured for 46 years.*
>
> *A group of Congolese children approached quietly. One girl, about ten years old, had a banana in her hand. Leaning over the safety rail she called out 'Danse! Grégoire – danse!' With bizarre, stereotype movements, the old male stood upright and twirled around once, twice, three times. Then, still standing, he drummed rapidly with his hands – rat-tat, rat-tat, rat-tat – on*

the single piece of furniture in his room, a lopsided shelf that was attached to one wall. He ended the strange performance by standing on his hands, his feet gripping the bars between us. The girl held the banana towards him and, righting himself, he reached out to accept payment … The gaunt image of Grégoire hung between me and sleep that night. How had he survived those long, weary years deprived of almost everything that a chimpanzee needs to make life meaningful? What stubbornness of spirit had kept him alive?

Sitting next to Grégoire with soft brown eyes, her body round and plump from years of inactivity, is the beautiful 40-year-old La Vieille, saved from a small cage in Pointe-Noire. We walk up the hill and sit on the grass. All that separates us from a group of chimpanzees is a fence. They sit, we sit. One fellow fascinated by my beard raises his hands and claps in amusement. Who's watching whom? They us, or we them? Other chimps race to join the mutual gawking session. We feel so connected to our friends across the wire. It is so peaceful, with the heavy tropical sky, the melancholy cry of a rain bird and the apes now silent. Then, as we leave, a wonderful sight: some 20 chimpanzees walking and running free across an open field. One of them is holding his keeper by the hand; that tenuous link between man and ape.

We camp on the beach between the ocean and a deep fresh-water lagoon. Somehow the day with the chimps affects us all, making us quieter and introspective. At sunset Ross catches a king fish. Cooked in tin foil on the fire, it tastes delicious. The waves crashing on the beach lull us to sleep.

Dispatch #49 – Lost

Next morning, via Deon's interpreting, a fisherman in a dugout tells us that there are still chimpanzees and gorillas in the surrounding forest. Wouldn't it be wonderful to see them? We pack up camp and follow the coast north towards Gabon. Sam is travelling with Babu and Bruce, who's now got a big grin on his face. Big Deon is with Ross and Anna. The beaches are wild and beautifully unspoilt. Thick rainforest and crystal-clear lagoons go right down to the ocean's edge. Tyres down to 1 bar, it's hard work for the Landies. Then there are river crossings and ferry rides, with Deon asking questions and directions as we go.

Now we're following a jungle track. It's not marked on the Garmin but the GPS tells us that somehow we've crossed out of the Congo and into Gabon. Pushing, slipping and sliding, engines growling, we use pangas and jagged shark's-tooth saws to cut away fallen branches. We're not going back now to find a customs and immigration post, as we're committed to an ever-narrowing jungle track that's meandering back down towards the beach. The thick canopy of trees overhead causes us frequently to lose our GPS signal. There are broken pole bridges, rainforest and swamps, and gorilla and chimpanzee prints in the mud. It's all humidity and sweat. The track's getting narrower and narrower. It's more overgrown and difficult. Because of the thick canopy of trees overhead we lose satellite signal again, and now it's getting dark. 'Where are we?' asks Mashozi, slapping at a persistent tsetse fly. 'Bloody lost by the look of it,' I reply, 'but the direction seems good.' We'll find out soon enough, or at least I hope so!

Gabon

Day 73, Country 6 on the Edge

Gabon is a forested jewel on the raw edge of Africa. Her vast, virgin rainforests are teeming with wildlife whilst there's glitz and glamour in the bustling major cities. Our dream is to track the pristine coastline and to find pygmy elephant, forest buffalo and, with some luck, chimpanzee and gorilla. The 800-kilometre-long sandy coastal strip of Gabon is a series of palm-fringed bays, massive lagoons, rainforests and estuaries. 'Très difficile', as they say in French. It won't be easy.

Dispatch #50 – Gooey Mud Holes

'Oh my God! The shit's hit the fan, she's going over,' shouts Mashozi as Ross's Landy, engine screaming, slides sideways into a deep water hole, his eyes wide as he fights the wheel. It's all in slow motion; mud drips from her chassis and for a moment her entire undercarriage is revealed. It's really quite indecent. There she goes, first with two wheels in the air, then down again as her backside slips into a gooey mud hole. Now her bonnet's in the air and one wheel's off the ground, still turning and throwing mud in every direction – bloody lucky she didn't go over. It's my fault; we should have walked through first but we didn't and so we push, dig and winch, and two hours later, covered in mud, Ross and I are out of trouble in the two Tdis. Now it's Bruce's turn in the overloaded Stomach. *'Are you ready?'* comes Ross's voice over the radio. *'One, two, three, GO!'*

Foot flat, second gear, low ratio. The other two Landies are joined onto Bruce's big TD5 130. The snatch ropes tighten as the Landies take up the bone-jarring shock. It's dark and everybody's tired out, there are no raised voices, just great teamwork with everybody determined to survive the edge. Thank God we've got big Deon Schürmann with us – he's as tough as nails. We have him hanging with the full weight of his 134 kilograms onto the side of the big Landy to stop it from tipping over into the rain-washed trenches.

This coastal track into Gabon is made up of river crossings and deep mud holes oozing with black goo – we get stuck for hours at a time, winching, pushing, pulling and digging. There are gorilla and elephant tracks in the mud. We inch forward, rebuilding plank bridges and swatting tsetse flies. The track is sometimes wide enough to take a Land Rover, at other times we walk ahead to cut and chop our way through. Sweat pours down our backs and drips off the tips of our noses.

BIG DEON RIDES 'THE STOMACH'

Bruce opening up a path through the forest

GABON - NOTES:
- IT'S A LAND OF LUSH TROPICAL VEGETATION
- KNOWN AS THE 'EDEN OF AFRICA'
- POPULATION ABOUT 1·4 MILLION
- RIVERS MAKE UP THE MAIN COMMUNICATION ROUTES –
- MADE UP OF 40 OR SO BANTU TRIBES, SOME OF THE LARGEST ARE THE FANG, ESHIRA, MBELE AND OKANDE.
- OUR BIG CHALLENGE IS TO FOLLOW THE COAST AND FIND PYGMY ELEPHANT.
- MALARIA IS BAD.
- CURRENCY IS THE CFA.

Dispatch #51 – Illegally in Gabon

'*I can hear the sea,*' comes Bruce's voice over the Motorola, and then in the Landies' lights we see the thick forest that's held us so tight opening up into grassland clearings with small coppices – it's beautiful. With tyres down we inch forward onto a squeaky clean beach on the Atlantic's Gulf of Guinea. There's a strong sea breeze, so no mozzies tonight. We wash the mud off in the sea and pitch camp. For the last 14 hours we've averaged 1 kilometre per hour; at this rate the journey around Africa will take us forever. We're illegally in Gabon and I feel ill at ease.

Dispatch #52 – Mayumba National Park

'What day is it, Mashozi?' 'Tuesday, I think, but I'm not sure which month.' We're losing track of time. Up early, there's not a human footprint other than ours, although we see small forest-elephant tracks around camp and a sitatunga mother and baby down on the beach. Then we see two rangers with rucksacks and radios, and when Deon speaks to them in French they tell us they're doing a foot patrol across the Mayumba National Park. It appears we crossed into it when leaving the forest last night. They look at the three Landies, the 33 country flags and the large South African flag decals on the bonnets. 'There's one of you ahead,' says a ranger with a broad smile, 'a white man from South Africa. You'll find him at the park headquarters in Mayumba.' We breathe a collective sigh of relief, at least there's a countryman ahead. We'll try to get to him before customs and immigration get to us.

Dispatch #53 – South African Hospitality

Closer to Mayumba, parts of the sand road are still paved with cobblestones, a sure sign that French colonists were here, slaving and logging and pushing into the jungle. We see an airstrip up ahead. '*Jeez!*' comes Ross's voice over the radio. '*We'd better get the hell out of here – let's get legally into the country first before we put our landing lights on and race down the runway!*' We pull a hard right back into the bush, away from the Mayumba airstrip, a control tower and a trickle of people climbing aboard a small aircraft.

A man on a moped leads us to South African Mike Markovina, a fisheries biologist who works with the Wildlife Conservation Society. What a great guy; turns out I know his dad. By patrolling the coast in a rubber duck, Mike's cut illegal trawling in the park area by half. He and wildlife photographer Linda Schunknecht allow us to set up a base camp in the grounds. We meet Quevain Makaya, a well-educated, English-speaking eco-guard team leader who will be loaned to us as a guide to help us through to Libreville. Mike and Linda introduce us to customs and immigration and out come our French letters of introduction and the Madiba Scroll of Peace and Goodwill. We pay for entry permits, and after a sweaty couple of hours, much rubbing of the pebble in the pocket and excellent French explanations by Big Deon, down comes the entry stamp with a bang. No need for a black mark on the sun visor here – I'm pleased to see that the Zen of Travel is still riding with us. Welcome to Gabon!

Dispatch #54 – Surfing Hippo and Iboga

Ross and Anna race ahead to an airstrip at Tchibanga and an oil plane that's going to get Deon out to Libreville and back to Joburg, family and work. We'll all miss him terribly. We're back to our core expedition members, plus Sam and Quevain, and together we take a ferry across the lagoon. The beautiful forests continue; that's the secret of this country, there are more trees than people. The wilderness extends forever. A 13-park national network of protected land that encompasses 11% of the country's territory has been established. More than 70% of Gabon is covered in pristine rainforest, home to the national bird, the African grey parrot. You can find forest elephant walking through patches of savannah grassland separated by clumps of forest, or padding softly down snow-white beaches. Gabon is one of the few, if not the only place on earth where one can see surfing hippo (and I don't mean yours truly). A clever hippo will sometimes swim parallel to the coast in search of better grazing off another beach, surfing in for a nocturnal feast and then swimming back in the early hours of the morning to catch a wave home.

Quevain, our tall 29-year-old interpreter, guide and new expedition member who calls me Dad, explains in his French-accented English that this place is famous because of a man called Malendi. 'People even come from Libreville to see him; many cars park here and the initiation ceremonies last several days.' Apparently Malendi is a *n'ganga*, a spiritual leader, who oversees rites of passage. 'Iboga, Dad, is a sacred plant,' whispers Quevain. 'It's used in coming-of-age ceremonies and ancient Bwiti initiation rites.' It's crazy stuff: sorcerers, vampires and mermaids all play a role in the traditions of Bwiti and it's said to have two to three million followers. 'You chew the root bark and travel into another world. You throw up for hours and stay awake for days.'

Quevain tells us that quite a few hallucinogenically inspired travellers seek out Bwiti initiation experiences to visit and communicate with forest spirits, and that ibogaine, the active chemical compound found in iboga, is now being used in Western societies for the treatment of drug addicts. 'But you must be careful – too much iboga and you can die. And remember, after the initiation it will take you about two

QUEVAIN JOINS THE EXPEDITION – HE'S A GEM

weeks to come down to normal.' I decide that now is not a good time to experiment with local customs; it's tough enough following the outline of Africa without iboga.

Dispatch #55 – A Smile as Wide as the Forest

Last night we camped in a forest clearing next to the beach, hoping to see pygmy elephant. It was just our three Landies, a fire, the camp chairs, simple food and some folklore stories from Quevain. The feeling of freedom in these unspoilt areas is making our journey all the more worthwhile. In Gabon most visitors fly from place to place; the roads are virtually non-existent and reaching one's destination is not guaranteed, especially in the rainy season. But now it's dry and the road to Gamba is a great adventure as we follow an overloaded bush taxi through jungle and savannah grass to the Mayonammi River, which the locals tell us means 'river that belongs to me'. But there's no sign of a ferry, just a wide channel of water, a few fishermen fixing nets and a dead slender-nosed, fish-eating crocodile with its neck chopped deep with a panga. 'It's a delicacy,' says the fisherman. 'We'll cut off a piece for ourselves, and the rest will go by bush taxi to Gamba.' The ferry arrives, just two pontoons, a deck and a Yamaha outboard. The skipper is from Benin and speaks English and his assistant, Fabrace, is a deaf-mute who directs us on board with grunts, hand signals and a smile as wide as the unending forest. The ferry costs 22 500 francs – about 400 rand – but the palmnut vultures and beautiful river are included for free.

Dispatch #56 – Kiwi John and the Zen of Travel

Gamba has a tarred road, fuel and cold beer. It's one of the operational centres of Royal Dutch Shell. The director of the park here says that to follow the beach up towards Port-Gentil is impossible, as there's a massive lagoon running into the sea and no ferry. So there's no way forward and we'll have to retreat and go hundreds of kilometres inland to get around it – I can't bear the thought. It's a hammer blow for the expedition. It reminds me of the Kunene crossing and the thousand-kilometre land detour to get from Namibia to Angola – all for 600 metres of river which we did by rubber duck afterwards anyway. The only way is to speak to the Shell guys who control the oil operation here and any transport north. We meet Kiwi John from the Shell compound, who

A FOREST OF HARDWOOD LOGS – WASHED UP ON A PARADISE BEACH.

offers us the use of his air-conditioned home and piping hot shower. You can buy hot bread and cold Regab beer from the clubhouse – bloody luxury!

We speak to one of the senior Shell men in Libreville, explaining the humanitarian and geographic nature of our journey. 'Phone back tomorrow at 9.30 a.m., and if all goes well we'll put your Land Rovers on a barge that will take you north across the Ndogo Lagoon, then into primary forest and a track that will take you to Iguéla in the north of Petit Loango Faunal Reserve. There's no guarantee that I can get permission, it will depend on a yes from the general manager who's on an oil plane right now flying to Gamba.' And so we camp in Kiwi John's garden and wait for the Zen of Travel to play its card.

Mashozi cooks up a giant pot of macaroni and we explore the coast. Then we get great news; Lady Luck is smiling on us again. Roger Ratanga, the Shell oil boss, turns out to be a great bloke. He was on the Gabonese team that monitored our first democratic elections. He fell in love with our country and has even bought a house in Cape Town, so he understands these crazy South Africans who are trying to drive around Africa. We meet at the clubhouse. He endorses the Scroll of Peace and Goodwill and agrees to load our three Landies onto the Shell barge that will cross the 30-kilometre Ndogo

Lagoon – the only way we can remain true to our objective of following the coast. And so we're off. It's paradise; there are some 300 islands covered in primary rainforest and then we're onto a jungle track. We travel all day through this pristine wilderness seeing elephant tracks everywhere – the animals being protected by Shell oil interests.

Our first pygmy elephant. He's beautiful –

Deep in the forest we come across an old logging camp.

Dispatch #57 – Four Days in the Life of an Expedition

We've got mud up to our knees and it stinks. There's much pushing, pulling and winching, but finally we're into a forest clearing. A chimpanzee runs across the path, notices us at the last moment and takes off for the safety of the woods. We've already seen gorilla tracks in the mud and heard and smelt them in the jungle. We camp in the rain. There's the grind of a smoky, wet-wood fire and damp bedding, but the early morning sun, the bird calls and thousands of butterflies lift our spirits. 'Look!' shouts Mashozi as a flock of African grey parrots settles noisily in a tree above our camp, making us a bit homesick for George, our African grey back home.

We find South African Jannie Fourie at Loango Lodge in the wilds of Gabon. He heads up a safari outfit called Operation Loango, started by an adventurous *Nederlander* Rombout Swanborn who's putting money into saving the forests and wildlife of Gabon. Jannie gives us a guide called Dimitri. I swear he's got a bit of pygmy in him. We'll leave at dawn down the Akaka River in search of forest elephant. Ross catches an African cubera snapper in the mouth of the Loango Lagoon and we eat it with the last of the Nando's sauce.

The early morning mist hangs over the river. As the sun comes out so do the tsetse flies. 'To the left!' shouts Bruce from the front of the expedition inflatable. And there he is, looking out from the green papyrus – our first pygmy elephant with his little Mickey Mouse ears and his small tusks, feet in the mud. He's small enough to duck through the thick primary forest, and he's beautiful. Shy sitatunga look up from their breakfast nibble of swamp grass, an African forest buffalo swims across the river in front of the boat, pelicans fly in formation over the endless forest, and Egyptian vultures look down on us from their leafy perch. We've never seen so many African jacana before. Bright malachite kingfishers dart between tall, green papyrus heads that sway in the wake of the boat. There are more elephant with every sweep of the river, and a lone hippo and a croc on a mud bank. After spaghetti and meatballs out of a can we sleep in a forest shack. Owls hoot throughout the night and we hear chimps in the forest.

Dispatch #58 – Chasing the Edge

The Cooper tyres, at 0,8 bar, squeak on the powder-white sand as we race against the tide. In the distance there's a shipwreck high and dry on the beach. As we approach it we see it's got a

THE ORANGE LIFE RINGS REMAINED TIED TO EACH LANDY'S BUSH BAR, SO BECOMING EXPEDITION GOOD LUCK TALISMANS AND CONFUSING THE HELL OUT OF BORDER OFFICIALS

'FOLLOWING THE EDGE'

thick anchor rope tied to a tree in the forest. There's no rust so it must have just happened, but there's not a soul in sight. It's eerie – like a ghost ship.

We see she's called the *Loba e Ndedi* and is registered in Limbe, Cameroon. Like pirates, the team climb a rope ladder hanging from the side. She's been ransacked but we find old sea charts for North and West Africa and orange life rings which we attach to the front of each Landy.

We push on. It becomes risky at high tide as we dodge waves and tall, dry mangroves, the setting sun and the Atlantic on our left. We're stopped by the wide mouth of the Nkoni Lagoon where, a metre from the shore, barracuda chase shoals of sardines. We set up a base camp. '*Ngiya khumbula ekhaya*, makes me think of Mozambique and home,' says Babu with a grin as he fillets a barracuda; the other one we give to a group of passing fishermen. The pristine, crystal-clear estuaries are as God made them – it's Africa's outside edge at its best. The sighing wind, the campfire, three Landies and some crazy, adventuring pilgrims attempting to circle the continent – it's all wonderful.

Dispatch #59 – A Special Delivery

Out with the choke, a few pumps on the fuel bulb, a pull on the rope and the Yamaha Enduro roars into life. The only way forward is in one of the expedition's Gemini inflatables. Three of the team will stay behind and take care of everything at the Nkoni Lagoon base camp. Bruce and Sam don't mind. They're like honeymooners in a small tent – all smiles, kisses and cuddles – but I hope Babu is okay and doesn't feel the odd man out. Ross, Mashozi, Annelie, Quevain and I will trace the mangrove backwaters into the great Ogooué River loaded with emergency supplies, extra fuel and sleeping bags. Ross plots a course on the Garmin GPS – as they say in their advertising 'we'd be lost without it'. Everybody's a bit tense; it's a race against time to Port-Gentil where we are collecting a 'special package' off the plane. Our grandson and youngest expedition member, Tristan, is joining us again after his last stint in Namibia. He's being escorted by 4x4MegaWorld fitment sponsor and good friend Adolf Waidelich.

At Port-Gentil he races into our arms. We take a sunset cruise back across the bay to a little island at the mouth of the great Ogooué River. Tristan is wrapped in Ross's jacket and waves break over the boat. Around the fire Adolf takes out the goodies: face cream for Mashozi from Liz, Adolf's wife, a bottle of Captain Morgan, two bags of Kudu biltong and dry wors, and stories from home. We role out a tarpaulin and sleep under the stars, all in a line like sardines, with life jackets as pillows. The next morning, to our horror, we find that village dogs have stolen the remainder of the biltong bag. We are devastated – all the dry wors and leftover kudu sticks are gone. We can't believe our bad luck.

It's five hours through the mangroves to get back to our base camp. From there we will have to go further up the Ogooué to Lambaréné. Here Anneke Veenswijk-Nel from the South African Embassy in Libreville has arranged for the scroll to be endorsed by the director of the Albert Schweitzer Institute, the organisation named after the Nobel Peace laureate and dedicated to alleviating suffering and injustice and creating a more equitable and sustainable future for our planet.

Dispatch #60 – Lambaréné

Lambaréné, a riverboat port on the Ogooué River and a busy trading and transport junction, is on the road from the south going across the equator to the capital of Libreville. It is divided into three areas, each separated by a bridge. Albert Schweitzer would turn in his grave; no longer is Lambaréné just a thatched village with only dugouts for transport.

Gone are the snakes, crocodiles and hippos. Now it's all blaring music and taxis – busy, friendly and colourful, with loads of character. We stay in the same high-ceilinged rooms used by the doctors and nurses who staffed the famous Lambaréné Hospital, founded in 1924 to treat lepers. One can feel Albert Schweitzer's legacy everywhere. The old hospital with its original furnishings and black-and-white photographs is a place frozen in time. Both the director and Professor Sadoo, head of the malaria institute at Lambaréné, endorse the scroll and confirm that our campaign to distribute mosquito nets to pregnant women and those with children under five is the best way forward.

Dispatch #61 – Crossing the Equator

We head for Libreville. Adolf rides with Mashozi and me; we're playing a CD bought in the market; great African sounds to a French voice. Porcupine, snake, turtle, crocodile, sitatunga, forest hog, buffalo, chimps and gorilla – smoked or dried – are hanging up for sale by the roadside. Despite Gabon's conservation ethic the sale of bushmeat is still an essential part of the culture. 'A big problem, this poaching, even fancy restaurants in Libreville sometimes serve illegal bushmeat. The people feel it's their right,' says Quevain, 'but new laws are protecting endangered wildlife.'

'*We're at 0° latitude!*' Ross's voice suddenly comes over the radio. We all tumble out of the Landies for an expedition photograph under the equator sign. The truth is our GPS indicates the sign is not exactly in the correct place. Still, we've crossed the line and that's what counts.

A FLOATING FOREST ON THE OGOOUÉ RIVER – SAD!

CROSSING THE EQUATOR

69

BRUCE COLLECTS FRESH DRINKING WATER – BUT WE STILL BOIL IT –

Dispatch #62 – Looking Ahead

Including Gabon that's 6 countries behind us now, with 27 still to come. Back in the Landies we have so much to think about: will the team make it through to the end, will I make it, will we survive, will the Landies endure? Things are still a bit shaky in Liberia; southern Senegal seems okay now but Western Sahara could be a problem for us. Algeria has had more violence, and the border is still closed with Morocco. We need special permission for Gadaffi's Libya, the Egyptian Red Sea border with the Sudan is still under dispute, Eritrea and Ethiopia could blow any day, and the dangerous Horn of Africa is beset by piracy and lawlessness. We've given ourselves a year – told the media and sponsors we'll be back on 25 April 2008 for Africa Malaria Day – but already we're running weeks late. I feel the pebble in my pocket – only time and the Zen of Travel will decide. We push on. Little Tristan's voice comes over the radio, breaking my reverie. '*Pops, are we camping in the forest? Is there a place to swim?*'

Dispatch #63 – Libreville, Capital of Gabon

Glitzy Libreville is very French, very busy, very expensive and very much controlled by President Bongo's Democratic Party of Gabon. He's been in power for more than 40 years. French military and political advisors serve him and he has a personal bodyguard of European mercenaries, Moroccan soldiers and 400 top-notch French airborne troops. The police roadblocks enjoy the diversion of stopping and inspecting our three travel-worn but colourfully interesting South African Land Rovers. Some of them are wanting bucks so I'm glad we've got Quevain with us to explain what we're up to. We have a few shit experiences that chalk up more black marks on the sun visor – but that goes with the territory.

Hotels are bloody expensive, but the Hotel Atlantique feels sorry for us and allows us to camp in the car park. It's a big letdown after the freedom of our normal beach and forest camps and the joy of a simple fire on the outside edge. We feel like hobos every time we're found washing in the basin of the hotel reception's toilets. Cities aren't great for us; they kill the budget and stop the flow of the journey.

As for the food, it's all croissants, small cups of coffee, long French loaves and imported ham and cheese – even the tomatoes are from France. We long for good *nyama*, bacon and eggs, and a nice, fat loaf of fresh, South African bread. Everything here is imported and costs a hell of a price.

All traffic comes to a halt when the president's Rolls Royce convoy comes through town with sirens wailing. But hey, there's peace here. Does Gabon need democracy if it's got a benign dictator like Bongo? What about Africa in general? It's an interesting thought.

Ross and I spread out the tattered *National Geographic* map on the bonnet of the Landy. It's overcast and humid. Bruce has found a pizza place and the team stands around, all chomping merrily. It's time to discuss the next move. I remember Jannie Fourie's words as we sat around the fire four days ago at Loango Faunal Reserve. 'Surely your outside edge expedition should include the Portuguese Gulf of Guinea islands of São Tomé and Príncipe? After all, they're linked to Africa by a volcanic pipe. Operation Loango will help you – phone us from Libreville.' I look out across the Atlantic – tempting, isn't it?

Off to São Tomé and Príncipe

Dispatch #64 – Island Style

Imagine our excitement when, after diving out of our Land Rovers into an old high-winged Donnier, we land on the bush airstrip just outside San Antonio – it's a dream come true. Ricus Delport is there to meet us on the island of

Príncipe. 'No crime here,' he says as he sees us looking around nervously for our rucksacks. We throw our kit on the back of an old Unimog that takes us down a track to Bom Bom Island Resort, which Ricus manages. It's one of the finest island paradises in the world. There are welcome drinks in coconut shells with red hibiscus flowers; an African grey called Chaplin that hops from shoulder to shoulder; air-conditioned chalets with hot water; a restaurant that looks like Lord Nelson's galley; and a Bar Pescador with an old, framed black-and-white picture of a massive marlin caught from a dugout canoe – it's all bloody luxury but already I'm worried about the cost and pull Mashozi to one side. 'Are you sure this is all on the house?' I ask. 'It's incredibly generous, the flight and all this.' Mashozi is not sure, so I find Ricus and explain to him that our expedition finances don't allow for this indulgence and that we'd be happy to sleep on the beach. Ricus laughs. 'I've got strict instructions from Rombout Swanborn, the boss, whom you met at Loango Lodge. It's all on the house, including meals and drinks. It's an honour for us to be part of your expedition here on Príncipe.'

It's like a dream world as we explore the old Portuguese-owned plantation homesteads, called *roças*, now overtaken by the jungle. São Tomé and Príncipe, believed to have been originally uninhabited, were explored by Portuguese navigators in 1471 and settled by the end of the century. They became a safe haven for the Portuguese, away from the real and perceived horrors of the Dark Continent, where the only mammals were bats and there weren't even poisonous snakes. It was a paradise to which they later imported slaves from Mozambique, Angola, the Gulf of Guinea and Cape Verde to work in the plantations. Intensive cultivation made the islands a major producer of sugar during the 17th century, and the introduction of coffee and cocoa in the 19th century brought new prosperity. By 1908 the island of São Tomé was the world's largest producer of cocoa, but working conditions for labourers were horrendous and in 1909 British and German chocolate manufacturers boycotted its cocoa in protest. An exile liberation movement was formed in 1953 after Portuguese troops quelled labour riots by gunning down and killing over a thousand *foros*, the descendants of freed slaves, who refused to work on the plantations. The Portuguese revolution of 1974 brought to an end the colonial era, and on 12 July 1975 Lisbon granted São Tomé and Príncipe independence.

For the expedition it's just wonderful knowing that instead of huddling around our normal campfire eating bean stew, we'll be feasting on a restaurant meal served up by the Indian chefs of Bom Bom. There'll be ice in our drinks and music in the air and later, by moonlight, we will negotiate the long footbridge to the perfect beach, to the crisp white sheets inside our chalets nestled between the coconut palms.

The next day we circumnavigate the small 19-kilometre-long, 15-kilometre-wide, jagged volcanic island. It's inhabited by approximately 5 000 people. Humpback whales cavort in front of Ricus's 28-foot boat called the *Blue Marlin*, which later lives up to its name as Adolf Waidelich tags and releases one of these monster fish. 'Pops,' says Little Tristan, 'this place, this is real paradise. Can we stay here forever?' We anchor the boat and swim ashore to where Ricus wants to build an eco-camp in the forest. 'Eco-tourism is the only way we can save this island. Already plans have been submitted for an oil terminal port in the next bay,' says Ricus.

'On the count of three!' shouts Ross to Tristan. The little guy shivers, and then leaps into midair from a high rock to land with a splash in a clear rock pool below. 'He's a brave little fellow,' says Ricus. 'Reminds me of a strange incident that happened nearby to a village boy who was out fishing with his father and went missing. The entire village turned out to look for him for days, but found nothing and presumed he had drowned. Eight months later a local fisherman spotted the child sitting on a rock with a monkey. He'd turned quite wild and they had to tie him up to get him back to the village. The eight-year-old little jungle boy only made animal sounds and it took him time to learn to talk again, but when he did he told his family and the psychologist who'd been assisting him that he had been looked after by the forest monkeys, who had kept him alive by showing him what to eat.'

Back on the *Blue Marlin*, to starboard are the sheer white cliffs of Barriga Branca, the father-and-son granite chimneys of João Dias Pai and João Dias Filho, and beyond, in the mist, is the almost thousand-metre-high Carriote Needle, all of which would have witnessed the coming of the Portuguese sailing ships in 1471.

At Príncipe's bush airstrip we meet President José Cassandra. He's a wonderfully gracious man, smartly dressed in a grey suit. He's interested in our journey so we chat about that as well as about his beautiful island. Everybody's relaxed,

Dispatch #65 – Take it Easy, Keep it Cool

São Tomé is equally beautiful. Off the edge of the *Dogs of War*-type airstrip are two old bullet-holed aircraft. Large, four-engined, tailwinged Super Constellations to be precise. During the Biafran War they served as a humanitarian bridge, flying out refugees from Nigeria. The were shot to shit on their last flight and just managed to limp into São Tomé, where we now sit drinking ice-cold Cola Creola beer in the shade of a wing. This one-time warplane is now a bar-restaurant known as Super Constellation, whilst its counterpart is being turned into a disco.

São Tomé is great. There are no traffic lights, the music's good, the food is spicy, polygamy is rife and the local saying is *leve-leve*, meaning 'take it easy, keep it cool'. The town and the island have got a wonderful buzz, but it's all really laid back. In the town square we find a pub famed for a rather unusual aphrodisiac cocktail called Pilolo atômica, or atomic penis. It's an apt name for a herb-filled drink that blows the top of your head off, and with each shot you get a free condom. 'It really works,' says the owner, Maria-João Pombo. 'People come from far and wide.'

There are only two factories on the island; the one makes chocolate and the other a lethal fruit-based schnapps called Mazotchi, several bottles of which are added to the expedition supplies. Our vision of completing the outside edge will include the exploration of other fascinating islands – those off the coast of Guinea, the Dahlak Archipelago off Eritrea, the Lamu Archipelago in Kenya, the Tanzanian Spice Islands of Pemba, Mafia and Zanzibar, and Mozambique's Quirimba islands and little Ilha de Mozambique.

and there's no show of guns or bodyguards as would be the case on the African mainland. Standing on the runway, with the equatorial sun beating down on our backs, I ask Castro, a San Tomian pilot, where he learnt to fly. 'It was in Libya on Russian MiGs,' comes the reply. 'There were more MiGs than students, and we were even allowed to practise using the ejector seats, never mind that the aircraft would then go into a pilotless crash.' And with that thought in mind we take off over the Atlantic to São Tomé.

Back to Gabon

Dispatch #66 – A Reality Check

It's 2 August 2007 and we're 98 days into the expedition. We've gone from rags to riches and back again, as in the car park of the Hotel Atlantique again we pitch camp like trailer trash, in the rain. It's a reality check after the luxury and paradise of Bom Bom Island. It's also a sad day as we say cheers to Babu, who's flying back with Adolf to South Africa and then back to his home and family in Bilene, Mozambique. He's been with us since the beginning as Portuguese interpreter and malaria prevention educator. We agree to keep in touch and arrange that Babu will meet us again next year on the Ruvuma River as we come down the coast from Tanzania into Mozambique, assuming, of course, that we make it.

As we wait for visas for Equatorial Guinea, Cameroon and Nigeria, it's South Africans to the rescue again as Anneke and her husband Riaan from the South African Embassy arrange for us to stay with their friends Henry and Maggie. They are delightful, and we form friendships of our own. The South African ambassador endorses the scroll and Riaan with his good sense of humour scribbles this sketch in the scroll:

The South Africans gather around for roast chicken cooked on a homemade 200-litre-drum Weber. Pilots Baksteen, Duim and Liam bring Mrs Ball's chutney, biltong and *mieliemeel* – all goodies from home that we miss. Fortunately there's still some Captain in the tank.

Henry, who heads up a security company, is lending us one of his employees, Noah, to accompany us north up the coast to Cap Estérias. 'Noah's from Cameroon and he speaks French and all the local dialects,' says Henry. 'If you have any shit, he's got my mobile number.'

Dispatch #67 – Cap Estérias

There's a pre-national-day cleanup happening in Libreville, and everyone's in a flurry. The curbs are being whitewashed, logs are being cleared off the beach and there are plenty of roadblocks everywhere, which result in a few ticks on the sun visor. We have to pull over and wait for an hour; it's customary as the president is passing through town. There are armoured cars with machine guns at intersections, armed troops in camouflage fatigues and then a cavalcade of government cars, screaming sirens and flashing lights. President Bongo is in a Rolls Royce followed by an ambulance 'just in case'. 'It's at times like these that they always hassle me, even though I've got a resident's card,' says Noah. 'They know from the way I talk that I'm from Cameroon. But they need us; we are the ones that do all the work in Gabon. The Gabonese are lazy – oil has made them that way. They just want to work in an office and wear a suit.'

Cap Estérias is just a few tired-looking expat beach cottages, with the last wooden shack merging into the forest. Some drunken fishermen are having a shouting match; sadly it's all about the price of a giant loggerhead turtle, still alive in the bottom of the boat. Noah tells us that it's custom here for the local people to hand over a turtle as part of the bride price or when a child is born. A wrinkled, sad-looking caretaker allows us to camp in the grounds of a derelict restaurant, with reserved signs on the tables and Christmas decorations still hanging from the ceiling. Looks like someone's broken dreams – high hopes that ended with a big Christmas bash before they flew off back to France. A stroppy French lady from down the road gives Noah the gears. 'You shouldn't be camping here!' she shouts. She's got a restaurant next door with proper toilets and lights. Grumpy old fart. Our tents are already up on the tip of the cape with palm trees and the beach beyond, just where we want to be. The Cap Estérias lighthouse is only a few metres away; it was built to warn ships of the long assegais of rocky reefs that jut out like long shafts into the Atlantic, but it's currently not working. 'Generator's fucked up,' says the caretaker, 'and we're still waiting for the old man (he means President Bongo) to do something.' We braai some French bangers from the supermarket in Libreville that cost more than R200 a kilogram. I wonder how on earth these poor local blokes survive. It seems years since we last had bacon and eggs, not to mention a 500-gram rump steak.

'ON THE EDGE'. A KETTLE, A FIRE AN ENAMEL MUG AND A TENT — LIFE CAN BE SO SIMPLE.

Dispatch #68 – Cocobeach
We are cruising through the town of Ntum, slowly in the red dust. Noah, Mashozi and I are in the Land Rover Mary Kingsley, Bruce and Sam are in Lady Baker, aka the Stomach, and Ross, Anna and Tristan are in John Ross. The comforting growl of the Tdi engines, the potholes and dips have become a way of life now, along with the Old Man Emu suspensions and deflated Cooper tyres soaking up the corrugations. And of course, there's the ongoing challenge to do our humanitarian work and stick to the edge.

Cocobeach is a small frontier town on the estuary that divides Gabon from Equatorial Guinea, and here we await news on permission to cross the border. We sit and drink Regab beer in a rustic plank-built bar owned by a friendly Ghanaian called Richard. It's part of a market that sells smoked fish, plastic shoes, second-hand clothes, colourful cloth, plastic basins, aluminium pots, and twine for making fishing nets. Everybody is worn out; we've been continuously on the move for months. Anna's got cramps and the squirts and she's on antibiotics – she's been ill for days and we're worried about her. Tristan's in the waves, relishing every opportunity to get out of the Landy and stretch his six-year-old limbs.

Dispatch #69 – Blue Monday
Monday morning, 9 a.m., and time for the moment of truth. We get the shocking news. For the first time the Zen of Travel seems to have abandoned us.

The expedition is refused entry into Equatorial Guinea. Our timing is shit. A botched coup has left alleged South African mercenaries rotting in the notorious Black Beach Jail in the island capital of Malabo. The whole affair hit world headlines and even Margaret Thatcher's son, Mark, was implicated in the attempt to overthrow the government of Equatorial Guinea. Now, to sour relationships between the two countries even further, a South African company building an airport in Equatorial Guinea has seized Cape Town properties owned by the ruling family due to non-payment. 'There's nothing more I can do,' says Anneke, 'I've tried my best.' What now?

Dispatch #70 – The Show Must Go On
The next morning we're feeling a bit better – stronger and more resolute. Ross works with the maps and GPS. Fortunately, Equatorial Guinea is only a small blob on the mainland coast and there's a road skirting the tiny country that can take us through the jungle into Cameroon. Little Tristan, head out of the window and hair blowing in the wind, is travelling with us. He sees a pig in a village and that sparks off the first verse of *Old MacDonald Had a Farm* … with an oink oink here and an oink oink there! Here an oink, there an oink, everywhere an oink oink! And so we oink, cluck, quack, meow and woof our way towards the Cameroon border.

Cameroon

Day 105, Country 8 on the Edge

Cameroon stretches from the fringes of the Sahara in the north to the borders of Gabon, Congo and Equatorial Guinea in the south. The occasionally active volcano of Mount Cameroon, rising from the outside edge, is the highest mountain on the west side of the continent. We would love to climb it a bit but we are arriving smack in the middle of the wet season and are expecting torrential rain. Crater lakes abound.

Dispatch #71 – The Scorecard

We cross the wide Ntem River into Cameroon. It seems to have more of a buzz than Gabon, but oh my, we go straight into a very surly bunch of customs and immigration officials, which results in a definite first black mark on the sun visor. I decide to do a bit of addition. The score so far is: South Africa 0, Namibia 0, Angola 23, DRC 11, Cabinda 9, Congo-Brazzaville 16, Gabon 41 (because of the paranoia in the build-up to National Day), the paradises of São Tomé and Príncipe 0 and now the scorecard has opened for Cameroon with 1. Just a reminder, to get a black mark you have to be bad-tempered, arrogant, impolite, threatening or aggressive, demand a bribe, wave an AK-47 around and yes, being pissed also helps. We prefer friendly negotiation, with lots of smiles and backslapping.

Fortunately, up to now, we've not paid a single bribe – no *money* has passed hands anyway, but as is the way of Africa, the odd pack of cigarettes, cap and T-shirt have been given out. *Getaway* magazines are also a great hit and together with good documentation and important letters of introduction they help smooth the way forward. But it's certainly not all about hand-outs. Luckily there are plenty of polite, friendly types who just wave you on or might keep you chatting out of curiosity. They're interested in the team and the vehicles, the malaria prevention branding, the Scroll of Peace and Goodwill and the 33 country flags. The fact that we are a team of South Africans helping to fight malaria in their country wins us huge points and certainly gives the scorecard a favourable balance. There are always some great comments, like 'Tell Mandela that John from Cameroon sends his regards'; 'What's going on with Bafana Bafana? A rich country like South Africa, and you can't play football?'; and 'Ah, you come in British cars – Land Rovers. Very strong. My friend, what have you got for me?' Africa – it's all good and all bad all at the same time. It's a challenging continent.

MUD AND MORE MUD – IT'S LIKE BLOODY SNOT ON A MIRROR

75

CAMEROON - NOTES

- 'BEWARE OF NASTY ROADBLOCKS' READS THE GUIDEBOOK
- MAKE SURE ALL DOCUMENTS ARE IN ORDER
- IT'S THE RAINY SEASON / ROADS COULD BE HELL
- FRENCH AND ENGLISH SPOKEN
- BEWARE COPS WANTING BRIBES
- WE SKIRT MOUNT CAMEROON
- SEEMS A FASCINATING COUNTRY, RICH IN CULTURE AND HISTORY

THE 'MUDBATH' TO NIGERIA —

Dispatch #72 – The Big Wet

How many times have you heard the words 'Africa is not for sissies'? One does indeed have to be hardy of spirit and mind to survive it. We've hit the rains in Cameroon and we're covered in baby-shit-brown mud from top to toe. Dashboard, steering wheels, gear knobs – it's all covered in goo. So is the outside of the Landies, which in the mist look like forest monsters that creak, groan, roar and shudder as we winch, push and pull them along some of the most difficult jungle track we've ever experienced. Some mud holes are deeper than the Landies and we have to pay some stroppy characters, many of them full of palm wine and the tree of knowledge, to help us cut an alternative path through the forest. It's ongoing – the tents and kit are all mouldy and smelling of damp from the constant wet of a place where rain is measured in metres. We're travelling with a pygmy bloke called Daniel. He's delightful, and tells me his favourite bushmeat is forest python wrapped in manioc leaves and steamed over coals in a hole in the ground.

Dispatch #73 – Kribi and Beyond

In 1856 a local chief signed a treaty with the English and later wrote to Queen Victoria inviting her to establish a protectorate over the area. A response to that letter and repeated other requests would have changed Cameroon's history. When the British Consul finally arrived in 1884 with a favourable response, he found that the Germans had beaten the British by only five days. Not surprising therefore that the old German-designed cathedral in Kribi is straight out of the Kaiser's Victorian-era Germany. Kribi is the first big town on Cameroon's outside edge. There are mopeds everywhere, the taxis are yellow, the central market is a mass of colour and the people are polite and friendly. After unpopulated Gabon, Cameroon has a stronger feeling of Africa. The people are jollier here and the salad and hard-boiled-egg sandwiches from the roadside stalls are made from proper bread – great, big, doughy English loaves, not those long, thin, full-of-air ones that we've had to put up with in Francophone Africa.

We make bully beef and atjar sandwiches on a Landy bonnet. Down at the beach the sea is a charcoal colour, the sand is biscuit brown and the weather is overcast. It's been a long and difficult mud road; slipping and sliding around logging trucks that were stuck in the mud, and doing humanitarian work on the way. At Plage de Lonji we pay 3 000 CFAs to camp in a shelter under some palm trees on a stretch of beach. There's a village full of Nigerian fishermen, the thick hardwood planks of their long boats held together with strong wire staples, and big, black mamas selling small, sugary, round doughnuts. 'Pops, they speak English,' shouts Tristan as he races into the waves to swim with the local kids. 'Cameroon's great!'

RITE TO SIGHT AND MALARIA PREVENTION –

Dispatch #74 – Douala and on to Limbe

After World War I, Cameroon was divided between the British and French under a League of Nations mandate, which means that in some areas English is the dominant language and in others, French. Douala, the biggest port and the industrial centre of Cameroon, is more French. We follow the dockside road – three right-hand-drive South African Landies, one behind the other. We've learnt the ropes by now and are used to driving on the 'wrong' side of the road with the front-seat passengers craning their necks and shouting 'Stop!' or 'Go!' or taking radio instructions from the leading vehicle, such as

'Careful, massive hole in the road/bridge washed away/truck coming'. After three-and-a-half months, the Landies, loaded to the hilt and invariably covered in mud, have become our homes and way of life. We know every sound, every smell, every squeak, every pitch and every roll as they work their guts out to follow the outside edge.

The area looks a bit dodgy and like most West African cities it's clogged with traffic, diesel smoke, taxis and market stalls. After crossing the Wouri River, we head north towards Limbe, hoping to get there before dark. 'Cops ahead,' comes Ross's voice over the radio. We show our *Carnets de Passage*, insurance papers, driver's licences, letters of introduction from the Department of Foreign Affairs, conveniently stamped and translated into French, and the Scroll of Peace and Goodwill. A few quick rubs of the pebble in the pocket, many *merci beaucoup*s and several handshakes later, we continue north up the coast through the rain and palm oil plantations. As always, everything is new and exciting, and we don't know what the next piece of the edge of Africa will look like. It's the joy of travel, small bite sizes, one day at a time. If we can get to Limbe today, tomorrow will look after itself.

Dispatch #75 – Limbe

Limbe, founded in 1857 by Alfred Saker, a British missionary, is still oh-so-English, and reminds me a little of another Limbe in Malawi. There are old colonial buildings; British Leyland and Bedford signs; well-maintained botanical gardens; a Victoria Bus Stop Bar and a Blue Whale Restaurant; Friendship and Guinness clubs; Market and Church streets; and a Mile 6 beach. This predominantly Anglophone city was called Victoria until 1983 and was the capital of the British section of Cameroon. The fish market is like a movie set – big woven baskets of silver fish, fish drying racks with smoke rising above, bicycles and dugouts, fish merchants and money changers and Ghanaian long boats with colourful flags and bunting, all dramatically backdropped by black volcanic sand beaches. There are also plenty of crooks, conmen and beggars and a greedy official catches Ross filming and tries to make a quick buck.

We set up a base camp at the Park Hotel Miramar, with its empty swimming pool and little bungalows. Strip steak and hot chips are prepared by a Rasta cook and served out on the veranda. I look around at the the team: Ross, with tired eyes and a few days' stubble on the chin, is working out logistics; Anna is making sure that Tristan doesn't fall off the cliff into the Atlantic; Mashozi is negotiating the price of the rooms; and Sam's setting up Bruce's tripod, helping him take pictures of the forested islands and another piece of the edge of Africa to add to the thousands already photographed. Daniel, our lovely pygmy friend from the forest, is looking quite overwhelmed. It's the first time he's ever stayed at a hotel. I pull out the tattered *National Geographic* atlas. Ahead of us is Mount Cameroon and the road that will take us to Nigeria.

Dispatch #76 – Mount Cameroon

It's Sunday and the local kids are all dressed up outside the Ebenezer Baptist Church. There are tambourines and drums, giving the hymns an African beat. Old Alfred Saker, the first missionary, would be pleased; there's even a monument to him down at the water's edge. Christianity here is alive and well and, much to the mirth of the rest of the expedition team, Mashozi and I get an impromptu sermon delivered to us by a Bible-bashing bystander through the Land Rover window as we stop at the market to buy bread and bananas.

Mount Cameroon is covered in mist. Debundscha, about 30 kilometres west from Limbe, is the second-wettest place on earth. As luck would have it, we are here at the height of the rains with no chance of climbing the mountain. It's bloody disappointing. It's bucketing down and there seems to

THE FISH MARKET IS LIKE A MOVIE SET

be no end to it. To the clicking of the old-fashioned Landy windscreen wipers and the characteristic cold-water drip onto the accelerator foot, we slip and slide through endless palmnut and rubber plantations. We stop to show Tristan how rubber is bled from the tree trunks and the tips of his fingers get stuck together with the white latex. For just a few seconds the mist parts to reveal Mount Cameroon; at a whopping 4 095 metres it's easily the highest mountain on the outside edge of Central and West Africa. It's a landmark sighting for the expedition and our spirits lift.

Dispatch #77 – A Night with a Madman
We stop to winch an old Peugeot out of a ditch. The driver and his girlfriend are both very appreciative, although she looks especially embarrassed, as if they were naughty schoolkids who'd been caught on their first date. In front of us there's a chain across the road, and a cheerful guy, dressed in black with a gold necklace and speaking pidgin English, says 'Special deal mon! Jus 5 000 francs you go tree cars. Very beautiful mon, you see when you go there.' And so we wind down a rainforest track to Lake Barombi Mbo. The forest rules in Central Africa, and down on the lakeshore the benches and circular cement plinths that probably once housed umbrellas, plastic chairs, drinks and music have been taken over by the jungle creepers. It's still a favourite hangout for lovers and soon the man in the Peugeot pitches up to be photographed with his darling on the edge of a wide, flat rock that juts out into the exquisite, circular lake. Others arrive by motorcycle, boys and girls four to a bike. Then, to add to the activity, a madman with a plastic bottle of holy water on his head appears on the scene. 'I'm not the child of Jesus!' he shouts in perfect English. 'I'm the son of God sent to save you!' 'Look Pops,' says Tristan, 'he's weed in his pants.'

We pitch camp. 'God bless you!' shouts the poor fellow as Mashozi and I put our dome tent on the floor under a derelict, corrugated iron roof that once served as a canteen for visitors. Bruce and Sam pitch their small blue-and-grey igloo on 'Lover's Rock'. Anna, Ross and Tristan push up their rooftop tent on top of the Landy and little Daniel moves his small tent alongside ours. At last light the Peugeot lovebirds leave for Kumba town. All is quiet until a delegation from the top of the hill arrives on a spluttering motorbike, made up of a girl called Gloria with a baby on her back and her near-blind father-in-

Our campsite at Lake Barombi Mbo.

law. 'You no pay!' she shouts. 'Oh yes we did,' says Mashozi. 'We gave 5 000 CFAs to the dude with the black T-shirt, trousers and gold chain. You were there Gloria, I recognise you. You helped him unlock the chain across the road.' 'Oh no, that man we don't know. He a thief, he taken your muney!' she returns. This is just too much for our man Daniel, and his hot pygmy blood starts to boil. 'You bad woman!' he shouts. 'You are in together with that man! Because my friends are white you want to cheat them. I don't like this corrupt business in Cameroon. I don't like!'

He's mad as a snake and changes to French. Gloria screams back insults – it's getting nasty. The madman returns. 'I'm the son of God!' he wails. 'Hallelujah! I will save you!' 'And the camping fee, the camping!' shouts Gloria. 'That is 5 000 also!' I do the old Greybeard handshakes thing (big smiles and lots of handshakes usually help in these type of situations) and urge them to keep cool. We agree on the camping fee, which gets handed over to the blind man. 'I'll lock the chain for your security,' he says, 'and in the morning I'll unlock it only when you pay the 5 000 entrance which the other man stole.' 'We'll see in the morning,' I reply. 'God is great!' shouts the madman, still balancing the plastic bottle of holy water on his head. Mashozi gives him half a loaf of bread smeared with peanut butter. The man of God rolls a joint the size of a banana and then disappears behind the clang of an old metal door. 'Look Pops,' says Tristan, 'he's sleeping right next door to your tent.' There's the smell of ganja and the godly incantations get louder. 'Go to sleep my friend, please go to sleep,' implores Mashozi. 'God be with you.'

Little Daniel slides the machete under his camp chair whilst Sam prepares some sausage and tough chicken over a smoky fire and Bruce goes through the day's pics on the laptop. We talk to Daniel about his life in the village of Nkoloveng, near the border with Equatorial Guinea. He explains how he survives from growing peppers, cassava, sweet potatoes and plantains. 'It a difficult life,' he says in his broken English. 'For the first year I could not give my wife a piece of soap, but now I live from my farming. My little boy Lambo is three years old and my wife has a four-month-old baby in her stomach.' He's a lovely man and it's such a shame that he'll have to leave us shortly when we cross into Nigeria.

All night the rain thunders down onto the corrugated-iron roof above us and every now and then a flash of lightning reveals our forest surroundings. Intermittent animal noises and wailing cries from our blessed man next door continue throughout the night, but in the morning he's quiet. The rain stops and the voices of fishermen netting small tilapia from their dugout canoes carry across the slate-grey waters of the mist-covered crater-lake of Barombi Mbo. One of them comes over to chat. 'Who's the madman?' I ask. 'We don't know who he is or where he came from,' he says. 'He lives here alone in the forest – he's demented, but he's a child of God like us all.' And so we pack the Landies in the mist to the sound of the madman singing 'Cumbaya, my Lord, cumbaya!'

Dispatch #78 – Nigeria Here We Come
'Quiet as you can, but keep the Landies running,' says Bruce over the radio before he slips out and quickly unhooks the chain that closes off the road. Then it's foot flat and we're through, even as Gloria and a gang come running down from the village. 'Bye-bye Gloria!' shouts Mashozi, giving her a big, innocent wave. And so we skid, slide, push and winch our way north. It's as slippery as snot on a mirror. There's a big, orange Magirus Deutz 4x4 truck down to its axles and blocking the track. They're using a block and tackle and have iron pegs driven into the road, but it won't budge. It takes us hours to get around it.

Breakfast is banana and bread. We are trying to reach the Cross River and then Nigeria, where we don't quite know what to expect, especially as we continue to get news of the kidnapping of foreigners in the Port Harcourt area. With us in the Landy is mud-spattered Nyning Ludhgha, a travelling mechanic who'd fallen off the back bumper of the Nissan that we had been following. 'I had been hanging like a bat until you rescued me,' he says in his delightful English. 'So you are going to Nigeria? Very dangerous! When I go to buy parts I dress in old overalls and slip illegally across the border, otherwise they just rip you off. Those Nigerians are ruthless.'

Another stop. Nyning gets out to assist us. There's a mud hole so deep it could swallow an entire Landy, but there's a road cut to the side, it's surface corrugated with poles cut from the forest. To take it, however, you need to pay the forest dwellers who've cut the track. It's another negotiation that leads to a shouting match and almost results in a punch-up between the forest dwellers. Nyning is thoroughly pissed off. 'You will have to pay,' he says, 'there's no other way. The problem is that the government gives money to fix the road but it gets eaten. They don't worry about us out here in the rural areas, especially because we're Anglophone.'

We push on. Up ahead, the Nissan Patrol that Nyning fell off blocks the road; it's stuck in the mud and won't start. Out comes our towrope. We're all pilgrims of the mud road to Ekok, heading for the Nigerian border. Nyning warns us again. 'They're a brutal nation – you'll need to be careful.' Last night I'd asked the team to be extremely diligent about security in Nigeria. 'Stick together at all times. Watch the vehicles, and keep them locked.' I probably sounded a bit paranoid but it's all the rumours: kidnapping, sex trafficking, drugs, armed robberies, scams and frightening traffic, with dead bodies on the highway being ridden over by the unstoppable flow of cars, oil trucks and motorbikes. What's making us even edgier, of course, is that we've got little Tristan with us.

We turn off on to a toll road.

Nigeria

Day 110, Country 9 on the Edge

Talk about Nigeria, one of Africa's great powerhouses, and people immediately think of violent crime, corruption, political unrest and scams – seems the country's got an image problem! But others say it's warm, friendly and exuberant, with a wild music scene. We're not sure what to think, but we'll be extra careful with our persons and property. Having Tristan with us makes us all nervous. We'll just have to put our faith in the Zen of Travel I suppose.

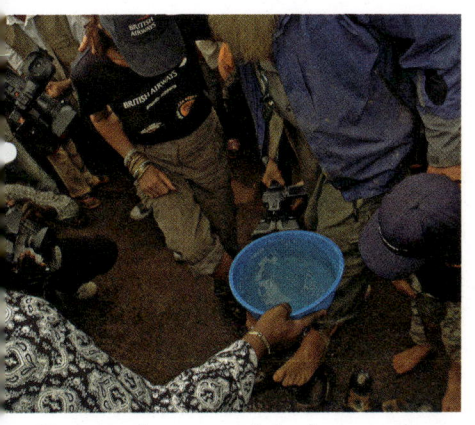

Despite the country's bad reputation, we are warmly welcomed to Nigeria, and the village president even washes our feet.

Dispatch #79 – Welcome to Nigeria

British Airways is a strong supporter of the expedition's One Net One Life malaria prevention initiative in Nigeria. We'd sent a message ahead from Cameroon but never in our wildest dreams had we expected such a welcome. Imagine the scene: here we are, barefoot at the border, trousers rolled up, covered in reddish-brown Cameroon muck, with mud in our hair, mud between our toes and mud even in my beard. The Nigerian welcome party, all smartly dressed, have crossed over to meet us. There are lovely British Airways girls in blue jeans and malaria prevention T-shirts and the TV cameras are rolling. High Chief Edem Duke, president of the Federation of National Tourism Associations, is heading up the occasion. He's a big man with a big heart. They produce a bottle of French bubbly and spray us and the three mud-splattered Landies. Welcome to Nigeria! We're zapped through customs and immigration without a single hitch. Instantly, perceptions of Nigeria change – this is the joy of travel. The warmth and friendliness of the people of Cross River State is infectious. Traditional dancers line the road and the president of the village produces a basin of water and washes our feet. Immediately we are off to distribute mosquito nets to mums with babies, spectacles to the poor-sighted and mobile libraries to schools. This is followed by more speeches and dancing and a detour inland to the Ebudu Cattle Ranch, a popular resort high up in the Sonkwala Mountains along the Cameroon border. Then there's another welcome party and more speeches and photos. It's all happening too fast.

Dispatch #80 – The Old Slave-Trading Port of Calabar

A convoy of cars and a police escort race us down to Calabar, a city perched high on the hills overlooking the Atlantic and the Calabar River estuary. Calabar gained

A LADY OF CALABAR IN TRADITIONAL DANCE COSTUME

NIGERIA – NOTES:
- A HUGE COUNTRY OF 924 000 KM²
- A MASSIVE POPULATION OF 140 MILLION AND GROWING
- BEEN WARNED THAT 'IT'S CRAZY'!
- CURRENCY IS THE NAIRA –
- ENGLISH IS THE OFFICIAL LANGUAGE, OTHERS INCLUDE HAUSA, YORUBA, IGBO, EDO AND EFIK
- NIGERIA ELECTED OLUSEGUN OBASANJO AS THE PRESIDENT IN 1999, AFTER YEARS UNDER THE DESPOTIC REGIME OF GENERAL SANI ABACHA.
- SEEMS TO BE A GROWING DIVIDE BETWEEN THE ISLAMIC NORTH AND THE CHRISTIAN SOUTH.
- SECURITY PROBLEMS IN THE OIL-RICH DELTA AREA.

prominence in the late 17th century when lucrative slave-trading city states were set up, mostly by the Efik tribe who sold off slaves from the interior to the Portuguese, Dutch, French, Germans and English. The rulers became rich and powerful. To emphasise their importance, they took on European names like Duke, Henshaw and James.

Malaria is rife here and, with the help of the British Airways team, we distribute life-saving nets to every single mother and child at the maternity hospital, but sadly we're too late for one little boy who's just died from the disease. The governor of Cross River State and members of the Royal House endorse the expedition scroll and there is a dinner party held in our honour at State House, complete with traditional dancers and musicians. I feel embarrassed to think that our perception of Nigeria was one only of lawlessness and scams. The old slave-trading port of Calabar is one of Nigeria's most likeable cities. Jimmy Inny, our British Airways host, tells us that Nigerian wives don't like their men to visit Calabar. The city has the most beautiful and enticing girls in the country, and apparently 'they know just how to look after a man'. The area is also believed to have Nigeria's best food – traditional culinary delights – and it explains why they say that if a Calabar woman cooks for you, you'll never leave town. High Chief Edem Duke is a gracious host, putting us up at his hotel and feeding us at his Chinese restaurant. Later, at Chief Edem's nightclub, we notice that Jimmy Inny was absolutely correct about the talented girls of Calabar.

Dispatch #81 – Trouble in the Delta

Be careful of the Delta area, we are warned. Over 90% of Nigerian export earnings come from crude oil, and the two states astride the mouth of the Niger River produce more than 85% of it. Billions of dollars of crude are extracted each year, but the wealth doesn't reach the local people and many of these minority communities are left in abject poverty. This disenchantment has led to severe clashes with the government, often resulting in torture and massacres. As a form of protest for this extreme retaliation, the locals have on occasion resorted to the occupation of the oil installations and kidnapping of foreigners.

Our plan was to launch our Gemini inflatables and explore the Niger Delta by boat, but the military and police are adamant that they won't allow it. So it's in the Landies again as, with sirens screaming, a police detail dressed in flack jackets and armed with automatics takes us on a high-speed detour around Port Harcourt, where, to avoid more kidnapping of foreigners, the military has recently taken hold of the city. '*Bumper to bumper. Please no stopping, it's dangerous! Move, move!*' come the anxious instructions from the police escort over the radio. We've loaned them one of our handhelds – it's good to be on the same frequency in case of emergencies, but they're pushing us to go too fast. Overloaded Landies, driving bumper to bumper at breakneck speed – it's crazy. Then there's a tap on my shoulder from the back seat. 'Pops, I want to wee,' says little Tristan. 'I'm desperate.'

'Can't stop, it's not safe,' replies Mashozi as she whips out her penknife, cuts the neck off a plastic water bottle and passes it to a wide-eyed Tristan. 'Here, you'll have to wee in this,' she says. 'And then you'll have to drink it,' I add with a grin as, with tyres squealing, we fly through a roundabout outside Port Harcourt.

After crossing the broad Niger River, we go to Onitsha where, in the pouring rain, the three Landies are mobbed in heavy traffic. There are hundreds of over-curious vendors and onlookers pushing against the vehicles, noses squeezed flat against the windows. Some climb onto the roof rack; it's out of control. And then, oh shit, an enormous, muscled Rambo with a shaved head, shotgun and machete peers through the windscreen. But it's okay; turns out he's part of the local militia that's moved in to ensure our safety. Over the radio comes another '*Bumper to bumper – move, move!*' followed by, '*The people, Papa King, they like you. It's the beard.*'

We reach Lagos where nothing but nothing can prepare you for the vast, chaotic, congested mass of people and vehicles, leading to a nightmare negotiation of the streets of the most populous city on the outside edge of Africa. Mashozi picks up a newspaper from a street vendor, and this is what Godwin Erapi has got to say in the local *Business Day*:

> *Embarking on a journey on most Nigerian roads today is akin to driving or cycling or running endlessly around a roundabout or [on] roads ridden with bomb craters with nowhere in mind. It is hard labour. For passengers on contemporary Nigerian roads, travelling or driving is like embarking on an endless journey as you are not sure where the trip will terminate and there is no time limit. You are both at the mercy of bloodthirsty, armed robbers and roads that lead to hell rather than your actual destination … And since the greater part of the contractor's profit has been stolen by government officials, the contractor builds a cheap, poor-quality road that would not last beyond the commissioning ceremony.* (22 August 2007, p. 15)

Dispatch #82 – Crazy Lagos

'Oh my God, watch out,' says Mashozi, as coming straight towards us on the wrong side of the dual carriageway is a seemingly out-of-control, crabbing fuel tanker. Only

NIGERIA IS NOT FOR SISSIES – ARMED COPS GUARD LANDIES & BALES OF MOZZIE NETS –.

There's every type of bush-meat at the market.

The beard, the gun and Robert Brozin of Nando's, who's come in to assist with malaria prevention —

yesterday, some thieves were burnt alive whilst trying to siphon petrol from a tanker that was on fire. The traffic is unbelievable! There are two or three people to a moped – no crash helmets – expertly ducking and weaving through the traffic. Some of them even have their handlebars bent inwards so as to better fit through the narrow gaps between the cars. Street vendors sell everything imaginable – hard-boiled eggs, cold drinks, plastic combs and toothbrushes; cures for gonorrhoea, gout and impotence; cow's horns and massive yams; meat-on-a-stick; cooking oil, maize meal, rice, pies, bread, groundnuts and bananas; and small plastic bags of drinking water. Commuters are eating and drinking on the move. It's a dangerous game of Dodgem cars, with dented, yellow busses and taxis, scarred from nudging their way through the potholed, puddled mess that makes up the craziest city we've visited yet. It's really no surprise that trucks, busses and lorries carry slogans like 'God's my pilot' and 'The Lord is my shepherd'. Believe me, to survive this lot you need a huge dose of divine providence.

With sirens screaming and blue lights flashing, our armed escort pushes a way through for the Landies. '*Careful, legless skateboarder ahead,*' comes Ross's voice over the radio. '*Quickly, look down. I can see him in my rear-view mirror, he's next to you.*' I can't bloody believe it, there's this little cripple holding on to my front-door handle, screaming along on a skateboard with white eyes against his smiling black face, grinning up at me. He's ducking in between the Landy wheels to avoid an oncoming car, then swinging out again, begging for money – playing with death. I pass him a few niara, about half a dollar's worth. 'God bless you, sir,' he shouts, and he's gone.

We meet the ceremonial King of Lagos, Oba Rilwan Akiolu, dressed in all his finery, complete with golden slippers, the First Lady of Lagos State, Mrs Abimbola Fashola, and the Royal household. They all endorse the scroll. Bob Thielcher from Protea Hotels in Lagos spoils us with luxurious clean sheets, ice in the Captain and warm hospitality. They too have joined our One Net One Life cause and here in Nigeria donate an extra thousand mosquito nets for distribution to the needy living in high-risk malaria areas around the city.

Dispatch #83 – Peri-Peri to the Rescue

As always, the South Africans really move in to help. Nando's opens up its sixth restaurant in Nigeria. It is a never-to-be-forgotten peri-peri bash and our expedition team members are the guests of honour. It has taken us more than four months and 16 000 kilometres to get here. Founder member Robbie Brozin, who joined us for a stint in Namibia, is here to meet us. He hands over a Help Nando's Fight Malaria cheque. They fly in celebrity chefs Clayton Sherrod from the United States and Citrum Khumalo from South Africa. The humidity is as thick as golden syrup, but they are determined to prepare the expedition a peri-peri feast. The ingredients are to be bought from the market at Beye on the Lagos Lagoon, just south of where we are camped at South African Marc Schreuder's cottage. At the colourful bazaar there are live crocodiles, snakes and turtles for sale, but the chefs stick to fish, greens, yams, groundnuts, pumpkin seeds and chillies for a beach banquet. David O'Sullivan from Radio 702 has also flown up to meet the expedition. Toes in the sand, waves crashing onto the outside edge of Africa, we party until late. The next day we distribute mosquito nets.

Dispatch #84 – King of Badagry

In front of the throne at the Royal palace we prostrate ourselves, face down, at the feet of the King of Badagry from where, as is custom, we greet him three times with the words 'Awee, Awee, Awee'. He is a dear old man and before presenting each of us with a certificate making us Pilgrims of Badagry, he endorses our scroll with the following words:

> *This is the greatest mission of the 21st century in the fight against malaria which has been ravaging the whole of Africa – it is the No. 1 killer disease. We appreciate your efforts and will continue to remember you for your Love for the people of this continent … His Royal Majesty, King of Badagry.*

The malaria prevention work is relentless, and we distribute more than 10 000 mosquito nets to mums and children in the Lagos area. It's a humanitarian journey that even takes us by boat and village mopeds into the swamplands around Badagry. Nigeria has a great soul; most people are friendly and hospitable, yet it's a country of extremes where tremendous poverty and wealth sit cheek by jowl. It's also undoubtedly a force to be reckoned with in Africa, and I'm sure there's no other place quite like it on the continent. For us it's been a fascinating experience – welcoming, exuberant and tough and an unforgettable chapter on the outside edge.

Eight days later we are completely exhausted and also saddened by little Tristan having had to fly back to school. For the time being we've lost our mascot, but happily he'll be back. Our escape from the traffic and feverish pace of Lagos is nigh. We overnight in a local hotel near the border. The next morning Ross treats himself for malaria. Slumped in the passenger seat, with Anna driving, he looks shocking. Benin, voodoo capital of the world, here we come.

HIS ROYAL MAJESTY THE KING OF BADAGRY

ONE NET – ONE LIFE.

85

Benin

Day 121, Country 10 on the Edge

Once known as Dahomey, the République du Bénin is probably the Gulf of Guinea's least-known nation. It's also the birthplace of voodoo, which was exported from here by slaves who were taken to the Americas, Cuba, Brazil and Haiti. We are imagining all sorts of interesting stuff, like fetishes and black magic, and are curious to see how the religion and practices compare with those of the sangomas back home.

LES SUTTON FROM LAND ROVER SOUTH AFRICA BRINGS IN A TEAM OF MALARIA WARRIORS —

Dispatch #85 – Cotonou

After the madness and chaos of the Nigerian roads, the little Republic of Benin is an oasis of calm, despite a history of coups. Sure, the sprawling city of Cotonou has tens of thousands of mopeds, all going flat out with two or three to a bike and still no crash helmets, but gone are the roadblocks and the adrenalin-pumping tension of Lagos. Our good friend Lesley Sutton, the Land Rover PR and media manager from South Africa, arrived at midnight with a team of adventurous journalists. In the spirit of Cotonou, we pick them up at the airport with local moped taxis, and a Landy, of course, to carry all their gear. None of them has ever been to the Gulf of Guinea before, but even so, they all happily agree to become malaria warriors. So we have a team of journalists who are not only providing valuable media coverage for our cause but are also assisting with the distribution of life-saving mosquito nets. They're a jolly bunch, many of whom have been with us before – good African travellers who are prepared to pitch their own tents, help cook and take what comes.

There's Pieter Oosthuizen, the motoring journalist from *Die Beeld* newspaper, who's a keen historian and has been reading up on explorer Mungo Park's Victorian adventures into West Africa; fun-loving Patrick Cruywagen, the bush editor from the magazine *SA 4x4*, who's keen to report on what, if we succeed, will probably be one of the greatest Land Rover adventures of all time; and freelance journalist Murray Williams, who's fit and tough and has already researched Benin, Togo and Ghana, the three countries through which they will be travelling. To add to the mix, there are the stalwarts from many previous adventures: the energetic Rob Till, professional stills photographer, and Rory Beattie, Land Rover's technical advisor, who's come to check out his three babies and to service them when we get to Accra in Ghana, and who is nicknamed '*Señor Mechanico*'. Tomorrow we're off to Ganvié, considered to be the largest lake village on the outside edge of the continent.

THE HUTS WERE BUILT ON STILTS ABOVE THE WATER TO AVOID ATTACK BY SLAVERS AND IT REMAINED THAT WAY —

BENIN - NOTES:
- A TINY COUNTRY WITH A COASTLINE OF ABOUT 100 KM / MALARIA BAD.
- TOTAL LAND AREA IS JUST 113 000 KM²
- FRIENDLY WITH A STABLE ECONOMY, EASY-GOING AND RELAXED, AFTER NIGERIA!
- POPULATION IS ABOUT 9 MILLION WHILST THE DE FACTO CAPITAL IS COTONOU OFFICIALLY IT IS PORTO-NOVO.
- HOME OF VOODOO — THAT'S GOING TO BE INTERESTING — NEED TO RESEARCH, GET TO KNOW MORE.
- USED TO ALSO BE ONE OF AFRICA'S BIGGEST SLAVE-TRADING CENTRES.

MUMS LINE UP FOR LIFE-SAVING MOZZIE NETS - MALARIA IS RIFE HERE.

a floating market

Dispatch #86 – The Venice of Africa

Ganvié is unbelievable. More than 20 000 people are living above the water in huts built on rickety stilts, with entire families commuting in dugout canoes – it's the Venice of Africa. There's a floating market of dugouts piled high with vegetables, fish and trade goods and even a few wonky little hotel rooms balancing above the shallow brown waters of Lac Nokoué. 'Ganvié means place of safety,' says our boatman. 'The village was called that because, during the slave trade, people here were safe from invasion by the Dahomey slavers, who for religious reasons were forbidden to extend their attacks over water.'

We're told that malaria is rife in Ganvié – it's a killer disease. Today's mosquito nets are funded by Durban-based Grindrod Limited, whose expedition slogan reads 'Caring for Africa'. The company would be proud to find our team of volunteers giving malaria prevention education and distributing its life-saving nets to mums who arrive at the little hospital by dugout canoe – with just a few centimetres freeboard – their tiny babies strapped to their backs. Most of these Tofinu-speaking women make a living from trading in fish that are trapped and grown in a network of branches that make up the underwater fences known as *akadja*. I can see the appreciation in the mothers' eyes – many of them know what it's like to lose a baby to the bloodsucking bite of the female *Anopheles* mosquito. Most of them have seen loved ones convulsing in fever or impotently watched whilst family and friends have submitted to the dreaded coma before dying from cerebral malaria. We personally place a net in each mum's hand, and they curtsey and demurely shake hands with us in thanks.

The rain clouds mercifully gather whilst sweat trickles down our backs. Behind the reeds, long barges quietly smuggle in 25-litre containers of fuel from Nigeria to be sold at roadside stalls, a Coke bottle at a time, to thousands of moped riders. Despite the harshest of conditions, Africa always seems to find a way. The village chief thanks us gratefully, but I can't relax. Back in Cotonou, with Anna looking after him, Ross is sweating it out with a terrible bout of malaria. He'd puked up the first four-pill dose of Coartem, so we gave him anti-nausea tablets, waited a while and recommenced the malaria treatment. It's scary isn't it, how sometimes we risk our own lives to save others?

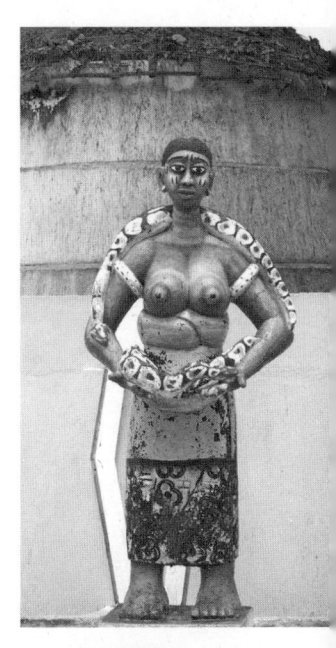

Dispatch #87 – Voodoo

Ross is still battling it out. If he hasn't improved by this evening we'll need to get him to a hospital for a quinine drip or consider flying him back home. It's as hot as hell. A statue of a priest gazes down at us from a Catholic cathedral across the road. In front of us a carved figure of a bare-breasted woman with scarification on her face handles two pythons. We're at the entrance of the voodoo python temple in Ouidah, where a cloth bloodied from sacrificed goats hangs from an ancient eroka tree. A man in traditional West African dress with six scars on his face drapes a python around my neck, and down in the pit there are more than 50 of its mates. Contact with the sacred pythons is said to give you vitality and protection. Once blessed, we make our way to the sacred forest of Kpasse to learn more about voodoo. Here, I touch the tree which, according to legend, the 14th-century-chief Kpasse had turned himself into in order to hide from his enemies. Thousands of fruit bats fly overhead, and voodoo statues are everywhere. There's a fertility god with a massive erect penis and a snake god that's eating itself. There's a voodoo god of protection, a god of thunder and lightning, a god of metal and a god of soil. To the accompaniment of drums, singing and dancing, His Majesty the voodoo king Mito Daho Mindji Kpassenon writes these words in the expedition scroll:

> I do appreciate what you are doing for peace and malaria.
> We voodoo people thank you for this great work.

ANNA AT THE PYTHON TEMPLE, ME MAKING NOTES AT THE VOODOO MARKET, VOODOO FETISHES AND THE VOODOO KING ENDORSING THE SCROLL — WE SHOULD BE JUST FINE —

The door of no return outside the voodoo capital of Quidah —

During a ceremony held in our honour, the king watches us through the fringe of gold tassels hanging from his wide-brimmed, embroidered hat. An aide twirls a large umbrella decorated with voodoo symbols above His Majesty's head. Another holds a long-handled, gold-bladed spear nearby. Amid much frenetic drumming and dancing, we are invited into a nearby hut where chickens are being sacrificed to the voodoo gods. Malaria is rife here. Later that afternoon, still in the sacred forest, we distribute mosquito nets – it's what we've come to do.

Dispatch #88 – The Door of No Return

Ouidah was once Benin's most important slave-trading port, where human flesh was sold for cloth, guns, beads and booze. In order to understand the slaves' final journey from Africa, we follow the Route des Esclaves, the sandy track walked by tens of thousands of slaves from the town slave market at Place Chacha, down to the beach some four kilometres away. The market was controlled by the Portuguese slave trader Francisco de Souza, or 'Chacha' as the bastard was nicknamed, meaning 'quick-quick'. The route runs down Rua Don Francisco de Souza, the road that has taken his name. It was De Souza who had the monopoly on the slave trade and had an army of 1 000 soldiers and 6 000 Amazon warriors, who were trained to use bows and were reputed to cut off one of their breasts if it impaired their ability to shoot.

Dotted along the slave route, past the old train station, are the royal emblems of the various chiefs of Abomey. We stop at the statue marking the Tree of Forgetfulness, which the slaves were made to circle, round and round with chained feet shuffling in the sand, women and children sobbing. They were forced to keep circling – men nine times and women seven – in a symbolic act of disorientation, so as to forget their previous life, religion and culture. The sad journey eventually brings us to the beach and the Door of No Return, a vast imposing arch decorated with bass relief images and metal sculptures of slaves in shackles. Some bits are missing, taken as souvenirs. It was through this arch that, along with the slaves, voodoo was exported far and wide.

Later in the cool of the afternoon, with a jolly man called Remi as my interpreter, I return to the fetish market in Ouidah's town square for an interview with a voodoo pharmacist. 'What would you use for love,' I ask, 'if you wanted to court a woman, get her to love you forever?' I scribble the answer as Remi translates: 'Take 16 (voodoo lucky number) *temikoukou* (small black beetles) and add a herb called *lema*. Then add 16 gall bladders from forest duikers and 16 from lambs, the head of a pangolin and more herbs. Next, add bits of your own hair, finger and toenails, grind it all together and burn it over a fire until it becomes a black powder. Sprinkle this onto the girl's food everyday until the powder is finished. She will come to you forever.' 'Forever?' I ask. 'Yes, forever.' 'And what if you should ever want to get rid of her?' I enquire. 'Oh,' comes the nonchalant reply, 'to break the power of the powder you just simply chuck all her stuff out of the bedroom and onto the street!' Okay!

On our way back to our expedition base camp near the Door of No Return, Remi tells me of Benin's difficult years: of the countless coups and the government infighting; of how the minister of interior was shot dead by the president's bodyguard when caught *in flagrante delicto* with *Madame* Kerekou, the president's wife; of how, in 1977, French mercenaries tried and failed to take Cotonou and of how Dahomey then engaged in a popular revolution that nationalised agriculture and industry in the name of socialism; and of further coups and unrest. 'But now it's much better – we have democracy!' says Remi. 'The people finally revolted – we'd had enough.'

Dispatch #89 – Two Expeditions Meet

It's wonderful when two expeditions meet. We'd first heard about three crazy South Africans who were 'surfing their brains out' from Cape Town to London up the West Coast when we were in Mayumba in Gabon. 'Ah! You've just missed the South Africans, the surfing dudes,' we were told. 'They couldn't believe the waves here in Gabon. They're travelling in an old Land Cruiser, you can't miss them.' And then again in Libreville, 'You've just missed the surfers,' said Anneke Veenswijk-Nel from the South African Embassy. And then, what a coincidence, they happened to drive past a backstreet in Cotonou where we were parked, so we arranged to meet near the Door of No Return.

The last time we'd met up with another expedition was way back in Angola and we were happy to meet fellow adventurers. What a party we end up having! We drink Captain Morgan from the Landy tank and dig out some highly prized flat chickens from the bottom of the Engel fridge that Marc Schreuder, the Nando's man in Nigeria, had organised for us in Lagos. With some Nando's sauce and a few fresh rolls, we turn the occasion into a never-to-be-forgotten, Mozambican-styled peri-peri feast.

Faces light up as we exchange stories of the outside edge: winching and pushing through the forests of Gabon, great surf spots and beautiful beaches, and hassles with bureaucrats (they love the black marks on the visor). The surfers' names are Michael 'Stone' Sternberg, Tim Harris and John 'Lucks' Fleming. The waves crash on the beach whilst we sit around a roaring fire. They stick their African Surfer decal into our Scroll of Peace and Goodwill. The next day they assist us with the distribution of life-saving mosquito nets and at Grand Popo, before we say 'Cheers!' and 'See you somewhere again up the coast of Africa', they ask us to do a naming ceremony for their old Cruiser. Ross, who's now up and about but still shaky on his pins after his worst bout of malaria ever, comes up with the Swahili name *Mze Kobe*, meaning 'The Old Tortoise'. The christening is completed when we sign on the back of their vehicle with a black marker. They want to stay on and surf some more. Good luck, fellow pilgrims of adventure. May we meet again somewhere on the outside edge. Togo here we come!

IT'S A LONG NIGHT WITH 'THE SURFERS'

Togo

Day 126, Country 11 on the Edge

Still tracking the edge, our next country is the République Togolaise, French-speaking West Africa's smallest nation. Togo is also a land of voodoo, which we've learnt does not signify religion, at least not in Africa, but is a word for a kind of spiritual being. Voodoo priests are particularly impressionable spiritually, and can be easily 'possessed' or 'mounted' by the voodoo, thus displaying its emotions through a human channel. Fascinating!

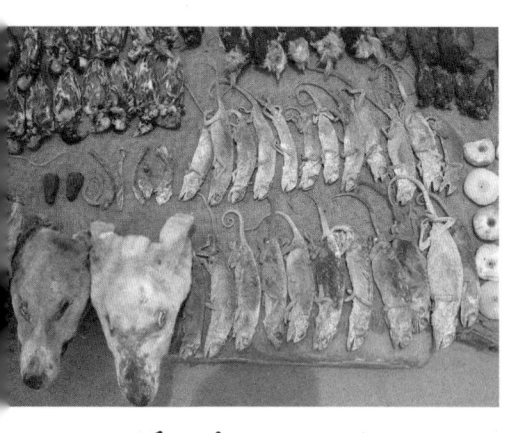

JEEZ! RATS; CAT, DOG AND HYENA HEADS; PORCUPINE QUILLS AND BABOON SKULLS — DRIED CHAMELEONS ARE ALSO A FAVOURITE.

Dispatch #90 – The Road to Lomé

We park the Landies under some shady trees at Hilakondji, at the border, where young girls giggle as they spread their colourful washing out to dry. Koffi, our French interpreter from Benin, helps Ross and Anna with the formalities out of Benin and into Togo. No black marks on the sun visor; maybe it's the voodoo belief that makes these two small countries so easy-going and friendly. Togo has had a rough time politically; over the last two decades thousands have fled the repressive regime and the country's wealth has plummeted. It's a far cry from the sixties and seventies when it attracted investors, expatriates and trans-Saharan tourists, with the pinnacle of that era being the 1975 Lomé Convention that promoted cooperation between African, Caribbean and Pacific countries and the then European Community.

With every seat taken by the journos and the Landy roof racks piled high with kit, we follow the coast towards Lomé. There are still signs of the old German buildings from Togo's first experience with colonialism, from when Gustav Nachtigel sailed into Togo in 1884 and signed a treaty with a village chief that made the then larger country a German protectorate called Togoland. It became the pride of the Reich; roads and railways were laid, wharves were built and the forest was cleared for cocoa and coffee plantations. When World War I broke out, the British and French overran the territory, forcing the Kaiser's soldiers to capitulate on 26 August 1914. After the war, a League of Nations mandate placed a third of the territory under British administration and two-thirds under French rule. The latter is currently known as Togo. The British attached their third of western Togo to Ghana, which now forms the Volta region of Ghana's Gold Coast.

At the village of Agbodrafo we count 78 people pulling in a community fishing net, straining against the big surf, whilst strong swimmers guide the net in from out at sea. We jump out of the Landies and lend a hand. Chanting and singing with

Following the crumbling edge of Africa to Lomé

Togo - Notes:
- A narrow strip of coastline only 56 km long
- Population of nearly 7 million, 800 000 live in the capital - Lomé
- Infamous for political corruption
- Much international pressure to improve human rights record and execute free and fair elections
- Still got the 'Landy Journos' with us - a jolly bunch.

the locals, we pull in half a tonne of sardines. We follow the crumbling edge of Africa where the old French-built road to Lomé has been eroded by the Atlantic waves. We see voodoo shrines and Catholic churches side by side and a small pub with a sign that reads 'Welcome to Under the Mango Tree'. We stop and pull out the long food drawers from the Stomach and lunch on fresh bread, bananas and tinned tuna. With rain threatening and everybody a bit worn out, we pose for a photograph of all of us sitting in a long West African fishing canoe with the words 'Are you ready for Jesus?' painted down the side. All the way down to Lomé people use watering cans filled from hand-dug wells to irrigate fields of vegetables, and there are piles of onions and tomatoes for sale on the roadside. The Togolese people of the outside edge, despite poor politics, make a plan to survive.

Dispatch #91 – Lomé

In the three Landies, the occupants all wide-eyed, we make our way down the Boulevard de la République with the Atlantic on the left and the downtown Grand Marché on the right. Grand Marché is Lomé's colourful central market and it's the hub from which all the major roads radiate out like the spokes of a wheel. It takes up a full city block and sells everything under the sun. There are fruit and vegetable displays like we've never seen before, and yams, cassava, spices and piles of homemade peanut butter. Go up to the first floor and you'll meet the celebrated *Nana Benz*, or 'Mercedes Mamas', who make a fortune from selling lengths of colourful cloth to buyers from the entire region and are often seen driving the luxury cars from which they take their nickname. There are imported Dutch wax prints, English and African prints, kente cloth from Ghana and indigo wraps from Guinea and Mali.

West of the market, we stop to photograph the Hôtel du Deux Février, a seven-storey, marble-and-glass tower built by Président Étienne Eyadéma in an ambitious bid to have the Organisation of African Unity's headquarters transferred to Lomé. The plan failed and now it is an expensive white elephant – another broken African dream. But one gets the feeling that, given the correct political leadership, little Togo, with its friendly, hardworking people, could quickly get up and get running again.

Dispatch #92 – The Fetish Market of Akodésséwa

Eight kilometres from Lomé is Akodésséwa, the greatest voodoo fetish market in West Africa. A fetish is an ordinary object imbued with sacred power, available as a voodoo charm. There are dried lizards and chameleons, dog heads, elephant feet, dead owls, porcupine quills, sitatunga hooves, baboon and hyena skulls, dried cat heads and bits of leopard skin. The voodoo medicine man chants incantations and rattles shells. Above the sweet smell of burning incense there's the stench of rotting flesh from the tens of thousands of bits of skin, bone and hair that adorn the fetish display tables outside. There's powerful muti here and customers come from as afar a field as Gabon, the DRC, Congo-Brazzaville, Ghana and Nigeria. I rub the pebble in my pocket.

Today's customer is from l'Afrique du Sud, he's got a great bushy grey beard and with a bunch of crazies is following the outside edge of Africa in Land Rovers and inflatable boats. Money changes hands and a small item is placed in an empty tortoise shell. Three times The Beard must repeat his name as each time he holds the tortoise shell to his chest. 'Kingsley, Kingsley, Kingsley,' he says softly. 'And remember,' says the voodoo man, 'you must give him three drops of water a year, just a little through the hole in the top of his head, and once a year give him a cigarette to puff through the small hole he uses as a mouth.' The clay-sculptured, white-chalk-dusted voodoo protection fetish is to protect the owner's home or possessions against theft. Later, observers are amazed to find it glued to the dashboard of a Land Rover that's decorated with the flags of the 33 countries that make up the outside edge of Africa. 'Let's hope it works,' says The Beard.

We'd left the Landies parked in Lomé and had all piled into two taxis to get to the voodoo market. Now, on the way back, our taxi driver stops at a roadside vendor and buys a cheap plastic Christian charm of Mary, Joseph and little Jesus with a halo around his head. He licks the rubber sucker and sticks it on the windscreen, allowing the holy family to dangle from a piece of string, bouncing, swaying and even jumping as we hit the potholes back to Lomé. Voodoo and Christianity, happily coexisting side by side.

Down on the beachfront there's a rather graphic sign that clearly indicates that it's illegal to shit on the beach. In the distance a long line of fishermen pull on their nets. At a rustic bar, under the palm trees, we drink Flag beer and eat cheap omelettes and French bread supplied by the smiling Togolese girls, whilst music by Jimmy Hope plays from a horn speaker. Just a short distance down the road, within the city limits of Lomé, is the border. The fascinating voodoo world of Benin and Togo is almost behind us. Ghana here we come.

OUR LITTLE PROTECTION FETISH

Ghana

Day 127, Country 12 on the Edge

Formerly known as the Gold Coast, Ghana was the first African country to regain its independence from Britain in 1957. Ghana is warm and hospitable with great national character; it is now one of the most politically and economically stable countries in West Africa. But for us, it's all about the joy of reaching an English-speaking country again as, the truth is, we've all got a bit 'francophoned out'. Another plus is that the locally brewed Club beer is excellent.

THE BEARD DOING HIS FOOT-STOMPING, BEARD-TWITCHING JIG —

Dispatch #93 – *Akwaaba*: Welcome to Ghana

Out of French and into English, we are still slowly working our way around the outside edge of Africa. Behind us now are 11 countries; 126 days; buckets of sweat; tens of thousands of mosquito nets; many deserts, rivers, lagoons, lakes, beaches, rainforests, sprawling cities and fishing villages; mud and more mud; and countless campfires. We continue with an almost fanatical determination to keep on tracking the outside edge of Africa.

The Ghanaian word for welcome is *akwaaba* and welcomed indeed we are. A Ghanaian British Airways team is here to meet us in full force. There's traditional dancing and drumming and a mosquito net distribution day at the Paramount Chief of Aflao's palace. Resplendent in robes, he sits on his gilded throne whilst near-naked women kneel on mats and pregnant women and mums with babies line up for their nets. The Paramount Chief endorses the Madiba Scroll of Peace and Goodwill. To drum beats, handclapping and much mirth from the journalists (especially Patrick Cruywagen from *SA 4x4*), I'm asked to do my half-Zulu, half-West-African foot-stomping, beard-twitching dance. It's become a bit of a signature piece which, embarrassingly enough, even gets onto local TV.

And so our humanitarian journey up the coast of Ghana continues, with further malaria prevention events and additions to the scroll doing a great job of making us feel positive and eager to continue our work:

> *Akwaaba! Welcome to Ghana, the land of people who love peace. We cherish and appreciate your concern for the welfare of ordinary Africans. God bless you – bravo!* (Director General of Education in Accra)

THE GHANAIANS ARE WONDERFULLY FRIENDLY

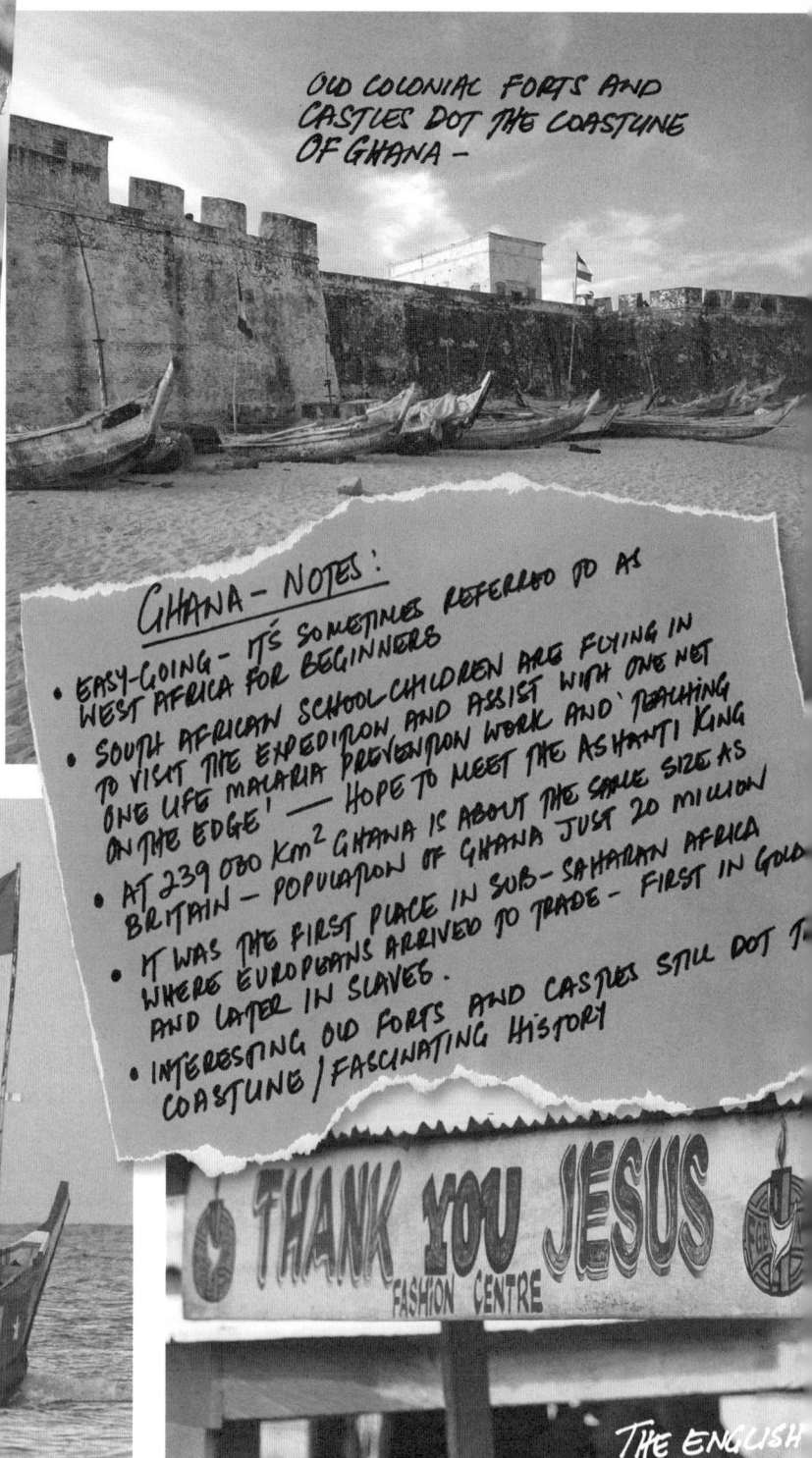

OLD COLONIAL FORTS AND CASTLES DOT THE COASTLINE OF GHANA —

COLOURFUL FISHING BOATS, EACH WITH THEIR OWN FLAG —

THE ENGLISH SIGNAGE IS DELIGHTF[UL]

GHANA — NOTES:

- EASY-GOING — IT'S SOMETIMES REFERRED TO AS WEST AFRICA FOR BEGINNERS
- SOUTH AFRICAN SCHOOLCHILDREN ARE FLYING IN TO VISIT THE EXPEDITION AND ASSIST WITH 'ONE NET ONE LIFE' MALARIA PREVENTION WORK AND TEACHING ON THE EDGE' — HOPE TO MEET THE ASHANTI KING
- AT 239,080 KM² GHANA IS ABOUT THE SAME SIZE AS BRITAIN — POPULATION OF GHANA JUST 20 MILLION
- IT WAS THE FIRST PLACE IN SUB-SAHARAN AFRICA WHERE EUROPEANS ARRIVED TO TRADE — FIRST IN GOLD AND LATER IN SLAVES.
- INTERESTING OLD FORTS AND CASTLES STILL DOT T[HE] COASTLINE / FASCINATING HISTORY

Thank you for flying the flag of our Rainbow Nation in a noble mission of saving and improving lives. (The South African Ambassador)

Dispatch #94 – Accra, Capital of Ghana

Our journey to Accra has taken us from the border town of Aflao down to Keta at the mouth of the Volta River, where a Rasta fisherman has the words 'Don't Jealous the Dread Man' painted in big letters on the side of his motorised fishing canoe. The Volta River estuary is about a hundred kilometres downstream from the Akosombo Dam wall, which has blocked the river to create one of the largest man-made lakes in Africa. The English signage on the way into Accra is delightful. There's a 'By His Grace' taxi, a 'God is Able' farm, an 'Amazing Grace International School', a 'God is Great' engineering works, a 'Blessing' fast foods, a 'Jesus Cares' business centre and a 'Faith in Christ' Rasta hair saloon.

Accra, the capital of Ghana, has a great buzz, especially down at the old Jamestown harbour, which is still referred to as British Accra. Here we count more than 200 handmade fishing boats festooned with flags. It looks like a scene from the old Viking days. Most of the boats are more than 20 metres long and about two metres wide at the beam, and have bases carved from single tree trunks. 'The fishermen use colourful flags of their choice. They can choose football club flags or Rasta colours, it's up to them,' says Yaó, our new Ghanaian friend and guide. Whilst Accra is considered a very safe city, I get the impression that the Jamestown harbour area is not the place you'd want to wander around on your own at night, despite the fact that fishing boats carry biblical slogans like 'God is One' and 'The Lord is Good'.

The fishermen are rough-and-ready and the area is well known for producing some of West Africa's best boxers. One muscled dude comes for a chat and the opportunity to practise his English. 'You must be a boxer,' I remark. 'No,' he replies, 'I'm a lawn tennis player and I represent Ghana.' It's a country full of surprises.

It was from here, in the 16th century, that the British traded slaves, gold and palm oil for guns. The old British Fort James now serves as a prison and a few inmates shout greetings from inside. The old colonial lighthouse still stands and if you give the lighthouse keeper a tip, or a 'dash' as they call it here, you can photograph it. Above the harbour is Accra's first hotel, the Sea View, which today is being used for a church service. Sanitation down on the beach is a shocker, and there are piles of stinking litter everywhere. Ghana's got a big population and in parts the infrastructure still needs to catch up.

Dispatch #95 – Weddings and Funerals

On Sunday we find ourselves east of Jamestown along High Street at the Kwame Nkrumah Memorial Park, honouring the leader who liberated Ghana from colonialism. It is thronged with wedding groups having their photographs taken. Ghana's great leader is buried here, along with his wife, and there's a statue of him pointing forward with the words 'Forward Ever – Backwards Never 1909–1972' inscribed below. Were Kwame Nkrumah alive today, I believe he would be proud of the nation he steered through the early years of independence from Britain. Despite the coups and 'kleptocrats', today's Ghana, which recently celebrated 50 years of autonomy, is full of hope as it prepares to host the African Cup of Nations football tournament. Nowhere thus far on the outside edge of Africa have we come across such national spirit, character and general friendliness. It's an easy country and it's no wonder some travellers refer to it as 'West Africa for beginners'.

Apart from football, weddings, music and Club beer, Ghanaians take funerals really seriously. The dead are often kept in the morgue for weeks whilst elaborate funeral plans are made. This includes the hiring of tents, caterers, musicians and entertainers; relatives coming from far and wide; and outfits being made. In some cases specialised, detailed, handcrafted coffins are chosen years in advance. Coffins in the shape of a Mercedes-Benz seem the most popular, followed by a body-sized passenger jet with all the livery. 'One thirsty fellow has decided to be buried in a giant bottle of Star beer,' says Eric who runs his own carpentry shop. 'Fishermen very often choose a wooden fish, or they commission an exact replica of their fishing boat. I can hardly keep up with the orders,' he says, handing me a card that reads 'Managing Director Eric, A Kpakpo – manufacturers of proverbial coffins and carvings'.

Whilst we are sitting in a bar having a few drinks with Yaó, he tells me that in the Ewe language his name means 'Thursday born'. 'That's how it works here,' he says. 'Every person takes on the name of the day of the week they were born.' 'But what if there are two Saturday children in the same family?' Land Rover's technical advisor Rory Beattie

An exchanging of flags

Handcrafted coffins: You can be buried in a boat, beer bottle or in a Merc

asks whilst sucking on a Club beer. 'Oh well, that's easy,' says Yaó, 'you get a Fat Saturday or a Short Saturday or a Smiling Saturday.' Bruce, poor guy, is looking like a real 'Sad Saturday'. Sam is leaving to go back to South Africa with the journos and she's making plans to go off to England on a working holiday. Bruce is going to meet her there after the expedition. It's tough for him, he's torn between finishing the expedition and being with Sam as soon as possible. I just hope he lasts. Rory, who's looking like a 'Thirsty Saturday', has just got back from servicing the vehicles. 'You can tell they've been through hell,' he says, 'but there's nothing major wrong with my three babies and our Cooper Tires sponsors have just sent up 15 new tyres from Durban. You're just carrying too much weight on the roofs – they're not meant to take three tonnes of mozzie nets each.' To stop the roof rack breaking, Rory has reinforced the roof of the long-wheel-base 130 that Bruce drives with galvanised piping, turning it into a Mad Max-looking vehicle. We say goodbye to the jolly team of Land Rover journalists. 'Don't worry about the vehicles,' says Rory with a lopsided grin, 'they'll make it. See you in Egypt.'

Dispatch #96 – Kids From Home Lend a Hand

It must be the first time in history that South African schoolchildren have been part of such a major humanitarian expedition. The children from Centurus Colleges who have been sponsoring John Ross, the Tdi Defender that Ross and Anna drive, have been getting a great education on Mama Afrika. They get regular history and geography updates, and their knowledge of the continent is improving dramatically. It's our way of making them part of our outside edge expedition, and the association is proving to be great fun. Already they've learnt about Namibia, Angola, the DRC, Congo, Gabon, São Tomé and Príncipe, Cameroon, Nigeria, Benin and Togo. It's a wonderful adventure and some of the lucky few from Southdowns, Tyger Valley and Pecanwood colleges get to fly into the capital of Accra to meet with the expedition, together with a group of rather jolly teachers and Trevor Glass, the founder of these fine schools.

It's wonderful to see the children's faces as they walk hand in hand with little Ghanaian kids through a rural school called The Lord is My Shepherd, where we drop off three mobile libraries and give malaria education and mosquito nets to every single child. There's even a ceremony in which a South African flag is exchanged for a Ghanaian one – it makes us feel proud. This is the sort of peace and goodwill that this expedition is all about.

At Bibiani we are hosted by Greg Hunter of Central African Gold, who is supporting us in the One Net One Life malaria prevention campaign. Greg and his team have organised a massive malaria prevention day, during which we distribute over 2 000 mosquito nets to mums with babies. There's the presentation of mobile libraries and a football match. The South African kids even get to do a fight-malaria skit in which they pretend to be *Anopheles* mosquitoes flying around a mother and child safely sleeping under a mosquito net.

The Central African Gold mine is within the great Asante Kingdom, where the people can trace their origins back to around the 11th century, when they arrived from the northern regions of the Savannah Belt to settle in the area of Lake Bosumtwi, an area that contained rich gold fields. After discovering this, they began to supply the precious metal to the Saharan caravans in the north and by the 17th century they were organised into dozens of small states trading with the Europeans, each vying for control of both the mines and the slave trade. Then along came a powerful fetish priest by the name of Okomfo Anokye who planted the seeds of two kum trees in separate locations, one of which flourished, indicating where the united Asante seat of power was to be established. The Asante capital was thus called Kumasi, taken from *kum ase,* which means 'under the kum tree', as the tree grew so large that the king often took shelter in its shade. The priest then evoked a golden stool from the heavens, which legend says alighted on the lap of Osei Tutu, who was thus named the first king. And so the throne-like Golden Stool became the most important symbol of the king's authority and national unity, and the great Asante nation was born.

By 1800 Kumasi had a population of about 700 000 people and trade was so brisk in the town's market that the king's servants periodically sifted the sand to collect loose gold dust. But then the wars with the British began and by the end of the 19th century the British had annexed the lands of the Asante as part of their Gold Coast colony. The Asante had given them a run for their money though, and so to humiliate them the British exiled the Asante King to the Seychelles. In 1900 the colonial governor Sir Frederick Hodgson demanded the Golden Stool be handed over for him to sit on. But the last laugh was on the British. Shrewd royal court members had foreseen such a development and had made a fake Golden Stool, and cleverly hidden the real one. More than a hundred years later the Asante remain one of the most powerful nations in West Africa.

The next day, to the accompaniment of drums, horn blowers and a praise singer, we have the privilege of shaking hands with His Royal Majesty Otunfuo Osei Tutu II, the current Asante King of Ghana. It was a ceremony we will remember forever: seeing queues of subjects bearing cases of schnapps as gifts to the Asante King, who graciously receives them whilst sitting on his Golden Stool, resplendent in fine robes and jewellery. Because of the weight of his royal majesty's gold arm bands, there's even a retainer to support his arm when shaking hands with the minions. In order to sit close to the king, the expedition team had to dress traditionally. So here we are all decked out in kente cloth whilst the praise singer heartily announces each group in a loud voice. The king's face lights up when the time comes to meet the Centurus Colleges' schoolchildren and he gets off his throne and greets them all individually – quite an honour indeed.

SOUTH AFRICAN SCHOOLCHILDREN ASSISTING WITH MALARIA PREVENTION

Before we leave, the palace scribe adds these words to the expedition Scroll of Peace and Goodwill:

The Manhyia palace seat of the Asante Kingdom is happy to be associated with this crusade to rid malaria … Africa is grateful.

King Otunfuo even gives the expedition a bottle of his precious schnapps. It's a great day, but sadly it's also time to say goodbye to our little malaria warriors, who fly home whilst we continue with our crazy adventure up the coast.

Dispatch #97 – A Humanist Turnabout

The Gold Coast of Ghana is peppered with a chain of ancient European-built forts and castles with approximately 80 fortifications of different types having been built over 300 years. First came the Portuguese, followed by other great sea powers like the Dutch, Danes and British, who were all competing for their share of gold, slaves, ivory and trade. We find forts and castles with names like Christiansborg, Good Hope, Amsterdam, William, Orange and St Anthony, and have great success in using these historic places as distribution points for malaria prevention work. Pregnant women and women with children under the age of five get a stamped Africa Outside Edge ticket, which they exchange for a life-saving mosquito net. It's a great humanist turnabout, being able to do charitable work in the same courtyards and on the very steps from which tens of thousands of slaves were exported to the New World.

The fishing harbour at Elmina is a riot of colourful hand-built, flag-flying fishing pirogues, once again with biblical names like 'God Bless' and 'Fish with Jesus' and aided mostly by 40 HP Yamahas. We use one to explore the coast – it's a wonderful change from being in the Land Rovers. The fishermen are noisy and boisterous. We nearly turn turtle in the surf, but then we're out into the Atlantic, Elmina Castle and Fort St Jago in the distance.

Back in the Landies, the humidity between rainstorms is stifling as we make our way to the Ivory Coast. Côte d'Ivoire has just come through a horrid time of civil war and we've been warned about security and armed roadblocks. Soon we'll be back in Francophone Africa and I know we'll miss the friendly 'hellos' of English-speaking Ghana.

ELMINA IS A RIOT OF FLAGS AND FISHING BOATS

Malaria prevention work is hugely satisfying when we are rewarded with such lovely smiles – what a wonderfully affable nation!

Côte d'Ivoire

Day 145, Country 13 on the Edge

'You are ill advised to travel here,' we read in the travel guide. It's referring to the civil unrest, during which time the large French expat population was evacuated. War raged here from 2002 until just before our departure from South Africa, so although everything seems to be under control now, needless to say we need to be conscious of our safety. In Côte d'Ivoire it's still referred to as 'the crisis'.

Palm oil plantations line the roads of Côte d'Ivoire.

Dispatch #98 – Off to a Bad Start

The border at Elubo is a dogfight. Seven bales of the expedition's life-saving mosquito nets destined for Côte d'Ivoire are impounded by customs. Given that the average mum shares a net with at least one infant, more than 2 000 mums and babies might go without life-saving nets. Out comes our Nelson Mandela-endorsed Scroll of Peace and Goodwill and the negotiations continue into the dark. Finally, thanks to the assistance of the South African Embassy staff in Abidjan, who send someone down to help, the nets are loaded up, passports are stamped and we are on our way. The cops are kitted out in flack jackets and tight-fitting camo outfits, sunglasses and red berets at a French-style angle, and have automatic weapons at the ready.

Accompanied by the frantic blowing of police whistles, we go through twelve roadblocks in the pouring rain. Bush encroaches onto the tarmac of what were once the best roads in West Africa. The click-click-whirr of Landy wipers on full goes hand in hand with the characteristic dripping of ice-cold rainwater onto the accelerator foot. Wheel-bursting spikes, logs and tyres cross the road ahead. There's yet another roadblock, with armed men in the rain wearing military ponchos whilst others peer out at us from under umbrellas. It appears that this is a major smuggling route out of Ghana and, to be fair, the large bales of mozzie nets on the Landies' roof racks do look a bit like contraband.

The rain is relentless. To make things worse Anna goes down with malaria. It's her first time and we dose her immediately with Coartem and settle on the palm-fronded beach at Grand-Bassam. The original French capital of Côte d'Ivoire from 1893 to 1900, it's now a dilapidated but charming place of crumbling old French buildings, palm trees, tired tourist resorts that once flourished, hopeful hookers and a massive lagoon that stretches all the way to Abidjan and beyond. The humidity at times is unbearable. Anna sweats it out with an intense fever and Ross ensures that she drinks

AFRICA OUTSIDE EDGE EXPEDITION — OFFICIAL

GRAND-BASSAM THE OLD CAPITAL

CÔTE D'IVOIRE - NOTES:

- OFFICIALLY THE REPUBLIC OF CÔTE D'IVOIRE. THE GOV DISCOURAGES THE USE OF THE NAME IVORY COAST, PREFERRING THE FRENCH NAME
- WITH AN AREA OF 322 462 km² CÔTE D'IVOIRE BORDERS LIBERIA AND GUINEA TO THE WEST, MALI AND BURKINA FASO TO THE NORTH, GHANA TO THE EAST AND THE GULF OF GUINEA AND THE ATLANTIC OCEAN TO THE SOUTH — WAS THE DARLING OF THE FRENCH COLONIES.
- POPULATION IS ABOUT 18 MILLION
- MALARIA IS RIFE, ESPECIALLY NOW IN THE RAINS
- GOOD AGRICULTURE — VERY FRENCH AND RECOVERING FROM POLITICAL UNREST — NEED TO BE CAREFUL!

loads of water with Rehydrate. An expedition like this is not for sissies and she's being very brave. The challenge is never to lose our sense of optimism and humour.

Dispatch #99 – A Palace Revolt

Three days later and Anna is over the worst of her malaria and it's time to hit the road to Abidjan. We completed the Gold Coast and now we're following the Ivory Coast, known as the Coast of Trinkets, with its countless small thatched, roadside stalls selling carvings, cloth, batiks, djembe drums, curved swords, treasure chests, baubles and beads. For Mashozi, any opportunity to view local crafts is a 'must-stop'. Instantly I go into defensive mode with familiar words like 'no budget', 'I'd rather you didn't' and 'no more room'. Mashozi gets on the radio. '*Ross, Bruce, please stop – Pops is being a grump.*' Ten minutes later and Mashozi has found an ape. I kid you not; it's an almost life-sized chimp carved from hard black wood and weighing a hefty tonne. 'What do you think?' she asks. 'Absolutely bloody not,' comes my instant reply, but the craftsman smells a deal and the sitting chimp is carried out onto the pavement for all to admire.

'Look,' says Mashozi, 'he's got a beautiful smile and he's even got his finger in his mouth – imagine him parked at the bottom of the stairs at home where you go up to the bar.' 'He's the weight of a human,' I snarl, 'and he'll take up an entire seat.' 'Oh, don't be such a spoilsport,' says Mashozi. The chimp salesman, sensing things aren't going his way, immediately drops the price by 10 dollars. 'It's not just about the money,' I complain, 'it's the bloody weight and inconvenience. Jeepers, every time we get stuck and have to lighten the vehicle we'll have to take the bugger out. Absolutely not. Buy something small and light,' I say before wandering off in a huff. There aren't too many tourists these days and the craft sellers are desperate for a deal. 'Pleez mister!' they cry. 'Sorry my friends,' I reply, 'I'm just looking.' There's no space in the Land Rovers and we've still a long way to go. Ross flashes his lights; it's time to hit the road.

The team safely in the vehicles, we drive off. A few minutes later I hear Ross over the radio. '*Pops, look behind you,*' he says, '*on the back seat.*' And there, concealed under a blanket behind Mashozi, is our newest expedition member. A huge bloody wooden ape, taking up far too much valuable room in an already jam-packed vehicle. 'Ross and Anna bought him for my birthday,' says Mashozi sweetly, 'it's just a few weeks away. We've already given him a name. It's Abu, the Ape from Abidjan.' 'Shit,' I mumble to myself, 'it's a palace revolt!'

Dispatch #100 – Abidjan

Abidjan, the gleaming high-rise commercial capital of Côte d'Ivoire, was once referred to as the New York or Paris of West Africa. For many years after independence from France in 1960, Côte d'Ivoire, and especially Abidjan, was the jewel of West Africa. Its strong economy, initially based on coffee and cocoa, attracted thousands of workers from neighbouring countries, and sizable numbers of French and Lebanese established themselves here. The president Félix Houphouët-Boigny ruled for 34 years and when he died in 1994, the *crème de la crème* of French political life, including President François Mitterrand, attended his funeral at Yamoussoukro, which Houphouët-Boigny had made the capital of the nation. A staunch Catholic, he also had the massive and grandly extravagant Basilique de Notre Dame de la Paix built there, inspired by St Peters in Rome, on a space cut from the jungle in the outskirts of what was the village of his birth.

Since the civil war, a lot of the commercial action that once made Abidjan flourish as the business core of West Africa has moved down the coast. Now West African commerce is based in Cotonou in Benin or Accra in Ghana and it appears that Senegal's Dakar has become the new French expat hub of West Africa.

For us the city of Abidjan is quite a culture shock. Fancy cars are driven by rich Lebanese and there are chic girls in tight jeans, all gold chains, mobile phones and high heels. It's a different world. We stretch the budget for a few items at an air-conditioned supermarket called Capsud. Mashozi ogles the imported French cheeses, hams and salamis and decides on a thin wedge of imported mature cheddar – bloody luxury. I spend time at the wine-tasting counter.

Before the crisis this city must have been a gem. There's still a bit of tension and roadblocks around and the elections have been postponed again. The contrast here between the rich and poverty-stricken is incredible: ankle-deep mud and six-lane motorways; corrugated iron shacks and 30-storey buildings; and dirty rags versus Paris fashions. A big billboard advertises that the American TV series *Desperate Housewives* is playing on CanalSat, French satellite television.

Dispatch #101 – Stop Malaria

We meet John Segbo, a delightful character who is determined to keep fighting malaria and heads up an NGO called Stop Malaria. He tells us there's a malaria crisis here and since the French were evacuated and civil unrest hit the country the organised malaria control programme has virtually stopped. The disease, he tells us, is the number one killer here, with approximately 300 people, mostly children, dying every day. We move in to help by distributing long-lasting mosquito nets at maternity clinics and outlying schools as well as in villages. The mums are lovely, with a great sense of pride and femininity. The pregnant women, some of them about to give birth, are wished *bonne chance* and *bon courage* as the crowd all clap their hands in appreciation with the presentation of each mosquito net. The poor-sighted elderly receive Rite to Sight spectacles. Whilst John Segbo interprets the malaria prevention message into French through the Land Rover speakers, the expedition team demonstrates how to use and care for the nets. There's singing, dancing, drumming and a bit of Johnny Clegg.

The humidity and the rain are endless as we travel on past massive lagoons and palm oil, rubber and coconut plantations. As we drive into the dark there are more police and army roadblocks, but John Segbo paves the way wonderfully. Near the small town of Grand-Lahou we find Françoise Stephenson, a delightful 70-year-old little lady who was born in France and then lived in England before coming to Côte d'Ivoire in 1992, where she fell in love with an Ivorian and went to live in his village. That's in the past and she now owns a few humble guest cottages and a bar in a clearing cut from a cliffside forest. 'It was terrible,' she says, talking about the crisis. 'Some French civilians were raped and killed; the soldiers came looking for me but I'd locked and barred the gates and my dogs chased them off. It seems better now.' She calls for the cook, a big smiling man from Burkina Faso who knocks up a fiery pepper soup and some beef brochettes cooked on a charcoal grill. It's served with rice, Flag beer and some Captain from the tank. 'Tomorrow we'll go feed the chimps. I'll take you to d'Azagny; there's a little island on a lagoon inhabited by a family of four. There used to be more, but when the trouble hit us the park officials disappeared and the chimps weren't fed. Many died from starvation and some drowned trying to swim to the mainland,' she tells us.

Up early, big Ivorian Bartholomew Koffi paddles us out two at a time in his canoe, loaded up with yams and pawpaws. Papu, the big father chimp, claps his hands in delight and scrambles down the mangrove branches to get closer. We throw yams and fruit; each chimp gets a chance to feast. What a great way of starting the day's journey!

Dispatch #102 – Sassandra and on to Liberia

The Landies creak and groan under the weight of the bales of mosquito nets as we take them to the hospital at the top

Food for the chimps. They are delighted – for us it makes a great start to the day.

of the hill in the colourful town of Sassandra, overlooking the Atlantic beaches and the beautiful Sassandra River estuary below. Later we walk out to the point, to the original French governor's grand residence. Now it's just a gutted ruin occupied by local villagers, who've planted neat rows of cabbages on the front lawn. 'Careful, no pics,' we're told. 'Behind the residence is now a prison.'

We're the only guests at the old run-down French colonial Campement Hotel. John and his pleasant little round squeeze named Jewel, with her two-toned wig, tight jeans and high heels, order tilapia, catfish, smoked prawns, steamed cassava and a fiery sauce to be brought down from a local restaurant. It's full moon and we eat with our fingers around a big circular table made from thick hardwood planks, under a cavernous veranda that runs straight out onto the beach. The beach is dotted with palm trees and colourful Ghanaian fishing boats anchored beyond the waves, and beneath the cliffs there's a broken jetty from which slaves, ivory, palm oil and rubber were once exported.

Over dinner we chat about the country's ongoing struggle for peace. John tells us that recent peace talks had been going quite well and that Thabo Mbeki had even assisted, but then President Laurent Gbagbo's plane was taken out by a rocket. Somehow he survived, but four of his bodyguards were killed, and now elections have been postponed again.

It's another night on the outside edge of Africa. There are stains on the sheets so we roll out our bedrolls. The mozzies are the size of catfish. The next day we head for war-torn Liberia. Some warn us not to go, and we are nervous as hell. After more roadblocks, some long-horned cattle and a red dust road, we fuel up at Tabou, our last town in the country. The customs and immigration people are friendly and we even share a Captain Morgan together, but, oh my God, Mr Big of the military is an evil-looking bloke and a hard nut to crack. He wants 15 000 CFAs just for permission to use the ferry across to Liberia. We can feel the tension.

Ross pretends to phone the embassy on the satellite phone. There's a flicker of concern in Mr Big's eyes, but he's not the sort of bloke you mess with. I turn to our friend. 'Plead with him, John. Explain again we're on a humanitarian expedition and that we're born-and-bred Africans, not rich foreigners.' Mr Big drops to 5 000 CFAs. I jump at the chance, although he'll still get a black mark on the sun visor. We say goodbye

THE FRENCH NO LONGER COME TO HOLIDAY IN SASSANDRA AND WE HAVE THE OLD HOTEL TO OURSELVES

to John Segbo and his little Jewel, who present Anna and Mashozi with traditional necklaces and earrings – such a lovely couple. The three Landies, one now carrying a wooden chimp, slowly roll onto the crumpled ferry in low-range first gear and cross the Cavally River into Liberia. Mashozi, between clenched teeth and groaning in pain with terrible nervous stomach cramps, mutters 'I wish we hadn't seen that *Blood Diamond* movie before we left home'.

Liberia

Day 152, Country 14 on the Edge

Seems it's a good time to follow Liberia's coastline. UN Peacekeepers have stabilised the country, the rebels have supposedly handed in their weapons and peace loving Ellen Johnson-Sirleaf has been voted in as Africa's first woman president. At the same time, it is a country with a dark past, and the nation is still licking its wounds from years of brutal conflict. Ever optimistic, we're going to give it our best shot.

Dispatch #103 – Haya All Doin'?

It's getting dark and we're feeling a bit uneasy. Mashozi has serious stomach cramps and has to stay in the Landy. On the Liberian side everybody's a bit ragtagged and speaking a crazy Rasta-type English. 'Haya all doin'? Welcome to Liberia.' They look at the Land Rovers and all the flags. 'Yaah come from Saa Africa – what's ya mission in Liberia?' People crowd into the immigration shack on the river. There are muscled dudes in tight T-shirts with cut-off sleeves. Finally the boss man stamps the passports. 'You're going to have to go into Harper to see immigration and customs,' he says. 'But it's dark,' objects Ross. 'Roads baahd, rainy season,' adds another. 'War's over,' says the boss man, 'yah'll be safe. Wilfred here will go with yah.'

And so we rumble into the bombed-out port town of Harper, capital city of the County of Maryland. We've never seen so many UN Peacekeepers in all our lives. Sandbagged sentry posts, blue helmets, flack jackets and guns at the ready. Kate, a lovely English girl, gives us permission to camp in the hospital grounds. She's working for a British organisation that has moved in to rehabilitate the hospital. 'The people are lovely,' she says, 'and they are sick and tired of war. They are so much friendlier than at Darfur, where I've just come from.'

Kate's right. Once over the initial shock of war-torn Liberia, we are overwhelmed by the welcoming and pleasant nature of the people, but oh how they've suffered – nearly 20 years of hell. People have been murdered, raped and mutilated, with their limbs cut off by the rebels. Guns were bought with diamonds. With immigration and paperwork sorted out, the scroll is endorsed at the government offices by the friendliest officials we've ever come across in Africa. They want to make a good impression – spread the message that the war is over and that it's now safe to visit Liberia.

We continue the daily challenge to track the edge. Never in this entire journey have we had it so tough; the rains are endless and mud holes deeper than the Land Rovers.

THANKS TO UN PEACEKEEPERS PEACE IS BACK ON THE STREETS AND THE MAMAS ARE TRADING

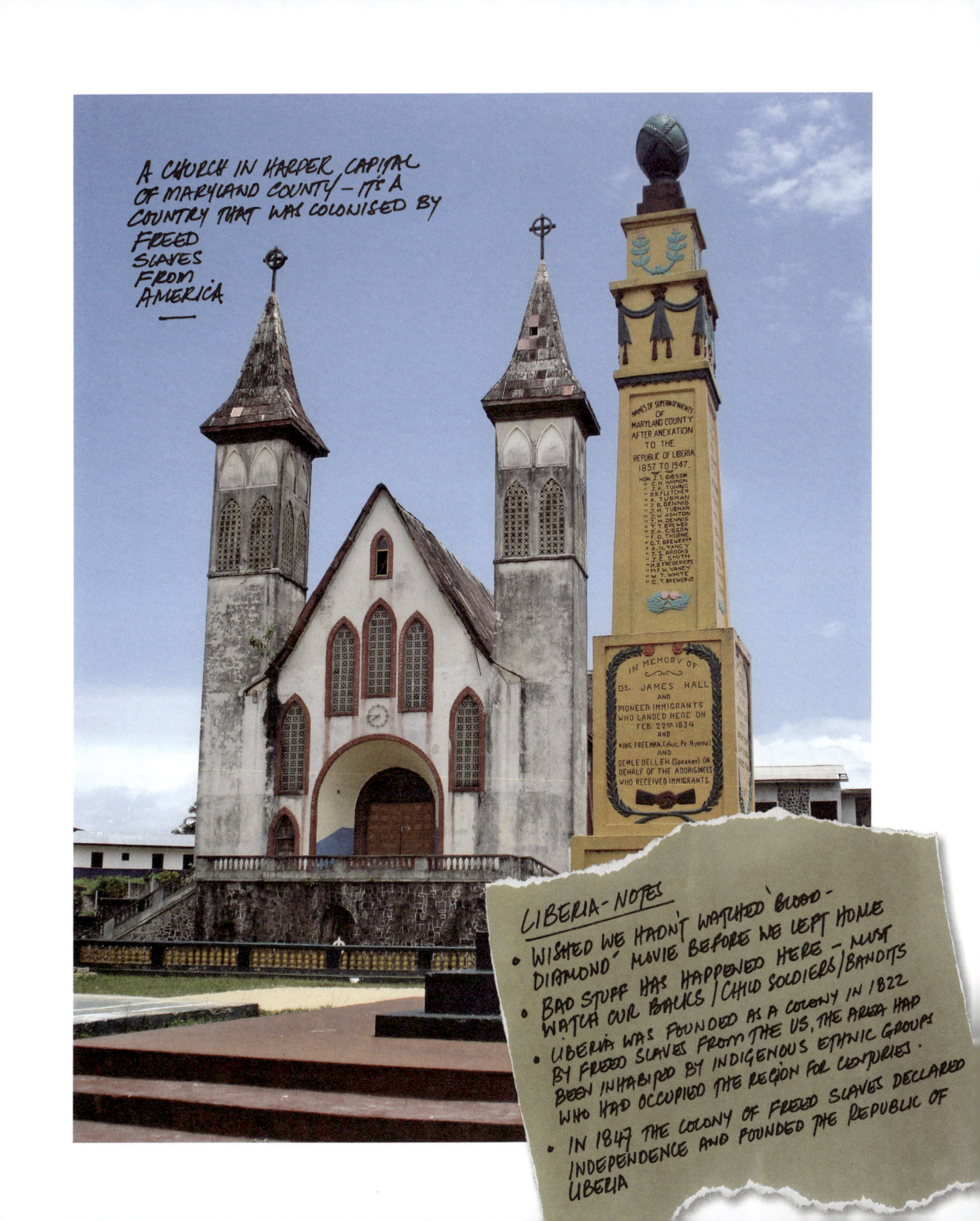

A church in Harper, capital of Maryland County — it's a country that was colonised by freed slaves from America

LIBERIA - NOTES

- Wished we hadn't watched 'Blood Diamond' movie before we left home
- Bad stuff has happened here - must watch our backs / child soldiers / bandits
- Liberia was founded as a colony in 1822 by freed slaves from the US, the area had been inhabited by indigenous ethnic groups who had occupied the region for centuries.
- In 1847 the colony of freed slaves declared independence and founded the Republic of Liberia

LIBERIA'S WOMAN PRESIDENT — AFRICA'S FIRST

Winches and recovery gear make you king of the road and hours are spent not just getting ourselves unstuck but helping the locals who limp along in battered, overloaded Hilux bush taxis. Winching and pushing, winching and pushing, red-brown mud everywhere.

In the back of our minds there's always the fear of an ambush. One night, as we prepare to sleep in a clearing in the jungle, some villagers come rushing out in the dark, amazed to find three Landies and a group of very muddy, travel-worn South Africans. They ring a village gong and a town crier spreads the message that we have come in peace, that there's no danger, and so they help us with firewood. Later the rain beats down on our rooftop tents.

The next morning we distribute mosquito nets to every pregnant woman and young mum in the village, and afterwards a lovely mama called Deborah joins us around the breakfast fire. 'It waah terrible,' she says in the sort of Deep-South lingo the Liberians speak. 'I waah only 12 when da rebels from Nimba come; their leader was Charles Taylor and they burnt our village to the ground. We ran to the forest but they shot my dear grandfather in fronta me, so we went to a refugee camp in Côte d'Ivoire. I sold fish and firewood to survive and finally a year later, in 1999, when the war waah over, we come back to our village. That waah the time that Mista Charles Taylor became president. But then it started all over again in 2003 and we had to run again. Our lives have been terrible. But now we are back and rebuilding our village

CAN YOU BELIEVE IT — THIS IS THE NATIONAL HIGHWAY

GRAGSBY FARM, SINOE COUNTY / DANCING WITH THE LOCALS

108

again. When we arrived, the UN High Commissioner for Refugees gave us some blankets, a tarpaulin to sleep under, cooking pots, some food and five dollah each. But there's no muney now and no jobs and we live from what we can grow in the forest. But at least I'm free and back in my home-born village. Ellen Johnson-Sirleaf, our new president, is a woman and we hope that she will treat us like her children.'

There are some poor-sighted, elderly people in the village and we are able to distribute spectacles. Their smiles of gratitude are endearing. They are now able to see clearly enough to read and do handcraft, and instant delight is written on their faces. As we pack up to leave, a man walks out of the forest holding a dead white-faced monkey, blood dripping from its nose. It's bushmeat for his pot tonight. Another man brings us a tame baby chimp. Mashozi offers it bits of orange and it gazes at us with soft, brown eyes as it sucks out the juice. 'No Mashozi,' I say, seeing the look. 'You already hoodwinked me into a wooden one.' The chimp owner shakes his head and says, 'The road ahead mon, it's baahd, real baahd. You can get stuck in a mud hole for weeks – bridges all gone.'

Dispatch #104 – Greenville Diesel in Mayonnaise Jars
The Landies, still with trademark red life rings attached to their bull bars, take a beating. I don't know how they keep going, grinding for hours through deep mud holes at crazy angles with wheels in the air. Then there's the horrible grating sound of the undercarriage scraping over the mud-hidden rocks, and gravelly mud clogging the brake pads causing them to screech in protest; the endless mud working like grinding paste on the brake discs. We are now in Sinoe County and it's dark, but there's no clearing in which to camp. Then we see a dim light and turn in to meet Joseph and Frances Mondubue at Gragsby Farm, part of an old rubber plantation. What wonderful people – they allow us to camp in front of their simple home and they help us with dry firewood. We all sing – us in Zulu and them in Sarpo, the local language. Anna and Mashozi cook up a camp stew.

It rains again in the night and the next morning Frances assists with distributing mozzie nets to pregnant mums and some reading glasses to the poor-sighted elderly. People arrive by the hundreds, shouting and running up the track to see the bedraggled strangers who sleep in tents on the roofs of their cars. With curious villagers peering over her shoulder, Frances slowly pens these words in the scroll:

As paramount chief of our chiefdom we welcome you. God's blessing for your bold adventure. While this team of navigators were with us we were given some mosquito nets and reading glasses. This was a great help for us, as most of us suffer from malaria ... The Good Lord will bless these people. We enjoyed the night they spent with us because Mr Holgate and his team danced and sang with us during the night. We also sat around the fire and chatted happily. (Paramount Chief of the Chiefdom – Botow)

The UN Peacekeepers wave us through the defences at Greenville. The Shell filling station in Johnson Street sells diesel decanted from drums into one-gallon Blue Plate Real Mayonnaise glass jars, with 'Quality since 1927, bottled in New Orleans' written on the label. One US dollar equals 60 Liberian dollars and you can change money in the street with the Lebanese diamond traders. We get into shit with immigration because Wilfred, the guy who'd been pushed onto us by immigration at the Côte d'Ivoire border, has no papers. They demand we pay him off; he'll have to take a bush taxi back to the border, a killing journey through the mud and rain on the back of a motorbike taxi. We give him some extra cash. 'Don't tell them,' he says, 'they'll take it off me.' Once that's sorted out we ask the immigration man if he can find us

Jeez! Thought we'd lost Ross in a pot-hole

mmm... mumbles Ross — it's a massive overdose of mud —

a workshop. His name is Major M Diggs and I think how sad it is how the former slave families lost their African names.

The alternator in Bruce's big 130 is not charging, drowned no doubt from a huge overload of mud and water. We end up at a bush mechanic's workshop called the Base, where mechanic Jouner Della keeps the local jungle taxis running. Battered old Hiluxes are welded and tied together with old motorcar tubing, bald tyres filled with gaters and spring

hangers 'shocked up' with bits of hard rubber. Fuel is gravity fed into carburettors via a 20-litre container and a length of hose. How would Africa ever possibly survive without its bush mechanics? So whilst we munch a tin of Exeter Bully Beef with some hot sauce and good local bread, the alternator is removed, cleaned, sorted and is running perfectly within an hour. No booking with an auto-electrician, no job cards, no tea breaks and no receptionists, showrooms or PR service calls. No invoice either, just 30 US cash and she's running like a dream. Bruce gives a sigh of relief. Now that he's got charged battery power again it's back to Bob Marley and he can download the hundreds of pics he's been taking of the mud road to Monrovia. Mashozi doesn't have to worry about the two chickens defrosting in the fridge either (although the sooner we eat them the better).

The Ethiopian UN Peacekeepers allow us to camp in a far corner of their base. There are searchlights, razor wire, armed, sandbagged sentry posts and the noisiest frogs we've ever come across. The next morning it's on through the mud, direction Buchanan. The pole bridges are a problem, many of them are washed away and we are forced to take detour after detour. There are also dangerous sinkholes – some of them deeper than the height of a man.

Dispatch #105 – Breakfast with Thomas Davix

On to the Cestos River in River Cess County we go. We camp in an old logging clearing where we meet Thomas Davix, who shares our breakfast of left-over peri-peri chicken, Nando's sauce, local rice and a mug of *Renosterkoffie*. 'It wah terrible,' he says, chewing on a bone. 'Ra-ta-tat-tat, those rebels just killing, the bodies piled up in the streets of Monrovia, and stealing cars and property. I hid in the Nigerian Embassy. I did odd jobs there and they looked after me.' I ask Thomas if the guns have all been handed in and whether the rebels have been reintegrated into society. 'Yes,' he says. 'The UN collected the guns and now without them the rebels are cowards. We have forgiven them; me despite the fact they killed my mother.' Sitting on one of our camp chairs with a panga in his hand, Thomas gives me a broad smile. 'I hope the loggers return,' he says. 'I used to drive a bulldozer for them; sometimes I got paid, sometimes I didn't, but it was a job.'

The Liberians we meet are just so open and optimistic. They are utterly sick of war and the only thing to hang onto is the belief that things will improve in the future. I guess when you've had it so bad it's the only way forward. We give Thomas a mosquito net to be shared with his wife and small boy. Ross helps him with some fishing line and hooks as there are big catfish in the river. We leave him some clothing and a little money – what a lovely man.

Dispatch #106 – Bananas and Bushmeat

We're pushing it. First, second and up into third and then back down into first or low-ratio difflock for the next mud hole or plank bridge in our path. Clutch, accelerator, brakes – the Landies go through absolute hell. Sweat drips through onto the khaki Melvill and Moon seat covers. They are starting to *nuka*, to stink. We pull into the jungle for lunch. 'Remembaah my name – I's Paatrick,' says a bare-chested hunter with a grin as he proudly shows us the antelope. 'Just caught it in a traap! Get me one a day, sell whole body for 700 liberties.' Blood drips from the animal's nose. 'Don't look,' I say to Mashozi, who doesn't like killing, as she and Anna dish up sweet corn, bananas, local bread and some sardines from the tailgate of the Land Rover. 'How long to Monrovia?' I shout to Patrick as he walks away with the antelope hanging over his shoulder, panga in his hand. 'Can take you a month, roads baahd mon! It's rainy season. Next town's Buchanan.'

Dispatch #107 – Buchanan Town

Buchanan Port once had a thriving steel mill with iron ore coming by rail from the mines inland. Now, like everything else, it's a bombed-out hulk, wrecked during the war. We park on the beach. There's a shipwreck on the rocks and a harmless madman who jumps behind the steering wheel of the Land Rover and pretends to drive. In town the market stalls are buzzing and one can sense we're getting closer to Monrovia.

Back in the Landies after a walk around town, the road improves and we stop to camp in a palm tree plantation. Robert B Falleh, the plantation owner, joins us around the stew pot. 'I can imagine the adventures you're having,' he says. 'I once went to Cameroon and whilst drinking beer I met a girl – she was really beautiful. We ended up in my room, but when I went through to the bathroom I came back to find that she'd stolen my money from under the tablecloth where I'd hidden it. That's the only time I've left Liberia – and I've never been out again.'

OH SHIT! WHAT HAPPENED TO THE BRIDGE?

'Will there be lasting peace? What will happen when the peacekeepers leave Liberia?' I ask Robert. 'Such degradation,' he replies, shaking his head. 'There are all these illiterate young men without jobs – that's the danger. The only way forward is education and job creation.' The drumming from a nearby village continues throughout the night and by early morning the gawkers have arrived. Robert helps us give out nets and malaria education to mums with babies. Breakfast is leftover stew and instant oatmeal porridge.

For the first time in days the Landies sing along in fourth and fifth; heavy tyres droning on the smooth tarmac, bits of muck dropping from the chassis and dried mud weighing down the front-wheel rim and causing a wheel-balance wobble. The road snakes through the Firestone rubber plantations, some of the largest in the world and now operating again after the war. We follow a white-painted, UN fuel tanker travelling with an armed escort, past the airport with UN helicopters parked in a row. Monrovia here we come.

Dispatch #108 – Monrovia, Capital of Liberia

Somehow we survive the mud road to Monrovia, capital city of Liberia, which is packed with UN vehicles and peacekeepers.

At Snapper Hill, with a view over Monrovia, we find a national monument to the first president of Liberia.

The US Embassy has taken over Mamba Point and there's razor wire and security everywhere. We meet Sékou Cissé, a delightfully friendly businessman who speaks French, English and the local languages and heads up Vestergaard Frandsen's PermaNet operation in Liberia, Sierra Leone and Guinea. Vestergaard Frandsen is the company from which we are drawing tens of thousands of life-saving mosquito nets, funded by the various expedition sponsors who care for Africa. These war-torn countries are crying out for help. We meet with the head of the National Malaria Control Programme. Radio, press and TV are present, all curious about the story of a South African humanitarian expedition tracking the outside edge of Africa and bringing help to war-torn Liberia. A message in the scroll reads:

> *The National Malaria Control Programme of Liberia is highly appreciative of your efforts towards peace and goodwill. We are thankful to you for the donation of mosquito nets to pregnant women, adding value to our initiative aimed at controlling and preventing malaria in Liberia. May God give you the energy to continue the good work.* (Tolbert G Nyenswah)

A convoy of 4x4s cruises past, lights flashing and sirens wailing. 'You'll never know which one she's in,' says Sékou, referring to the president. 'She might be in the bullet-proofed saloon Mercedes-Benz, the Geländewagen, or not be in the convoy at all. The important thing right now is that she doesn't get taken out.' I'm pleased to see that Ellen Johnson-Sirleaf's residence is a simple one down near the beach on the airport road. We stop for traffic whilst travelling along Broad Street up to Snapper Hill, and a young man comes up to the Landy window. 'They chopped me in the war,' he tells me with a toothy grin, showing me the stumps he has for arms. I give him a few Liberian dollars and he offers me a stump. I touch it with the flat of my fist, West African style, then to the heart. 'You from South Africa?' he asks. 'I'll pray for you, my brother.'

The traffic police, dressed in American-style uniforms, wave us on. We get to the top of Snapper Hill, the highest point in Monrovia. There are young men in singlets and jeans lying around between the ramparts and cannons, and there's plenty of security. There's an old lighthouse and a monument to the first president of Liberia. 'Hey, nigger,' says one of the young men looking at me. 'Saw you on the TV, you and your family giving out mosquito nets! God bless you, man!'

Dispatch #109 – The Horrors of War

Sékou pays a Nigerian peacekeeper 20 bucks to allow us all to climb to the top of the bullet-holed shell of the multi-storied

Ducor Palace that was occupied by rebel forces. 'Before the war this was one of the most prestigious hotels on the west coast of Africa,' he says. Now the flotsam and jetsam of child soldiers have been moved out and all that remains is graffiti, old discarded clothes and endless views over a city that struggles to shake off the mantle of terror.

Sékou points over to Providence Island, to the place where freed slaves from the US first landed in 1822 before settling in Liberia. 'It's crazy,' says Sékou. 'This tiny minority of emancipated slaves, who had African roots but American names, brought with them the Bible, guns and a smattering of American education and ruled over the local majority for nearly a hundred years. We were colonised, so to speak, by a small group of black settlers who exploited the masses. It was like your apartheid in South Africa, except here it was black on black. But eventually the people had had enough and it was no wonder that when Master Sergeant Samuel Doe overthrew the government in 1980, shooting the hated ministers on the beach in Monrovia and declaring himself president, the local people danced in the streets, happy to see the oppressors gone.'

But then Liberia turned on itself in a terrible civil war. Charles Taylor, an ally of President Doe until he was accused of embezzlement, led an armed uprising and took control of the country in 1989. Taylor's claim to power did not go unchallenged, and ten years of brutal civil war followed before he was voted in as president. The warlord Taylor had won through sheer ruthlessness, masterminding the recruitment of child soldiers in Sierra Leone and using now infamous blood diamonds to pay for guns and ammunition to fuel the conflict. Tens of thousands were killed, raped and maimed, with the child soldiers themselves sowing terror.

'It was the beginning of the end,' Sékou says, looking at me sadly. 'They were just kids, the rebels, with cocaine rubbed into razor blade cuts in their foreheads. They would say "Hey old man, fall like a palm tree!" and so, at attention with their hands at their sides, respected members of society were made to fall backwards onto the concrete. If they put out a hand to save themselves they were shot dead, and if they fell straight like a chopped-off palm tree the back of their heads would hit the concrete and split open like a coconut, leaving them to die on the street. Or crazy on booze and drugs they would grab a pregnant girl, debating "Boy child or girl child?" before cutting her stomach open for the answer. Horrible! I don't know what got into them,' he says with tears in his eyes.

Charles Taylor was finally arrested in 2006 and sent to The Hague, where he was put on trial for war crimes by the UN-backed Special Court for Sierra Leone. But the poverty-stricken victims, many with butchered arms or legs, still beg on the streets of Monrovia and Freetown. I think of Mugabe in Zimbabwe who, fearing he too might be indicted for war crimes, refuses to step down. Africa, it's all so crazy. I chat to a Nigerian peacekeeper from Calabar. He's thrilled to hear that the expedition visited his city. 'Fire and brimstone,' he says, 'that's what will happen to Liberia when the peacekeepers leave.' I hope he's wrong.

Dispatch #110 – The Road to Sierra Leone

The Landies head for the border with Sierra Leone, three in a line with Mashozi and me up front. At a police checkpoint a man with red eyes shouts out angrily: 'Pull over man! I'm from drug enforcement. Gonna search your car.' He's full of shit and becomes the only Liberian to score a mark on the sun visor. That night we follow a footpath and camp in the bush. It's not very pleasant – overgrown and wet – and we bunch together on our camp chairs around a smoky fire under the pulled-out Land Rover awning, trying to get out of the soaking rain. We keep it jolly though with a bit of *nyama*, some carrots and *dop* – after all it's Mashozi and my 40th wedding anniversary. But somehow the rain gets into the roof tent, so we have wet bedding!

The next morning Bruce complains bitterly about the smell. In the rain the poor fellow had inadvertently pitched his tent over a pile of human turd. 'Let's get out of here,' he says. Down the road we meet Sékou and his team at a school where we're having a malaria prevention event. Later, Alfred, a little man who speaks perfect English and works with Sékou, rides in the Landy with us as part of the One Net One Life team. 'There are a lot of frustrated people,' he says. 'They want to see immediate improvement, like jobs, money, electricity, better housing and transportation.' At the border we eat 'potato green' – a Liberian delicacy of sweet potato tops mashed with rice, meat and fish. A big billboard reads 'Mine and trade our diamonds legally' and at immigration a framed picture of Ellen Johnson-Sirleaf smiles down at us benevolently. God bless her, Liberia sure needs her.

Sierra Leone

Day 161, Country 15 on the Edge

Founded as a homeland for freed slaves, mention the name of this once-wealthy West African country and people immediately think blood diamonds and drug-crazed, boozed-up rebels and child soldiers. It's a shocker, 50 000 people were killed, more than three-quarters of the population displaced and 20 000 left mutilated – but now the war is over. However, I am still a bit worried about post-war Sierra Leone and our security.

Dispatch #111 – Blood Diamonds

The border crossing has the ex-British feeling of Malawi or Zambia. Alfred, who's travelling with Mashozi and me, tells us that after the British military had brought peace to Sierra Leone in May 2000 British advisors remained on to rebuild the army and the police, hence the new uniforms and rather polite manners. Sékou Cissé is still with us, and is leading the convoy in a pick-up piled high with mosquito nets for our ongoing campaign. He crosses here all the time and knows the ropes. He loads up a couple of blue-uniformed Sierra Leone cops who are heading down to Freetown for an off-duty weekend. 'Will be good for the journey,' he explains to Mashozi and me with a wink. Bruce too will have company. A beaming Sergeant Alex – round face and big smile below a smart police beret – will ride with him in the Stomach.

And so in a cloud of dust we're off into Sierra Leone. 'It was the diamonds and the greed that destroyed our country,' says Sierra Leone-born Alfred, as we bounce along the potholed red dust road. 'At the time of independence from Britain we were a rich country, but greedy governments and coups ate the wealth. Charles Taylor, the warlord who became president of Liberia, financed his war there with our diamonds. His rebels were called the RUF, the Revolutionary United Front. They crossed the border from Liberia, killing, raping, looting and butchering and using child soldiers to terrorise the villagers. Girls were raped and forced into sexual slavery to become soldiers' wives, and chiefs and village elders were executed. Child soldiers were sometimes forced to execute their own parents and rape women old enough to be their grandmothers. Given Kalashnikov's AK-47s, booze, drugs and crazy names, they spoke in Krio slang, partied to rap music and became the rebel leaders' killer dogs of war. It was terrible. I ran with my family and went to live in Conakry in Guinea; it was impossible to stay. Their leader, backed by Taylor, was a crazy man called Foday Sankoh. He'd been jailed in Pademba Road Prison in Freetown for seven

A FEW YEARS AGO KIDS LIKE THESE WERE TAUGHT TO KILL AND MUTILATE –

ONE NET – ONE LIFE

We demonstrate the importance of tucking the net in under the sleeping mat or mattress

SIERRA LEONE – NOTES:
- Official language is English
- Blood diamonds and greed, that's been the problem – but now it's coming right –
- Capital is Freetown, area is 72 325 km², with a short but beautiful coastline of about 300 km.
- Most of the population are Mende and Temne with a smattering of Europeans & Lebanese.
- The descendants of slaves are known as Krios –

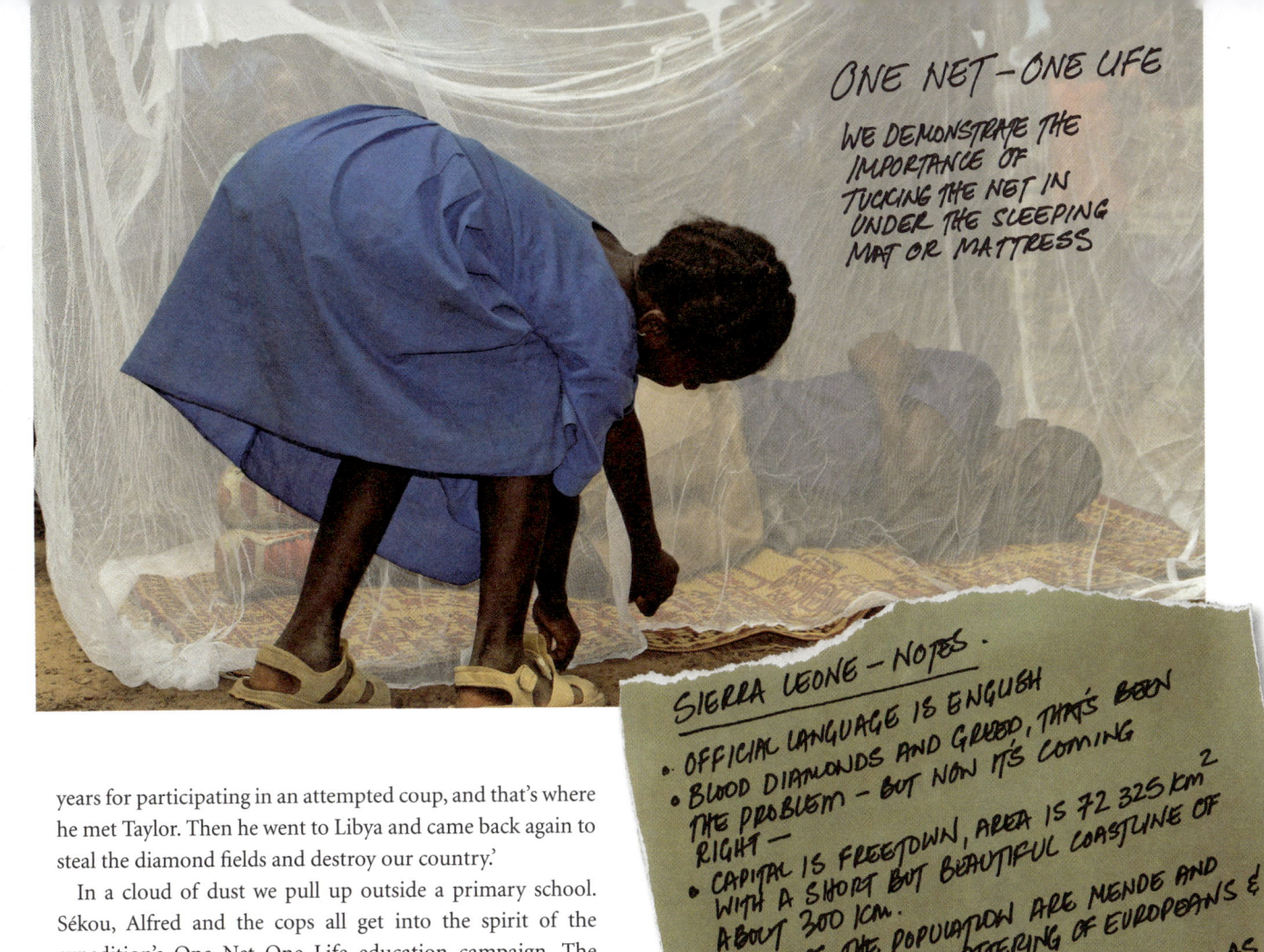

years for participating in an attempted coup, and that's where he met Taylor. Then he went to Libya and came back again to steal the diamond fields and destroy our country.'

In a cloud of dust we pull up outside a primary school. Sékou, Alfred and the cops all get into the spirit of the expedition's One Net One Life education campaign. The kids and teachers love it. Holding the nets in the air, they sing and dance in the dust. They are all neat in their little post-war, peacetime school uniforms – so much hope after so much pain. Bruce asks a few of them to climb up onto the expedition Landies for a picture; it causes a stampede and soon the three Landies are covered with waving schoolkids. A few years ago kids like these would have been taught to kill and mutilate. Let's hope that those days never return.

Dispatch #112 – The Road to Freetown

We reach an intersection and the cops jump out and ask questions. Sékou comes over to our Landy. 'Bad news,' he says, 'the ferry over the Mao River is down; this is the problem in the rainy season. We'll have to push inland, basically following the Liberian border to where there is a bridge.' We pass Faro and Zimmi, various hills, valleys, twists and turns, rubber plantations and old narrow British-built Bailey bridges. Mashozi sits with her sandalled feet up on the dashboard. I drive with my left hand on the thick padded steering wheel, right arm out of the window, with an occasional glance into the cracked wing mirrors to check for Bruce's and Ross's dust and an ear open for any transmission or engine change of tone. The air flaps are wide open, the Garmin GPS is attached to the windscreen by a big round rubber suction device, the handbrake's rubbing against my left calf and the radio microphone's near at hand in case of emergencies. In between watching the dashboard gauges and swerving to avoid crabbing overloaded taxis, and goats, chickens, cyclists and village pigs, I share some groundnuts with Alfred and Mashozi. Everything is new and exciting; we never know what's around the next corner. It's all about the Zen of Travel, and the pebble in the pocket.

The traffic increases. Alfred tells us we're coming up to Kenema. We pull into a filling station as we're all low on diesel, and pay with local leones. People mob the Landies, but at least we can communicate in English. They're intrigued and full of questions. 'All the way from South Africa?' 'Why aren't you black?' 'You drove here, in these cars?' 'You came through Liberia?' 'You sleep in those tents on the roof?' 'South Africa is rich – it also has diamonds, yes?'

The market is colourful and bustling, and we buy the expedition staples of bananas and bread. Diamonds were discovered here in 1931 and every second shop, many of them owned by shrewd Lebanese traders, buys these precious stones. 'We're about 300 kilometres southeast of Freetown,' says Sékou. 'I'll go in front; please drive carefully. The police with us will handle any roadblocks, but you'll need to be wary of livestock and trucks with no lights – the road can be dangerous.' It's getting dark, so we stop to wash the mud and dust from the headlights. We're tired out and our policy is not to travel at night. It's a difficult one; we're with Sékou and his team and they've been so incredibly helpful all the way from Monrovia. Sékou's also got a house in Freetown and he's offered to put us up. We push on.

It's a nightmare of potholes and unlit trucks loaded with firewood and charcoal. Through the mist and rain we pass one-eyed taxis, the wipers click-clicking away. '*Sékou's going too fast, it's crazy,*' comes Ross's voice over the Motorola. '*You're right, I'll flash him.*' I reply. '*It's too dangerous, even if he knows the road.*' Sékou pulls over; he's a bit of a cowboy and drives this road all the time. He laughs. 'Sure I'll slow down. The road's better after the Masiaka intersection,' he says. We push on through the rain along with overloaded Peugeot taxis all headed for Freetown. We drive on past the town of Bo, home of the Mende people, still known for their secret societies. Mile 91 is a busy intersection. There's loud music, young men drinking local gin and a man with no arms begging for food and coins. 'He's been chopped,' says Alfred. 'There are many that have to beg to survive, but now there are some aid organisations that care for the amputees.' Past taxis and street markets, we keep going. '*Watch out,*' warns Ross, '*there's a stark-naked fellow walking down the middle of the road!*' Alfred laughs. 'Ahead of us is the town of Masiaka. It used to be called Mile 41 but former president Siaka Stevens changed it to Masiaka. From there the road improves.'

It's well past midnight by the time we cruise into Freetown's East End. It's as rough as a goat's kneecap. We see prostitutes in the lamplight, people sleeping on the street and on rubbish heaps, young dudes hanging around in groups and others on noisy mopeds. 'It's a tough area,' says Alfred, 'you shouldn't walk here alone at night. But don't worry, not all of Freetown is like this.' He's right, high up on Spear Loop Hill, overlooking the sea, is Sékou's three-storey mansion. 'Welcome to Freetown,' says Sékou. He shows us our rooms; we flop into bed to be woken a few hours later by the muezzin's pre-dawn call, urging the Ramadan fasters to keep it up. 'Imagine how lovely it would be to have a day off,' says Mashozi, pulling the sheet over her head.

Dispatch #113 – The Battle for Freetown

Freetown lies at the northern end of a 40-kilometre-long mountainous peninsula. Bruce makes two cups of coffee and we sit on the balcony overlooking the beautiful Atlantic beaches, best known of which is Lumley Beach on the north of the peninsula, just around the corner from Freetown. I explain to Bruce that ours certainly aren't the first South African accents to be heard here. In 1995, with the RUF rebels about to take Freetown, Executive Outcomes, made up mostly of South African mercenaries, was contracted by President

Valentine Strasser. He promised the mercenaries concessions to mine diamonds in exchange for their finely honed skills. It took the professional soldiers of Executive Outcomes less than ten days to clear the area, and by August 1995 they had the diamond fields back under Freetown's control. The South Africans turned the tide on the war by retraining army units as well as organising the Kamajors traditional hunters, who had already formed self-defence groups, into well-armed, anti-rebel militias who could protect their communities from rebel atrocities.

Later Strasser was ousted in a coup by his own followers. Elections were held despite the RUF attacking villages and chopping off people's legs, arms and hands to keep them away from the polls. The new president, Ahmad Tejan Kabbah, cancelled the Executive Outcomes contract, and the RUF and its allies took the city back. By this time, the Economic Community of West African States Monitoring Group, ECOMOG, had taken up the fight against the RUF. This multilateral armed force was helped by a British security firm, Sandline International, with links to Executive Outcomes.

It's amazing that Freetown is still standing. In January 1999 the third battle for the city began with the launch of RUF's Operation No Living Thing, in which the rebels massacred over 6 000 civilians, cut off people's hands and feet, destroyed property and retreated, taking hundreds of captured kids with them. Thousands of UN Peacekeepers were sent to Sierra Leone but the RUF retaliated by kidnapping 500 of the Zambian and Kenyan members. Charles Taylor, along with other warlords, had by this time moved in to take Liberia, and 150 000 civilians had been killed. He'd made a personal fortune from Sierra Leone diamonds, even using them to launder cash with international terrorist rings like al-Qaida and funding the elections that made him president of Liberia.

The UN Peacekeepers were, it seems, incapable of keeping the peace in Sierra Leone. The staff of *Médecins Sans Frontières* were kidnapped by RUF rebels, UN hostages were taken and a UN helicopter was shot down. The RUF took hold of the Kono diamond fields again and a peace deal, which included Charles Taylor, floundered. The shit once again hit the fan – who cares for peace when it's diamonds you're after? In May 2000 Britain moved into Sierra Leone with a full military force. Operation Palliser came into effect and the RUF rebels were finally cleared out. Foday Sankoh was arrested, stripped naked and paraded through Freetown's streets before being handed over to the government. Thanks to the British, in January 2002, eleven years after the RUF rebels had crossed into Sierra Leone from Liberia, President Kabbah declared the war in Sierra Leone to be over.

We meet with Dr Baker, head of the malaria control programme, and he and his team endorse the scroll. We go on to distribute nets at the Murray Town Barracks School where the kids are lovely – they smile and there's light in their eyes. Malaria is rife here and we feel we're helping to make a difference. We have sunset beers under thatched umbrellas at a beach bar on Lumley Beach. Two girls, bead sellers, sell us some charming necklaces. Music plays and new cars cruise the beachfront. There's a great vibe; peace has returned to Freetown's outside edge. We buy two fat rotisserie chickens and fresh bread and go back to Sékou's house on the hill for a feast.

Dispatch #114 – The Old Town

Freetown Land Rover services the three Landies. You can tell they've been through hell – there's lots of mud and grit from Liberia and the brake pads have worn right down. The workshop staff and manager all gather round for photographs and a scroll signing. Wherever we go, the warmth and the friendliness of the people are overwhelming; after so much suffering to be so good-natured is incredible. We can't get over how different Freetown is from the other West African coastal cities, with its wonderfully hilly layout and the bays and beaches of the Freetown peninsula. The best place to start exploring Freetown is from the Cotton Tree, a magnificent old silk cotton tree older than the town itself. Slaves were sold from under the tree and the story goes that in 1787 a group of so-called Black Poor immigrants and 60 white women, who'd been deported to Sierra Leone, gathered here as the very first colonists from England. Their original settlement was destroyed, and the current city was founded in 1792 when these first settlers were joined by former American slaves. Down by the waterfront is the Slave Gate through which freed slaves walked from the ships to an unknown future in Africa's Free Town. An inscription still reads:

Royal Hospital and Asylum for Africans Freed from Slavery by British Valour and Philanthropy CE *1817.*

IT'S ALL ABOUT DIAMONDS

MALARIA EDUCATION AND BEDNETS TO SCHOOLS IN FREETOWN – DOING WHAT WE CAME TO DO. PEACE AFTER HORRIFIC VIOLENCE

... an aged and crumbling tumble of sagging streets, clapboard and cement-block buildings ... today, urban decay and the scars of war have eaten so deeply into the fabric of the town that it seems as though only a strong breeze would bring the wood-panelled houses down. (2003, p. 624)

It's late afternoon. We buy supplies, fuel up and head for the border with Guinea.

Dispatch #115 – The Road to Conakry

We pull off the road and into the bush. It's raining softly. Little Alfred is intrigued – it's the first time he's camped with us and he gets his own small pop-up tent alongside Bruce. Up go our roof tents, out come the camp chairs and the box of pots and pans, a table and the braai grid. Soon a fire's going, the kettle's on and we're having a 'drop'. 'Is it like this every night?' he asks. 'Yes, most nights,' says Mashozi, as she and Anna chop some meat and veggies for a stew. Alfred's lovely – intelligent and very kind. I ask him about the Krio language we've heard people talking. 'Most people speak it,' he says. 'It's a mix of English and various African languages.' Alfred gives us examples: '*Howdee bohdee?*' is 'how are you?' 'I'm fine' is '*bohdee fine*' or '*no bad*'. 'Goodbye' is '*we go see back*' and 'how much?' is '*ow mus?*' 'I want to go to the toilet' is an easy one to remember, it's simply '*ah wan wet*' and 'Sierra Leone' is abbreviated to '*Salone*'.

The rain gets heavier and we move our chairs under the Land Rover awning. 'The West Side Boys rebel camp was down in the valley there,' says Alfred, pointing. 'They were a real bunch of gangsters, but their worst mistake was when they kidnapped a 12-man Royal Irish Rangers patrol. The British SAS and the parachute regiment hit them at dawn with big Chinook helicopters and chain guns. The rebels were running round in their underpants, firing wildly. The British rescued all the hostages; it was called Operation Barras and put an end to the West Side Boys and their rebel leader Foday Kallay, who was taken prisoner.'

Up early, we pass hundreds of people walking to market with baskets of maize cobs, yams and bananas and bundles of firewood balanced on their heads, swinging upside-down chickens by their feet. Soon the passports are stamped, a bamboo pole goes up and we cross into Guinea.

We also can't get over the very British feel of Freetown – there's a Leicester Peak, a St Charles Church, a Regents Village and there are York, Kent and Sussex beaches. There are also areas of Aberdeen, Wilberforce, Gloucester, Wellington, Hasting and Waterloo. The narrow streets are crowded with bicycles, traders and pedestrians, as well as old, dilapidated, pastel-coloured Creole houses with rust-red corrugated iron roofs and dingy alleyways that make the place look like a *Blood Diamond* film set. Graham Greene's novel *The Heart of the Matter* was set here in Freetown during World War II. Our battered *Rough Guide to West Africa* aptly calls Freetown:

Guinea

Day 164, Country 16 on the Edge

The great waterways of West Africa, including the Gambia, Sénégal and Niger rivers, all start in the République de Guineé, giving it the nickname 'African Palace of Water'. Guinea is often referred to as Guinea Conakry to distinguish it from other Guineas of the world. It was for many years one of Africa's most secretive and isolated states, only recently opening up to the outside world. Sounds fascinating – we can't wait to get our teeth into it.

BACK TO BLOODY FRENCH BREAD – HOW WE MISS THE BIG, FAT S'AFRICAN LOAVES –

Dispatch #116 – The Road to Conakry

The bamboo pole goes up and we make our way out of English-speaking Sierra Leone and into no-man's-land. With 9° 10' 27" N and 12° 57' 32" W on the Garmin, we enter the République de Guineé. Back into French territory we go. Give me the old British colonies any day. The slow sweat of a border crossing trickles on but little Alfred, who is still travelling with us, helps us along. He's a great guy – just half a brick and a tickey high. He escaped from Sierra Leone during the trouble and made Guinea his home, so he speaks perfect English and French and understands both worlds.

I sit and watch a typical border scene unfold. Customs and immigration officials in blue uniforms and black berets are doing their thing. Shouting and screaming, they order two terrified mamas with five little kids to get out of a Peugeot taxi. With all their humble bits of luggage they have to report to 'Mr Big', who's hiding from the sun on a chair under a rusty corrugated iron lean-to that's about to collapse. Big stomach, big nose, big muscles, big boots and big thick neck – Mr Big looks like a comic character out of a French cartoon. Pointing with his stick, he makes them unpack everything, and then he takes his pick: a thermos flask, a small bag of rice and some bananas. Finally, before stamping their documents, he demands some cash. They pack up their kit and walk forlornly down the road and the next Peugeot taxi to take them on to Conakry. The whistle blows again, and again more money and goods change hands. It's always the ordinary, humble people who have so little that suffer the most. 'Calm down Pops,' cautions Ross, 'you've been getting a bit uptight with officials lately – it's not worth it.' Alfred returns with a smile, carnets and passports in his hand. 'Let's get out of here,' he says, 'they're full of shit.'

We fuel up the Landies. The coast road to Conakry runs between the North Atlantic and a range of hills that remind me of the Lebombo mountains at home.

Through the streets of Conakry, capital of the République de Guinée — It's the Wild West —

GUINEA – NOTES
- CAPITAL: CONAKRY
- POPULATION: 9.6 MILLION
- AREA 245 857 SQ KM.
- BORDERED BY SIERRA LEONE, LIBERIA, CÔTE D'IVOIRE, MALI, SENEGAL AND GUINEA-BISSAU
- BECAME A FRENCH COLONY IN 1891 AND THEN INDEPENDENT IN 1958 –
- CURRENCY IS THE GUINEAN FRANC
- OFFICIAL LANGUAGE IS FRENCH, WHILE OTHERS ARE FULA, SUSU AND MAUNKÉ –
- STRONGLY ISLAMIC / RICH IN MINERAL WEALTH

Malaria is rife but the people are lovely —

Coupon for a Mosquito net

In the Landy Alfred tells Mashozi and me something of the history of Guinea. It seems that when General Charles de Gaulle offered French colonies immediate independence or membership to the French Community as a step to autonomy, Guinean leader Sékou Touré rejected the offer, declaring, 'We prefer poverty in liberty to riches in slavery.' The French took the rebuff badly; they sabotaged infrastructure, cut off all financial and technical aid and withdrew massive amounts of capital. Guinea went socialist, nationalising farms and industry, and eventually the economy failed and the country became isolated. Touré imagined all sorts of conspiracies against him; thousands were imprisoned or executed and about 250 000 Guineans fled the country.

But, Alfred tells us, it was the people who finally brought about change. In 1977 there was a market-women's revolt against the government's plans to stop private trade. Some local governors were killed and police stations burnt, but it was the power of the people that changed things. More recently, in 2006, Guineans again took to the streets in protest against poor living conditions, bad roads, unreliable electricity supply, high prices and a lack of jobs. Even teens, women and children armed themselves with sticks, stones and petrol bombs and revolted. Over 200 people were mowed down by the military, but they got their message across and now things are much better. 'You'll see when we get to Conakry,' says Alfred.

We pass through small villages, rice fields and narrow bridges, and eventually reach the outskirts of the city. Small Renault vans used as taxis, roofs piled high with bags of charcoal, overtake us at breakneck speed. An overloaded old Peugeot station wagon races past with six in the back, four in front and the driver hanging halfway out the window. It's loaded on top with a gravity-defying pile of luggage, two big bunches of green bananas, three goats, some yellow, plastic cooking-oil containers and two extra rooftop passengers holding on for dear life. There's a strong feel of Islam here, the Ramadan fast has started and food stalls are busy preparing for after-sunset sales. Whistles blow and the vultures pounce: vehicle papers, passports and vaccination cards are demanded. It's all a scam to try and get bucks and results in a black mark on the sun visor.

Conakry is a long, thin, rough-and-ready city built on a peninsula that juts out into the Atlantic. Our businessman friend Sékou Cissé organises discounted rates at a hotel down on the beachfront; he's well known here in Conakry. Malaria volunteer Hugh Roe has flown in from South Africa to join the expedition for a while. He and his wife Tessa were part of the Land Rover convoy that saw us out from Cape Town and then stayed on as volunteers up the South African coast. He's full of fun and adds a fresh spirit to the expedition. The next morning we meet at Sékou's offices and with the PermaNet team put together a One Net One Life malaria prevention plan for when we return in two weeks' time – time enough I hope to break away inland, east across Guinea into Mali and down the Niger River. So, loaded up with fuel and supplies, we say goodbye, for just a short time, to the outside edge of Africa. It's a strange feeling, but the time has come to take George's ashes to Timbuktu.

A Side Trip to Mali

Dispatch #117 – Taking George to Timbuktu
My father-in-law George, Mashozi's dad, loved Africa with a passion. His great dream was to one day visit the mystical, mythical southern-Saharan city of Timbuktu. Unfortunately he died before he ever made it, but his ashes were kept in a screw-top jar in Mashozi's clothes cupboard should we ever go that way. So when we took off from the Cape of Good Hope, escorted by a record-size convoy of 347 Landies, there was old George amongst the supplies in one of the pull-out Landy drawers. It became a bit of an expedition joke – that he might get confused with curry powder and be eaten.

George would have loved the adventure: the Sperrgebiet, the Skeleton Coast and the great sand ocean of the Namib; the crossing of the Congo; the forests and pygmy elephant in Gabon; the challenges of Cameroon, Calabar and Lagos; the voodoo ceremonies and fetish markets of Benin and Togo; Ghana's historic forts and castles; and the other crazy adventures that have unfolded along the edge of Africa.

George was a great humanitarian and would have felt for the people of war-torn Liberia and Sierra Leone and their suffering, that included the butchering of limbs by drug-crazed child soldiers. Were he alive today, he would have been a key player in the distribution of life-saving mosquito nets. With smiles and handshakes he would have assisted with the giving out of mobile libraries and writing materials to village schools and with spectacles to the poor-sighted in remote villages. We often sat around a fire debating the time and effort it would take to break away from the coast to take George all the way to Timbuktu, essentially a thousand-kilometre detour inland from Guinea. But Mashozi was adamant: 'We'll be scattering George's ashes into the Niger River outside Timbuktu and that's that.'

At last light, six months and 16 outside edge countries into the journey, we cross on a ferry into the ancient city of Djenné, which boasts the oldest and biggest mud mosque in the world. It's the end of Ramadan and thousands come down to the water's edge to pray. The women and children are beautifully adorned – the little girls with jewellery, plaited hair and make-up, and the ladies with henna-painted designs on their hands and feet. There's a lot of poverty here, however, and sanitation is poor and malaria is a killer. It's the start of the Feast of Eid and we follow the custom of going from door to door to give gifts, a mosquito net to each mum.

Three days later we move on. Our interpreter's name is Moise, but because he's so talkative we call him Noise. He's quite a character and thinks Mashozi is the bee's knees. We camp on the edge of the Bandiagara escarpment. Below is Dogon Country and endless views over to Burkina Faso. All my life I've wanted to visit Dogon Country; it really is a dream come true. At the village of Teli we explore the cliffs, the mud granaries with their little conical roofs like witches' hats and the red-brown mud villages built into the cliff faces. It's full of mysterious people whose predecessors were pygmy-type folk, known as the Tellem, a community the current Dogon people believe had magical powers that could make them fly or transform themselves into giants and climb up to their cave dwellings in a single step.

Back along the Niger, we arrive at a mud-built, Fula-speaking village a little downriver from Mopti. The big Gemini inflatables land with a thud as they are rolled off the roof rack of the Landy. The entire village turns out to watch as these crazy South Africans sweat it out: inserting boat boards, bolting on the Yamahas and then loading the inflatables with bales of mosquito nets, basic supplies, boat fuel and George, and finally launching into the sticky heat of the 20 000-square-kilometre inland delta of the Niger. One Landy will remain in the village. Hugh, Bruce and a man called Mohammed will take the other two across the desert to Timbuktu. The boat party of Mashozi, Ross, Anna, Noise and myself will continue on our own.

Water levels are the highest in over 20 years and many of the mud villages have been swallowed. Malaria is rife here and the appreciation from the pregnant women who receive nets is overwhelming as they sing and dance in jubilation. In the heat of the day we hide from the sun and we sleep wherever we end up at the end of the day. The river is massive. One of our pontoons explodes like a rifle shot, ripped by a jagged piece of metal as we pull alongside a Niger River trading vessel. We patch it in the cool of the evening; the next morning there's still a slow leak but we pump as we go.

Days later, beaten by the sun and with about a tablespoon of boat fuel left in the tanks, we arrive at a broad sweep in the river outside the ancient trading city of Timbuktu. '*Safari njema* – have a good journey,' whispers Mashozi, using a Swahili farewell to say goodbye to George as, with tears in her eyes, she unscrews the bottle and sprinkles his ashes into the Niger, his final resting place.

Dispatch #118 – Mythical Timbuktu

Finally we enter ancient Timbuktu where Bruce and Hugh have come to meet us in the Landies. It's a dream come true. I sit in the mud-walled courtyard where Major Gordon Alexander Laing, the first white man to enter Timbuktu, had stayed before joining a camel caravan to take him north across the Sahara Desert. Two days later he was stopped by the Tuareg and killed with a spear through the heart. In the same house, an artist, using a quill pen, transcribes words of another, more ancient scroll onto a page of ours. Translated from Arabic, they read:

> *Salt comes from the north, gold from the south, money from white man's country; but God's words, holy things, interesting tales, we can find them only in Timbuktu.*

Camel caravans continue to carry trading salt to this archaic wonderland and the Tuareg still wear robes and turbans and fight the desert heat by drinking daily cups of sweet Mali tea. It is all as George had imagined. That night we celebrate Mashozi's 60th birthday out in the Sahara with the tribespeople. A Tuareg boils up some traditional tea in an ornate, handcrafted kettle and it is served thick with sugar in small glasses on a dune on the edge of the world's largest desert. Looking south from where we sit with our six candles in the sand, we see the lights of Timbuktu twinkle in the distance; to the north it's pure darkness, we see just the beginnings of the track in the desert that leads to Tamanrasset in Algeria and the Mediterranean.

The desert folk in their indigo blue or black turbans dance in the sand. We suck on the bones of a succulent sheep. 'What a beautiful kettle,' says Mashozi as Mohammed the Tuareg pours her another glass of traditional tea. 'It's yours,' I say. 'Happy birthday.' We'd arranged for Noise to buy it in the market earlier that day as a birthday surprise. He also adds an agate and silver ring, and Bruce a pendant and carvings wrapped in a small piece of cloth. Ross and Anna had prematurely spoilt Mashozi with Abu the Ape from Abidjan, who still takes up space on the back seat of our Land Rover.

The Tuareg sing a haunting melody, but the birthday party comes to a sudden end when Bruce gets stung on the toe by a scorpion. The poison soon spreads up his leg and the gland in his groin becomes swollen and sore to the touch. He lies writhing in agony as a Tuareg *marabut*, a traditional holy man and healer, pushes and prods his toe, nodding wisely every time Bruce groans in pain. 'He won't die,' Noise assures us, but we feed him some antihistamine from the medical kit anyway. The Tuareg roll their carpets up and go back to their desert camp, and we head back to Timbuktu.

Dispatch #119 – Biltong and Rugby

I realise that the journey is running into months when I start thinking of home pleasures and things South African. You know, like Marmite; ice in the Captain Morgan; sleeping in until late or lazily reading the Sunday papers with the dogs curled up next to the bed; and being called to dinner at the end of the day knowing that it's a *regte* braai instead of bean stew in a battered pot over a smoky fire. This gets me thinking

MASHOZI EMPTIES GEORGE'S ASHES INTO THE NIGER OFF TIMBUKTU —

of biltong and the incredible bad luck we've had in getting sticks of our favourite wet and fatty.

First there was Big Deon Schürmann, who told us he was bringing in 20 vacuum-packed sticks, rolled up and hidden in his canvas bedroll when he came to meet us in Congo-Brazzaville. The entire bedroll was nicked. Next came Adolf Waidelich, our Land Rover fitment sponsor from 4x4MegaWorld, who knew about our plight and was going to sneak two big packets, one of impala dry *wors*, the other of sticks, into Gabon. After much restraint on the first night, deciding to savour the stash, we awoke the next morning to find that some dogs had stolen into camp and guzzled the lot. Finally came Hugh Roe, but the moment I saw his face in Guinea I just knew it. 'The the whole b-b-bloody lot was confiscated in Bamako – not even bribes and negotiations would work,' he stammered. I saw the look of shock and horror on the team's faces.

A Tuareg pours tea with Mashozi's birthday kettle.

Now in this ancient place we have a modern-day dilemma. The Boks have made it into the Rugby World Cup final and we're up against England – it's Africa against Europe. So we leave the dusty streets of Timbuktu with the inflatable boats rolled up on the Landies, cross the river on the Niger ferry and race through the potholes and scrub, dodging cattle, donkeys, camels and goats in our frantic quest to see the game. It starts at 7 p.m. local time. Luckily we phoned ahead and a hotel in Savare town was tuning into the match for us.

Two minutes to kick-off, it's a race against time. At the sight of our three Landies, a policeman rushes forward, his hand up to stop us and whistle blowing furiously. '*Let's go!*' I shout over the radio after making sure he's not carrying an AK-47. We wave and swerve, foot flat and acting stupid, and race into the hotel grounds. There's a small TV with a bunny-ear aerial set out with chairs under a tree in the courtyard. We all stand to attention, fists clasped to our chests for the South African national anthem. The commentary's in French and the picture's a bit snowy but who gives a shit, South Africa is bringing home the cup. The local Malians are as excited as we are. We embrace and shake hands. In broken, French-accented English, they shout: 'We are happy, so happy, it's a victory for Africa.'

Back in Bamako, capital of Mali, and over a thousand kilometres from Timbuktu, I swerve for a man pushing a hand trolley loaded with a single block of salt – a link to the trade routes of Saharan Timbuktu and the great Niger River. Finally we make our way back to Conakry on the coast of Guinea to continue the ongoing challenge of tracking the outside edge. Taking George to Timbuktu has been an unforgettable and worthy diversion.

Back to Guinea

Dispatch #120 – Saving and Improving Lives
We're back in traffic-choked downtown Conakry, back on the coast of Guinea, at a school for the deaf. The children are bright-eyed and beautiful. To greet us they wave both hands in the air. Braving the humidity with us is Isaac Kekana, South African Ambassador to Guinea. Branded in a South African-flag T-shirt, he makes us feel proud to be members of the Rainbow Nation, assisting us in giving each and every child a

long-lasting mosquito net and a pack of exercise books and pencils. Then, with a police escort, we're off to the general hospital where every mother and infant receives a life-saving net. You would think that we would have become battle hardened by now, but still the emotion hits you in the pit of your stomach: the look in the mother's eyes and the desperate poverty, with children dying from malaria because the mums cannot afford a simple mosquito net.

In the children's ward we place a net on each bed. As we move from child to child down the corridors the smiles of appreciation and handshakes from their parents are heart-warming. A poor electricity supply with constant power cuts has little premature babies' lives, two and three to an incubator, hanging on a thread. Now there is a mosquito net for each mother and infant, and at least they will be safe from malaria when they get home. A Ministry of Health official makes a speech and the Minister of Lands and Mines endorses the Madiba scroll in support of malaria prevention. The media scribble in their pads and local TV and radio are present. Ambassador Kekana writes:

Viva the expedition, viva.

A journalist pulls me aside. 'Congratulations,' he says in his French-accented English. 'Hand to hand to each mama, it is the only way. If you give the bales of nets to the officials, they sell them in the market – and these poor people, they will never get.'

I look at the team, working so hard to make a difference, with their One Net One Life malaria prevention T-shirts soaked through with sweat. Mashozi is having a tough day. Earlier in the maternity ward she ran out for a bit of a cry, then came back again. She never gives up. Bruce rolls another bale of 100 nets off the top of the Landy. Out comes his Leatherman and he cuts the straps, then the nets are untied and placed on a table. Today Sékou and Alfred do the malaria prevention education 'talk up' to the mums, translating why and how to use and care for the nets over the Landy sound system. Two assistants help Mashozi and Anna hold up a net; they give a demonstration with a mother and tiny baby lying underneath. Then Ross and Bruce get the mothers into queues with the help of local community workers, and Mashozi and Anna give each mum a coupon – one coupon one net.

The pushing, the shoving, the bruising, the heat and the crowds – there are not always enough nets to go around and I see the desperate looks on the mothers' faces. They know that a net can keep their babies safe. The challenge of refusing greedy officials' demands to take bales of nets elsewhere, doing the malaria education and physically putting a net into each mum's hand is tougher at times than the geographic struggle of travelling the outside edge. It's emotionally draining and physically tiring, but always worthwhile.

The next day, with local malaria prevention volunteers, we make our way past the notorious camp Boro where many anti-government supporters were tortured and killed. Some were even hung from a bridge over the highway as an example to others. Careful not to be seen taking pictures of the bombed-out palace, and loaded with mosquito nets, we launch into the Atlantic. Our purpose is to reach the islands of Roum, Kassa and Tamara where small island-village communities are desperate for mosquito nets. Tomorrow we will load up the Landies and head up the coast to the ex-Portuguese colony of Guinea-Bissau. Like Mozambique and Angola, it had a long war of liberation followed by a bitter civil war. We don't quite know what to expect.

Dispatch #121 – The Road to Guinea-Bissau

The spotlights on the bull bars cast a wide beam illuminating the elephant grass, which is taller than the battered Landies. Tired and worn out by the persistent rain and humidity, we reverse, go forward, and reverse again to flatten it, allowing us a patch big enough to camp on. The rain hits us again and we dive for our tents. Up early we push on – the mud, water holes and deep river crossings make it really slow going. I chat to Omar on the radio – he's a new expedition member who joined us in Conakry and is now travelling in Bruce's Land Rover. He's a mature 24-year-old who lost his mother in the war. He learnt English in Sierra Leone and speaks French and the local languages. '*Omar, at the next village, ask if there's a ferry and if people are still crossing into Guinea-Bissau and if the border post is open.*' A little while later I get the answer: '*Yes, Papa King, yes. There's a ferry and the people they are crossing and the border it is open.*' I give a sigh of relief. I'd been worried. The road had now become just a narrow, hardly-used mud track – it certainly didn't look like the *route nacionale* to an international border.

We stop the Landies and ask again at the next village. Omar gives a big grin. '*Yes, there's a ferry,*' he says and so we push on. First and second, low-range difflock, grinding and growling through the mud. With water cascading over the bonnets and the vehicles constantly swaying and jerking, the heat and humidity intensifies as we inch up the coast. 'Watch out!' shouts Mashozi as I swerve for a goat and slide sideways into a deep, slimy mud hole. Ross winches me out. How much more can these poor vehicles take? The Garmin GPS shows we've reached the river boundary between the Republic of Guinea and Guinea-Bissau. We're stopped by a rusty chain across the track. A man in a tattered blue uniform jumps out from under the thatched eaves of a hut. 'Where's the ferry?' we ask, quite irritated. 'It hasn't worked for a year,' comes the reply, 'it's got a big hole and the engine's broken. The government people from Conakry said they'd come and fix it but they've forgotten about us. You'll have to turn back.'

I feel sick. Two days of slogging down a rotten road to nowhere and now we have to go all the way back. But then I cool down and see the humour of it all. How stupid, I've travelled enough in Africa and I should have known how these things work by now. 'Is there a ferry?' I'd repeatedly asked. YES, had come the reply – but I'd failed to ask if it was working. 'Are people crossing?' I'd asked. YES, had been the reply – but that was probably in dugout canoes. And 'Is the border open?' YES, the border IS open, but I suppose that's if you arrived on foot or by bicycle, then crossed by pirogue or swam and risked the crocodiles.

We slowly turn the Landies around and stop under a tree for a bully beef sarmie. Anna slaps at her skin. There's a type of fly here that bites like hell and leaves a blistery welt on your skin that itches and burns like crazy. 'Always happens at the end of the rainy season,' says Omar. Later we learn that further up the same river is another ferry. 'Is it working?' I ask. 'Can it carry Land Rovers like these? When did you last see it?' 'We can't say,' comes the answer. 'It's a long way away but we have heard that people cross to the other side …'

THE BEARD & OMAR

AT LAST! A WORKING FERRY INTO GUINEA-BISSAU.

126

Guinea-Bissau

Day 189, Country 17 on the Edge

This is one of the smallest and least-known countries in West Africa. What interests us about this part of Africa's outside edge is the Bijagós Archipelago, which makes up the largest group of islands found along the West African coast. It boasts more than 40 islands, only some of which are inhabited. It's going to be a nice change of pace to explore them by boat, a little holiday from the road so to speak.

ROSS AND ANNA CONNECTING WITH THE OUTSIDE WORLD.

Dispatch #122 – Mozambican Flavour

Eventually we find a working ferry and cross the Rio Corubal into Guinea-Bissau. The cashew nut trees and war-torn Portuguese buildings remind us so much of Mozambique and we all get a little homesick. After frenetic Francophone Conakry, the small, relaxed city of Bissau is alive with bars and music and even has an annual Rio-type carnival. We wander out onto the wharfside at Pidjiguiti, where half-sunken wrecks line the old jetty. Security follows us around; taking photos is forbidden and they're a bit edgy. I wonder if this is because of all the drug trafficking that's said to go on here. The UN Office on Drugs and Crime estimates that a tonne of pure Colombian cocaine is rerouted through this small West African country every day. It was here at this same waterfront on 3 August 1959 that a dock-workers' strike for a living wage took place and police opened fire at point-blank range, killing 50 men and wounding more than 100. In *The Rough Guide to West Africa*, José Emilio Costa, who took part in the strike, tells his story:

> *This old captain friend of mine, Ocante Atobo, was leaning against the wall of the office shed. When the line of police reached the spot where he was, an officer suddenly raised his gun and shot him point blank in the chest. Ocante collapsed in a pool of blood. For a split second everyone froze – it was as if time stood still. Then hell broke loose. The police moved down the pier, shooting like crazy into the crowd. Men were screaming and running into all directions. I was over by my cousin Augusto Fernandes' boat, the* Alio Sulemane. *Augusto, who was standing next to me, had his chest shot wide open; it was like his whole inside was coming out. He was crying: 'Oh God, João kill me please.' But it wasn't necessary; when I lifted his head from the ground he was already dead …*
> (2003, pp. 500–501)

OUR ISLAND CAMP – JUST 90 METRES LONG BY 30 WIDE.
BIJAGÓS ARCHIPELAGO OFF THE COAST OF GUINEA-BISSAU.

A 'TYPICAL' OUTSIDE EDGE CAMP – AND IT'S PROBABLY STEW AGAIN

Guinea-Bissau – Notes

- REMINDS US OF MOZAMBIQUE – MAKES US A BIT HOMESICK / IT'S AN EX-PORTUGUESE COLONY
- ONE OF THE WORLD'S POOREST COUNTRIES WITH TWO-THIRDS OF THE POPULATION LIVING BELOW THE POVERTY LINE!
- BEEN HAMMERED BY WAR / STILL GOT PROBLEMS WITH UNEXPLODED LANDMINES
- POPULATION 1.5 MILLION
- PORTUGUESE IS LITTLE USED, MOST PREFER THE STREET VERNACULAR OF 'KRIOLU'
- THERE'S A STRONG CAPE VERDE INFLUENCE AND ALSO A SMALL CHINESE POPULATION FROM THE FORMER PORTUGUESE COLONY OF MACAU —
- EXPLORE THE ISLANDS

The massacre and the police interrogations that followed lit the spark for armed conflict, and the War of Independence against the Portuguese raged until 1974, when Guinea-Bissau became the first Portuguese colony to gain full sovereignty. Sadly only two decades of relative peace followed before civil war broke out in 1998, bringing the country to its knees. But now there's peace.

We meet with the Minister of Health and arrange to distribute life-saving mosquito nets outside Bissau. Our Scroll of Peace and Goodwill in support of malaria prevention is endorsed by the local governor and a Guinea-Bissau Foreign Affairs representative. Looks like everything's okay and we all instantly like the place and the laid-back Guinea-Bissauans. Once again, the place has that feeling of old Mozambique, with flat chicken, prawns and imported Sagres beers from Portugal. There's a sprinkling of Cape Verde islanders and good music called *gumbe*, which is always sung in Kriolu. It would be lovely to hang around.

Dispatch #123 – Escape to the Islands

Outside the bombed-out palace, with near-naked, white clay-faced tribesmen around the Landies, we meet Steve who, with a team of experts, is lifting landmines in the interior. He directs us to a place on a river north of Bissau where we go about preparing to launch the expedition boats into the Bijagós Archipelago. Made up of more than 40 islands, it is the largest island group along the West African coast and a must for any outside edge expedition. The closest island to the mainland, Bolama, is 25 by 5 kilometres wide. As always, the humidity is mind-sapping.

Apparently the islands attracted the imagination of British expedition members as far back as 1792, when Phillip Beaver, aged 26, set sail from England with 274 prospective settlers. The group even included a legislative council and a governor who had been chosen in the Globe Tavern in London. By the time they got to the Bissagos Islands of the archipelago in their two ships, *Hankey* and *Calypso*, half of the passengers were already down with malaria. The expedition seemed doomed; the adventurers were attacked by Bijagós warriors, who kidnapped several women and children. Phillip Beaver only managed to secure their release by buying the island for £77 worth of iron bars. When the *Calypso* set sail for Sierra Leone, more than half the surviving expedition members decided to see if the grass was greener there. Only 13 of the remaining 91 who stayed behind on Bolama survived malaria. According to our 'bible' for the area, *The Rough Guide to West Africa*, a typically laconic entry in Beaver's journal reads:

Sun 2nd Dec. Killed a bullock for the colony. Died and buried Mr Webster. Thermometer 92. Three men well.
(2003, p. 520)

Only Beaver and five others survived the rains of the following year. He and a companion sailed back to England in May 1794, musing that it had been an 'ill-contrived and badly executed, though well-intended expedition'. I hope we have better luck.

There's the familiar smell of outboard fuel and the sweat of pumping the pontoons, inserting the boards and bolting the tough Yamaha Enduros onto the transoms of the two 6-metre-long One Net One Life Gemini inflatables. Then there's the loading up and tying down of camping equipment, first-aid kit and clean clothes; basic supplies and some Captain from the Land Rover water tank; paper maps and the Garmin GPSs; and bales of life-saving mosquito nets for remote island communities. It's low tide and hot as hell by the time we snake through the mangrove swamps and out into the sharp chop of the waves of Guinea-Bissau's warm North Atlantic. Pelicans fly overhead in perfect formation. We find an island filled with birds and baobabs, and Ross catches a good-sized barracuda. Another island is knee-deep in shells but it's too rocky to camp on and somehow the spirits don't seem right.

INTERESTING COMPANY A WILD BUNCH GATHER AROUND THE LANDIES

BRUCE & BIJAGÓS PERI-PERI BARRACUDA

By late afternoon, the setting sun an orange ball in the west, we find our island paradise – 90 metres long by just 30 metres wide. It has a beach and a lone baobab tree and there's plenty of firewood, and not a human being in sight.

It's been a hard grind lately and it's just wonderful to be out of the Landies for a while and free from the crush of people. We all desperately need time out. Ross and Anna fillet the barracuda whilst Egyptian vultures dive and swoop over the sharp-toothed, big-eyed carcass. With his shirt off, map of Africa tattooed on his back and looking a bit skinny after all the months of hard travel, Bruce chops the fillets into chunks. Next he fries them up with hard round onions from the Central Market in Bissau, and adds some precious Nando's Hot Peri-Peri Sauce. We all sit with our backsides in the sand under a starlit sky, helping ourselves thumb-and-forefinger, African style, to succulent pieces of Bijagós peri-peri barracuda. There's no menu, no bread or salads, no music or TV, no cellphone reception and there's not a soul in the whole wide world that knows where the bloody hell we are, other than that we are somewhere on the outside edge of the continent.

The next day Omar, Bruce and I deliver mosquito nets to women and children on a small island where most of the fishermen are from Senegal, so Omar does the malaria education in French and Madinka. He's a great lad, proving yet again that it's travelling with local people that brings a journey alive.

Dispatch #124 – On to the Casamance

A few days later we're back in the Landies, inflatable boats rolled up and floorboards and motors stashed. Refreshed from the visit to the Bijagós Archipelago, it's time to head for the border with Senegal's Casamance area. Until recently there was a travel warning by the British Foreign Office and the US State Department, but Omar, who's been asking the locals, says it's safe now and that apart from the danger of landmines in certain areas, the separatist conflict is over.

As we are leaving Guinea-Bissau, Mashozi notices that the immigration officer is struggling to read our passport details. Out comes a pair of Rite to Sight spectacles. He tries them on and beams with delight, stamps the passports, poses for a quick photograph and the next moment we're out of Portuguese territory and into French. We pass though a well-armed military checkpoint, past a billboard that warns against landmines and into Basse-Casamance, the southernmost part of *la République du Sénégal*. Guinea-Bissau has been a refreshing outside edge gem – *obrigado*!

CLOSER TO THE CASAMANCE BORDER. A GRAPHIC SIGN WARNS US ABOUT THE DANGER OF UNEXPLODED LANDMINES

Senegal

Day 193, Country 18 on the Edge

The outside edge of French-speaking Senegal is broken by the Gambia, a small ex-British colony that really only occupies the Gambia River and its banks. Strange isn't it, how in the European Scramble for Africa little thought was given to local tribes and cultures, and the region has had trouble for years. We hear that Senegalese music, popularised by Youssou N'Dour, Orchestra Baobab and Baaba Maal, is some of the best in the region and is certainly worth paying attention to.

Dispatch #125 – The Basse-Casamance

Out of Guinea-Bissau and we're into the troubled Casamance region, which is sadly also Senegal's most beautiful area. Fortunately, there's peace now between the largely non-Muslim Casamance Separatists and the Islamic Dakar government, although the separatists have been violently lobbying for independence for years. Peace talks had been going reasonably well until the MV *Le Joola*, a ferry carrying passengers mostly from the Casamance area, capsized in stormy seas on its way to Dakar. At least 1 863 people died and the prime minister and the head of the navy were sacked, but there's still a great deal of bitterness in the Casamance, where the Jola people, from whom the ferry took her name, are still highly critical of the government's handling of the crisis.

A good road takes us into the riverside port of Ziguinchor, which is worth heading for even if just for the exotic name. We find rooms in a little hotel on the wide Casamance River where brightly decorated fishing pirogues line the banks. The waiter, Jean-Pierre, speaks delightful French-accented English. When the trouble hit the Casamance, he spent time in nearby English-speaking Gambia. Now he's back. 'I'm a Jola,' he says, 'this is my country. It's the richest part of Senegal and we wanted our independence, but there's peace now.' I ask him about the road to Cap Skirring, as it's important that we get to the outside edge of Senegal's southernmost cape. 'It's safe,' he says, 'you can go. They've repaired the roads, the ambushes have stopped and the landmines are being cleared.' 'And the malaria?' I ask. 'It's bad,' he says. 'Too many mosquitoes, especially where they are growing rice.'

At a little school that we stop at, called École Carounate, the teachers and children can't believe it. All the way from *Afrique du Sud*, three Land Rovers roll up with mozzie nets for every child. Omar interprets and the teachers endorse the scroll in French.

THE ROAD IMPROVES. PEACE HAS COME TO BASSE-CASAMANCE

THE CASAMANCE RIVER AT ZIGUINCHOR —

ANOTHER CAPE BEHIND US —

SENEGAL - NOTES
- POPULATION IS ALMOST 13 MILLION
- TOURIST FRIENDLY BUT THERE HAVE BEEN PROBLEMS WITH REBELS IN THE SOUTHERN BASSE-CASAMANCE AREA — SAID TO BE THE MOST BEAUTIFULL REGION
- TOLD/WARNED TO BE CAREFUL OF LANDMINES IN THE SOUTH
- FRENCH IS THE OFFICIAL LANGUAGE WHILST THE INDIGENOUS WOLOF IS SPOKEN BY THE MAJORITY — LOOKING FORWARD TO REACHING DAKAR AND THE MOST WESTERLY POINT OF THE AFRICAN CONTINENT — A YARDSTICK FOR THE OUTSIDE EDGE EXPEDITION —

'These funny people from a place called South Africa brought us mosquito nets. Their steering wheels were on the wrong side!'

Dispatch #126 – And We're Out Again

Across the Casamance River we continue through beautiful forests and past lakes. Before the unrest, this area was a great favourite, especially with French adventure tourists and expats from Dakar keen on mountain biking, kayaking, hiking and camping. You could lose yourself here for days. Inexpensive *campements* offer bungalows or camping. Omar asks a few questions, and everybody assures him that the trouble is over and that the bush fighters have returned to growing cannabis. It's more profitable and less risky.

This is an odd piece of Africa's outside edge, with the Basse-Casamance being split from the rest of Senegal by a tiny country grandly called the Gambia. So in a short space of time not only did we exit Portuguese-speaking Guinea-Bissau and cross into French-speaking Casamance, but now we're going to pass through English-speaking Gambia, re-enter French-speaking Senegal and then cross into Arabic Mauritania. Confusing, isn't it? There's a strong security presence, sandbagged outposts and lots of guns as we exit the Casamance into the Gambia.

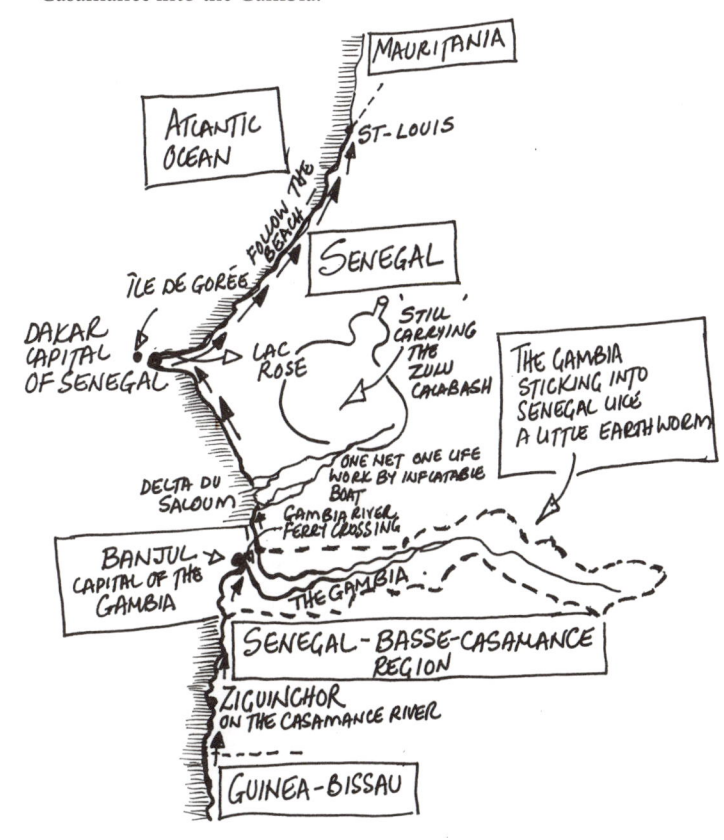

The area is a beautiful mixture of tall hardwood forests, endless lagoons and creeks, mangrove flats and long white beaches. On the beach at Cap Skirring we meet Mohammed, who's got a small palm frond-thatched chophouse – just a few rickety tables and chairs and a sea-sand floor. Mohammed rushes out to borrow some cutlery. His mate races to the market and an hour later there are dodgy cheese and tomato omelettes and coffees all round and it's back to bloody French bread. Omar is the interpreter and Mohammed tells us he is the sole survivor of a boatload of 'illegals' who'd been discovered at sea trying to get to the Canary Islands and on to Europe. 'It happens all the time,' says Omar, 'people are desperate. The families club together – if only one of them can get to Europe and get a job, there would be enough money to keep them all alive.' 'We didn't make it,' says Mohammed. 'A storm came and the engine broke. We finished the water, and everybody died except me.' We pay for the breakfast in CFA francs and shake hands with Mohammed. 'Would you do it again?' I ask him. 'Yes,' he says quite definitely, 'some of this money you give me now will go to the boatman.'

133

The Gambia

Day 194, Country 19 on the Edge

With only about a hundred kilometres of coastline, this friendly, easy-going country consists of little more than the wide mouth of the Gambia River and 11 300 square kilometres of riverbank. From October to April there's a massive influx of sun worshippers from Europe and Britain, so it's probably going to be a bit posher than we're used to, with the hotels and shops being set up for the tourists. Should be an enjoyable piece of cake.

DEAD AND RESTING ON THE 'OUTSIDE EDGE'

Dispatch #127 – Off to a Good Start

Right from the start, when we were given our Gambian visas in Guinea-Bissau, we were impressed. It was a public holiday, yet the Gambian ambassador graciously agreed to meet us at his home. We sat on his veranda, had small glasses of sweet tea and explained our journey. He endorsed the scroll, sent for his staff and issued the visas there and then. 'Gratis,' he said. 'No charge. Your journey is good for Africa and you'll love the Gambia – it's ex-British, very civilised, has good hotels and restaurants. It's also friendly and we love having visitors – you'll see.'

Shake, rattle and roll; the heavy-duty Old Man Emu suspensions continue to ride the corrugations and potholes out of southern Senegal's Casamance area and across into the Gambia as we follow an overloaded Peugeot 504 bush taxi up the Atlantic coast. The road soon improves and all of a sudden we're into another world, the likes of which we haven't seen in months. '*Look,*' comes Ross's voice over the radio, '*on the left. The sign.*' I almost crash into Bruce below a sign that reads 'Full English breakfast served ALL day'. It's tourist season; lots of Brits and Europeans wander around in shorts and bikini tops, beach thongs, hats and sunglasses, very pink from the African sun. There are English pubs, English fish-and-chips shops, Rasta beach boys, big tourist hotels, music and the smell of suntan oil. Bumsters gather around the Landies, pleasant and friendly. 'Hey man, you need hotel, change money, want a girl, need a guy, need a guide? Welcome to the Gambia man – how long you stay?' I look at Mashozi – this is not the outside edge we've come to love, with the African villages, the deserted beaches and a simple campfire at night. Maybe we've gone a bit *bossies*. '*What do you think?*' I ask the others over the radio. '*It's another piece of the outside edge and I guess we need to experience it,*' comes Ross's not-too-enthusiastic reply. '*Can't believe all the white chicks with the black dudes,*' chuckles Bruce. '*No chance here for you anyway,*' answers Ross, '*you know you've got Sam waiting.*'

134

Busting Banjul, capital of the Gambia –

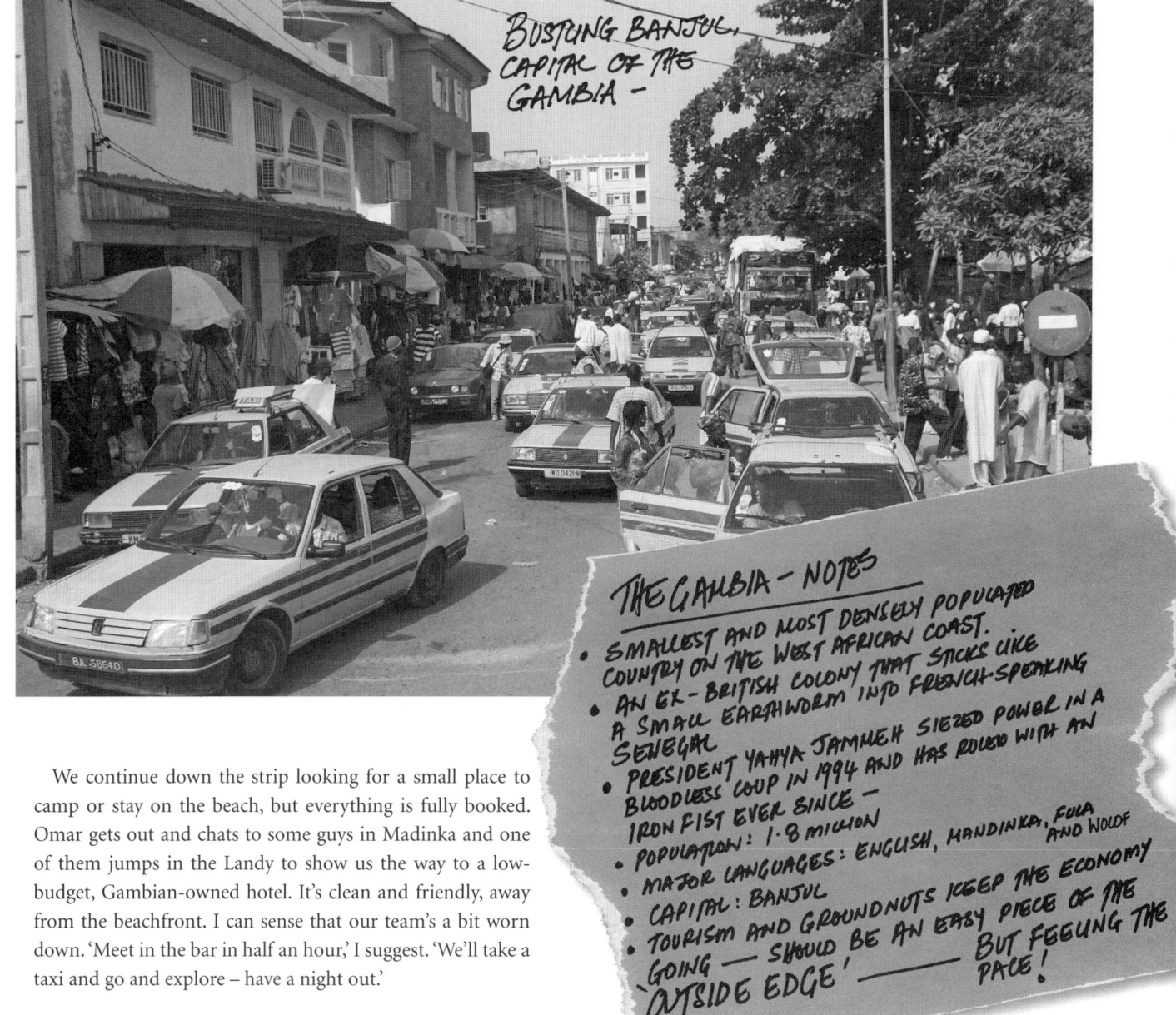

THE GAMBIA – NOTES
- SMALLEST AND MOST DENSELY POPULATED COUNTRY ON THE WEST AFRICAN COAST.
- AN EX-BRITISH COLONY THAT STICKS LIKE A SMALL EARTHWORM INTO FRENCH-SPEAKING SENEGAL
- PRESIDENT YAHYA JAMMEH SIEZED POWER IN A BLOODLESS COUP IN 1994 AND HAS RULED WITH AN IRON FIST EVER SINCE –
- POPULATION: 1.8 MILLION
- MAJOR LANGUAGES: ENGLISH, MANDINKA, FULA AND WOLOF
- CAPITAL: BANJUL
- TOURISM AND GROUNDNUTS KEEP THE ECONOMY GOING – SHOULD BE AN EASY PIECE OF THE 'OUTSIDE EDGE' –––––– BUT FEELING THE PACE!

We continue down the strip looking for a small place to camp or stay on the beach, but everything is fully booked. Omar gets out and chats to some guys in Madinka and one of them jumps in the Landy to show us the way to a low-budget, Gambian-owned hotel. It's clean and friendly, away from the beachfront. I can sense that our team's a bit worn down. 'Meet in the bar in half an hour,' I suggest. 'We'll take a taxi and go and explore – have a night out.'

Dispatch #128 – Chicken, Beer and Bumsters

All washed and scrubbed, in creased shirts and longs, we pile into two battered, rickety, green-and-yellow taxis. We've tried to look presentable, especially Bruce, who's admitted to wearing whatever smells the least. The ride is not expensive – it's just a few dalasies each for the delight of experiencing a nerve-wracking, bum-numbing, pothole-weaving, traffic-swerving, Senegalese music-blasting ride to the beachfront. 'There are tourist taxis,' says Omar, 'but it's better to take local ones like these – they're cheaper.' Omar is wonderful to have along; he's excellent company for Bruce, who's still a bit lovelorn, and has become a great friend and wonderful expedition team member, always adding local colour and information. He speaks six West African languages, his Sierra Leone English is delightful and he's great with malaria prevention work. Bruce is still teaching him a few words of

ARCH 22 - BUILT TO COMMEMORATE THE COUP OF 22ND JULY 1994

AFTER THE WILD STRETCHES OF COASTLINE, GAMBIA SEEMS A BIT TOURISTY FOR US - HEY, BUT ITS SAFE, ENGLISH-SPEAKING AND FRIENDLY -

Zulu and Omar greets me every morning now with a big grin and a '*wenzenjani*?' meaning 'what's happening?'. I just wish he could do the whole journey, but his West African travel permit and his available time will only allow him to travel with us as far as Dakar in Senegal, from where he'll have to take a bush taxi back to Conakry in Guinea. Omar has taught us a few Madinka words too; most Gambians speak Madinka and it's a common West African language. 'How are you all?' is '*ali be kayira to*?'; 'yes' is '*haa*', 'no' is '*hani*' and 'okay' is '*awaa*'; 'thank you very much' is '*abaraka baake*'; 'let's go' is '*ali nga taa*'; 'do you have any bananas?' is '*i ye banaanoo soto le bang*?'; and equally important is '*jelu le mu*?' or 'how much?'.

We put two tables together at a pavement restaurant. 'It's good and cheap,' says Omar, who's fallen in line with Mashozi's budget. The friendly waiter speaks English. 'We learn it in school,' he says. A musician strums a kora and sings sad ballads in Madinka. It seems odd to be surrounded by sunburnt tourists with London and Manchester accents swilling cold beer and G&Ts, whilst England's winter is just six hours away across the Atlantic. The bumsters are at work outside and Omar tells me that it's every family's dream that their out-of-work, out-of-school son should marry a foreigner, so bringing extra money to the family and village. Fit young Rasta bumsters chat up older European women for sex, money and a hopeful future. Foreign men easily find an attractive young prostitute; it's part of the Gambian scene.

136

White people in West Africa, says Omar, are called *toubab*. He thinks it's the corruption of the word for doctor or maybe it's from the English words 'two bob', meaning two shilling. We drink ice-cold, fairly strong Gambian lager called Julbrew. Ross and I each do a full chicken with chips and veggies – it's delicious. Bruce gets beef stroganoff and Mashozi, Anna and Omar go for English fish 'n chips. Mashozi even finds South African white wine on the menu.

We talk about the journey ahead; we have to be on the Saloum River in Senegal in three days' time where, together with Richard Nyberg from the United States Agency for International Development (USAID), we're planning a big malaria prevention event on the Bassoul Islands at the mouth of the river. In addition, Nando's will be flying in a celebrity chef to Dakar from the USA. It appears the guy staged a dinner where he raised 5 000 US dollars for mosquito nets, and now he's coming out to help distribute them and cook the expedition a celebratory meal. 'Let's get there a day early,' suggests Ross, 'so as to give ourselves time to set up base camp and prepare the inflatable boats.' It's a good call. Tomorrow we'll explore Gambia's short coastline and take the ferry from Banjul over the Gambia River – there's never enough time.

Dispatch #129 – Banjul and Across the River

'*Please photograph the cemetery,*' I ask Bruce over the radio. It's unusual to have so many graves right on the beach and there's this monstrous arch ahead. Mashozi pages through *The Rough Guide to West Africa*, our traveller's bible. 'It's called Arch 22,' she says, 'Banjul's monument to President Jammeh's regime.' We drive through the arch, a massive cream-coloured, freestanding monument that spans Independence Drive. Mashozi reads on, telling us that it was built to commemorate the coup of 22 July 1994. There's a great view of Banjul from the top, clearly showing its location on an island surrounded by ocean, river and mangroves. The top floor houses a display of ethnographic material and at the foot of the arch is a gilded statue of a soldier holding an infant, supposedly representing the rescue of the nation by the military coup.

In the days when the Gambia was a British colony Banjul used to be called Bathurst. It's still a bit English; the coastal road takes us past the Atlantic Hotel, the Royal Victoria Hospital, State House, the Albert Market on Russell Street and on to Liberation Street (formerly Wellington Street), where we wait in line at the busy ferry terminal, in the thick humidity and heat, hoping to cross the Gambia River before dark. We could write a book just on outside edge ferry crossings. This one has all the usual colourful, organised chaos and, of course, there are some military guys who push into the front of the queue and foreigners must pay in foreign currency. There's a big arch that inspires confidence, saying 'Welcome to the Banjul Ferry Terminal'. A pavement chophouse cooks us a bit of chicken, served with sweet potatoes and bananas over a charcoal grill. A Rasta man offers us grass. 'So sorry about Lucky Dube, mon. Too much crime in South Africa mon – I'll pray for you, brother,' he says.

The area is a colourful mass of trade happenings and there are chickens, goats, fish, sweet potatoes, groundnuts, bananas, beans, cheap sunglasses and shoes, and hawkers selling cold drinks and biscuits. There's also cooking oil, sugar, rice and plasticware. I feel sorry for a refugee from Sierra Leone. 'Been here nine years,' he says. 'Ran from the war – go back to what?' I buy a box of chocolate crunchies from him. Omar is getting pissed off. 'What's happening – when will we get to the other side?' he wants to know. I give him a smile, 'It's Africa my friend.' And so we wait, wait and wait. The tension grows; navy cops control the crowd, time marches on and people roll out their prayer mats. More hawkers come, this time it's an endless stream of belts, hats, CDs, DVDs, shirts, peeled oranges and cashew nuts. And then six hours later it happens; a siren goes and amidst a mad rush of buses, bush taxis, cars and lorries, we hit low ratio and ease the Landies in first gear up onto the already overloaded ferry. We lock them and climb onto the upper deck. 'What about the kit on the roof?' asks Bruce. 'Let the voodoo protection fetishes from Benin do their job,' I reply, 'I need some air.' And so we cross the Gambia River at last light.

I love these river crossings, they are so much part of the outside edge journey. A perfume seller in Islamic robes dabs a sample onto the back of travellers' hands. No one seems to mind, then he gives his spiel and sells a few bottles. The mud-brown river is wide and the tide is running; the lights of Banjul fade behind us as we roll off the ferry in the dark at the Barra terminus. The area is heavily populated and it's difficult to camp, so we decide to push on in the dark to the Gambian border post at Amdallai where, as usual, Omar does a great job with sorting out the paperwork. And so, for the second time in just a few days, we enter Senegal, this time north of the River Gambia through the border post at Karang. There's never a dull moment.

Back to Senegal

Dispatch #130 – Yoghurt with a Kick

Pretty cool border crossing – no black sun visor marks here. Across the River Gambia, it's out of English and back into French. Despite the fact that Senegal was France's oldest African colony, only about 20% of the population understand French and the main language remains Wolof. Over the radio Omar tries to teach us all a bit. The standard greeting is pretty easy and is the same throughout Islamic Africa, '*assalām 'alaikum*', meaning 'peace be upon you' with the response of '*wa 'alaikum assalām*', 'and upon you be peace'. Then we get into the slightly more difficult stuff like '*jàmm nga am*?' and '*mangi fi rekk*' meaning 'how are you?' and 'I am fine'. 'What's your name?' is '*naka nga tudd*?', 'I'm going/goodbye' is '*mangi dem*' and, probably the most important, '*jërëjëf*' is 'thank you'.

White dust, yellow grass, ancient baobabs, mud huts with conical thatched roofs, mule-drawn, two-wheel buggies called *calèches*, battered overloaded Peugeot 504 *taxi-brousses*, brightly coloured old Mercedes-Benz minibus taxis and villagers in the fields reaping groundnuts all make up the colourful Gambia–Kaolack road. The mind-numbing humidity of the Gulf of Guinea is behind us now; here it's more of a dry heat. We dodge the *calèches* into Kaolack; we need to fuel up and get supplies. It's a crowded, hot, windy, dusty Islamic market town with a beautiful mosque said to have been funded by Saddam Hussein. Mashozi finds a Lebanese-owned general store; in West Africa they're always the best and sell everything, even the odd under-the-counter bottle. She waits her turn to be served behind a robed man who looks around furtively and whispers to the Leb behind the counter who, in turn, fetches a cardboard tray of what looks like plastic yoghurt containers. There are more whispers, money changes hands, the goods are quickly loaded into the boot of the man's Peugeot and he speeds off into the dust. Mashozi raises her eyebrows. 'It's a good line,' says the Lebanese storekeeper in a pommie accent. 'Cheap gin or whiskey disguised as yoghurt for those who don't want to be seen to drink.'

We head for Foundiougne on the south bank of the Saloum River where we're going to set up an expedition base camp for a joint USAID–One Net One Life malaria prevention exercise down the river to the delta islands of Bassoul, joined, can you believe it, by an American celebrity chef and his team who are catching a ride with the USAID team from Dakar – there's never a dull moment. Apart from the geographic challenge to track the outside edge, we must remain true to the ideal of using this adventure to improve and save lives.

Dispatch #131 – Down the Saloum

We rent a rustic French expat cottage on the banks of the Saloum River just outside the dusty village of Foundiougne. Two French ex-legionnaires are booking out, complete with fishing rods and a group of sexy Senegalese girls – the men are returning to Dakar and then on to France. 'It's no life. Europe is shit, we miss Africa,' says one of the men. 'And how is South Africa?' 'Good,' I reply, 'good.' '*Bonne chance!*' he shouts, as they roar off into the dust Dakar Rally-style in a battered yellow Land Cruiser. Genevieve, the lovely Senegalese caretaker, and her family are wonderful. She speaks French and we've got Omar to translate.

The next day, early morning, Mashozi and Anna get to work sorting out boat supplies. I go into the village to get some more boat fuel and drinking water. Ross, Omar and

Bruce take the other two Landies down to the water's edge to prepare the boats. I get back to find the two big 6-metre-long Gemini inflatables floating again, each with their 30 HP Yamaha Enduros bolted onto the transoms. We'd last used them in the Bijagós Archipelago off Guinea-Bissau. We load fuel, drinking water and supplies. The team from Dakar, together with members of the local health authorities, is ready and waiting upstream for us with a 12-metre long local pirogue loaded with 15 bales of long-lasting, insecticide-treated mosquito nets.

Things are looking good – it's great when a plan comes together. We've contacted Richard Nyberg, the leader of the Dakar team, to tell him we're on our way. Then comes the embarrassment. Ross's Landy goes down to both diffs, it's like sinking sand and the incoming tide is pushing fast. Bruce slowly moves in with the Stomach; first letting the tyres down to 1 bar, he spools out the winch cable. Ready, steady, go! Down Bruce goes; the heavy 130 onto its belly, completely stuck. Smoke billows from the winch and there's the smell of burnt electrics – it's cooked! Richard phones to find out where the hell we are, and I quickly explain our predicament. 'You mean you've come all the way following the coastline from Cape Town and you can't get your backsides off the banks of the Saloum?' he says in his American accent. 'Must go, see you shortly,' I answer.

We bring in the third Landy and join all three with snatch ropes: one, two, three, go! They won't budge. Ross's Landy is sinking fast, the rising tide now a metre from his rear wheels. Oh shit! Imagine losing them now, it will probably mean the end of the expedition. Hardly a word is spoken. The team sweat with the exertion and in minutes everything is offloaded from Ross's Landy, including everything on the roof racks. It's at least a tonne of kit – even the spare wheels and fuel jerry cans come off. Now the water's lapping against the back wheels. We deflate the tyres to 1 bar all round, two long planks from the wreck of an old fishing boat are dug in under the front wheels and mud ladders under the back. We know we'll have only one more chance at this and then the tide will take us – how bloody embarrassing! More air is let out of Bruce's tyres, the mud is dug away from under the diffs and a longer snatch rope is tied onto my Landy, which is still on dry ground. The river is washing against the rear wheels. The tide is coming up fast; it's a race against time.

SENEGAL IS CERTAINLY TOURIST FRIENDLY

AT THIS STAGE WE'VE STILL GOT TIME ON OUR HANDS – AND THEN THE TIDE COMES RACING IN AND WE NEARLY LOSE A LANDY –

We unload the Stomach – now there's a mountain of kit up on the beach. The back Landy's exhaust is gurgling under water. Radios on, Ross, Bruce and I get behind our steering wheels. Ross's voice comes through, '*Good luck guys. Second gear, low-range difflock. One, two, three, GO!*' We drop the clutches. There's that chassis-jarring whiplash of the kinetic tightening of the snatch rope. '*Go! Go! Go!*' comes Ross's radio voice. Mashozi claps her hands above her head and ululates like a Zulu, and there's the burning smell of Land Rover clutches. Slowly and agonisingly, like pulling a reluctant tooth, we free ourselves from the sucking, gooey clutches of the rising tide of the Saloum River. 'Shit, that was close,' says Bruce, who like all of us is covered from head to toe in mud.

The illustrious chef Wilbert Jones from Chicago is very American. He's never been to West Africa or on an inflatable boat before and has got his older, female chaperone with him. 'Please do your best; he's quite a celebrity. He gave a dinner party and raised money for mosquito nets,' says Rachelle, the easy-to-get-on-with South African girl from Nando's who's put the whole thing together. 'I hope you've brought him lunch,' she adds. 'Goat, snake or fish?' I ask pointing to a dented aluminium pot with sandwiches inside. Mashozi glares at me, but I was joking about the snake. Ross is in the other Gemini with Bruce, Anna and Omar. Richard Nyberg, a really friendly easy-going fellow, is in the big pirogue with the health authorities.

The wind has come up and we're all getting splashed. 'Put your windcheater on, Wilbert,' says the chaperone as we hit the sharp edge of an incoming wave and he almost bounces off the pontoon into the delta. Mashozi shows him where to sit and how to hold on – she's good that way. 'Kingsley,' says Wilbert the chef, 'dyaa mind if we drink some o' that dark 'n foamy rum Rachelle told me about?' I shout to Ross – he's got the cool box. Out comes a bottle and rolling with the boat it gets poured into dented enamel mugs and Coke is added – only one drink each, we're here to work. The tension eases and Wilbert Jones starts to relax. The delta is beautiful as we snake through the narrows between the mangroves.

Dignitaries and mums from the five island villages are there to meet us, each village community dressed up in their specific colours. What a wonderful day: there's traditional dancing and singing, malaria education and a life-saving net for every single mother. Wilbert shakes hands with the mums and smiles. Ross films, Bruce takes stills and I do my Zulu foot-stomping, beard-waggling jig. As usual, Anna and Mashozi do a great job of distributing the nets. The USAID team handle all the protocol. 'We hear about it on the radio, or read about it on the news, but this humanitarian help never usually reaches us,' says the village president. 'Now for the first time people come from Dakar, from America and all the way from South Africa to help us fight malaria.' The musicians beat their calabash drums and the mamas dance with the nets. With a pebble in my pocket, we're doing what we came to do.

That night there are rattles and djembe drums and traditional dancing and singing around the fire. Music is what Senegal does best. 'It's a slave dish,' says Wilbert of the food he's prepared. 'Black-eyed beans served with sweet potatoes and wild spinach.' I take my hat off to him – this famous man who's travelled a great distance to help others and on an open fire has cooked our humble team a celebratory meal at a place on the Saloum River that most people have never heard

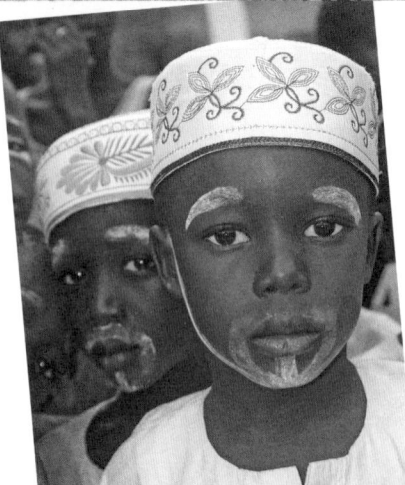

WHAT A GREAT DAY AT THE MOUTH OF THE SALOUM RIVER. SINGING AND DANCING, USING THE ADVENTURE TO IMPROVE LIVES –

of. It's delicious. We're early to bed, stiff and sore from the morning battle to free the Landies. Chef Wilbert Jones adds these words to the scroll:

11 Nov 2007 – What an adventure – I love watching Discovery Channel in America, but now I can tell everyone about the real thing.

Dispatch #132 – South African Hospitality

We reach bustling Dakar by way of Djifer, Palmarin, Nianing, Mbour and Rufisque, the route a mixture of fishing villages, baobabs and tourist-trap beaches. Then we get to the hooting, jostling commercial sprawl of hustlers and vendors; slums and smart, white-painted, South-of-France-look-alike villas; restaurants, markets, bars, clubs, hotels and beaches; and music, soccer and wrestling matches that make up Senegal's three-million-strong capital and one of the most liveable cities on Africa's west coast.

Never have we known such hospitality from our fellow South Africans. Led by Derrick Williams from the embassy and his family and friends, we are welcomed by the waving of a South African flag and a gift of biltong and Amarula. Their kindness and appreciation for what we are attempting to achieve is quite overwhelming. We get invited to a real South African braai. There's André Jacobs, the eccentric councillor at the embassy, Piet Bosduif from Benoni, who's famous in Dakar for his *boerewors*, Steven and beautiful Mariana who cook up a real hot Durban curry and the Van Zyl family who, concerned for our wellbeing, buy us sacks of vegetables for the road ahead and lend us a driver and a vehicle to carry extra bales of mosquito nets towards the Sénégal River. The next day we meet lovely Thembi Majola, South African Ambassador to Senegal, Cape Verde, Mauritania, Guinea-Bissau and the Gambia. She writes these words in the scroll:

> *To my fellow compatriots. Your epic journey along the coast of Africa to bring awareness and physically to distribute treated mosquito nets to expectant mothers and mothers with babies up to five years is clearly a noble act … a very personal experience that has touched many people in a most direct, personal life-saving way. I salute this noble expedition and want to express my deep respect and pride in the humanitarian work you are achieving at a great deal of personal cost. I wish you Godspeed on your journey, and am proud that you fly the South African flag, representing South African resilience, a caring spirit and a will to succeed. Hambani kahle!*

SOUTH AFRICAN AMBASSADOR THEMBI MAJOLA — SHE MAKES US PROUD —

Dakar is free and easy with great food and music and a relatively safe environment. It's no wonder that it has replaced Abidjan as the French expat centre of West Africa. There's also a buzz around the forthcoming Dakar Rally, which this year is leaving from Lisbon in Portugal.

Dispatch #133 – Africa's Most Westerly Point

Dakar is situated on the double-pronged Cap Vert Peninsula. The southern spur contains the heart of the city, with cliffs and coves running along the coast and Cap Manuel and the main port area situated along the more sheltered eastern side. The other prong is called Pointe des Almadies, and that's where we're heading. We're now carrying another scroll, this one from South African National Parks with a message encouraging a conservation partnership with its neighbours in Africa, as well as the three stones which were taken from Cape Agulhas, the southernmost tip of Africa. At a ceremony facilitated by the South African Embassy, we place a stone and pick up another at des Almadies, the most westerly point of Africa. That's the official dispatch – truth is we were expecting a wild, rocky, uninhabited Atlantic point, but in Africa things are rarely what you expect. Imagine our surprise when

WE REACH AFRICA'S MOST WESTERLY POINT NEAR DAKAR —

Derrick Williams and the delightful team of South Africans escort us past the reception, swimming pool, lawns and near-nude bathers of a Club Med situated on Africa's westerly tip, or should I say nipple. 'Eyes straight ahead,' I caution the team, as with our South African flag and Cape Agulhas rock we step over and around near-naked, sun-bronzed bodies and out onto Africa's most westerly point. The manager of the club buys us drinks in the pool bar and endorses the expedition scroll with a flourish of:

Bon courage, bonne chance, bonne continuation and good luck!

Dispatch #134 – Place of Dreams and Legends

We park the Landies and take the chaloupe from the ferry station off Boulevard de la Libération near the beautiful old art deco, French-colonial railway station. Just 20 minutes out into the Atlantic, we get our first sighting of the colourful historic slave-trading island of Île de Gorée. Just 900 metres long by 300 metres wide, it's now a UNESCO World Heritage Site. In the north is Fort d'Estrées, perched on top of a high, sheer basalt cliff face, below which is a little town of time-worn, pastel-coloured old colonial buildings, draped with bougainvillea and shaded with palm trees and giant baobabs.

We round the stone-built castle in the south and tie up at the jetty near a small, sandy beach. There's a wonderful buzz; the Île de Gorée art and music festival is on the go to the sounds of djembe drums, blues, jazz and rap. Attractive girls in braided hair and tight jeans mingle with Rasta men in colourful ethnic outfits and there's the smell of ganja in the cobblestoned alleyways.

The Portuguese were the first to use the island as a trading base in the mid-15th century. Dutch adventurers captured it in 1588, naming it *Goede Reede*, meaning 'good roadstead'. The Portuguese regained control but lost it to the French in 1678. Thereafter the island was repeatedly captured and recaptured in war games between the French and the English, who were intent on controlling the trade in spices and humans. Today Gorée remains a place of dreams and legends, dotted with batteries and canons – vestiges of the battles that shook the island.

We wander through the cobbled streets past the old colonial buildings that once belonged to slave traders, merchantmen and administrators. Some were slave warehouses and others were residences, home to love affairs between famous historical figures who were not allowed to bring their wives to Senegal and beautiful slave girls who were called *signares,* from the Portuguese word *senhora*, meaning 'lady' or 'dame'. These love affairs led to a golden age in which the *signares* of Gorée, daughters of white colonists and slave women, controlled much of the wealth and power on the tiny slave-trading island.

There's more ganja in the air and row upon row of stretched canvases of colourful Senegalese art interspersed with market stalls and mamas selling beads, baubles, bracelets, colourful cloth and clothing. Up near the top of the hill we find Rasta families and artists living in the old gun emplacements and bunkers. One particularly colourful character, quite stoned, has a tame monkey called Booboo. There's the soft, low whistle of circling yellow-billed kites overhead. We see big, white tethered goats with twisted horns and long, elongated testicles and cats of every description at every corner. Glancing into courtyards through narrow doorways, we see families squatting around basins of rice, fish or goat meat and eating with their fingers; they are smiling and happy and there's music playing.

Down at the jetty the music continues. Île de Gorée is a place of happiness and, unlike the other Gates of No Return places we have visited on the west coast's outside edge, its colourful inhabitants seem more intent on celebrating the present than crying over the past. Back in Dakar, it's our last night in Senegal. With our new-found South African friends, we all gather at a humble restaurant overlooking the Atlantic. Musicians sing and play xylophones, drums and rattles, and the moonlight dances on the ocean. Tomorrow we follow the coast north to St-Louis and Mauritania.

Dispatch #135 – The Road to Mauritania

We loved Dakar but as always it's good to be on the move again, following the outside edge. It's also a sad time as we say cheers to Omar – he's become a great friend and we'll miss him sorely. He hugs us all warmly and cries a little. We're fellow pilgrims of the road with shared adventures that we'll remember for the rest of our lives. North out of the city we make our way to Lac Retba, also known as Lac Rose. This is Senegal's version of the Dead Sea, a photogenic setting of women salt gatherers on a pink soda lake. Then it's the familiar outside edge, tyres down to 1 bar over the dunes and onto the beach for the 200-odd-kilometre journey to St-Louis. It's complete freedom again – wide open beach – the Landies humming along at 60 kilometres per hour, with Ross and Anna leading, followed by Mashozi and me, and then Bruce. There are villages and scores of brightly coloured fishing boats, baskets of fish coming off the beach, and colourfully dressed mamas sitting in groups buying from the catch. Mule-drawn carts laden with silver fish move between the boats and still they're going out for more – it's a bonanza. A boat flips in the large waves and people rush to help. They turn it back over, clean the outboard and give it another go – their boat skills are excellent.

We set up a base camp on the southern tip of the peninsula near the Hydrobase, an old staging post used by seaplanes operating the early airmail service between Europe and South America. The city of St-Louis covers a piece of mainland coast at the mouth of the Sénégal River, which is linked by bridges to N'dar Island and a long spit of land that makes up the opposite bank called the Langue de Barbarie Peninsula.

THE EDGE OF THE ISLAND OF GORÉE

NEAR ST-LOUIS – THE PILCHARDS ARE RUNNING. IT'S A PROTEIN BONANZA

WE FOLLOW THE BEACH FROM DAKAR TO ST-LOUIS

Being in St-Louis, with its faded colonial buildings, colourful fishing boats, horse traps and blue-and-white-robed Wolof who look like they've stepped out of the Sahel, is like reliving an old French-West-African movie. It's the oldest French settlement in West Africa and until 1958 it was the capital of Senegal and Mauritania. Like Gorée, it too is a UNESCO World Heritage Site. We have the Atlantic on the one side, and the mouth of the Sénégal River on the other. Camping in the dunes, we are lit by just a small fire on the edge of a mysterious continent.

North of St-Louis on the road to Mauritania, with the help of the Ministry of Health, we distribute the last of our West African supply of mosquito nets to schools and orphanages together with Rite to Sight spectacles for the aged. Africa's high-risk malaria belt is behind us now. The One Net One Life campaign will begin again in earnest on the east coast of Africa, where extra malaria warrior volunteers and vehicles will come in to support the campaign and the almost daily challenge of fighting malaria.

There's a lot of activity planned around the week of Africa Malaria Day on 25 April in Mombasa, Kenya. That's a good few weeks and 12 countries away, and there's no guarantee we'll make it. Sitting around the fire that night I ask the following question: 'Was the West African malaria campaign worthwhile? With all the day-to-day effort and planning, the loading and unloading of bales of nets, broken roof racks, dealing with boats and lorries, the sweat and the crowds, the manic pendulum that swings from desperate poverty and sadness to jubilation and fun, and all the media effort of the journalists, radio, TV and press, was it all worth it?'

In sending the clear and simple message to mums and mums-to-be that to avoid getting malaria they and their children must sleep under an insecticide-treated mosquito net, tens of thousands of lives have been kept safe. So was it worth it? Of course it was. Mauritania here we come.

Mauritania

Day 209, Country 20 on the Edge

The République Islamique de Mauritanie covers more than a million square kilometres, a third of which is known as Zone Vide – the Empty Quarter. It's not surprising that it's a country with one of the lowest population densities in the world. Our plan is to use the beach where the world's greatest desert is washed by the North Atlantic as our 1 268-kilometre outside edge highway. Memories of the Namib are still fresh in our minds.

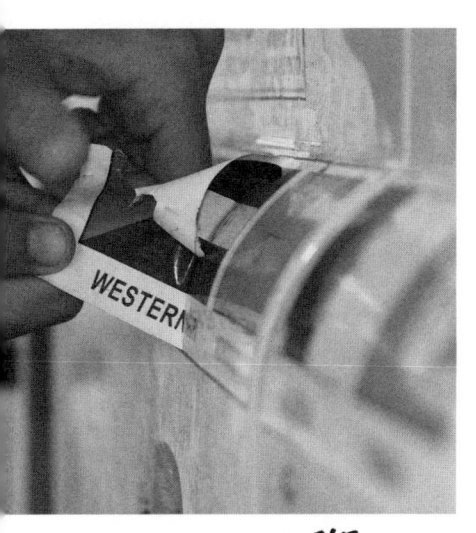

PEELING OFF THE WESTERN SAHARA STICKERS – WE'LL REPLACE THEM LATER.

Dispatch #136 – Nouakchott, Place of Winds

Across the Sénégal River into Mauritania and we're caught in a sandstorm; sand in the hair, eyes, mouth, nose, ears and beard. Sand in the food and in the bottom of our battered enamel mugs of early morning coffee. Sand in the canvas bedrolls and in the engine oil. But no sand in the Captain Morgan – sadly, it's all gone. Booze is not allowed here, in fact it's strictly forbidden. Bruce says even our faithful, secret tank is empty.

We're following the outside edge of the Islamic Republic of Mauritania where the wind-blown sands of the Sahara are arrested by the North Atlantic. After the storm it is unimaginably beautiful; the dunes have been washed smooth by the wind. At night, around the fire, the stars shine brightly down on us and we hear the distant cry of jackal. Balaclavas, beanies, socks and jackets – the freezing desert nights bring back memories of Namibia's Skeleton Coast, but that's 18 outside edge countries and seven months ago. In the early morning, with not another person in sight, we gather around the Landies to peel off the Western Saharan flags which represent the next country up the coast. The Sahrawi Arab Democratic Republic, or Western Sahara, has been annexed by Morocco and the flying of its flag has been outlawed.

On the low tide thousands of seabirds rise like clouds in front of the three expedition Landies. Wild camels on the dune tops, also following the outside edge, are silhouetted against the sun. We pass big men in blue robes and white turbans riding up the coast at low tide in old Landies. Foot flat in third and fourth, engines growling against the headwind and sand, we finally crawl into Nouakchott, capital of Mauritania. The muezzin's call to prayer has the blue-robed men gathering outside the Grande Mosquée, also known as *Mosquée Saudique,* as it was built by the Saudis. Old 190 Mercedes-Benz diesel taxis hoot for business; the drivers, in turbans and

THE SAHARA — GREATEST DESERT OF THEM ALL.

MAURITANIA - NOTES
- ALCOHOL IS ILLEGAL / FORTUNATELY THERE'S NOT MUCH CAPTAIN LEFT IN THE SECRET TANK —
- OFFICIAL LANGUAGE IS HASSANIYA ARABIC
- THE CURRENCY IS THE OUGUIYA
- THE CAPITAL IS NOUAKCHOTT.
- AN 'ERG' IS A DISTRICT OF SHIFTING SAND DUNES AND A 'BARCHAN' IS A MOVING CRESCENT-SHAPED DUNE WITH A CHARACTERISTIC CREST — THE CHALLENGE OF THE SAHARA COAST IS AHEAD OF US / WE'LL FIND OUT!
- FEMALE CIRCUMCISION IS STILL PRACTISED IN THE SOUTH —— THE BEACH AND THE SAHARA DUNES WILL BE 'OUR HIGHWAY' —

OUTSIDE NOUAKCHOTT

sunglasses, drive as if they are wandering on camels through the desert with no thought to indicating or hand signals.

We ask a blue-robed pedestrian for directions and he shrinks back from us as if we were the devil. 'Americans,' he mumbles to another aggressively. '*Afrique du Sud. Janub Efrekia*,' we say our origin in two languages, proudly pointing to the South African flags on the Land Rover bonnets and then uttering the trademark bywords 'Nelson Mandela' and 'Bafana Bafana'. The mood changes and we're ushered into the Lebanese-owned *Le Prince* restaurant for the biggest shawarma and chip sandwiches you've ever seen. Nouakchott in the local Arabic Hassaniya language means 'place of winds', an apt name for a city that is *sjamboked* by sandstorms for more than 200 days a year. Maybe it's a good thing, because when the wind stops the bloody flies come out.

Dispatch #137 – The Fleas of a Thousand Camels

In all our years of travel we've never been so badly treated at an embassy. The humiliation is like a kick in the stomach. Despite the fact that we have an appointment with the Moroccan ambassador himself, and that his embassy had already been contacted by both the Moroccan and South African embassies from Dakar and been given all the details of our humanitarian and geographic journey, it seems to mean nothing. Something has gone terribly wrong. We're kept waiting for two hours whilst the staff inside smirk and drink tea, glaring at us from time to time through the open door. The message is clear: the Moroccans at their embassy here in Nouakchott do not want anything to do with us. All of a sudden the ambassador is conveniently 'not in the country' for nine days and the door is closed in our faces.

I go back down to the receptionist. I can sense she's embarrassed. Finally I get someone who'll speak English – yes, they know about our journey, but have got strict instructions not to grant us visas for Morocco. As the Moroccans occupy Western Sahara, this embassy holds the keys to not one but two countries on our outside edge path, and the refusal extends to both. I pull out all the stops – the Mandela-endorsed Scroll of Peace and Goodwill, press clippings and letters of introduction in French and Arabic. They won't even look at them. 'Go back to South Africa; get your visas there. There's nothing we can do for you,' they say. The situation is getting tense and I can tell we're about to get thrown out. I gather up my things. 'Thank you. Have a nice day,' I say, holding my hand to my heart, Arab style, all the while thinking 'the fleas of a thousand camels upon you – you rude shits'.

I see the looks on the team's faces; to remain true to our outside edge challenge we have to be able to follow the coast from Mauritania up through Western Sahara and Morocco, all of which needs a Moroccan visa. We're all gobsmacked. After having come so far and achieved so much, is this now the end of the journey for us?

Dispatch #138 – Never Say Die

We need to find a base camp where we can have time to think. '*There's a place called Terjit Camping, it's in the guidebook. Seems the Dakar Rally crowd use it – it's a sort of 4x4 overlander's camp*,' says Anna over the radio. It turns out to be a collection of thatched huts on a windblown stretch of beach just outside the capital, next to the fish market – ideal for an emergency base camp. With carpets and mattresses on the floor inside our new home, desert style, we sit in a circle eating bits of fatty, bony lamb and couscous with our fingers. 'What now,' asks Ross, 'what are the options? Let's first try the official routes.' He sets up the satellite phone outside. The first call is to Derrick Williams at our embassy in Dakar. He's done so much for us in the past but now can do no more. 'We've hit a brick wall,' he says. Next call is to Charl Möller in Rabat, Morocco. 'I'll come straight to the point,' says Charl. 'Diplomatically, South Africa is out of favour here for supporting Western Sahara's bid to get their country back from Morocco. The fact that you are a South African expedition, which will be coming out of Mauritania in South-African-registered vehicles, has already come to the ears of Moroccan security. They're edgy. The problem is that with all the high-profile humanitarian work you've been doing they think you'll try and make contact with the poor Sahrawi people, who are agitating for a settlement. It's a cold war with most of the Sahrawis in exile in refugee camps deep in the Sahara. It's not a good situation – you're just in the wrong place at the wrong time. Your expedition has become too prominent and if we keep on pushing you'll be totally banned from coming in.'

I come back inside and give the information to my small circle of adventure pilgrims. There's a shocked silence – we're overcome with disappointment. Do we move with all our kit back to Dakar, leave it there, close down the expedition, all go back home for Christmas, apply for clean passports and apply to fly to Morocco as normal tourists, then come back here and give it another shot? 'Too expensive, we don't have the budget,' says Mashozi like a true expedition bursar. 'And what about detouring through Algeria and then coming in through the top?' offers Bruce, looking at the map. 'Can't work,' replies Ross. 'Word has it that the Algerian–Moroccan border is closed. Seems there's been some terrorist activity and on top of that Morocco's pissed off with Algeria for supporting Western Sahara's claims for independence too – it's a mess.' 'What about one of us flying from here to the UK with all the passports and applying for tourist visas from there?' suggests Mashozi. 'A good idea,' says Ross, 'but if the embassy sees the Mauritanian stamps in our passports and knows we were right here, they could smell a rat.'

We're frustrated and in need of some lateral thinking. Some would call it a need to get pissed. Bruce confirms once again that the Captain in the secret tank is finished. 'Hey Bruce, try racing the Landy up a nearby dune to increase the angle,' says Ross. 'See if you can't squeeze out a few drops. Pretend you're working underneath the vehicle whilst we keep on brainstorming.' He comes back later covered in sand, his head wrapped in an Arab scarf with only his eyes showing, and plonks down a transparent plastic water bottle that's three-quarter filled with a dark liquid, which with all the heat and sloshing around has become thick and treacly. As we sit in our little thatched hut behind closed doors with another sandstorm beginning to rage outside, the liquid remedy in an enamel mug with some Coke is quite delicious, and quite illegal. 'Who needs to go home the most?' I ask. 'If we had to choose one of the team to go back to South Africa, who should it be?' 'It should be Ross,' says Mashozi, 'he needs to see little Tristan and he's good at sorting out these things.'

The decision is made. We phone Derrick Williams in Dakar and they organise a cheap flight to Joburg. It's all hush-hush and this time we're going under the radar. Anna is sad to see Ross go – they've fallen deeply in love. With all our passports, clean-shaven in long trousers and a collared shirt and with a small rucksack on his back, Ross takes the connecting flight from Nouakchott to Dakar. The future of the expedition lies in his capable hands – it's a huge responsibility. Back at Terjit the camp seems empty without him.

Dispatch #139 – The Waiting Game

We sit it out at Terjit and wait. There's the monotony of heat, flies, wind and sandstorms, but it's an opportunity to write up these notes in the journal:

Each day starts with the kettle on the gas ring – coffee for Bruce and Anna, Twinnings, milk, no sugar for Mashozi (from her secret stash) and black Rooibos for me. The talk is about our current situation. What if Ross can't sort out the visas? What if the Mauritanian authorities find us here with no passports? What if Ross fails to get a visa back into Mauritania? What if Ross succeeds but the Moroccans smell a rat, and even with visas we're not allowed into Western Sahara? What if … what if … what if …? There's no roaming on our cellphones here, so we rely on a daily fixed-time satellite phone call to Ross. He's been delayed in Dakar where Derrick Williams is helping with important paperwork. He flies to Joburg tomorrow – hold thumbs! The tension is getting to me. I walk on the beach, barefoot on the low tide on the edge of the Sahara with the wind tugging at my beard, a cloud of dust over Nouakchott and brightly coloured Senegalese fishing boats anchored against the breeze. We can't abort the expedition – we've been through so much.

We do our afternoon jaunt into Nouakchott to buy a cooked chicken with rice, chips, salad and bread from the Lebanese. Called 'chop chop', it's all packed together. It's great value and the yellow dog in camp called Duke, which Mashozi has adopted, loves the bones and leftovers. It's close to prayer time and hundreds of men in blue robes, sunglasses and turbans hang around the Grande Mosquée drinking mint tea, smoking cigarettes and shisha pipes, playing cards or just talking, spitting and twiddling their worry beads. Their robes are flowing, voluminous affairs with kangaroo-type pouches in front for cigarettes and cellphones; much of their time, it appears, is taken up in constantly rearranging the metres of cloth that enfolds them. Collectively, they look rather like a whole lot of Roman film extras in a Julius Caesar movie, waiting to be called onto set.

As Westerners, we're largely ignored. The Dakar Rally comes through here; it starts again shortly and they're used to seeing colourfully branded off-road-looking 4x4s. But that's not the case with the black Africans who request help, money and lifts. Visitors to Mauritania like us, they're from Senegal, Ghana, Burkina Faso and Nigeria. Most of the manual work here is done by black Africans; young men on the move, learning French and skills and slowly working their way up, with or without papers, all with the one objective of somehow getting to Europe. There are even some poor fellows from Liberia, leapfrogging north, country to country. 'You been to Liberia, Monrovia?' they ask. 'We ran, brother, we ran from the war. Got here as refugees, now we working like slaves. No muney to get back home, but to get home, what for? Families all been killed, property taken. We need to get to Europe.' Incredibly, a master-slave mentality still exists in this country and it was only in July 1980 that slavery was officially abolished.

South of Avenue Gamal Abdul Nasser the stalls of the Marché Capitale are piled high with the flowing blue dra'as that the men wear and the colourful malahfas worn by the women. The sandy lanes of the food market, the Marché Cinquiéme, are a kaleidoscope of fish sellers, homemade peanut-butter vendors, and sheep and goat sellers. There are also colourful pieces of cloth; pots and pans; plastic basins and buckets; fruit and vegetables from Senegal; camel saddles and carpets; and donkey carts and dented cars. On the corner are fully armed police officers; there's an ongoing battle here between the light-skinned Hassaniyan Arab population and the black-skinned Mauritanians in the south.

In the late afternoon, after prayers, our base camp out at Terjit becomes a bit of a lover's lane. Wealthy Arabs, dressed in their robes, cruise along in their smart 4x4s, silver Mercedes-Benzes and black BMWs with delightfully feminine girls in their colourful malahfas. The amorous couples walk on the beach and paddle in the waves. Once the sun goes down the laughter and giggles increase with more than a cuddle. But if they're going to taste the fruits of love on the dune outside our hut, I wish they wouldn't leave their banana peels behind.

We get a cryptic call from Ross from Joburg. The passport work is done and they have been submitted to the Moroccan Embassy together with the necessary paperwork. We'll know the result in five days' time. We go back to Rue Alioune, the good and cheap fast-food street. We try Ali Baba's – it's got a Nigerian cook named Care who speaks good English. He's a young welterweight boxer, desperately trying to get to Europe. He cooks us steak, egg and greasy chips and serves it with fresh bread. 'How's life in Nouakchott?' I ask. 'Tough,' comes the reply, 'I'm black and Christian.' We laugh. 'Where do you get a drink?' I ask. 'Easy,' he says, 'ask any taxi for the VIP Club. Whiskey and girls; it's even got a disco. Even in Nouakchott, my friend, people are people.'

We sit out on the small veranda eating and watching the men in robes float by. Mashozi suddenly puts down her knife and fork. 'Whose is that?' she asks, pointing at a small daypack that's lying unattended in the corner and that's been there since we sat down. 'Let's get out of here!' Care comes running out. 'Don't worry,' he says, picking it up. 'I know who forgot

Mashozi in a nomad's tent – our expedition base camp at Cap Tagarit.

The team on top of a dune

Then we get a message from Derrick Williams in Dakar. Ross has been trying to get hold of us; he's leaving at 2 a.m. tomorrow by road from Dakar via St-Louis with a driver, and we must meet them at the Rosso border. We leave Bruce to look after the camp and race through the desert, Anna, Mashozi and I in one Landy. We park outside the big, blue military security gates close to the northern bank of the Sénégal River; men in uniforms and guns want us to move on. I'm so busy concentrating, trying to explain that I want to park where I can be seen as I'm picking somebody up, that I hardly notice the top of a child's head at my window. I think it's another street urchin begging, with a cut-open tin can, as is the custom. And then there's a familiar little voice that gladdens our hearts. 'Hi Pops! I'm back on expedition.' It's little Tristan followed by Ross and Mama in his flowing robes, turban, sunglasses and cigarette – the man who'd helped us across the border 12 days ago. 'Hello Father,' he says, giving me a big hug. 'I brought you Ross and the small boy.' Inside the Landy Ross passes me my passport and gives me a wink. Inside is a Moroccan visa. *Halala*! The effort is worthy of congratulations. We're back on expedition!

Dispatch #140 – Back on the Edge

Closer to Nouakchott Ross gets on the radio. *'Hi Bruce, we've got the visas! Pack up camp; we'll catch the low tide.'* It's a wonderful feeling. With the tyres down to 1 bar and all the water and diesel tanks full, we ride the tide north, determined as always to follow the outside edge. Here it's all about fishing villages on the beach, camels in the desert, windstorms, bitterly cold nights and the beauty of the Sahara. We carry on past Cap Timiris, around the massive Bay of Saint John, or *Baie de Saint Jean*, with the barren sandstone islands of Cheddid, Touffat, Kiji and Tidra to our left. At Cap Tagarit we sleep, out of the wind, in a desert nomad's tent on hard mattresses on the floor. We eat lamb and fish on the coals and drink small glasses of sweet tea. There's not a footprint on the beach. This area is part of a protected desert coast park called the Blanc d'Arguin National Park – it's a paradise for aquatic birds. Mashozi's been digging for something in the back of the food drawer – it lands with a thud on the Sahara sand. We can't believe it, all the way from the Ashanti King in Ghana, it's the bottle of schnapps he'd given us. 'I'd clean forgotten about it,' she says. 'Cheers, your majesty!' says Ross, pouring

it here.' 'It was just a feeling,' says Mashozi, 'crazy I know. It's just the way some of the people look at us, I thought it could be a bomb.' She's right, there is some hatred for Westerners here; it's a country with some strong Iraqi affiliations. Since 9/11 we live in a changed world. Nouakchott and the waiting game at Terjit are getting the better of us.

us a tot each and raising a mug. After all the stress we've been under the bottle cheers us up no end.

The next morning Ross sets a course on the Garmin GPS as 20° 20' 23" N and 16° 15' 2" W. Tristan, chewing fatty biltong from home, sits on his dad's lap. He's learning to steer. We're trying to follow a coastal track through the Sahara but the windblown sands have obliterated any signs. There's a feeling of wild freedom – just three battered Landies and a little expedition team against the backdrop of the largest desert in the world.

Dispatch #141 – Nouadhibou

Out of the desert, driving into Nouadhibou, we pass one of the world's great railway rides, the immensely long iron-ore trains that each bring an average of 22 000 tonnes of crushed rock out of the interior down to the coast for export. It's a way of travelling north to Algeria and you can load your vehicle, sit inside it on a flatbed perhaps and travel for 12 hours up to the mines in Zouîrat. In the past, this train was frequently attacked by the freedom-fighting Polisario guerrillas, as initially Mauritania had also claimed a stake in the country. These attacks were amongst the reasons why Mauritania abandoned the fray and sued for peace, letting Morocco take over its illegal share of the country.

Nouadhibou, meaning 'Jackal's Well', is a flat, unassuming town set on the eastern side of the Cap Blanc Peninsula. It seems much more relaxed and easy-going than Nouakchott. South of the port in Baie de Cansado we find a ship's graveyard of 26 abandoned fishing hulks, scuppered, we're told, for fraudulent insurance claims. Inexplicably, there are thousands of fish rotting on the beach. The lighthouse out at the point of Cap Blanc might desperately need a paint job, but for us reaching this spot above the high chalk cliffs means we have survived the desolate Saharan coastline of Africa's least populated country. We take the Landies to the very edge; below us in the Atlantic surf frolic some rare Mediterranean monk seals, *Phoques moines*. Close to where we're parked is a line of white-painted stones and, beyond that, a no-go landmined area and Western Sahara, into which, if all goes well, we'll cross tomorrow. Our Garmin GPS coordinates read 20° 46' 12" N and 17° 3' 0" W.

Back in Nouadhibou Ali welcomes us into his overland camp. It's called Camping Baie du Levrier and there's secure parking for the Landies. We take our shoes off and sit on cushions on carpets in an open-sided desert nomad's tent where, once again, even though an ice-cold beer would be more appropriate, we go through the serious business of tea. Poured from a height into small glasses, the drinking of several glasses of bitter green tea, thick with sugar, is one of the most important rituals in Arabic Africa. 'You have visas for Western Sahara?' asks Ahmeida al-Baseid, a busy little turbaned fellow who specialises in getting people across the border. 'Tomorrow I go with you.'

The muezzin's call to prayer reverberates through the small, high window into our box-sized room, which is just big enough to take two mattresses on the floor. Breakfast at a nearby café is made up of custardy-type sticky buns, cheese, omelettes and strong coffee. Ahmeida helps us out of Mauritania. Thank goodness we've got him as we have all sorts of hassles, and unbelievably we leave the country with another mark on the sun visor.

We're all a bit tense and grumpy – ahead of us is the Western Saharan border which we still need to cross. Ahmeida says goodbye and warns us about landmines on either side of the road. The Moroccans have built a fancy border post in the shape of an imposing medieval gatehouse. This is the moment of truth. '*Hold thumbs and good luck*,' comes Ross's voice over the radio.

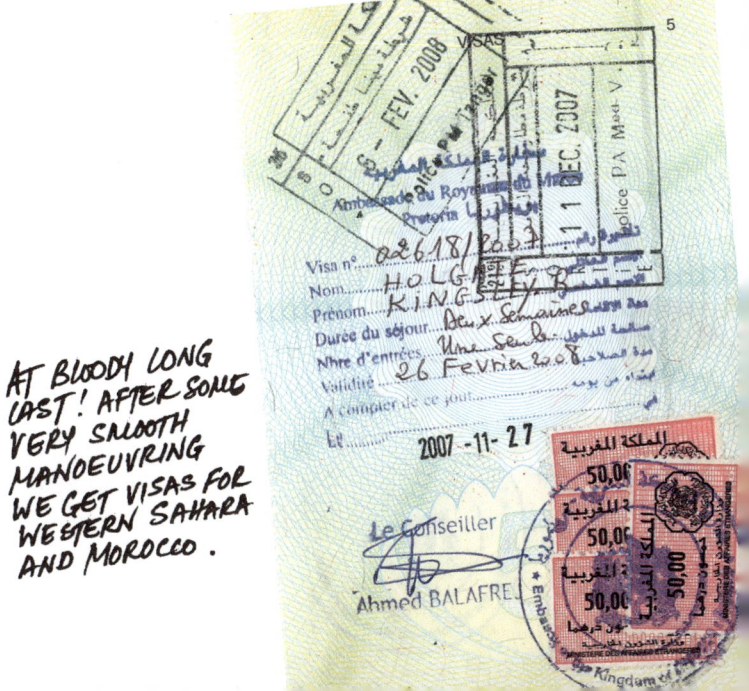

AT BLOODY LONG LAST! AFTER SOME VERY SMOOTH MANOEUVRING WE GET VISAS FOR WESTERN SAHARA AND MOROCCO.

Western Sahara

Day 224, Country 21 on the Edge

Originally known as Spanish Sahara but now occupied by Morocco, Western Sahara has a rugged coastline with some of the world's richest fishing grounds. It also has some of the world's biggest phosphate mines. No wonder the Moroccans want it – there's probably oil. After all the effort, tension and time spent worrying about getting us visas, we just hope they don't turn us away on arrival. Here we go!

It's just too dangerous to leave the road.

Dispatch #142 – *Hier Kom die Bokke*

With our hearts in our mouths we hang around the Landies whilst Mashozi lines up with our passports. Despite the ceasefire, Moroccan security forces are on high alert, meaning sniffer dogs are abroad and vehicle searches are the order of the day.

I had warned the team: 'Given the touchy situation with South Africa supporting the true inhabitants of Western Sahara, let's be low-key and not push the fact that we are South Africans.' Little Tristan got the story wrong and on arrival starts singing '*Hier kom die Bokke*!' As it turns out everything is okay, however, and the officials are really friendly. 'Mandela a great man,' they chirp. 'Bafana Bafana useless – what happen? And your country getting the World Cup?'

Once through immigration, I get pulled in for an hour session with Mr Mohammed of customs. He's a kind, moustached man who tells me that he 'jeest luuves to speek Eengleesh'. His accent is like Shirley Valentine's Greek lover in the famed film. 'Ah,' he says, 'I once meet an Eenglish girl – very very bootiful. Mustafa, she say, you must to stop the smoking, too much coughing. She leave, I still too much smoke, too much coughing. I like Beatles music, I like Eengleesh – international language. I like speek.' And so patiently we fill in a green document transferring all vehicle details from the international carnet (the vehicle papers approved almost globally) onto a uniquely Moroccan one. 'This green paper, for all police to see – very important. And to hand in when you leave Maroc, otherwise beeg trouble.'

Then my friend Mohammed suddenly becomes serious. 'This place Maroc, and the border military,' he says firmly. And so the search begins: look, prod, feel, underneath and on top. They've even got their own ladders to get up onto the roof racks. 'For bombs,' says Mohammed, 'your own safety.' This time there's a German Shepherd cross, straining at its trainer's lead and smelling the vehicles. 'May I?' asks Mashozi, taking out a box of Beeno's that she keeps for stray dogs. The sniffer dog loves them and the trainer gives up – the six-hour-long border crossing into Moroccan-occupied Western Sahara is over. 'Goodbye, be careful – landmines!' shouts Mohammed in his best 'Eengleesh' as he waves us into the wasteland of miles and miles of desert, a few camels and a bitterly cold wind.

By now, the next military outpost, forever aware of security in this battle-scarred region, would have noticed three little specks, one behind the other, moving slowly across the vast desert expanse of Moroccan-controlled Western Sahara. Zooming in with their binoculars they would have noticed that these were not camels, but rather three battered, South-African-registered Land Rovers. 'Right-hand drive, must be those South Africans that have just crossed the military checkpoint out of Mauritania,' I imagine the sergeant mumbling. 'It's the man with the big beard, they've got the flags of all the countries around the edge of Africa on the side of their vehicles. They've come all the way from Cape Town – they must be bloody crazy.'

They're right, we must be bloody crazy. But with the Zen of Travel, a pebble in the pocket and a Scroll of Peace and Goodwill, we're nine months into the journey with 20 outside

'The Moment of Truth'

WESTERN SAHARA – NOTES

- WEDGED BETWEEN MAURITANIA AND MOROCCO THE LAND AREA OF WESTERN SAHARA IS 266 000 km²
- MOST OF WESTERN SAHARA WAS ANNEXED BY MOROCCO IN 1976 – TURNED INTO A WAR
- MOST OF THE POPULATION LIVE IN EXILE IN REFUGEE CAMPS IN THE SOUTHERN SECTION OF ALGERIA'S SAHARA –
- BUT THE PROBLEM IS NOT OVER – THE PEOPLE OF WESTERN SAHARA WANT THEIR COUNTRY BACK AND THE AREA IS STILL LITTERED WITH UNEXPLODED LANDMINES.

Lit by a torch, this simple pile of stones marks the Tropic of Cancer.

edge countries behind us. It's foot flat on the accelerator, using third and fourth gears against the howling headwind. Ross's voice crackles over the radio, '*No power, we'll have to stop. Dirty diesel.*' The wind howls across the gravel plains of the Sahara and white horses gallop across the North Atlantic. It's such a forlorn place. Ross cleans the separator and we're off. There's no fuel in the next village so we siphon from the jerry cans.

Dispatch #143 – Tantalising Tagines

All the way up the coast from Senegal there's been an excited buzz around the forthcoming Dakar Rally, which this year is going to take place from Lisbon to Dakar. There's also a bit of international controversy surrounding the glitzy event that has so much money thrown at it but travels through some desperately poor areas. Western Sahara used to be a Spanish territory, and had been under Spanish rule for more than a century. In the early 1970s the local people, known as Sahrawis, began to resist Spanish colonialism and formed the *Frente Polisario* liberation movement. In 1975 the territory was on the verge of gaining independence from Spain. Spain had even agreed to a referendum, but then the Green March happened in which Moroccan troops, followed by King Hassan II and 350 000 unarmed Moroccans and accompanied by much waving of flags and Korans, marched into the territory to claim Moroccan sovereignty.

Spain was eager to avoid a colonial war and in a clandestine agreement handed the administration of the disputed area to neighbouring Morocco and Mauritania, in what was supposed to be a tripartite administration along with the local Sahrawis. Morocco and Mauritania thought they would clobber the nomadic Sahrawis and the whole thing would be over in a couple of weeks, giving them shared control over the region. But they hadn't banked on the tough fighting spirit of the men in the small *Frente Polisario* army who, in their old battered Landies, knew the Western Sahara like the backs of their hands. The outcome was a terrible guerrilla war that lasted for over 16 years, with the local *Frente Polisario* freedom fighters refusing to back down.

Fortunately there is currently a ceasefire whilst the UN sends millions every year trying to organise a seemingly never-to-happen referendum. The armistice gives us the opportunity to inch up the coast of a country that's said to be the world's last remaining colony. It's a country occupied illegally by Morocco with most of her own citizens living in exile in refugee camps in southern Algeria. South Africa, along with 71 other countries in the world, supports the Sahrawis' right to self-determination, as does our Outside Edge Expedition.

Here there's no turning off to camp in the dunes. Signs warning us to 'Beware Landmines' line the road and there are frequent police checkpoints so we decide to head on through the night, stopping only to shine our torches onto a small pile of rocks marking the Tropic of Cancer. To keep me awake Mashozi reads me pieces out of the food section of the guidebook and in turn I feed these tasty morsels of gastronomic information to the other Landies by radio. One of the dishes that has us all salivating is a sort of *potjie*, called a 'tagine'. It's a basic beef or lamb stew with vegetables in an earthenware dish covered by a conical lid that is left to slowly simmer over a charcoal fire. There are also some very refined variations: *barrogo bis basela*, a lamb stew with prunes; *safardjaliyya*, beef stew with quinces; *sikbadj*, lamb with dates and apricots; and *tagine bel hout*, a fish stew with tomatoes, ginger, saffron, and sweet and hot peppers. Black olives are invariably added to the honey-flavoured sauces; apples and pears may also be thrown in. We've been living a bit rough lately – following the coast of Mauritania along the beach where the Sahara flows down to meet the North Atlantic, camping in the dunes at night with constant sandstorms. Sand in the food, in the coffee and between your teeth.

By the next morning we're through the landmine fields and arrive in the Moroccan-occupied garrison town of Dakhla. Past the police checkpoints and into the old town, we follow a street lined with pavement restaurants. '*Look at the Basotho hats*', comes Ross's excited voice over the radio, referring to the conical tagine stewpot lids. We pile out of the Landies. What a pig-out: fresh tomatoes, carrots, avocados, olives, cucumbers and feta cheese; plates of lamb chops, just like those little Karoo ones with the crisp fat on the side; then the tagines. There is a communal gasp of appreciation as each conical pot lid is lifted to reveal a steaming lamb *potjie* served with bowls of couscous. Bread, which accompanies every meal, is considered sacred and you will see people kiss it in reverence. Never wasted, it is gathered up at the end of a meal and broken into breadcrumbs for sweets. Diesel in Dakhla works out to be R4,48 per litre. Good food and cheap diesel – it's a winning combination.

Dispatch #144 – A Terrorist Attack

Then we hear the bad news: four French tourists have been gunned down on the side of the road in Mauritania, the area that we've just come through. The Mauritanian interior minister blamed the senseless killing on a regional al-Qaida terrorist gang. The sole survivor of the attack, the family's father, was seriously injured and was flown to a hospital in Dakar, Senegal. We all think back to what sitting targets we could have been – a simple fire next to the three Landies with their rooftop tents, and our little grandson Tristan with us. Ahead of us is Algeria where 37 people have just been killed by a suicide bomber. A few days later, as a result of death threats, the Dakar Rally is cancelled.

Up the coast from Dakhla it's real outside edge stuff as the Landies follow tableland cliff edges that fall away into the Atlantic – it's wild and dramatic. On past Laayoune, the UN peacekeeping vehicles remind us of Liberia. With a Garmin reading of 27° 40' 17" N and 12° 57' 21" W, we stop at the little village of Tah. It's 10.45 a.m. on 8 December 2007. Little Tristan slides down the slippery slope of the commemorative monument that marks the original frontier between Western Sahara and Morocco. There's a small roadside motel and café aptly called *Laliberté*. Red Moroccan flags fly everywhere. Now we're in Morocco proper. Directly across the Atlantic are the Canary Islands and up the coast Casablanca, Rabat, Tangier, and the mouth of the Mediterranean. It's all so new and hugely exciting.

3 LANDY SPECKS FOLLOWING THE 'EDGE' OF WESTERN SAHARA

LITTLE TRISTAN SLIDING DOWN THE SLOPE OF THE FRONTIER MONUMENT –

Morocco

Day 225, Country 22 on the Edge

We have arrived at the gateway to the Mediterranean, with exotic names like Casablanca, Tangier, Marrakech and Fez. After having travelled north up the coast of Africa, then west around the bulge of the continent, it's going to feel strange to reach Tangier and turn east along the Mediterranean coast, with Gibraltar and Europe just across the water. Being at the top of Africa is certainly a breakthrough, having travelled all the way from the bottom.

Dispatch #145 – Morocco

The road is made for such an expedition; it hugs the outline of Africa, going around Cap Juby to the town of Tarfaya, first established as a trading post by an eccentric Scotsman called Mackenzie, who in the mid-19th century built a fort on a tiny rocky island that he grandly called Port Victoria. The Landies sing along; Morocco is very tourist-friendly and at the sight of a foreign vehicle the police wave you on smartly. Wow! No black marks here. It is rich in history, culture and colour; boasts ancient medinas, kasbahs and souks; and offers spectacular scenery, beaches, the snow-capped Atlas Mountains and the Sahara – the greatest desert in the world. No wonder it's a paradise for tourists.

Already we're coming across other adventure travellers, mostly from Europe, travelling by motorbike, 4x4 and camper van. After the coast of Mauritania it seems strange not to have the outline of Africa to ourselves. We reach Tan Tan, from where the Green March started, and then it's on to the walled city of Tiznit, famous for its silversmiths. Here at the Souk des Bijoutiers, the jewellery market, we watch the craftsmen working delicate silver filigree into heavy Berber bracelets and necklaces. Tristan of course likes the swords and daggers. We push to the old Spanish enclave of Sidi Ifni and in the early evening follow the traffic into the bright lights of the playground resort of Agadir – a new city that's risen out of the ashes of an earthquake that on the night of 29 February 1960 killed 15 000 people and made more than 20 000 people homeless when 3 650 buildings were destroyed. It's now been rebuilt into an international sunshine coast tourist resort. We can't believe it, there's an English pub with footy on the telly, draft beer, full English breakfasts, fish and chips and Western music. For the British visitors who need to escape some of the 300 days of sunshine a year, there's even a pub called the Bar Fly. It's all so European and touristy.

We are delighted. Morocco is a cultural gem – music, dance, ancient walled markets, silversmiths, Berber bracelets and necklaces, medinas, kasbahs and souks

Morocco - Notes:

- Kingdom of Morocco - at times I thought we'd never make it.
- Population 31.6 million
- Capital city: Rabat
- A rich cultural blend of Arab, Berber, European and African influences.
- The Kingdom is the most westerly of the North African countries known as the Maghreb.
- Strategically situated with both the Atlantic and Mediterranean coastlines
- Exciting mix of medieval walled cities and souk markets - the largest city is Casablanca - money is the Dirham

Morocco at last

We follow the outside edge cliff-top road and camp out of town at a tourist trailer park. It's all so strangely civilised after the lonely desert nights on the beach or in the Sahara dunes. It's also getting closer to Christmas and that time on expedition when the team starts talking about home. From Mauritania we'd sent a satellite email to Lin Glass at British Airways, dropping a hint about how wonderful it would be if we could visit home for Christmas. She said she'd try. Bruce is especially pensive; little Sam left us in Ghana quite a way back, and he's taking strain.

Dispatch #146 – Beautiful Essaouira

Mashozi's got the *Insight Guide to Morocco* and the well-used, dog-eared *National Geographic African Adventure Atlas* on her lap, and the three Landies keep on swapping snippets of information over the radios. Berber peasants sell small bottles of oil on the roadside; this argan oil is painstakingly pressed by Berber women from the olive-like fruit of the low, thorny, bushy argan tree. 'Apparently it's unique to Morocco, and only grows along this southwestern seaboard. It's not only used for cooking but also as local medicine, treating everything from stomach ailments to heart failure,' says Mashozi, reading from the guidebook.

We're tracking the coast, heading for the ancient port town of Essaouira. *Insight Guide to Morocco* tells us:

> *Until quite recently the town was known by its Spanish or Portuguese name, Mogador. It was founded in the 18th century by Sultan Mohammed ben Abdullah as a free port [or pirate enclave] for Europeans and their Jewish agents engaged in trans-Saharan gold, ivory and slave trading.* (2007, p. 263)

In 1952 Orson Welles chose the town as the location for his film, *Othello*. We're not disappointed. The Atlantic beach stretches against its fortified walls. Inside the ramparts is the old trading town with blue-and-white houses, colourful craft and carpet shops, sidewalk musicians and cafés and the ever-enticing smell of tagines, the contents of which continue to provide a gastronomic adventure. We climb up onto the fortifications where old cannons face Îles Purpuraires, famed for its medieval farming of a type of shellfish that produced a purple dye that was much in demand in 1st-century Rome.

Forever on the move, we continue out past the fish market, where you can sit down and order your favourites, cooked straight from the sea. We park the Landies and give Tristan a chance to race down the beach and into the waves. Poor little guy is getting Land-Rovered out – aren't we all?

We arrive in Casablanca – how romantic the name, although it's nothing like its sin-city image in the classical Hollywood movie that appropriated its name. It's an exciting metropolis where the streets are choked with traffic, noise and diesel fumes. With an unofficial population estimate of over five million people, it's one of the largest cities on the African coast. Despite the modern, high-rise buildings, billboards, clubs, restaurants and fashion houses, it's also a city with extensive poor areas called *bidonvilles*, or shanty towns, many of which are hidden behind high walls, known to the locals as walls of shame.

A Quick Dash Home

Dispatch #147 – Christmas in South Africa

We park the three Landies on the pavement outside the old Casablanca Hotel and that's where we get the good news. British Airways, one of the expedition sponsor partners, is going to fly us home for a short festive season break. We can't believe our luck – it's a wonderful last-minute rush. Early the next morning we leave the Landies with Land Rover Morocco for servicing, and Charl Möller, the acting South African ambassador from Rabat, whisks us through the diplomatic gate at the airport. Hey presto, the next moment we're having bacon and eggs at Heathrow before getting on a plane home. What a treat! The dogs go mad and George the parrot talks to us in Zulu. We haven't seen families or friends for months, not to mention the long absence of *boerewors* on the braai, hot showers and soft beds. – all this from the luxury of our own home without having to put up a bloody tent. It's sheer pleasure! And for Bruce it's bliss to be back home at the family castle in Shongweni with Sam next door.

At home we listen in amazement to fellow South Africans complaining about high prices, the electricity crisis, politics and how tough things are. The truth is that when you've travelled from Cape Town to Casablanca through 21 African countries, you appreciate what a wonderful paradise we live in and just how lucky we are in South Africa. Our biggest challenge is to be more optimistic and sort out the crime, but we've got a great country – the best on the continent.

Back to Morocco

Dispatch #148 – A *Boerseun* from Casablanca

Back in Casablanca our break has given us more than enough heart to continue tracking the edge of Mama Afrika. To meet us at the airport is Charl Möller and the newly appointed Charge d'Affaires for the South African Embassy, Nthuleng Seleka. With them is also a smiling, round-faced Christiaan Bornman, our new expedition member and interpreter for Morocco, and can you believe it, he's a young 20-year-old *boerseun* from Pretoria who speaks excellent Moroccan Arabic. He greets us with a big grin and an Arabic handshake to the chest, saying, 'Howzit you okes, welcome back to Casablanca'. Christiaan and his family have been in Morocco for seven years doing valuable humanitarian work with the Berber people in the High Atlas Mountains. He was home-schooled and in the taxi tells us that he learnt Darija, the local Arabic dialect, on the streets of the medieval walled city of Fez. He has brought with him a big tub of *tuisgebakte boerebeskuit* and in our bags, now safely through customs, we have some biltong, the odd bottle of Captain and a giant bag of spectacles to add to our Rite to Sight campaign.

Dispatch #149 – Hashish Country

We struggle to get the Landies out of Land Rover Morocco's crowded car park. It's full of Supercharged Range Rover Sports and the latest in big, high-speed BMWs. 'We can't cope, business is booming,' says the French-speaking manager. 'A lot of it is paid for with dirty money from the drug lords in the north who need fast getaway cars. You must be careful when you go there, to the area called the Rif. People will try to sell you hashish and the police jump at the chance to imprison naive foreigners,' he warns.

Christiaan, our interpreter, tells us that it is indeed a big problem here and that the Rif Mountains in the north of Morocco are internationally associated with the massive cultivation of hashish. Although theoretically illegal in Morocco and the Spanish enclaves of Ceuta and Melilla,

MOROCCO HAS A FASCINATING OUTSIDE EDGE—

CHRISTIAAN THE BOERSEUN FROM CASABLANCA.

hashish or 'kif', as it's known, has not been criminalised and trade is brisk and expanding. This hidden export industry has an estimated annual value of more than 500 million US dollars and a European street value of 10 times that amount.

Dispatch #150 – Naked in the Atlantic

Back in the Landies, which are still battered but now cleaned and serviced, we cruise Casablanca's playground. We make our way across the beachfront Corniche d'Ain Diab, famous

THE REMAINS OF THE HASSAN TOWER IN RABAT → AND IN THE SAME SQUARE THE FAITHFUL COME TO PRAY OUTSIDE THE MAUSOLEUM OF MOHAMMED V

in falling pregnant come here, he says. They stand naked in the Atlantic and let seven waves crash against their bodies. A lady with kind eyes and beautiful, smooth, brown skin paints henna designs onto Annelie's hand and around Mashozi's ankle. The wind blows cold from Europe.

Dispatch #151 – The Tallest Building on the Edge

Following the Corniche, we pass the old 1920s lighthouse on the point, which is surrounded by shacks. As is the case all over Morocco, most of the shacks have satellite TV dishes. There are tens of thousands of dishes. 'It's a crazy society,' says Christiaan, 'on the one hand so purist and on the other tuning illegally into Europe's porn channels.'

Further on is the Hassan II Mosque; it's the largest single building that we have come across thus far on the outside edge of Africa. It's the gift of a grateful nation to its previous sovereign on the occasion of his 60th birthday in 1989. The magnificent building, complete with library, museum, steam baths and conference facilities, was designed by French architect Michael Pinseau and financed by voluntary subscriptions. Built on the seabed, with water on three sides, it complies with the Koranic saying 'Allah has his throne on the water'. Cedar wood from the Middle Atlas, delicately carved, and marble from Agadir and Tafraoute were used in its construction. The detailed craftsmanship is truly unbelievable.

To find the 750 million US dollars needed for construction, special officials collected contributions from every home in the land, and some employers deducted a percentage from their workers' wages. The late king's highest officials are said to have fallen over themselves to be generous. The prayer hall, with an electricity-operated sunroof over the central court, has space for 20 000 worshippers whilst another 80 000 can pray on the surrounding esplanade. The marble minaret covers 25 square metres and is 175 metres high, making it the tallest religious building in the world, beating the Great Pyramid of Cheops by 30 metres and St Peter's by 40 metres. It took 35 000 workers 50 million man-hours to complete the building. Visible for hundreds of kilometres out to sea, this is one of the largest mosques in the world. A laser beam points like a giant finger from the top of the minaret towards Mecca, and can be seen from 32 kilometres away. In the expedition journal I scribble:

for its restaurants and nightclubs. At its western limit, there's a small rocky outcrop called Sidi Abderrahman, a picturesque cluster of white tombs and little rabbit-warren houses accessed by pilgrims at low tide. We take off our shoes and wade across. It's a place of the occult where people speak in whispers and burn incense and herbs to cure sickness. A lady arrives wearing a smart coat and dark glasses. She seems harassed. Money changes hands and a moustached man smoking a long-stemmed hashish pipe sacrifices a black fowl with a single swipe of a sharp knife. Still flapping its wings, the fowl is thrown over the edge of the rocks. Without looking back the lady walks down the steps and is pulled through the shallows to the mainland in a big black tractor tube. Next in line is a beautiful girl dressed in the very best of designer clothes. I wonder what she's come for. Christiaan is a wealth of information. Young girls who are having difficulty

750 million USD, that's a load of money for a country that has so much poverty, but then again it's brought a lot of pride to the nation.

Dispatch #152 – The Calabash at Cape Spartel

The journey up the coast from Casablanca is proving a great outside edge experience, sometimes with our Landies just a metre from the brink of a steep cliff that plunges down into the ocean. Rabat, the capital city, is beautiful. It's made up of an old lighthouse on the jagged edge of Africa, backdropped by five kilometres of ramparts, and was once a pirate stronghold. High on a hill overlooking the city, we visit the remains of the Hassan tower that was destroyed in the earthquake of 1755. We hear the Friday call to prayer and hundreds of pilgrims arrive to worship in the large open space dotted with the remains of old stone columns. Colourful royal guards on horseback man the entrances to the square and traditional water sellers pose for pictures. Christiaan leads us up the steps to the mausoleum of Mohammed V and his son Hassan II. He tells us that at the funeral of the latter an estimated two million Moroccans flooded Rabat's streets to say farewell to their king. We gaze down at his marble tomb in the knowledge that we've reached the heart of the kingdom.

The road to Tangier hugs the Atlantic coast and parts of it remind us of South Africa's Cape Peninsula. It's an area that's been heavily influenced by Spain and Portugal, with most of the Moroccan ports having fallen to either of these forces at one time or another. The Landies growl on – it's winter and we're all wrapped up in scarves, jackets, longs and boots. Behind us is the heat and humidity of West Africa. We stop at Cape Spartel for a team shot. Nine months ago, 347 Land Rovers escorted us out of the Cape of Good Hope, the most southwesterly point of the continent, and now we're at this, the most northwesterly cape. Outside the lighthouse we hold up the Zulu calabash that's carrying cold South Atlantic water from this landmark's southwesterly counterpoint, and pour a little into the North Atlantic Ocean. If we're successful, we'll return to the Cape of Good Hope to empty it, but that's still many months, 11 countries and lots of *vasbyt* away.

Dispatch #153 – Tangier and the Tomb of Ibn Battuta

Reaching Tangier and the mouth of the Mediterranean is a yardstick for the expedition and we're all chuffed to be here.

ANNA AND A TRADITIONAL WATER SELLER –

Reaching Cape Spartel. It's a yardstick for the expedition.

161

The port city has a wonderfully colourful history. Morocco was split between France and Spain by the signing of the Treaty of Fez in 1912, and Tangier became virtually an international zone with much cultural diversity. A later statute in 1923 made this loose recognition formal, sharing Tangier between Spain, Britain, France, Portugal, Holland, Belgium, Italy and Sweden. According to the *Insight Guide to Morocco*:

> For the next 33 years Tangier was a centre for unregulated financial services, prostitution, smuggling and espionage. (2007, p. 112)

Barbara Hutton, the Woolworths heiress, had a house in Tangier and was famous for her notorious parties. Her gatherings included Flamenco singers and belly dancers and even tribespeople on camels carrying loaded rifles to perform their ceremonial dances. Malcolm Forbes, the late but famed American billionaire publisher who had strong links to the Arabs, also had a house in Tangier. One of his most extravagant parties was his 70th birthday celebration in 1989 that is said to have set him back a cool two million US dollars. Guests, including Elizabeth Taylor, Henry Kissinger and the Gettys, were entertained by hundreds of drummers, belly dancers, acrobats and Berber horsemen.

We take digs in the downtown Holland Hotel. It's a bit ropey, but there's safe parking for the Landies and it's a short walk to the kasbah. There's still an English church in Tangier and Mustafa, the caretaker who's been here for more than 30 years, points out the grave of David Herbert, whose tombstone reads: 'Born 3 October 1908. Died 3 April 1995. He loved Morocco.' Herbert was a famed British socialite and memoirist, and was dubbed as the Queen of Tangier. Muriel Louisa Phillips's tombstone simply reads: 'Artist, painter, friend.' Walter Harris, correspondent for *The Times*, died here 4 April 1933. 'He loved the Moorish people and was their friend' is written on his tombstone. The honourable Sir Reginald Lister, British Consul General to Morocco, died at his post of malarial fever on 10 November 1912, aged 47 years.

There's still a Sunday service and, although the numbers have dwindled, the white flag with the red cross of St Andrews still flies above the church. Outside the gate Berber women in big straw hats sell homemade cheese, circular loaves of bread and fresh herbs. We hire Chico, an illegal guide, to take us through the kasbah in search of the lady who has the key to the tomb of one of Africa's greatest travellers, Ibn Battuta. For me it's a bit of a pilgrimage – I want to pay my respects to one of the greatest Arab geographers and travellers of all time.

Born in Tangier in 1304, Battuta set off on a pilgrimage to Mecca, but his intended trip of around six months became a 29-year journey in which he vowed never to travel the same route twice. His incredible journeys took him east to India and China, south across the Sahara Desert to Mali and Niger, and down the East African coast to Somalia and to what is now Kenya and Tanzania. We finally gain access to his tomb, which is only about 1.5 metres long and draped in green cloth. This was a man who talked about snow-capped mountains on Africa's equator and the Mountains of the Moon long before the European Victorian explorers like Burton, Livingstone and Stanley ever ventured into Africa. Back in Morocco, in 1344, Ibn Battuta related his adventures to the Sultan of Morocco and was asked to dictate an account of his journeys to a young scribe called Ibn Juzayy. Translated into English, the book was delightfully called *A Gift to Those Who Contemplate the Wonders of Cities and the Marvels of Travelling*, a bit of a mouthful that has become shortened to *El Rihla*, or *The Journey*, and was used as a guidebook by other travellers.

We pay some money to the key lady and make our way through the narrow streets of the kasbah to the palace at the top of the hill, where snake charmers perform for us by pulling frighteningly big, shiny, black cobras from a wooden box. Massive old Portuguese naval guns point across the Straights to Gibraltar and to the right is the house Matisse, the famous painter, lived in. Cops are everywhere but the drug scene is still active in Tangier. A junkie outside the door of a dingy alleyway shop has a syringe dangling from a vein in his arm. 'Hey mister,' he says, 'you American? Come, I give you a good fix.' Our guide Chico is properly pissed off. 'We don't need this rubbish,' he says. 'They give Tangier a bad name.'

At Café Baba the coffee is strong enough to stand your teaspoon up in. This was an old hippie hangout in the sixties and there's a black-and-white picture of Keith Richards of the Rolling Stones dressed in a hairy sheepskin jacket and pulling on a long-stemmed hashish pipe. Chico looks out across the sweep of the half-moon beach. 'In the old days there were just a few beach bars and hardly a light at night, now it's just a mass of modern hotels and apartments, many owned by Arabs from the oil-rich states and tourists from Europe. The old Tangier is over and a new era of tourism seems to be taking over.' Tomorrow we leave Tangier to continue following the outline of Africa.

Dispatch #154 – The Mediterranean Rif

The wild Mediterranean coastline of Morocco known as the Rif is the most continuously dramatic, craggy landscape that we've yet come across on the outside edge of Africa. It's like a continuous Chapman's Peak Drive, one mistake of the Landy steering wheel and you'll plunge hundreds of metres down into the Med. The dramatic coastline, known for its illegal hashish cultivation, runs all the way from the Spanish enclave of Ceuta, south and east down the coast to Al Hoceima, Ras el Ma, the beautiful lighthouse of Cap des Trois Fourches, the second Spanish enclave of Melilla, the massive lagoon of Nador and on to Saidia to where Moroccans escape the city heat at beachfront apartments on the Mediterranean.

It's too built up for us to camp so Christiaan finds us a cheap, out-of-season backstreet apartment for the night and a car guard to watch the Landies. So we have beds, showers, a kitchen and a lounge. Dinner is three plump rotisserie chickens, chips and bread whilst we watch Algeciras TV news and learn that there've been more killings across the border in Algeria. Our journey along the entire coastline of Morocco is now virtually complete. Tomorrow we'll try and cross into Algeria. Some say it's possible, others not.

Dispatch #155 – Seven Days and Big Bucks

Tight security and no photos allowed. We're stopped at the boom and Moroccan police, customs and plain-clothes security all gather around the Landies. The border security post is backed up by a big military fort flying the red Moroccan flag high on a nearby hill. 'It's the Algerians, they closed the border,' say the Moroccans, shaking their heads dismally. 'Not good country,' says a man with a clipped moustache and a leather jacket, the type you don't mess with. There's a big ginger cat biting its way into a black garbage bag. The red-and-white boom is closed and the whole place has got a sorry air of neglect. There is absolutely no way they'll let us across into Algeria. Christiaan tries his best to negotiate. We've heard that cheap fuel from Algeria is smuggled across all the time,

THE CAP DES TROIS FOURCHES LIGHTHOUSE

ONE WRONG TURN AND WE'LL END UP IN THE MED.

'THE RIF' - THE WILD, RUGGED, HASHISH-PRODUCING MEDITERRANEAN COASTLINE OF MOROCCO.

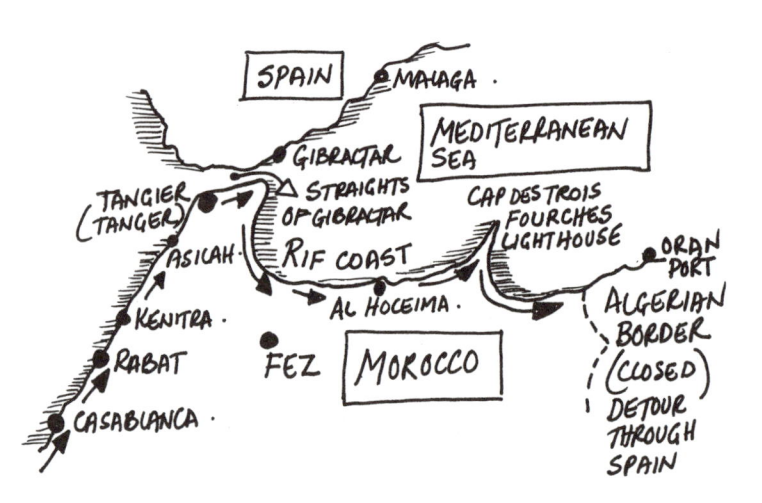

We liked the humour – 'The Beard' heading for Fez with a fez on his head.

but for us foreigners in our three South African Land Rovers it's strictly no go. There've been incidents and the Moroccans are concerned about al-Qaida terrorist groups crossing into their country, as well as the ongoing dispute with Algeria over its backing of the Polisario movement in Moroccan-occupied Western Sahara.

It's a massive blow – we'd hoped for a miracle. Now we'll have to return to Tangier and put the Landies and ourselves onto a ferry across the Straights of Gibraltar to Spain. We'll then have to follow the coast for 700 kilometres to take another ferry across the Mediterranean from Alicante to Oran in Algeria before backtracking to the other side of the boom where we now stand – seven days and a massive dent in the budget to do just 100 metres of the outside edge. Damn it! Why can't Africa sort its indabas out? Sadly, the Zen of Travel has temporally abandoned us, but we've come this far and we're certainly not giving up now.

Dispatch #156 – The Ancient Walled City of Fez
I give the pebble in my pocket a reassuring rub as slowly we turn the three Landies around. Instead of complaining, we decide to make the most of it and keep it exciting. So rather than backtracking all the way to Tangier down the coast of the Rif, we detour via ancient Fez, where we find cheap rooms on the third floor of the Hôtel de la Paix on the broad palm tree-lined Hassan II Boulevard. Mohammed the car guard assures us that *inshallah*, for a fee, the Landies will be safe on the crowded street. Mohammed the receptionist speaks a bit of English and throws breakfast into the room rate. Mohammed the porter points to the antique lift. 'Be careful,' he says, 'it only takes two people.' But the rooms are clean and much to Mashozi's and Annelie's delight there are baths and hot water.

The next morning we stand on a hill overlooking the ancient, walled medina of Fez and meet Berber community leaders who've travelled down from the High Atlas Mountains with Christiaan's parents. Through our Teaching on the Edge programme, we hand over soccer balls, books, pens, rulers, crayons and colouring-in books for the kids, as well as Rite to Sight spectacles for the poor-sighted.

Fez is fascinating. The call to prayer from scores of mosques rises up to meet us, as do the sounds of the thousands of people who live in a maze of alleyways, madrasas, markets

We hand over learning materials, soccer balls and Rite to Sight spectacles.

'The Beard' overlooking the ancient walled city of Fez.

still feels a hidden, frozen-in-time place – a chipped-and-battered, secretive North African jewel.

Our noses tell us we're getting closer to the medieval tanneries. Crafts and trades of the medina have remained almost unchanged for a thousand years. We are given sprigs of mint to stick up our noses to help against the stink of fresh animal hides steeped in urine to make them supple. Men crouch and balance over stone vats as they dip and soak the hides in natural dyes, and roofs and walls are thick with drying skins. It's back-breaking work that is handed down from father to son. The souks are full of the finished products – bags, jackets, wallets and belts. At one time, whole libraries were sent to Morocco to be 'Morocco bound' and tooled with gold.

Tinsmiths, carpenters, gold and silver jewellery makers, stonemasons, carpet makers, butchers, grocers, nougat sellers, live chicken sellers, painted doors, olives, spices, necklaces of dried figs, bakeries, restaurants, coffee shops and tea houses are just some of the activities, sights and sounds that assail the senses in ancient Fez. It's Saturday night, we're footsore and desperate for grog – not always an easy thing to find in Islamic North Africa's Maghreb where boozing is generally frowned upon and in some cases totally outlawed.

and mosques that make up what is believed to be the most complete example of medieval Islamic civilisation in the world today. We pass through the keyhole arch of Bab Boujeloud, one of the main entrances to the medina, and we're into a world that Salim, our guide, tells us has 970 streets, 344 quarters, 470 mosques, 8 gates, 350 000 people and foundations that date back to the year 789. All 1.5 km² of this wonderland are enclosed within 14 kilometres of wall.

There are no cars allowed in Fez, but you might get run over by an overloaded donkey or a mule. It's mysterious and exotic and, for all the friendliness of the people to us strangers, it

The medieval tannery at Fez – skins and hides soaked in urine. It's back-breaking work.

A mosaic of Bacchus, god of wine and intoxication!

Volubilis —

Dispatch #157 – Saturday Night in Fez

We go underground, down the steps, into the dimly lit Nautilus Bar. 'Music American', says the barman with a grin as *Hotel California* blares from two little speakers that are placed either side of bottles of gin, whiskey, brandy and Pernod. Sadly, there is no Captain Morgan, so we go for West African-brewed Flag beer. A couple cuddle on a couch and at a table in a corner a group of moustached, middle-aged men drink up a storm with their girls. Moroccans smoke with a passion and everybody puffs away to the sounds of Elton John followed by George Michael belting out his hit, *Faith*.

There's a jolly buzz and peals of laughter as, at the corner table, a large-busted girl's chair collapses, leaving her spread-eagled on the floor, looking up with a bemused grin at the circle of moustached men who leap up to take pictures of her on their mobile phones. The place is getting lively. In comes the banjo player and soon everybody is clapping and dancing. Plates of artichokes and peeled radishes are offered as snacks. More Flag beers, midnight and a frightening bar bill chase us off to bed. I wake up fully clothed.

Dispatch #158 – Volubilis

The name sounds like I feel, even with the help of three Disprins and a few cups of coffee. En route to the Tangier ferry, we stop off at the ancient Roman ruins of Volubilis, which in the year CE 45 was the empire's most remote base. The Lisbon earthquake in 1755 damaged the city and it fell into ruin. It only came to the attention of the outside world again when two foreign diplomats stumbled upon it at the end of the 19th century.

Christiaan finds us a guide named Khalid of Nazareth. His father worked as a cook for the resident French archaeologist from 1933 to 1976. 'I used to help my dad in the kitchen,' says Khalid. 'I got to know the visiting students, learnt some English and qualified as a guide. When I was 14, I was an actor in the movie *Jesus of Nazareth*, filmed at my village. I was in the stable with Joseph and I made enough money from the movie to buy my mother a house and some olive trees. That's why they still call me Khalid of Nazareth.'

And so, with Khalid, we explore ancient Volubilis, from the Tangier gate down the broad, flagstoned Decumanus Maximus carriageway to the Triumphant Arch. What a grand lifestyle these ancient Romans must have lived, with lavish public baths that provided a meeting place to chat, do business, exercise, eat and drink, and grand houses with elaborate heating systems providing hot water and steam for baths and heat. The mosaics on the floor of these vast houses are still in excellent condition. There's Bacchus, the god of wine and intoxication, in a chariot being pulled by panthers (I know the feeling). The house of Venus has a stunning mosaic of Hylas being abducted by nymphs and the bathing Diana being surprised by Acteon. It boggles the mind; there's Bacchus again discovering the sleeping Ariadne, and Orpheus, the god of music, charming wild animals with the playing of his lyre. There's also a mosaic of nine dolphins, believed by the Romans to bring good luck, and the sea goddess Amphitrite is in a chariot being pulled by a seahorse.

Khalid of Nazareth leads us down to the forum, the public square where the Romans would hold daily political debates. 'A Roman surprise,' he says with a shy grin as he points to a stone carving of a large erect penis and testicles. 'It's the pointer to the bordello.' Steam baths on the lower level and the cubicles with girls on the upper – a great favourite with the Roman soldiers. By this time my hangover has moved from my head to my dragging feet and my stomach's a bit dodgy. 'Ah! The latrine,' says Khalid from Nazareth pointing to a line of holes where the Romans could sit and talk politics whilst abluting. 'Politic you know,' he says in broken English, 'it has no smell. This big square rectangular stone basin, it's Vomitarium. The Romans when too much full from feasting would take a feather to tickle the back of throat – whoosh! Make the big vomit to empty stomach so they could eat and drink more.' I feel nauseous – and so ends our journey of the ancient 2 000-year-old Roman city of Volubilis. Algeria via Gibraltar and Spain, here we come.

A Long Detour via Gibraltar and Spain

Dispatch #159 – The Long Way Round

Soobh Fegr, the dawn summons. It's one of the five calls to prayer that marks the Muslim day. It's a dark morning at 5 a.m. and the Moroccan customs officials are a bit edgy. The Rif area of Morocco grows one of the world's largest hashish crops and Tangier is renowned as a smuggling port. An icy cold wind blows across the Mediterranean. We say goodbye to Christiaan, our South African guide – he's been an absolute star. Mysterious, romantic Morocco will, in our minds, always remain one of the most colourful and easy places to travel along the outside edge of Africa.

With the expedition Landies being lashed down onto the bottom deck of the ferry, the expedition team rams in coffee and ham sarmies on the top deck. Pork has been a bit off limits of late and it's really a bit of a treat. How ridiculous. Here we are being prisoners to North African politics, having to detour through Spain so as to get into Algeria. It plays hell on our bloody budget, but at least we get to visit the Rock of Gibraltar where, under a Union Jack flag and with a Battle of Trafalgar poster on the wall, we're served big glasses of pale ale and plates of fish and chips at the Lord Nelson pub. The joy of hearing our own language is delightful and there's a wonderful feeling of freedom after Islamic North Africa. We ask ourselves what the hell we are doing in this little British outpost when we're supposed to be circumnavigating Africa by land. But that's the Zen of Travel and you have to roll with the punches.

Dispatch #160 – The Spanish Coast

It's all too damn expensive, we're in the land of the euro and the diesel price is a killer. We hug the coast, the three Landies slipstreaming behind each other. Then, to speed things up, we break inland through Granada, the Sierra Nevada topped with snow, past villages where the inhabitants have tunnelled into the hills to live like moles underground. It's exciting but it feels strange to be off the African edge. We feel a bit guilty, as if we have deserted a faithful friend. The next day we're in Alicante, playground of the rich, and that night we leave European shores aboard the *El-Jasier II*, destination Algeria.

English beer, fish and chips and the Straights of Gibraltar – a crazy detour to get around the Morocco-Algerian border –

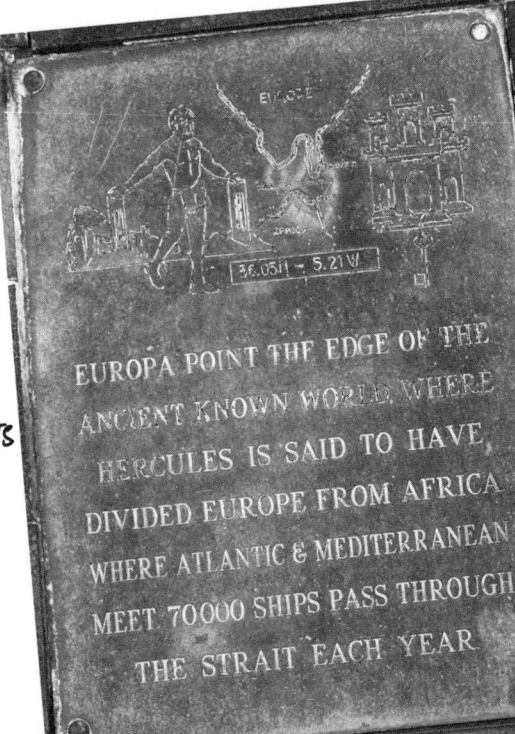

EUROPA POINT THE EDGE OF THE ANCIENT KNOWN WORLD WHERE HERCULES IS SAID TO HAVE DIVIDED EUROPE FROM AFRICA WHERE ATLANTIC & MEDITERRANEAN MEET 70000 SHIPS PASS THROUGH THE STRAIT EACH YEAR

36.05N – 5.21W

Algeria

Day 289, Country 23 on the Edge

Beset by internal strife, the security situation in Algeria has worsened. Backed by our Department of Foreign Affairs, our biggest humanitarian challenge thus far will be taking learning materials and Rite to Sight spectacles to the Sahrawi refugee camps deep in the desert. In Moroccan-occupied Western Sahara it was difficult to meet with the true people of that country, but now we can complete the puzzle. We are nervous.

We return the Western Saharan flags to their rightful spots on the Landies as soon as we are safely out of Morocco —

Dispatch #161 – Come what May, Destination Algeria

We're on the night ferry, the *El-Jasier II*. Built in Seville in 2005, it's rolling uncomfortably as we cross from Alicante in Spain to Oran in Algeria. It's packed with people trading on foot with bundles and bags – second-hand shoes, baby-feeding bottles, cartons of cigarettes, nappies, toilet paper, blankets and mattresses. Those with vehicles have loaded fridges, washing machines, bicycles, furniture, TV sets and microwaves. Others are trading in brand-new cars. Some have cabins, some sleep on the decks. There was rough weather during the night and people have puked everywhere. We steal into the Algerian Port of Oran at sunrise. It is a customs and immigration nightmare; full of vehicles being stripped and searched and everywhere there are hugs and handshakes, whispers and smiles and deals being done.

There's a terrorist scare on the go and a travel warning has been released. Several bombs have gone off recently and the UN Headquarters in Algiers was targeted. We are nervous as all hell. But what a welcome. 'Ah! *Afrique du Sud* – South Africans. You are most welcome.' Down come the entry stamps with a bang. There's security everywhere, along with flack jackets and automatic weapons. A pretty Algerian security lady who speaks English explains the situation. 'You need security wherever you go. Foreign visitors are not allowed to move without it,' she says. Because of the recent upsurge in terrorist activity in Algeria the authorities don't want us killed it seems. She talks in Arabic into her radio, and then smiles. 'Looks like you are expected,' she says. 'Red Crescent is waiting for you – seems your expedition is doing a good job. You're going to the refugee camps at Tindouf?' I nod. Seems the truth is out. She helps us change dollars into Algerian dinars and we buy vehicle insurance. Super-friendly people, no black sun-visor marks here – not yet anyway.

The boom goes up and we follow the flashing lights of a heavily armed police escort – we have one in front of our three Landies and another guarding the rear. Accompanied

A view over Oran.

ALGERIA - NOTES
- AFRICA'S SECOND LARGEST COUNTRY
- ITS 2,381 MILLION KM²
- CAPITAL: ALGIERS
- ITS BORDERED BY MOROCCO, MAURITANIA, MALI, NIGER, LIBYA AND TUNISIA.
- OVER 90% OF THE POPULATION ARE SUNNI MUSLIMS. BERBERS ARE THE LARGEST ETHNIC GROUP
- MAIN LANGUAGES ARE ARABIC, FRENCH, BERBER — MUST FIND A LOCAL TRANSLATOR
- SECURITY SITUATION IS POOR. ISLAMIC ACTIVISTS WANT TO TAKE OVER THE GOVERNMENT; FOREIGNERS ARE BEING TARGETED — ARMED CONVOYS?!

"IN OUR OLD LANDIES WE EVEN TOOK THE FIGHT TO NOUAKCHOTT, CAPITAL OF MAURITANIA."

AFRICA
OUTSIDE EDGE EXPEDITION

OFFICIAL

We meet Ammi and his family. He's from the Red Crescent — so hospitable, they even dress us up in local costume.

by sirens screaming and uniformed men talking on their hand-held radios, we zigzag through the streets of Oran. Plain-clothes men who now appear in front of the Landies usher us into a parking garage. The gates close behind us with a clang. We shit ourselves. What now? Then suddenly it's through a side door with our bags, armed security on either side. Djamal, the manager of the Hotel Adef, speaks delightful English. 'Welcome to Oran, we haven't seen tourists for years. Passports please – mother name, father name, date of birth, passport issued when and where, and what your occupation?' We introduce ourselves and explain our journey. Djamal, wearing a mustard-coloured jacket, grins broadly. It's *Fawlty Towers* at its best. 'We have restaurant, we have bar, we have room service. We have best nightclub, beautiful ladies. Mashozi and you, Papa King – we give you biggest room in hotel, view of the sea. But please not to walk outside.'

We pull back the curtains of our ornate, cavernous room to reveal a grain silo, a scrap metal loading dock, hundreds of shipping containers of different colours, a tall brick chimney, the ferry that's just brought us from Spain and beyond that the Mediterranean. We bang on the gurgling water pipes that date back to French colonial times and then run the tap again. Finally there's the hissing of steam and the spitting of hot water. After a quick wash we find we are the only people in the dining room. The staff are delightful. 'Welcome to Oran. Tomorrow the security police will pick you up and take you to Mr Ammi from Red Crescent. Ammi, he's a good man,' says Djamal.

Dispatch #162 – Filling in the Gaps

Some weeks ago, on our journey up the coast of Western Sahara (located exactly where the name says it should be – on the western edge of the Sahara), it had been impossible for us properly to meet the legitimate citizens of the land. They are a proud people called the Sahrawis. Now, thanks to the efforts of our Department of Foreign Affairs and an invitation from the Sahrawi Arab Democratic Republic, in exile in the south of Algeria, we're going to get the opportunity to complete this section of the outside edge puzzle. Until now, for security reasons, this meeting has been kept secret. Adrenalin pumps, and I feel the smooth pebble in my pocket as we head off at breakneck speed in a heavily armed convoy. There's the gendarmerie in a vehicle in front, then Ammi Bol-la from the Red Crescent in an old, white diesel Patrol, then the three Landies. It's a 3 000 kilometre there-and-back dash to the refugee camps. The Landies are heavily loaded with learning materials, Rite to Sight spectacles and deflated 2010 South Africa World Cup soccer balls that we picked up in Oran. Ahead, more gendarmes stop the traffic and wave us through; they're very efficient. In the villages armed men in the roadside olive groves sweep the area. Surely with all this attention we're like sitting ducks, especially as the government and police are the terrorist targets?

Dispatch #163 – The Road to the Refugees

Ross comes on the radio asking, '*What about diesel?*' I flash my lights. Ammi and the military cops pull over quite agitated. 'Diesel,' I say to Ammi from the Red Crescent, 'we need to fuel up.' He speaks to Mr Moustache, the tall grizzly-looking lead cop, and he's onto his radio. 'On the right ahead,' says Ammi. Security fans out around the filling station. Mashozi grins when we give her the receipt. In oil-rich Algeria diesel is cheaper than drinking water. The cops are agitated. I feel very exposed – what if my family gets shot up? Is it worth the price? We must be crazy. How the hell did we get into this?

We drive from police post to police post, changing guards and vehicle escorts as we go. They're all very professional and friendly, offering us cigarettes and strong coffee. 'Bafana Bafana no good, just like Algeria. Lazy, eat too much,' says one gendarme, part of a crowd gathered around a coffee-shop TV set in the cold. Egypt's playing Cameroon in the Africa Cup of Nations final in Ghana. They'd much rather stay and watch the game than escort us down a long road to a landless country.

Morocco had dropped napalm and phosphorous bombs on tens of thousands of Sahrawis, mostly women and children, who then fled across the border into Algeria where they were granted asylum. Here they were allowed to build refugee camps in an area of the desert considered uninhabitable. It's a place where temperatures reach a scorching 40 °C in summer and plunge below freezing in winter. Sandstorms, called siroccos, rip through the refugee camps without warning. Flash floods wipe out entire tent neighbourhoods, destroying everything in their path. Here, in the southwest corner of Algeria near the border with Morocco, nearly 200 000 refugees are struggling to survive in this inhospitable part of the great Sahara Desert. South Africa is one of 72 countries that recognise the Sahrawians' right to independence; we are going to try and do our bit to help.

Dispatch #164 – Iron Camels of the Desert

It's the first time ever that three battered South African-registered Landies pull into the mud houses and tented areas that make up the refugee camps. The Western Saharan flags are back where they belong, between Mauritania and Morocco, on the sides of the vehicles. This is the most uninviting part of the Sahara that we've ever seen, but surprisingly the residents are full of pride and passion. After all these years in exile, they still long to get their land back. Our interpreter's name is Hamadi Bachir. He's a deeply intelligent man who speaks excellent English. 'Every family has a martyr,' he says. 'I lost four of my family in the war.' Ammi, our friend from the Red Crescent who has travelled with our convoy from Oran, says, 'I will rather die than live under the Moroccans. When Morocco and Mauritania invaded us they thought we were just a bunch of desert nomads and that the war would be over in a couple of weeks, but we fought them for over 10 years and by the time of the UN-brokered ceasefire, we'd given them a bloody nose. Our advantage was that we knew the desert like the back of our hands. We were known as the nomads of the clouds, forever wandering with our livestock in search of water.'

'And of course we had these,' say Ammi and Hamadi, tapping the bonnet of my much-travelled Land Rover Tdi. 'Our series 2 and 3 Land Rovers were our armed vehicles. We added extra fuel tanks, machine guns, RPGs and even anti-aircraft guns facing both ways. We got to know these vehicles inside out and even took the fight as far as Nouakchott, the capital of Mauritania, with our iron camels of the desert. Even today, it's the old Landies that are the backbone of transport in the refugee camps, hauling water, supplies, people, livestock and food – we can't do without them.'

Dispatch #165 – The Refugee Camps

A bone-jarring, teeth-loosening corrugated track takes us through to a local school in another camp, where we give out piles of learning materials and, best of all for the kids, footballs that are stamped '2010 World Cup, South Africa'. At the hospital we distribute spectacles to the poor-sighted. Over 80% of the population of the refugee camps are women and children. That night we meet the February 27th Women's Group, which is a kind of boarding school, its name a commemoration of the day the Sahrawi Arab Democratic Republic was founded in 1976. These tough, friendly women are wonderful; they are the backbone of life in the camps. Against unbelievable odds these ladies, many of whom have lost their husbands and sons in the war, have continued to build a nation and organise education, health and hygiene. We sit cross-legged on hand-woven carpets in a high-walled, peak-roofed tent. Dinner is couscous and camel. Outside there's a sandstorm. The brave matrons share some of their stories with us. One of them sobs with emotion as she tells us of their long walk across the desert to Algeria, sharing whatever food and water they could find, making fires

2010 SOCCER BALLS AND LEARNING MATERIALS FOR THE REFUGEE KIDS.

Dispatch #166 – The Wall of Shame

'It's a great travesty of justice,' says Hamadi, 'the world should recognise our plight. We are a nation in exile, with the Moroccans now having built a sand berm armed with five million landmines and more than 150 000 troops, so keeping us out of our own country.' The Moroccan Wall, or Wall of Shame as Sahrawi sympathisers call it, is approximately 2 700 kilometres long and took about six years to build, but has sadly not received much international attention.

There's a concert in our honour. Dancers are draped in flags and the audience of mostly women stand and wave peace signs in the air, their faces wrapped in headscarves and passion in their eyes. We're dragged up onto the stage and wrapped in hand-stitched green, red, black and white flags with a red crescent moon and star in the centre. All they want is to have their country back and South Africa is supporting a UN initiative for a free and fair referendum. The Minister of African Affairs, Mohammed Yestem Breissat, arranges a sunset dinner out in the desert where we sit cross-legged in the Sahara, eating homemade bread and camel kebabs. Later that evening, in a simple mud-built palace, the president of this little country in exile, Mr Mohamed Abdelaziz, endorses the expedition Scroll of Peace and Goodwill with these words:

> I warmly welcome these great adventurers of our dear sister South Africa. We in the Republic salute and commend this initiative that promotes peace on the continent and helps to eradicate disease ... With your great journey you have united the sons of our continent, and shortened the distance – please continue this great effort.

Kind and unassuming, he presents us each with a bangle engraved with our names and the flag of his country – we feel humbled by it all.

Albeit in exile, we've met the proud people of Western Sahara, so filling in this piece of the outside edge puzzle. We turn the Landies around. The Algerian military police meet us outside the town of Tindouf, and district by district groups of armed men and vehicles escort us back from village to village. Flash floods in the desert turn it into a nightmare journey. Two days

AND SO WE MEET THE PRESIDENT IN EXILE, MR MOHAMED ABDELAZIZ – HE'S A LOVELY MAN.

and raking the hot coals into small depressions in the sand so as to make a warm bed for the tiny babies.

The stories of their flight and the hard life in the camps are written in deep-etched lines on their faces. Even though they have very little, their hospitality is boundless and they pamper us, even giving us trinkets and desert robes to wear. 'We've even started an egg-laying plant,' says Ammi proudly, 'enough to give each refugee two eggs a month.' Next morning in our mud-walled quarters breakfast is a bowl of boiled eggs, fresh fruit and bread. Mashozi kicks me under the table. 'That's enough for 10 refugee families for a month,' she whispers. People with so little sharing so much – we feel awkward.

later, in the dark, with blue police lights flashing, the security gates clang behind us once again at the old Hotel Adef. Djamal, the manager, is delighted to see us alive.

Dispatch #167 – Oran

Back in Oran, with its beautiful old French colonial buildings such as the grand opera house modelled on the one in Paris and apartment blocks with ornate balconies, covered shutters and neo-classical details, one can tell that the French had been here for more than a century. Unlike other African countries colonised by the French, here the fight for independence from 1954 to 1962 cost more than a million Algerian lives. The fighting grew increasingly bitter when militant French settlers formed a secret underground army that went on a bloody campaign of reprisals against the National Liberation Front. Sadly, liberation in Algeria never brought peace and in the last 10 years an estimated 100 000 people have been killed in a civil war sparked off by the government cancelling an election that a radical Islamic party was assured of winning.

Since 1993 all foreigners have been under a *fatwah*, which is a religious opinion on Islamic law issued by a recognised authority. In this case, the *fatwah* promotes a sentence of death and more than 100 foreigners have been killed. Khaled, a friend we have made in Oran, explains about our constant security: 'It's really difficult, the government doesn't want the embarrassment of foreigners being killed, so the cops are under strict orders to make sure you guys stay alive. They're serious about it; if you get killed on their watch the cops will not only lose their jobs but face stiff prison sentences.'

Still Khaled manages to smuggle us out of the hotel without security and with his wife and friends we go up to the Fort of Santa Cruz that overlooks the city. It's a wonderful break from the constant surveillance. That night they entertain us at their home in nearby Aïn el Turk, which in French colonial times was a summer retreat. 'Now it's a centre for cabaret,' says Khaled. 'All night, every night. There are girls galore and you can drink until dawn.' We find Algerians to be some of the most generous and hospitable people we've come across – if only they could have peace. In Khaled's car and followed by one of the Landies, we backtrack to the Moroccan border at Oujda within sight of where we'd been turned back by the Moroccans. There are diesel smugglers everywhere, but we just had to do it to remain true to the outside edge.

Scenes from the refugee camps – ladies from the February 27th women's group endorse the scroll with Mashozi.

Dispatch #168 – Across the Meridian

Khaled puts us on the road out of Oran, then waves and hoots a farewell. Such wonderful friendships and hospitality. 'It's our trademark,' he laughs, 'look what happened to the French. We were friendly to them and they stayed for a more than a hundred years.' With Khaled's help we'd given the police escort the slip – I know it's reckless, but the sense of freedom is wonderful as we travel east across the Greenwich Meridian en route to Algiers.

Truth be told, we are dog-tired and all the security makes us edgy. The good thing, however, is that despite the current

Home Sweet Home.

terrorism threats the Algerian people are superbly friendly, especially when they hear that we are from *Janub Efrekia* – that's how you say South Africa in Arabic. But our freedom couldn't last – we're stopped at a big police roadblock. They're pissed off: where's our escort? We phone Khaled, he calms them down and on the phone explains to us that the thick-forested broken country ahead is considered very dangerous. It appears there's been some recent action. We wait for hours for a senior man to arrive, and our passports and papers are checked. Now it's getting dark. With cops in front and behind and an armoured car at our side throwing searchlights into the thick forest, we're taken to a hotel in the dark and given strict instructions *not to move* until the next morning when an escort would take us through to Algiers. We've managed to procure some cheap whiskey. Grogging is generally frowned upon, even so we have a few *dops*, all of us sitting on the floor and beds in our hotel room. The next morning, dressed in full leathers, jodhpurs and boots and, looking very much like actors in a German SS movie, cops on motorbikes escort us to the South African Embassy in Algiers.

Dispatch #169 – Algiers

The South African Ambassador is Mzuvukile Maqetuka, and he and his team can't do enough for us. There's tea and cake and the writing of messages in the expedition scroll. The ambassador is concerned about our security and loans us the embassy's trained-in-South-Africa security man – a big, tough, streetwise Algerian called Hafed. He's really pleasant and speaks reasonable English complete with a bit of Afrikaans and South African slang. In Algiers, Hafed organises us six plain-clothes cops and a guide from the police station above the Casbah, and they throw a *cordon sanitaire* around us. Residents move inside their Turkish-built, rabbit-warren homes in this stopped-in-time UNESCO World Heritage Site. Some kids throw a big-bang Guy Fawkes cracker and the men with the guns drop to the floor – everybody's a bit tense. The kids run down an alleyway howling with laughter. Few foreign visitors come these days and it's out of bounds for embassy staff, says Hafed.

This was a freedom-fighter's refuge against the French. Hafed buys some *chema* from a stall. 'You roll it into a wad and push it inside the gums. It keeps you calm,' he says. You need it here, especially in a place with 475 alleyways, 280 dead ends and hundreds of secretive, flat-topped houses that make ideal hideouts for urban terrorists. Hafed organises us a room at a good price at an old private hunting lodge set in beautiful grounds outside the city. It seems to be a haunt for businessmen with girls. Throughout the night there's the clicking of high heels on marble floors, the distinctive sounds of porn channels on the TV and much giggling and laughing. In the early morning we are greeted by the muezzin's call to prayer, a howling dog and sunrise over Algiers. Hafed arrives with his lovely girlfriend; she wants to meet us before he leaves with his little bag of clothes to escort us to Tunisia.

Dispatch #170 – The Road to Tunisia

Hafed's serious radio voice comes over the air from Bruce's Landy. 'Papa King …' 'Go ahead, Hafed.' 'Yes, Papa King. Police *say to drive little bit fast – three people killed here one day before yesterday.'* So we go flat out through towns and villages, all sirens and blue lights, with the cops stopping traffic to wave us on. Thank God for our Old Man Emu suspensions and permanent four wheel drive. 'Far more chance of being killed in a car crash,' says Mashozi, as following the cops, engine screaming, we overtake a truck on a blind rise. It's all too Rambo-ish.

The Algerian coastline is unbelievably beautiful and in parts much like the Rif coast of Morocco. It is also like a continuous Chapman's Peak Drive, with steep cliffs falling away into the Mediterranean and Cap Carbon looking very much like our own Cape Point, complete with baboons and lighthouse. But there are no foreign tourists other than our three Landies and a posse of well-armed friendly Algerian police.

At the beautiful town of Bejaia the pace calms down. We get a new escort and continue following the coastal twists, turns and tunnels into Jijel at last light. Armed cops guard the little hotel where we pay 3 200 dinars per room. It's not bad, and each room has an arrow showing the direction of Mecca for prayer time. Everybody's really friendly. The cops case the street joint where we want to eat kebabs whilst others watch the Landies where they're parked behind the hotel – don't want them blown up. The voodoo protection fetishes from Benin should keep them safe.

Hafed's a star; he does a wonderful job of translating and is great company for Bruce. I chat to him about the current security situation in the country. I sense he's concerned for our safety – it's a bad time. I suggest an early morning call. I chat to the cops, telling them we should try and get out of Algeria by tomorrow night. They are keen, and I'm sure they want to be rid of the responsibility of this crazy outside edge circus. We're all tired and a bit jittery. The next day brings more cops, more running the gauntlet and more watching every situation. We see a covered Peugeot van on the side of the road – who's inside? Then there are some young bloods shouting from a street corner – are they armed? Our eyes are out on stalks as we go through thick forests, although admittedly the countryside and coastline are beautiful. Is there danger waiting outside a cop shop for the next convoy? Surely that's when we are the most vulnerable? Attacks on police stations are common here. Dog-tired, our last cape is Cap Rosa. It's a beautiful, small fishing harbour, that also includes the remains of an old Turkish Fort and a small lighthouse.

Our three Landies bridging the gap.

Bruce puts his camera on its timer and we grin for a rare full-team shot on the Greenwich Meridian.

Following flashing police lights in the dark gives you a headache. We hear a muezzin's call to prayer as we go through El Kala. This is where our last Algerian police convoy leaves us. We hoot and flash our lights in thanks. Hafed does a great job of getting us out of Algeria; it's wonderful to have an embassy man with us! He just flashes his Algerian security card and down goes the exit stamp. I let out a sigh of relief. The people have been lovely but not to die for. Tunisia here we come!

Tunisia

Day 301, Country 24 on the Edge

With its ancient Roman cities and coliseums, vibrant medinas and beautiful beaches, Tunisia is a jewel in the North African crown. Influences from Italy, Spain and France give the country a sophisticated European feel and the rich texture and vibrancy of Arabia give it a kaleidoscope of colour that attracts thousands of tourists. Lucky, because unlike its oil-rich neighbours, Tunisia's economy relies on agriculture and tourism. For us, Tunisia means reaching the northernmost tip of the African continent.

THE LIGHTHOUSE OFF AFRICA'S NORTHERNMOST POINT —

Dispatch #171 – Crossing into Tunisia

The border people all seem very relaxed but the police commissioner herds us into his office. I explain that there's a delegation meeting us at Bizerte and then a ceremony at Africa's northernmost point. He's very polite, offering smiles, handshakes and little glasses of sweet mint tea. We look a bit travel-worn and rumpled, which leads him to rub a stick of perfume on the backs of our hands. Mind you, we probably do smell a bit. There are more small glasses of Arabic tea and yet another slow page-by-page scrutinising of each passport with a furrowed brow, ash falling off the end of his cigarette and side whispers to customs and immigration men who are called into his office one at a time for extra effect. 'What you are, what you do, name of bank? Your mother name, your father name?' he asks. We've seen it all before and know what's coming. With a big, friendly smile I remark to Ross in Zulu that I sense we're going to need the black pen for another mark on the sun visor. He nods and answers in English, 'Yes, Tunisia is very beautiful.'

There's yet more tea, more offers of cigarettes, more smiles of friendship and more whispers to his colleagues before finally the police commissioner invents a visa problem which he indicates, in the friendliest manner, can easily be sorted out. Then comes the bombshell, the one we've been waiting for. *Baksheesh* – a bribe, a backhand, money. Mashozi loses her cool. The next minute she's got her cellphone out and phones Danie Meyer, the South African ambassador in Tunis, who is expecting us. 'Do you want to speak to our ambassador?' she asks, handing the phone over to Mr Nice. 'Explain to him that you want money!' Mr Nice backs off, down comes the passport stamps and six hours later, in the early hours of the morning, we even get a police escort into town. It's this sort of bureaucratic crap that wears us out so, taking out the felt-tipped marker, Mashozi opens the scorecard for Tunisia. Hafed's pissed off. 'It's because it is out of season, late in the evening and we're the only people, so he thought he could play with us. You should see this border in summer – thousands of Algerians cross here to have holidays, the girls with tight jeans and T-shirts and then covering up with conservative headscarves and Islamic dress as they cross back into Algeria. For young Algerians like me Tunisia is our playground. We love it – it's so free.'

Everybody's tired and a bit Land-Rovered out. What's killed us is having been over-policed in Algeria. We've been missing the freedom of camping wherever we end up on the outside edge and just doing our own thing. What we're really yearning for, however, is a good old braai and some *dop* – even a slice of South African-type bread would be a great. But a serious treat, however, would be rump steak, *tjops*, a curl of *boerewors*, Nando's sauce, and some biltong, wet and fatty. Home pleasures are all about pouring a double Cappies, having mates around and throwing the odd bone to the dogs whilst wearing shorts and no shoes, walking *kaalvoet*. I guess all we need is a day off.

Dispatch #172 – Africa's Northernmost Point

From the Algerian border we travel past a series of beautiful lakes, forests, green fields, white-walled villages with blue doors and shutters, spring flowers and rich agricultural lands. Tunisia was once the breadbasket of Rome. '*We're approaching the port of Bizerte,*' says Ross over the radio. '*Isn't it wonderful – no roadblocks and no security hassles. It feels so free.*' We all agree. Bizerte is so clean and colourful, with gaily painted fishing

TUNISIA - NOTES:
- *HOME OF THE ANCIENT CITY OF CARTHAGE*
- *POPULATION IS 10.4 MILLION, CAPITAL IS TUNIS.*
- *AREA IS 164 150 SQ KM, MAJOR LANGUAGES ARE ARABIC AND FRENCH*
- *FASCINATING HISTORY, BEAUTIFUL BEACHES TUNISIA IS LOVED BY TOURISTS*
- *FOR US IT MEANS REACHING THE NORTHERNMOST POINT OF THE AFRICAN CONTINENT A GREAT FEELING AND A YARDSTICK FOR THIS CRAZY JOURNEY TO TRACK 'THE EDGE'*

THE S'AFRICAN, TUNISIAN AND EXPEDITION FLAGS, THE SCROLL, A CONSERVATION STONE, THE EXPEDITION TEAM AND HAFED – WE'VE REACHED THE NORTHERNMOST POINT OF AFRICA.

boats behind the sea wall of the old port. It's a special moment as we're heading for Cap Angela and the northernmost tip of Africa, and we know we're close. In first and second gear, we bounce down a small dust road, its potholes still full from last night's rain. We pass a shepherd dressed in an old, blue dustcoat herding nine sheep; a small forest, and a moustached man on horseback; emerald green fields; women washing clothes at a water pump; spring flowers; a tethered donkey, four cows and a man in a red jacket; and at last we get there.

We pile out of the Landies. We've talked about this moment for weeks – it's such an important yardstick for the expedition. Danie Meyer, the South African ambassador to Tunisia, his wife Mynie and a group of VIPs are here to meet us. Imagine the scene: the expedition team, worn out and ragtag from the tense journey across Algeria, and the Tunisians, all dressed in suits as they endorse the same Peace and Goodwill scroll that's now been written in by presidents, kings, ambassadors, paramount chiefs, government ministers and Nobel Peace Prize laureates Archbishop Desmond Tutu and Nelson Mandela. If we survive this crazy journey and return to the Cape of Good Hope, we would like to hand the scroll back to Mr Mandela. To the flashing of media cameras, we hand over a symbolic conservation stone carried all the way from Africa's most southerly point and pick up one from here to be taken back down to Cape Agulhas. With the South African flag flying, I feel proud of our little team and all the good work we've achieved; it seems like a miracle.

Dispatch #173 – Home away from Home

Danie and Mynie must have taken one look at us and known we needed some TLC; some good old home life. They take us to their residence in Tunis, where again we see our national flag flying outside. Ali the guard opens the blue wrought-iron gates and Wagter the black Labrador wags his tail and pants with excitement. Here we can wear shorts and go *kaalvoet* and there are crisp white sheets, showers and a keg of beer. Earlier that morning, Danie and I had gone to his favourite butcher where, in true Tunisian fashion, the head of the day's slaughtered cow, camel, goat or sheep is displayed outside the shop to indicate the meat is fresh. This evening is everything we've been dreaming about. Bruce is cooking; the *tjops* and steaks are sizzling on the coals and there's crumbly *phutu pap* with onion and tomato gravy and motherly Mynie's fresh homebaked bread. We wash it all down with bottles of South African wine and there's fun and banter around the braai.

Danie takes a bit of cheese and a rat trap into Ross and Anna's Landy – their vehicle has got a resident rat and it's been getting into everything. When he comes back we discover our host is a keen historian. 'Tunisia is a paradise,' he says. 'It's rich cultural and social heritage is thanks to the many empires that have come and gone in this part of the world, from the Phoenicians to the Romans, Byzantines, Arabs, Ottoman Turks and the French. The ancient city-state of Carthage is just a few minutes' drive from here. Hannibal, the famed military commander and tactician, invaded Europe from there. Imagine taking an army from North Africa across the Mediterranean and then using elephants to transport them over the Alps to invade Europe – a spectacular feat. It so enraged the Romans that they came back here and destroyed the old Carthaginian Empire, and it is even said that they ploughed up the fields and sowed them with salt. Today there's a railway station called Carthage Hannibal.' Danie goes to check up on the Landy, comes back with a grin. 'There were two rats,' he says. 'I got them both.'

Dispatch #174 – Tunis and Ancient Carthage

Since independence from France in 1955 Tunisia has been one of Africa's most stable and moderate Arabic countries. What a difference between here and the stricter nations in the region; the people here seem happy and relaxed. There's an energy to Tunis, the capital city, with its beautiful white-domed houses and the blue coastline of the Gulf of Tunis. The country's been liberalised, women have equal rights, polygamy and Islamic fundamentalism are outlawed and one feels safe on the streets. The mainstay of the economy is tourism, but fortunately for us it's out of season and the millions that visit haven't arrived yet. This little North African country is a melting pot of so many nations; most people here are better educated and one senses that they feel more a part of Europe, which is quite different from the other Arabic countries.

On Mount Byrsa, amongst the old stone ruins and pillars of the ancient Phoenician trading capital of Carthage, stands a beautiful Roman theatre. At first glance we can already see why Carthage is now a UNESCO World Heritage Site. Fezari Mabrouk, an old wrinkled tourist guide, gives us a toothless grin. 'Listen,' he says as he claps his hands to show off the acoustics of the Théâtre Antique de Carthage. 'It holds 10 000 people,' says Danie Meyer, who's showing us the sights of Tunis. Miriam Makeba performed here in 1972 and, more recently, so did Johnny Clegg. Above the amphitheatre, as proof of the Tunisians' religious tolerance, stands a beautiful 19th-century French Cathedral which is now used as a cultural theatre. It's a lovely clear day. Looking out from Mount Byrsa, we can see the old ports of Carthage and, beyond them, across the Gulf of Tunis, we can see all the way to Cap Bon. It's a fascinating piece of the outside edge, which the Carthage tourist brochure sums up quite nicely:

> *For three thousand years the history of Tunisia has been made along these shores – Phoenicians, Punics, Romans, Vandals, Byzantines, Arabs and Muslims, Crusaders, Spaniards, Turks and French, like so many waves breaking on the shore throughout the never-ending cycle of the years ...*

Danie Meyer is in his element. 'Legend has it,' he says, 'that it was the beautiful Princess Elyssa from Tyre who founded Carthage, the New City, on African soil. After she discovered her brother and co-ruler, Pygmalian, had murdered her husband, Princess Elyssa fled her homeland in present-day Syria with some loyal followers. Tired from the long sea voyage, she wanted a place to settle with her people, and found the headland that used to be a Sidonian Phoenician trading post to her liking. The African chief she began negotiating with was afraid that they might settle in too large numbers, so she requested that he allow her just as much land as a hide of a cow could cover. The natives agreed to the modest proposal, but Elyssa, displaying some of the cunning of her infamous great aunt Jezebel, resorted to a trick. She had the hide cut into very thin strips which encircled a wider area than she appeared to have requested. The African chief, who by this time had fallen for her charms, relented, and the place was named Mount Byrsa, which means 'ox hide'. And that's said to have taken place in 814 BCE.'

Now, 2 822 years later, in the car park on Mount Byrsa, you can have your photograph taken with a man dressed as a Roman Centurion, and there's even a fake throne and live falcon, postcards, miniatures of the Carthaginian (or Phoenician) and Roman busts and old coins for sale. I'm so glad it's out of tourist season. We say goodbye to Danie and Mynie Meyer;

We all clap to test the acoustics of the Théâtre Antique de Carthage.

they've added so much to the Zen of Travel, not only by being there for us at Africa's northernmost tip, but also for making Tunis and ancient Carthage come alive.

Dispatch #175 – Carthage to Sousse

It remains constant. It's like a drug, a security blanket, if it's not there we go into a decline, it's our reason for being, it's always on our left – it's the outside edge of Africa and it's beautiful. John Ross, Mary Kingsley and Lady Baker (alias the Stomach), three South African-registered Landies, carry a Scroll of Peace and Goodwill in support of malaria prevention, a calabash filled with Cape of Good Hope seawater, a pebble in a pocket and some special stones. We're following the coastline of the Gulf of Tunis along cliffs, beaches and green fields. We reach Korbous. I'm looking for a pharmacy, but we're lacking French and Arabic as Hafed's gone back to Algiers. I find one, where I rub my stomach and blow out my cheeks. It's all the great hospitality in Tunis. The man and his wife behind the counter get the giggles. I give a grimace: 'Con-sti-pa-tion,' I explain, rubbing my rounded belly again. 'Ah! *Lax-a-tif*,' they say. I get a bottle of powder and a measuring spoon. It works like a bomb – literally! From El Haouaria, we look back some 50 kilometres across the gulf to where the outline of the white buildings of Tunis is clearly visible. Offshore are the islands of Zemba and Zembretta and across the Mediterranean, out of sight, lie Spain, Italy, Sicily, Corsica and Sardinia.

We round Cap Bon and then return south along the Gulf of Hammamet. After Algeria, there's such a wonderful feeling of freedom – we stop where we like, we can photograph the sights and there are no roadblock hassles. Parts of the coast

DRINKING ALL THE STOCK AND HAVING FUN BEFORE CROSSING INTO 'NO BOOZE' LIBYA

The old fort on Jerba Island.

remind us of our own Cape Peninsula. Ross is navigating. '*Let's push for the town of Sousse,*' he says over the radio. For the first time in a long time we feel like tourists, enjoying good roads and good food. Then we get a reality call from Theo Albrecht from the South African Embassy in Tripoli, Libya. He'll meet us in three days' time at the Libyan border. 'Please, you must be on time – it's CRITICAL,' he says. 'Things aren't easy here but your paperwork seems to be coming through – let's hope for the best!'

Sousse, one of the oldest ports on the Mediterranean, dates back to the 9th century BCE when it was founded as a Phoenician trading post. Today it's the third-largest city in Tunisia. For us the attraction is the ancient medina, the old walled market built in 859. We abandon the Landies and let Mohammed take control of our destination, hands on the reigns and a cigarette in the mouth. We hear the clip-clop sounds of shod hooves on the tarmac and whispered commands to the two beautiful horses as Mohammed skilfully manoeuvres our horse carriage from where we've parked on the beachfront up to the bustling medina. We can feel the heartbeat of the local culture as we stroll through a labyrinth of winding alleyways, past hundreds of vaulted souks – the market stalls that sell everything from shisha pipes to carpets. We see coffee and spices, antique Berber jewellery, sunglasses, saucy underwear, belly-dancing outfits, birdcages, engraved copper, leatherwear and bridal gowns. Mashozi buys me a long brown robe, a sort of cassock that we've mostly seen worn by farmers on the roadside. Then, to complete my new wardrobe, she adds an Arabic headscarf. Mashozi gets herself a beautiful Berber shawl – we're spoiling ourselves today.

Back in the Landies, driving slowly out of Sousse, a man runs out from between a pavement shop of mopeds, points at me and shouts, 'Hey Hannibal, can I come along?' Mashozi gets the giggles. She's heard me being called Bin Laden, Papá Noel, Ali Baba, Jesus, ZZ Top, William Wallace, Zorba the Greek and Christopher Columbus, but Hannibal is a first.

Dispatch #176 – Roman Thysdrus

Danie Meyer had ringed it on our map. We see it from a distance, a giant ochre-coloured plum pudding. The sheer bulk of the largest of all Roman monuments in Africa is breathtaking. Situated in the modern town of El Jemm, the huge stone-built coliseum provided seating for a whopping 45 000 spectators. We walk through the dungeons and see the iron rings where the prisoners and wild animals were tethered, and then climb the stairs to sit at the top of the grandstand. It's easy to imagine what went on here: wild beasts fighting to the death; gladiatorial skirmishes as re-enactments of various myths; and Christian martyrs and prisoners being thrown to the lions. The Romans, it appears, loved the practice of public slaughter. The coliseum here in Thysdrus, an area made wealthy from olive oil production, was, after the coliseum in Rome and the amphitheatre in Santa Maria Capua Vetere, the largest in the Empire. Outside the coliseum, where tourists take camel rides, Mashozi bargains for three red felt fezzes. 'Why three?' I ask. 'One for you, one for Ross, and one for Abu the Ape from Abidjan.' The latter, might I add, is still taking up space in the back of our Landy.

In El Jemm you can buy factory-made Roman pottery, Roman busts and columns, and even slabs of mosaics depicting gladiatorial scenes from the nearby coliseum of Thysdrus. It seems as if the Romans have never left.

Dispatch #177 – Jerba Island and Beyond

We mustn't miss our deadline for the Libyan border meeting. We still don't have visas; it's a niggling worry at the back of my mind and the next outside edge challenge. The city of Sfax and the offshore Îles de Kerkenah are behind us as we travel down the Gulf of Gabes heading for Jorf, the ferry point for the tourist mecca of Jerba Island. Three battered South African Land Rovers, loaded to the hilt, carrying a man with a beard and a scruffy team – it's natural that the no-nonsense-looking security man gives us so much attention. Jerba Island, with its idyllic palm-fronded, white-sand beaches and rows of hotel complexes, can't afford another tourist attack like the one that took place in 2002 in which 20 tourists, mainly German, were killed by a lorry load of explosives. The old fort is magnificent and the harbour at Houmt Souq has replicas of old three-masted schooners for hire, for both sightseeing and booze cruises, whilst the dockside is stacked with hundreds of terracotta clay pots used as traps for catching octopus for tourists' tables.

We sit out on the point watching the colourful octopus boats. A cop on a moped wants to know what we're up to, why all the Landies? Pointing a finger to the side of my head, I tell him we're crazy, that we're trying to follow the edge of Africa. But his English is bad, and he swears blind that I've said he's crazy! Now I'm marched off to the police station for insulting a policeman. The plain-clothes guys with sunglasses and leather jackets get called in. 'Cool it, Pops,' says Ross. After much scrutinising of papers and passports we all shake hands, jump in the Landies and head out along the tourist road via Ras Tourgueness.

Jerba claims to be the land of the locust eaters, celebrated in Homer's *Odyssey*. These days the locust eaters have been replaced by thousands of sun worshippers: German, Dutch, Swedish and Italian. It's all been a bit too much for us and already I'm feeling a sense of nostalgia for the rough and raw adventures of the outside edge. Whilst I can't deny that it's a wonderful piece of Africa's outside edge, it's simply too touristy for us and we push on over the causeway to Zarzis on the mainland, where fat sheep are tethered to butchers' stalls and smuggled diesel from Libya is being sold on the roadside. Tunisia, with its warm heart and friendly manner, has been an easy and charming experience; it's no wonder that it's such a sought-after tourist destination. Let's just hope it survives Islamic fundamentalism.

Tomorrow 11 a.m. is our deadline for entrance to Colonel Mu'ammar Abu Minyar al-Gaddafi's Socialist People's Libyan Arab Great Jamahiriya – I just hope he lets us in. Apparently he's just closed the borders to fellow Africans as there are too many immigrants from West Africa; it seems he's courting Europe instead. Theo calls again to confirm our meeting at the border. 'See you tomorrow,' he says over the phone, 'but please understand, nothing's guaranteed so hold thumbs.'

Libya

Day 307, Country 25 on the Edge

Mayebabo! Alas, the Socialist People's Libyan Arab Great Jamahiriya is difficult for independent travellers, and it's a huge rigmarole to get in. We've had our passport details officially translated into Arabic and stamped and stapled into the back page of our passports, filed our detailed itinerary and paid a small fortune to a tour operator and a tourism police officer to meet us at the border so that they can watch our every move across the country. But there's still no guarantee of getting in ...

LEPTIS MAGNA.

Dispatch #178 – We're Through!

A massive billboard of Colonel Mu'ammar Gaddafi welcomes us to the *Jamahiriya*, or State of the Masses, of Libya. 'It's a stroke of luck,' explains Theo, our embassy man. 'Someone who plays tennis with a relative of Gaddafi heard of your predicament and the right word was whispered into an official ear.' And so, with paper and signature in hand, Theo and Assad, our friendly official tour operator, spent the last six hours in a mammoth paper-shuffling, border-post negotiation, which resulted in new Libyan expedition documentation and Libyan, Arabic-script number plates, now attached to each Landy. *Alhumdillah!* We are through!

The road to Tripoli is aptly named the Highway of Death. Fuel smugglers carrying cheap Libyan petrol and diesel through to Tunisia drive like bloody lunatics, ducking and weaving through the traffic and into the face of oncoming vehicles. Burnt-out wrecks litter the side of the highway. In Libya fuel is only 17 South African cents a litre; it's less than half the price of drinking water. There's no import duty on cars and big petrol V8s thunder past. Whilst women need a driving test to get a license, Libyan men qualify automatically. Meet the drivers in a coffee shop and they'll very politely wish peace upon you with the traditional *assalām 'alaikum,* but put them behind the steering wheel and they turn into cowboys with an aggressive disrespect for your life. 'Allah is the patron saint of brakes,' says Assad with a grin. We're warming towards him – he's professional, friendly, speaks good English and has a great sense of humour. Our minder, however, is a young, glum-looking, plain-clothes cop who speaks only Arabic and is already frustrating the hell out of Assad by constantly asking 'What are they saying, what do they mean and why are they laughing?' as he eyes us up and down suspiciously. With his fancy, sharp-pointed, leather shoes, Mashozi has already nicknamed him 'Twinkle Toes' and the name sticks.

ROSS ANNA MASHOZI THE BEARD ASSAD

46037 46038 46036 46037

HAMMING IT UP WITH OUR NEW FRIENDS AND LIBYAN NUMBER PLATES
TWINKLE TOES

LIBYA - NOTE:

- HASSLES TO GET IN - I SUPPOSE THE EXPEDITION THING IS CONFUSING, AND ARRIVING IN OUR OWN LANDIES - EASIER IF YOU FLY IN AS A TOURIST.
- CAPITAL CITY IS TRIPOLI
- THE 1 759 540 KM² LAND BORDERS ALGERIA, TUNISIA, EGYPT, SUDAN, CHAD AND NIGER
- THE LIBYAN FLAG IS INTERESTING, IT'S THE ONLY NATIONAL FLAG IN THE WORLD WITH NO DESIGN OR INSIGNIA - IT'S JUST A UNIFORM GREEN
- PRESIDENT SINCE HIS SUCCESSFUL COUP IN 1969, MU'AMMAR ABU MINYAR AL-GADDAFI IS STILL REFERRED TO AS 'BROTHER LEADER AND GUIDE OF THE REVOLUTION'

TEACHING ON THE EDGE

Dispatch #179 – Libya's Capital of Tripoli

In Tripoli, Mashozi and I stay with Theo and his family. Ross and Anna move in with Buks and Susan de Vry and Bruce with Caiphus Malope – all wonderfully hospitable South African Embassy staff. There's an alcohol-free cocktail party in our honour and the ambassador endorses the scroll. We visit the British, the international and a local government school to talk about the expedition and have a gig with a jolly gang of South Africans who even make their own *boerewors*.

Today Assad is dressed in an embroidered waistcoat, called a *farmla*, over a blue-and-grey-pinstriped kaftan robe, and on his head he has the typical *taghiyha*, the black fez of Tripoli. The outfit is completed by sandals and round 1960s rock-star shades. The Landies are parked and we're taking a walk through time in the capital. There's no English language signage in Libya, only Arabic, and the streets are called sharias. Twinkle Toes follows at a distance as we walk down Sharia Omar al-Mukhtar, named after a national hero who led the freedom struggle against the Italians. 'They made a Hollywood epic about him,' says Assad proudly. 'It's called *Lion of the Desert*.' Anthony Quinn plays the hero, Rod Steiger is Mussolini and Oliver Reed is the Italian villain, Colonel Graziani, who hanged poor Mukhtar in the end. 'Look,' says Assad, pulling out some money. 'The Lion of the Desert's face is even on our 10 dinar note.' Assad tells us more about the Italian reign. 'From 1911 until the end of World War II the Italian time was not good for Libya. They took over completely, killing or exiling at least half of our population. What made matters worse was that Libya became the battleground for the World War II desert campaign. Even now, large minefields still remain, killing our people,' he says.

The old Italian casino with marble pillars from Leptis Magna is now a bank. 'Please, no photographs,' says Assad, looking across at Twinkle Toes. We walk through Green Square, with green flags everywhere, and pass the Red Castle that overlooks the port where Assad's father took him for his first swim. At the northern end of the medina, the Arch of Marcus Aurelius, the only Roman monument left in Tripoli, still stands. I can just imagine how it must have been in Roman times – a wealth of slaves, ivory, gum arabic, gold and coliseum-bound wild animals, brought from the African interior across the Sahara, passing through this gateway between the desert and the sea to be shipped across the Mediterranean to Rome. In Roman times this place was full of travellers, merchants, camels and small *foundouks*, hotels for the passer-through. Even wheat for Rome's bread was grown in Libya's green mountains. 'You understand Papa King,' says Assad, peering over the top of his spectacles, 'it was the wealth of Africa that kept Rome alive, and it is still the same today. It's our top-quality oil that drives Europe.' In a narrow backstreet a group of West Africans scurry like rats as they see Bruce pointing his camera. 'It's a problem,' says Assad, 'thousands of illegal immigrants from West Africa pay hard-earned money to unscrupulous human traffickers to bring them across the Sahara. They hope they can use Libya as a springboard into Europe.' We'd come across gangs

The Green Mosque in Tripoli.

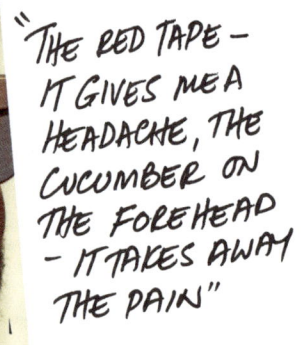

"THE RED TAPE – IT GIVES ME A HEADACHE, THE CUCUMBER ON THE FOREHEAD – IT TAKES AWAY THE PAIN"

An old Roman bridge on the edge of Africa

Leptis Magna.

of hopefuls throughout West and North Africa, young men from Nigeria, Ghana, Cameroon and even Liberia, leaving their families behind and running from poverty in their desperation to get to Europe, but only a small percentage of them ever make it. It's sad.

Up early on a public holiday, smiling children hang out of car windows as crazy, suicidal drivers overtake us at breakneck speeds over blind rises and around corners. It makes the blood run cold. We enjoy steamed mutton with rice and strong coffee at a dusty roadside café, where the people are friendly and well dressed. At least Gaddafi has spread the oil money around by supplying housing, electricity and subsidised food, and most Libyans seem content with their lot. We make our way to the ruins of the Roman city of Leptis Magna.

Dispatch #180 – The Roman City of Leptis Magna

Some of the finest Roman ruins outside Italy are to be found along Libya's Mediterranean coast. It's hard to think that this is the same African outline as South Africa's Cape Peninsula, Namibia's Skeleton Coast, the rainforest coast of the Gulf of Guinea, crowded Lagos, voodoo Benin, war-torn Liberia and Sierra Leone. Leptis Magna, the richest and most magnificent of all the Roman cities in Africa, is surely one of the most spectacular scenes along the outside edge. Our dusty boots take us over the well-worn slabs of the paved street of the Via Colonnata that runs down to the grand outdoor theatre that seated thousands. We sit in the top row; below us is the stage and beyond that the Mediterranean and Europe.

Lovely Libyan spices and legumes.

The German Mausoleum at Tobruk

At Tobruk Mashozi and Anna place flowers at the base of an unknown S'African soldier's grave —

No English signage in Libya

Dispatch #181 – The South Africans at Tobruk

Assad stops in a town to make more photocopies of our permissions letter – he's going through them like confetti at a wedding. Each roadblock claims one, and there are many roadblocks. We continue our drive following an old Italian road along the outside edge of Africa to reach the Commonwealth War Cemetery outside Tobruk, where a mix of British, Australian, Canadian, Indian, New Zealander and South African soldiers lie buried – a total of 3 670 men and 1 woman. It's late afternoon and a cold wind blows across the desert. We park the Landies. The sky is grey and leaden and the atmosphere is heavy. Ahead of us is a monument to fallen South African soldiers, in both English and Afrikaans:

Sacred to the memory of our gallant comrades of the First South African Division who made the supreme sacrifice during the battle for Cyrenaica, November–December 1941.

In the bitter struggle to relieve the siege of Tobruk, this division was the only all-volunteer contingent. We walk slowly between the long, neat rows of the gravestones of our countrymen: Van Reenen, Van Rensburg, Van Staaden, Van Niekerk, Van der Merwe, Bates, Macintyre, Adams, Ehlers and Gillespie, Moleke, Mosifane, Ndhlovu, Goqo, Cohen and Rosenthal. Each gravestone has our old national motto, 'Eendrag maak Mag', meaning 'Unity is Strength', circling the head of a springbok.

That morning Annelie and Mashozi had picked a huge bunch of wild flowers growing between the ancient ruins of Apollonia, once the port for the Roman city of Cyrene, high on the hills behind it. They now find the gravestone of an unknown South African lying between that of Private Claassen and Corporal CJ van Vuuren. It's a simple stone that under the springbok head reads: 'A soldier of the 1939–1945 war – Known unto God.' We call for a minute's silence as the girls place the flowers and a small South African flag at the foot of the grave. It brings a lump to the throat and a dash of colour to the sombre surroundings. A dog barks from the flat roof of a nearby mud-brick, Arab house. Sheep and goats graze beyond the neat, brown, sandstone perimeter wall. Especially poignant are these words from Laurence Binyon's poem inscribed on a headstone:

They shall grow not old as we that are left grow old:
Age shall not weary them, nor the years condemn.
At the going down of the sun and in the morning
We will remember them.

Dispatch #182 – The War in North Africa

The war in North Africa, in which South Africans played a prominent role, was key to the overall success of the allies in World War II. The British Army was in Egypt to protect the Suez Canal, the use of which significantly reduced the time it took ships to sail between Europe and the Far East. If Britain controlled the Suez, then Nazi Germany and the other Axis powers could not use it. Also, if the Allies could build up bases in North Africa, there was always the potential to launch an attack on what Churchill called the 'soft underbelly of Europe', meaning Italy or Yugoslavia. By 1941 the Italian army had been all but beaten and Hitler had to send German troops to North Africa to clear out the Allies. The German force was led by Erwin Rommel, one of the finest field marshals of the war. In March 1941 Rommel attacked the Allies in Libya and by May that same year he had all but pushed them back into Egypt. Only Tobruk held out against the Desert Fox.

In June 1941 British General Archibald Wavell started Operation Battleaxe to help the siege of Tobruk. It failed, as the Allied force was too small to defeat Rommel's Afrika Korps. Churchill sacked Wavell and replaced him with General Claude Auchinleck, who planned an attack on Rommel for November 1941. The attack succeeded and Rommel was forced to retreat, but then he reorganised and hit back. The tough seesaw battle for this inhospitable coastline continued until June 1942, when Tobruk fell. A total of 35 000 Allied troops were taken prisoner, which was more men than Rommel had at his disposal.

Later, Bernard Montgomery was put in charge of the British Eighth Army, composed of men from the United Kingdom, South Africa, Australia, New Zealand and India, and on 23 October 1942 he launched the greatest artillery barrage the world has ever known. The attack was directed against the combined might of the German and Italian forces entrenched near a remote desert railway station in Egypt, whose name is now recorded for all time in the annals of war as El Alamein.

Rommel was forced to retreat. Trapped between the Eighth Army and the advancing American forces from Algeria, he wanted to evacuate troops before the inevitable happened, but Hitler expressly forbade it and sadly Rommel the military genius was flown out of North Africa alone. From here the Eighth Army, including the Seventh Armoured Division forever remembered as the Desert Rats (because they'd gotten so used to living in holes in the desert), teamed up with other Allied units and drove the enemy westwards through the desert all the way to Tripoli. Approximately 130 000 Germans surrendered and by May 1943 the war in North Africa was over, proving that Hitler's army was not invincible.

As we leave the cemetery through the wind and the dust, I am touched by the number of South Africans who distinguished themselves, writing their country's name in the pages of glory in the history of war. I look back at the basket of wild flowers and our red, blue, green, yellow, black and white flag fluttering in the wind. It's almost dark by the time our three dusty expedition Land Rovers, each with the South African flag decal on its aluminium bonnet, continue their journey to track the outside edge of Africa. Mashozi gets a text message; it's from old friend David O'Sullivan of Radio 702 who wants to do a link-up. We pull over and on the edge of the Sahara explain in a few words to the South African listeners something of the emotion of the war graves of Tobruk. It's hard to believe that a country like ours, whose young men had fought and died for justice and freedom, would in its history go on to entrench the hated race policies of apartheid – fortunately now over.

Two days later we say goodbye to Libya and the last massive billboard of an always youthful Mu'ammar Gaddafi, the now-familiar, full-face image of the caring colonel wearing aviator shades and a pillbox-style chechia perched on thick, black, curly hair, his nose up as he looks out across some distant Sahara horizon. 'Please, no photographs,' says Assad, 'no pictures of the old man. It could cost me my job.' Assad, kind and intelligent, has been good to us. 'Don't worry,' I say, putting my hand on his shoulder, 'we understand. Thank you my friend, thank you for bringing us across Libya.' Why worry about billboards, I think to myself? We've got the full-face Gaddafi T-shirt bought from the craft shop at ancient Leptis Magna and a copy of his Green Book in which he sets out his doctrines for the *Jamahiriya*. Whilst we might have felt boxed in and controlled, the outside edge of Libya has nevertheless been a fascinating experience.

Egypt

Day 314, Country 26 on the Edge

Ever since the ancient Greek historian and traveller Herodotus first described Egypt as 'the gift of the Nile', she has been capturing the imagination of all who visit her. We are excited to be back in the ancient land of pyramids, pharaohs, hieroglyphs, temples, kings and queens, gods and goddesses, mummification, tombs, time and trade. El Alamein, ancient Alexandria, the mouth of the Nile and the Suez Canal are all important expedition yardsticks.

THUMBS UP! WE'VE EVEN GOT YELLOW NUMBER PLATES — WELCOME TO EGYPT

Dispatch #183 – Werrcom to Egypt

'Yaba al-Hajj,' says a grinning Egyptian immigration officer as he stamps my passport. Apparently that means 'an old man that has made the pilgrimage to Mecca'. 'It because of your beard,' he says in broken English. 'Okay,' I nod, thinking that's a change from being called Bin Laden or Father Christmas. Mr Nasser at customs looks at me forlornly. 'Your international carnets for the three Land Rovers, they are good,' he says. They bloody well should be, I think, especially as Egypt demands that you put up three times the value of each vehicle as security with the Automobile Association. 'Ah,' he says, 'but the rest, you'll need plenty money. Money for vehicle inspection and then license and insurance fees.' It's getting dark. We're sitting on the kerb. With his finger, Mr Nasser scribbles a total in the Saharan sand. It reads '245'. 'Egyptian pounds?' I ask. 'No,' he says, 'dollars, American dollars.' I raise my eyebrows. You mean 245 US for three Land Rovers?' 'No, it's for each. Total,' he says, wiping the old amount away with the palm of his hand and drawing the figure 735 in the sand. Mashozi has a fit as she puts on the interior light and punches the calculator. That's nearly R1 700 per vehicle. After the exorbitant fees to get across Libya it's a devastating budget killer. 'Don't worry, I give receipt. Werrcome to Egypt,' says Mr Nasser with a big smile.

The sun sets over this forlorn place, over the litter and the smell of piss. Why, I ask myself, must Africa always have to be so bloody difficult – wonderful yet frustrating at the same time? Police fail to read the engine numbers, so they string a piece of wire through the injector pipes and clamp on an embossed seal. It takes hours. 'To stop theft,' says Mr Nasser. 'We need to know that your Land Rovers are not stolen. Customs will remove the seal when you leave Egypt.' 'I ask you, with tears in my bloodshot eyes, Mr Nasser,' I say, 'would five people who have been travelling for more than 300 days, with passport stamps and visas to prove it, and who are carrying letters of introduction in

Arabic and a Madiba Scroll of Peace and Goodwill in Landies piled with kit and rooftop tents, which even have 33 flags of African countries on the side, would they really be travelling all this way in stolen property?' 'Keep calm Pops,' says Ross, who's looking a bit worse for wear with a few days' stubble and wearing an old woollen beanie and a large green jacket. 'Just pay the bucks.' The mosque blares forth its sunset message as a half-dead skinny bitch with four yellow pups wanders across the lamplight. Three bored, sloppy-looking Egyptian soldiers with AKs hanging from their shoulders lean against a hole in the wall that serves as a tuck shop. 'We need 30 US more,' says Mr Nasser. 'It's for the computer.' 'Shit,' growls Mashozi. 'Pay up,' says Ross. 'It's for plastic ID cards.'

Six-and-a-half hours later, with battered yellow Egyptian number plates, plastic ID cards, insurance papers, receipts and stamped carnets and passports, we roll into Egypt down a winding mountain pass to the town of Salum. Here we find a cheap and friendly hotel that serves us bits of mutton with chips and salad and offers rooms with broken bed boards, sheets like carpets and much banging and crashing of bedsprings from an amorous couple next door.

Dispatch #184 – Visiting the Dead

After Gaddafi's Libya, Egypt feels wonderfully free and welcoming as I scribble these words in the tattered journal:

EGYPT NOTES:
- *FULL NAME IS THE ARAB REPUBLIC OF EGYPT - POPULATION 76.8 MILLION — WOW! THAT'S A LOT OF EGYPTIANS —*
- *CAPITAL IS CAIRO, MAIN LANGUAGE ARABIC AND THE COUNTRY HAS AN AREA OF 1 MILLION SQ KM*
- *GENERALLY RELAXED AND TOURIST FRIENDLY BUT A BIT UPTIGHT AT TIMES BECAUSE OF SECURITY ISSUES — TOURISM PROVIDES A BIG SLICE OF THE ACTION AND THEY DON'T WANT ANY HASSLES WITH OUR EXPEDITION GETTING TAKEN OUT —*

THE EGYPTIAN FLAG FLIES ABOVE THE CITADEL IN ANCIENT ALEX

There's a sandstorm brewing and a sombre moment as we walk between the domed sandstone gatehouses, either side of which are sculptured lionesses cradling cubs. A black-and-white dog lying on the plinth of a memorial cross somehow breathes life into the dry Western Desert surroundings of the 1939–1945 War Cemetery in Salum, where friendly caretaker Essa Elarabi lovingly tends the graves of 372 fallen South Africans who died fighting for the just cause of freedom. 'My father was here in 1946, and then my brother from 1977 until 2004 and now it's me,' Essa proudly explains whilst leaning on a rake. Like in Tobruk, we walk between the long lines of springbok head emblems. There are familiar South African names like Pretorius, Rust and Van der Westhuizen and between an unknown grave and that of Private F Walker there's our namesake: perhaps a distant relative, a Lieutenant JJ Holgate of the Royal Durban Light Infantry was killed in action on 13 December 1941, aged 32. Further along Egypt's Mediterranean coast, the Italian monument to its World War II dead is like a high-domed cathedral. Here there are no gravestones, just hundreds of marble plaques bearing good Italian-Christian names like Giovanni, Cesare, Antonio, Constantino, Mario and Giuseppe, surrounded by desert dunes and sea. In the visitor's book a Canadian has written, 'In war there are no winners – only losers'.

'Guten Tag, wie geht's?' asks caretaker Monam Raouf who's standing to attention at the German monument, immaculately dressed in white robe and headscarf. 'Do you speak any English?' I ask. He does, and in the shade of this giant mausoleum he tells me his story. 'We were nomads living in the desert with our flocks. My grandfather gave this area to the Germans 11 years after the battle. The bits and pieces, the remains of 4 700 German dead, were gathered up from the El Alamein battlefields 5 kilometres away and each placed in a small wooden box. So behind these 14 beautiful arches, built from sandstone taken from Marsa Matruh and standing here on these granite floor slabs, there are now 4 700 boxes buried,' says Raouf, pointing. 'There are still the scattered remains of another 1 200 of Hitler's men there in the desert, as well as those in the sea from the airmen who were shot down and drowned.'

Upstairs in a small museum are wreaths and faded black-and-white photographs of young men in uniform and pictures of the small wooden boxes of body fragments being loaded onto a truck out in the Western Desert.

We stop the Landies to photograph a memorial that marks the place where the South African forces outspanned at El Alamein. Further down the road are the Commonwealth war graves. It's a very emotional place, made even more special by the arrival of Lesley Sutton from Land Rover who's flown in again with a group of South African journalists, most of whom had been with us in Benin. They meet us as we place a wreath and a small South African flag beneath the gravestone of an unknown South African soldier. We page through the long list of the dead, seeking family and friends. Anna finds a Muller, Bruce a Leslie, Mashozi an Adams – most of the young men were in their twenties. The gallantry of some of these men was formidable and under Gurney I read:

During an attack on strong German positions at Tell-El Eisa on 22 July 1942, the company to which Private Gurney belonged was held up by intense enemy fire. Heavy casualties were suffered, all the officers being killed

CARETAKER MONAM RAOUF AT THE GERMAN MAUSOLEUM NEAR EL ALAMEIN

or wounded. Private Gurney without hesitation charged and silenced two machine-gun posts. At this stage he was knocked down by a stick grenade, but recovered and charged a third post, using his bayonet with great vigour. His body was found later in an enemy post. By this single-handed act of gallantry in the face of a determined enemy, Private Gurney enabled his company to press forward to its objective. The successful outcome of this engagement was almost entirely due to his heroism at the moment when it was needed.

The longest tank battle of World War II fought here at El Alamein in Egypt changed the direction of the war and helped bring about Hitler's defeat.

The men who fought and died out here in the Western Desert wouldn't believe what has happened to this once remote coastline. Here, the outside edge of Africa has been taken over by holiday developments – it's all bricks, concrete and mortar, packed one against the other. This is where tens of thousands of Egyptians flee to for their annual holidays to escape the heat and pollution of Cairo. Rommel, I think, would have turned in his grave. Alexandria here we come.

Dispatch #185 – Bustling Alexandria

Filled with some four million people, bustling Alexandria is Egypt's major port and one of the most historic cities on the entire outside edge of Africa. Established in 332 BCE by Alexander the Great, who's buried here, the city became a major trade centre and focal point of learning for the entire Mediterranean region. Its ancient library held some 500 000 volumes and the Pharos of Alexandria, a lighthouse that was amongst the tallest man-made structures on earth for many centuries, was one of the Seven Wonders of the Ancient World.

Driving the battered Landies into Alexandria, well that's an adventure all on its own. It entails constant dodging of old black-and-yellow Fiat taxis, horse-drawn carriages and carts, donkeys and pedestrians. We've gotten used to driving on the 'wrong side' of the road by now, as we have been doing it since Angola. Our passengers, in an act of survival, have learnt to shout 'Go!' or 'No! No! No!' to avoid accidents. This practise comes in handy, yet again, as the driver of an old, dented Bedford, carrying live camels to the meat market, swerves out in front of us – it's scary.

The longest tank battle of World War II was fought at El Alamein – it was the end of the road for Hitler. The remains of 4 700 German dead were each placed in a small casket.

The only way forward is to drive like an Egyptian: hand on the horn and foot on the accelerator, hesitate and you are pushed out of the traffic flow. It all adds to the adventure. Most Egyptians are polite and friendly, and especially curious at the sight of three battered right-hand-drive, South African-registered Land Rovers with orange life rings still tied to their bull bars driving along the 20-kilometre-long gauntlet of Alexandria's crowded Mediterranean beachfront, known to all Alexandrians as the 'corniche'. Mashozi, who is in charge of the budget, negotiates a good deal at the Windsor Hotel on El Shohada Street. It's an old, faded colonial building, built in 1906, which harks back to British days. They agree to arrange safe parking for the Landies – vehicle security is always a major consideration in cities, as within easy reach on the roof racks are extra fuel containers, roof tents, the rolled-up Gemini inflatable boats with their floorboards and other essential expedition kit. We've been lucky up until now; could it be the voodoo protection fetishes from Benin, one in each Landy?

THE GOVERNOR OF ANCIENT ALEXANDRIA ADDS A MESSAGE TO THE SCROLL

Travel-worn and a bit rumpled, we pile our dusty kit and cameras in the hotel's foyer – no camping tonight. Security looks us up and down. So as to better explain our odyssey we show them the flags of the 33 countries that are stuck to the outside of the Landies – it's an excuse that always seems to work. A bellboy in a blue uniform and a creaking, antique lift take us to our high-ceilinged bedrooms. Tall, squeaking shutters open up onto a crumbling balcony with views over the old harbour and the 15th-century, medieval fort of Qait Bey, which guards the entrance to the Eastern Harbour. Underwater excavations here have led to the discovery of ancient columns and statues that could have been part of Cleopatra's palace. Down in the King Edward Lounge, we are served ice-cold Egyptian beer – a welcome change from the 'No booze, big dry' of Gaddafi's Libya. A pianist tickles the ivories of a baby grand piano. Dinner is served in the elegant Queen Elizabeth Dining Hall, where smiling, white-jacketed waiters hover below high-ceilinged frescos. It's like a scene out of an old black-and-white movie. The menu is massive. I go for the soup and the spaghetti carbonara. Everything seems so clean; what a change from dented pots on an open fire and eating with a spoon whilst balancing your chipped, enamel plate on your lap.

Through a large arched window our table has a view of Alexandrians on the move. We see attractive girls in headscarves and jeans strolling with their lovers. The sounds of hooting, jostling taxis are accompanied by the clip-clop of ornate, horse-drawn carriages with large wooden-spoked wheels and brass lanterns. My mind goes back to our 1993 crossing of the continent in open boats that ended here. The journey completed, we stayed in a nearby small back-street hotel where I scribbled these words in the Cape to Cairo journal:

In the evening, seated on the balcony of a dingy hotel overlooking the ancient streets of Alexandria, I write my final notes in the sweat-stained expedition journal. Horse traps lit with old carriage lamps clip-clop past. The muezzin's call to prayer floats on the Mediterranean night air. An old ceiling fan creaks and groans above me. The adrenalin drains from my body. The journey is over!

I page to the front of the journal. Inside the cover an old friend scrawled this quotation from the famous Victorian explorer HM Stanley: 'For the traveller who is a true lover of wild life, where can she be found in such variety as in Africa, where is she so mysterious, fantastic and savage, where are her charms so strong … her moods so strange …' Like Stanley, my soul has been claimed by Africa.

That was 15 years ago and here we are back again. Not much has changed in Alexandria, except then it was the finish of an expedition; on this one we're only two-thirds of the way through. Now there's a new governor of Alexandria, but the beautiful palace is the same. At 11 a.m. the next morning we are ushered from our three Landies with great pomp and ceremony to meet His Excellency, General Adel Labib, who welcomes us to his historic city. We receive wonderful gifts and he endorses the Scroll of Peace and Goodwill in support of malaria prevention with these words:

In the name of Allah, Alexandria Great Governorate was honoured to receive your wonderful group. Your model must be replicated in the whole world and not just in Africa as we are in need of such [a] wonderful model which is preserving humanity and helps needy people.

Dispatch #186 – Rashid and the Mouth of the Nile

'*This is crazy*,' comes *Señor Mechanico's* voice over the radio. Rory Beattie from Land Rover is back again to service his

192

'babies' and is driving the visiting journalists, none of whom has been to Egypt before. They can't believe the traffic as we continue to dodge the donkey carts and overloaded trucks as we make our way to the ancient town of Rashid, known internationally as Rosetta. An old Ford swerves for a donkey cart and sends a pedestrian flying. Here old American cars from the sixties still serve as taxis, ferrying passengers up and down the banks of the Nile. At the old French fort on the banks of the river we find the exact place where the Rosetta stone was unearthed by Napoleon's soldiers in 1799. The basalt slab, which dates from about 196 BCE, was inscribed in Egyptian hieroglyphs and ancient Egyptian and Greek. This combination of written languages enabled a Frenchman called Jean-François Champollion to finally decipher the Pharaonic language, so opening a window on Egypt's incredible past. To succeed in our quest to follow the coast of Africa, we must now reach the western mouth of the Nile where, after a journey of 6 695 kilometres, it flows into the Mediterranean.

The tourism police are all over us like a rash; seems like it's a sensitive military area. Then, to make matters worse, we bog one of the Landies down to the axles. Security men huff and puff as they help us push, aided by the winch cable. They're getting pissed off, seems that memories of the Israeli attack from across the Sinai are still fresh in their minds. And then, to make them even more frustrated, we have to go through the ritual of pouring some calabash water, transported all the way from the Cape of Good Hope, into the Nile. Then we get our journalist friends to endorse the scroll whilst sitting on the banks of the longest and most historic river in the world. There's never a dull moment. It's a yardstick for the expedition.

Dispatch #187 – Turning the Landies South

The Mediterranean edge of the Nile Delta is fascinating – there is an abundance of reed beds and a lake on which fishermen sail tall-masted, lateen-rigged, shallow fishing dhows called feluccas. The Nile is the lifeblood of Egypt, especially here in the Delta. There are palm trees and water buffalo in green fields, horse carts laden with vegetables and the largest pumpkins we've ever seen in our lives; a rich harvest in the desert. We cross the second mouth of the Nile at Dumyat and then a causeway linking blobs of land that takes us into Port Said at the entrance of the Suez Canal. There is lots of chatter on the Landy radios – everybody's chuffed. This is a great turning point for the expedition, as for the first time we swing the Landies south and homewards down the east coast of Africa. It's a wonderful feeling. On our left is the 163-kilometre-long Suez Canal. Opened in 1869, it remains one of the greatest feats of modern engineering, linking the Mediterranean to the north of the Red Sea and severing Africa from Asia. We park the Landies next to the canal at Port Suez. It's a strange experience, as with the sun setting over the Red Sea Mountains, giant ocean-going ships pass us like camels in the desert. It's a special time.

I sit at the graffiti-covered base of a monument to Ferdinand de Lesseps – the French consul to Egypt who headed up this incredible Suez Canal project. Earlier we'd been reading up about it in the guidebook. The canal, which had cost the lives of thousands of labourers, had been completed in a fanfare of celebrations in 1869 and Pasha Ismail, the khedive of Egypt, set out to impress the world. In Port Said the extravaganza began with fireworks and a ball attended by 6 000 people. They

VISITING JOURNOS

SCENES FROM RASHID AT THE MOUTH OF THE NILE.

THEN TO ADD TO THE TENSION — WE GET BOGGED DOWN

AND SO WE EMPTY A LITTLE CALABASH WATER INTO THE MOUTH OF THE NILE

included many heads of state, such as the emperor of Austria, the prince of Wales, the prince of Prussia and the prince of the Netherlands. The parties continued for weeks. Two convoys of ships entered the canal from its southern and northern points and met at Ismaïlia, where a new palace had been constructed. The Suez Canal was declared open and Africa was officially separated from Asia. But the imported champagne, the parties, fireworks and piss-ups had cost Pasha Ismail dearly. In Cairo he'd even built an opera house and the Pyramids Road so that his most important guest, the French Empress Eugénie de Montijo, could travel in the luxury of her carriage to the Great Pyramids. The celebration and resulting debts nearly bankrupted the pasha and to appease his creditors he had to sell off shares in the Suez Canal company to the British government. This resulted in Britain gaining control over Egypt, which lasted until the 1952 revolution.

On the shores of the Red Sea we have a rip-roaring bunfight. Lesley Sutton, who does Landy PR and normally doesn't *dop*, is the instigator. There's a belly dancer and the expedition team all use the kit that's been given to them along the way to dress up as Arabs. The next day, feeling like death, we detour to Cairo to apply for visas for the Sudan, Eritrea, Djibouti and beyond. Some say our route is not possible, that it's too dangerous, but we'll just have to see.

Land Rover puts us up at a fancy hotel whilst *Señor Mechanico* and Ross do a great job of servicing the Landies with the help of Land Rover Egypt. Roland Reid, General Manager, Marketing and Sales for Land Rover South Africa, flies in to wish us well; his Landies have made it to Cairo.

We spend our last evening with the visiting journalists watching the evening Sound and Light Show that brings alive the Great Pyramids of Giza, of Cheops, Chephren and Mycerinus, and the Sphinx, the mythical winged monster with a woman's head and lion's body. We're at some of the world's oldest tourists attractions. The Pyramids Road was only paved when President Jimmy Carter visited. There's the buzz of traffic in the distance.

Dispatch #188 – The Zen of Travel

We sit out on a jetty over the Nile. Feluccas sail gently past; beyond the water are the city skyscrapers, mosques and traffic. Roland and I discuss the journey and I explain it's not only following the edge of Africa that's a difficult physical and mental challenge, but that it's also the planning and logistics of all the humanitarian work that's taxing. There are some days when we are overcome by the desperate need of people.

Many are amazed by what a small South African family and a team of volunteers can achieve. 'How do you do it?' and 'Where do you find the energy and the people to help, and how do you handle the tough logistics?' 'How can we lend a hand?' they want to know. 'Well, how about loaning us a lorry to carry 3 000 mosquito nets, along with your company driver and a few helpers, just for the next two days,' we reply. And that's the secret.

Heading south with the Suez on our left – a great feeling!

This journey is much bigger than us. Most people have a desire to help others and somehow our crazy adventure touches their hearts and they become Good Samaritans, adding to the Zen of Travel that controls our journey, come what may. People we've never met before in our lives, many of them expatriate South Africans, come to the rescue, providing food, accommodation, extra vehicles, boats and logistical help. South African ambassadors and their staff get involved in the humanitarian work, as do ministries of health and education. I go on to explain to Roland that it's this Zen of Travel and the Good Samaritans we've met that have helped us get this far. We shake hands; he's flying off to Joburg. Our two nights of Land-Rover-sponsored luxury in Cairo are over. It's back on expedition – we need to find a cheap hotel and parking for the Landies. The next lot of visas will be a challenge.

Then we get this email from a Belgian fellow by the name of Fred Leemans who lives in Cairo, who tells us he loves adventuring in southern Africa and has picked up the crazy story of our humanitarian journey in *Getaway* magazine. Apparently he has every issue from 1993 and has carried them with him in boxes to wherever he's been posted, and they gave him our email address. We've never met the man before, but the next moment he is our guardian angel in Cairo, helping us with all sorts of logistics – visas for Sudan and Eritrea, a driver to drive us around busy Cairo, a meeting with the governor of the Red Sea, and he even tries to lobby for us to enter an Egyptian military area.

Fred opens up his house and his bar to us, and when my grandson Tristan arrives with expedition volunteer Big Deon Schürmann, more bedrolls are rolled out on the floor. Shahira, Fred's lovely Egyptian wife, serves endless plates of food. A shared sense of adventure and a love for Africa bind us all together. Two days becomes ten as we wait for visas and paperwork. We gather at sunset around the back of the Great Pyramids where few tourists go. We can hear the drone of Cairo's traffic in the distance. Bruce captures the Leemans family, Freddie and Shahira and their two little boys Salim and Seif-Alexandre, and the expedition team on film. All of us are holding different issues of *Getaway* magazine – the link that brought us to these Good Samaritans who typify the sort of wonderful help and friendship that pushes us along. And so, with visas for Sudan, Eritrea and Djibouti on board, we leave the pyramids behind and head back down to the Red Sea coast. Down to a coast of dive resorts and international hotels, to Zafarana, Hurghada, across the Tropic of Cancer and on to Marsa Alam, where the governor of the Red Sea endorses the scroll and promises to phone ahead to give us clearance to cross the Egyptian border into the Sudan at Bir Shalatein.

Dispatch #189 – Crossing Lake Nasser

We are not supposed to be here, but after the Egyptian military turned us back from the border with Sudan we had no option but to be taken by a police escort to Aswan on the upper Nile, from where we hope to take a 300 kilometre-long ferry journey to Sudan. It's a bloody nightmare. When it comes to bureaucracy and paperwork the Egyptians seem to take the cake. I don't know if the Pharaohs invented all this need for paper or if it was Alexander the Great. I am sure that during the 70-odd years the British were here, they too played a role. Anyway, the Egyptians have mastered it. It takes us a tolerance-testing three days of shuffling paper to get on the passenger ferry, but the problem is that the Land Rovers have to go separately on a hopelessly overloaded flat-bottomed, antique barge aptly named *The Aswan*. It's bloody scary; they only just fit on and have to be roped down in case of a storm. 'Have there ever been any mishaps?' I ask the captain. 'Oh yes,' he says. 'A few years ago a ferry boat caught fire and more than 400 people drowned.' I check the barge out. Its ancient Marine diesel engine leaks oil, the bilge pump is already at work and the wheelhouse is just a bench by a massive wheel that

WITH PAPERWORK IN HAND FOR THE SUDAN, ERITREA AND DJIBOUTI - WE LEAVE CAIRO AND THE PYRAMIDS.

the skipper steers with his feet. Chains and a cable run to the rudder. The only lifeboat sits under a load of trade goods and there's no navigational equipment. It will be a miracle if our Landies get to the other side.

The passenger ferry, well, that's quite an adventure. It's packed to the gunnels, full of Nubians making their way from Egypt to Sudan with trade goods. They have everything except the kitchen sink: fridges, TVs, satellite dishes, expired medicines, kiddies' toys, fancy shoes and Made-in-China trinkets. The galley serves bean stew and boiled eggs, and sleep is impossible. In the morning the skipper blows the horn as we pass the Abu Simbel temples, where at the larger Great Temple four famous colossal statues of Ramses II sit majestically facing the rising sun. It's a magnificent sight; each statue is over 20 metres tall and they are flanked by smaller statues of the pharaoh's mother and his beloved wife, Nefertari, as well his first eight children. Ramses II built a second temple close by, the Small Temple, which was dedicated to Nefertari and the ancient goddess Hathor. In the 1960s, as work progressed on the river's dam wall, these irreplaceable temples were threatened with being swallowed forever beneath the rising water and silt of Lake Nasser.

Fortunately UNESCO moved in. A cofferdam was built to hold back the encroaching water of the new lake, whilst Egyptian, Swedish, Italian, French and German archaeological teams began to move the massive structure. At a cost of about 40 million US dollars, the temples were cut up into more than 2 000 huge blocks, weighing from 10 to 40 tonnes each.

ACROSS THE WATER STANDS MAJESTIC ABU SIMBEL - IT'S MAGNIFICENT.

They were reconstructed inside a specially built mountain, 210 metres away from the water's edge and 65 metres higher than the original site. The project took just over four years. The temples of Abu Simbel were officially reopened in 1968, whilst the sacred site they occupied for over 3 000 years disappeared forever beneath the grey-brown waters of Lake Nasser.

The captain sounds the horn again. This time it's to tell us that we're now in the Sudan. Wadi Halfa here we come.

Sudan

Day 341, Country 27 on the Edge

We've got visas for Africa's largest country, but we've had to enter via Lake Nasser instead of overland via Bir Shalatein along the outside edge. So now we have the dilemma of how to cross the Nubian Desert back to the coast. There's also civil war in the south and the situation in Darfur is making things volatile. Sudan is one of the least visited countries in Africa, as various ongoing conflicts mean much of this vast nation remains off-limits.

LITTLE TRISTAN DRESSED IN A SUDANESE TURBAN — ONE DAY HE'LL READ THESE SCRIBBLED NOTES —.

Dispatch #190 – Half-swallowed by the Nile

To much blowing of the ship's horn we pull into the port at Wadi Halfa. It's really just a couple of cement slipways that angle into Lake Nubia plus an arrival-and-customs shed. Down goes the stamp with a bang – welcome to Sudan. Mr Haider, the Nubian clearing agent, has a friendly crinkled face and kind eyes beneath his immense snow-white turban. 'Ah,' he says, ruffling Tristan's hair. 'You are the people with the three Land Rovers. Hopefully they will come. We love Land Rovers; the old ones opened the desert for us. That was the time of the old Wadi Halfa before it was swallowed by the high water. The Egyptians, they call it Lake Nasser, but we call it Lake Nubia. The old Wadi Halfa was a beautiful town on the Nile – now our original homes and date palms are under water. The construction of the Aswan Dam in Egypt caused flooding here, you see. We got paid some compensation but most of the money ended up in the pockets of the government officials. It was not a good thing. Come, one of these old Land Rovers will take you into town.'

Enclosed by sand floors, mud walls and a woven-palm-frond ceiling, supper is camel meat and Nubian bread. The entire expedition team is packed into two rooms of the Nile Hotel, but it's still bloody luxury. Most of the other travellers sleep on beds under the stars in the open compound. I toss and turn throughout the night, worried sick that the Landies might not make it. If they have a storm out there, the whole lot could turn turtle – try explaining that one to the Land Rovers' sponsors. For us, with 26 countries now behind us, it would mean the end of the expedition.

Dispatch #191 – 'Please, just five more minutes'

Halala! Alhumdillah! We all leap up from our dusty breakfast table in the market square in Wadi Halfa to 'congratulations' and 'thank God' all round. We hug and shake hands. Our worst nightmare is over – the three Landies have survived the

The challenge of crossing the Nubian Desert — destination Port Sudan.

SUDAN – NOTES:
- Largest country both in the Arab world and in Africa – it's the 10th largest on the planet
- We've been here before on a 1993 Cape to Cairo journey – not too much has changed
- All sorts of hassles in the south of the country but the N.E. and the coast are OK
- Patience the size of the Nubian Desert – that's what's needed.

300-kilometre journey and the barge, we hear, has just tied up down at the port. We grab our kit, jump in an old Series II Landy taxi, pay our two Sudanese pounds each and shoot across a dusty plain down to the water's edge. There they are, still roped down onto the deck, and all the kit still secure on the roof racks. The Egyptian captain, in his dirty overalls, gives us a toothy grin. 'We came as quickly as we could through the night. There was a wind, we had trouble with the engine and your Land Rovers, they are heavy,' he explains.

People swarm all over the barge, unloading trade goods from the hold. It's wild confusion and the police won't let us offload until we've got a paper from customs. Customs won't give us the paper until they can find old Mr Haider, the clearing agent, who's gone missing. 'Just five minutes,' says the customs officer, squeezing all five fingers of his right hand together and heavenwards in an upwards movement, which, in the Sudan, where you need patience as wide as the Nubian Desert, can mean anything from a day to a month. Two hours later we find Mr Haider with his big white turban and his crinkly smile. 'The system,' he says, 'not good. No electricity so computer can't print customs receipt – you wait just five minutes.' I phone Mr Saleh, the ship's agent in Aswan. 'They won't let our vehicles off,' I explain. 'Just five minutes,' he says. The captain of the barge is jumping up and down; he wants the Land Rovers off so that they can unload more goods from below. We go back to the police. 'Just five minutes,' they say.

We find Mr Haider wandering around the customs hall, smiling and shaking hands with all and sundry. 'Just five minutes,' he says. 'Just five minutes.' The sun beats down mercilessly. The electricity is back on but the computer man has gone with the key. He will be back in just five minutes. The Sudanese people are generally very kind and hospitable, but it's a difficult country, one of the world's last wild frontiers. It is no wonder that local Arabs are uncertain, as an age-old proverb questions if Allah laughed or cried when he created the Sudan. I think he probably did both.

Five minutes become five hours. By 3 p.m. we at last have some action. Helped by planks, two iron ramps, ropes, human hands and the ship's engine, the unloading of the Landies becomes a precarious gravity-defying operation, confused all the more by everyone and his dog shouting directions and a fight breaking out to one side. We manage to smooth the chaos over by the promise of some *baksheesh* if they don't drop the Landies into the lake. It's a bloody miracle, but finally the three Landies that have gone through so much stand side by side on *terra firma*. We wait for customs for 'just five minutes'. 'Just five minutes' we wait for security police. I am getting thoroughly pissed off. The inefficiency is boundless, or is it just a way of placing obstacles in the way of visiting foreigners? We fork out 50 US dollars per vehicle for clearing and then, despite visas that cost 100 US each, there's another 50 US per person for the pleasure of having one's passport stamped by immigration, where 'just five minutes' turn into two hours whilst the cops beat the shit out of an illegal immigrant who is handcuffed to his mate.

There's a whole group of these illegals shuffling along in handcuffed twos. A youngster falls to the ground and gets kicked into gear by a big Nubian cop in a blue uniform and beret. There's a group of young girls, also illegal immigrants, who start screaming and wailing in protest. It's pandemonium. 'This is the Wadi Halfa way,' says another cop with a grin as he cocks his AK. Ross drags little Tristan away from the ugly scene that's brewing. 'They come here illegally to our country from Ethiopia, we find them on the ferry with no papers,' says the cop. 'They try to get to Israel – can you believe? Yes, Israel,' he says with absolute hate and disgust in his voice. They hope to get into Egypt, and then from Sinai into Israel, where they get asylum before trying to get to Europe. You wait – just five minutes. Big boss will arrive.' Finally Mr Big does arrive, but we must please give him just five more minutes as he first sorts out 'this matter of the illegals' before attending to our little Five Minutes Brigade. Big Deon Schürmann, our ex-rugby-playing expedition member, would love to throw a few punches. Ross is getting tense and holding himself back, whilst Mashozi is outraged. 'Why do you hit him when he is down like a dog?' she demands. 'Not your business madam, you wait five minutes.' Bruce puffs on calming cigarettes and Anna holds a wide-eyed Tristan.

Finally, we hear the magic words. 'Welcome to Sudan,' says the Sudanese officer with a big smile as Mashozi helps him stick countless revenue stamps onto our forms, and then it is just another five more minutes as photocopies of each passport are made and another bloody five more minutes as a passport photograph is attached to each one. At last we're out of the police/immigration compound and make our way past the sad, desperate eyes of the hopefuls who are being loaded into a big-wheeled, fat-tyred, cross-desert bus. 'They will be in trouble when they get to Khartoum,' says a cop. 'It will be the end of them.' I wonder what he means.

Out of Wadi Halfa, we follow the old 1890s British railway line that General Kitchener's forces laid at an astonishing rate of half-a-kilometre per day. He was intent on getting across the Nubian Desert to Khartoum to wallop the self-proclaimed Mahdi, a religious leader who was to be the redeemer of Islam, and who was slowly overwhelming the British forces there.

We make camp in the Nubian Desert: chairs in a semi-circle, chicken on the coals, feet in the sand, the warm desert wind blowing and stars shining overhead. Sadly there's no alcohol, it's strictly forbidden, but nevertheless, we have an overwhelming sense of freedom. 'Tristan, it's time to go to bed. Up you go, into the rooftop tent.' The little seven-year-old looks up at his dad from where he's been braaing his own meat on his own little fire, his cheeks full of sheep fat. 'Just five more minutes, please Dad,' he says as he puts the fingers of his little hand together in the typically Sudanese gesture. 'Please, just five minutes.'

Tomorrow we will attempt to cross the vast, waterless Nubian Desert, following a line on our Garmin GPSs – it's a somewhat dangerous thousand-kilometre journey. If we make it, it will reconnect us to the Red Sea coast somewhere near Port Sudan, so bringing to an end the long detour

"PLEASE DAD! JUST 5 MORE MINUTES," PLEADS LITTLE TRISTAN.

1000 KM ON A GPS LINE BACK TO THE COAST AND PORT SUDAN

FOOLISHLY WE DECIDE TO GIVE IT A GO

around the Egyptian military area and the disputed section of the Egyptian–Sudanese border. This odyssey of sticking to the outside edge takes a little longer than just five minutes.

Dispatch #192 – Crossing the Desert

Ross is the navigator, and his is the biggest responsibility. Eyes fixed to his Garmin GPS above the Land Rover dashboard, he tries to follow endless dry riverbeds, known around here as 'wadis'. We hope they will lead us safely across the rugged moonscape and through the steep razor-back mountains that run in formidable ridges across the dunes and gravel plains of a desert seldom travelled. Most tracks across the Nubian Desert lead south, following Kitchener's old British railway line from Wadi Halfa to Omdurman and Khartoum at the confluence of the Blue and White Niles – a line that was built too late to relieve General Gordon who was besieged there by the Mahdi. *Lonely Planet Egypt & the Sudan, A Travel Survival Kit* quotes a much older text, *Cook's Traveller's Handbook for Egypt and the Sudan*, published in 1929, as saying:

> *The Dervishes rushed to the palace, where Gordon stood on top of the steps … and in answer to his question, 'Where is your master, the Mahdi?' their leader plunged a huge spear into his body. He fell forward, was dragged down the steps, and his head having been cut off was sent over to the Mahdi in Omdurmân. The fanatics then rushed forward and dipped their spears and swords into his blood, and in a short time the body became 'a heap of mangled flesh'. The Mahdi professed regret at Gordon's death, saying that he wished he had been taken alive, for he wanted to convert him …*
> (1990, p. 384)

Khartoum was a scene of cruel massacre at that time, but our journey takes us far away from there. We must head east-by-southeast, in a thousand-kilometre challenge to reach Port Sudan on the Red Sea. If we'd known what we were in for we'd never have attempted it. I guess it was a little foolish, especially with seven-year-old little Tristan on board. After five days we are about to give up. Diesel and water are beginning to run low and we are shredding tyres on the ragged black, volcanic, sharks-tooth rocks. It's late afternoon and the wind is howling across the desert.

Do we abort the journey and head due south back towards Kitchener's railway line? 'We've worked so hard to get this far east,' says Ross, 'and to give up now would be a bloody shame.' Big Deon tallies up the water and the diesel. 'There are two-and-a-half jerry cans of water and 12 litres of bottled drinking water. It's the zigzagging searches for a way through the mountains that are killing the diesel consumption,' he says with a serious frown. Directly ahead of us is a narrow gap in the mountains, a dry riverbed, but it's to the north and the Egyptian border, not the way we want to go. 'Let's give it a go,' says Ross, forever the optimist. Okay, I nod, and the three Landies difflock in low ratio to grind through the gap.

We pass some nomads with camels. I stop next to a woman wrapped in a shawl; she has a leathery face and a gold nose ring. 'Port Sudan?' I ask, pointing east. She shakes her head. 'Suakin?' I ask then, using the name of the ancient Arabic slave-trading port that's just south of Port Sudan. She nods vigorously and points up the riverbed. '*Shukran*, thank you,' says Mashozi. The Garmin points north, totally the wrong direction, but then as we drive it slowly swings north-by-northeast and finally due east as the wadi narrows and gets closed in by the hills. Is this another blind alley? If so, we'll have to turn back. And then we get the surprise of our lives. There's a small track, a recent cutting that leads us through the mountains. '*Direction's great*,' comes Ross's voice over the radio. We bounce along over the rocks; ahead of us are a few buildings, water tanks and the sound of a generator. '*I hope it's not military*,' comes Deon's voice over the radio. '*No*,' agrees Ross. '*We don't want to get into shit and get turned back.*' But luck is on our side; it's a friendly Jordanian gold-exploration company and we learn that they had cut the track through the mountain. We're offered ice-cold Pepsis and our jerry cans are filled with drinking water. 'Follow the track; just follow the track. You can be in Port Sudan in two days.'

Dispatch #193 – Woolly Heads

But it's not that easy. The journey entails more lost trails and riverbeds; a real slog through rough, broken mountain country and desert scrub. We keep on getting lost. It's hell on the Landies, but somehow they just keep going. 'Oh shit!' says Ross, looking up from the early evening campfire as eight tribesmen with long swords and huge woolly-afro hairstyles pad silently towards us on their camels. 'Let's keep calm and friendly,' I mumble to the team. I greet them with an '*assalām 'alaikum*' as they come straight through our camp. Only one of them raises a hand in acknowledgement whilst the others scowl and disappear into the night.

Little Tristan puts his hand on my knee and with big, wide eyes in the dark whispers, 'Woolly Heads,' his imagination running wild. 'Are they bandits? Will they come back?' he wants to know. Later that night after Tristan's gone to bed, we dress Bruce up in a Nubian djellabah and turban, panga in his hand with a head torch around his neck lighting up his face. I shake the canvas of Tristan's tent. 'Woolly Heads, there are Woolly Heads in camp,' I whisper. Eyes wide, Tristan's little face appears behind the mosquito gauze as Bruce walks out of the bush shouting '*assalām 'alaikum*!' Later on, for fear of nightmares, we explain it was only Bruce and a joke, but the little fellow will never forget the Woolly Heads of Nubia.

Two days later and running on empty, the three battle-worn Land Rovers rumble into Port Sudan, established by the British in 1905 to facilitate the export of cattle, goats, camels, cotton and sorghum. We race to the airport to get Big Deon on a flight to Joburg via Khartoum and Cairo – he's a sucker for punishment. I wonder when we'll see him again. Covered in dust, we grab a room in a rundown hotel where at least the beds are clean and there's a shower. I would kill for a beer but there's no such luxury here; they do serve a non-alcoholic variety however. 'Come on, let's give it a go,' says Ross. 'We'll pretend.'

Dispatch #194 – The Virgins of Suakin

South of Port Sudan, the island of Suakin is cloaked in myth and legend. Its name translates to 'place of jinn'. Apparently, Queen Balqis of the Saba Kingdom of Yemen, or the Queen of Sheba as she is also known, sent seven virgin maidens to King Solomon in Jerusalem. On the way to the Holy City, however, a storm drove the ship off course to Suakin; shortly after, all the girls were pregnant. They claimed they had sexual relations on the island with a *jinn*, a supernatural fiery creature mentioned in the Qur'an. Very little still stands at the old port, it's really just a maze of coral-built ruins. We stand in the shade of Lord Kitchener's old headquarters. Across the bay in the new port there's a modern ferry that takes pilgrims across the Red Sea to Jiddah in Saudi Arabia, en route to Mecca.

The old British-built railway station at Port Sudan. Later we get into big shit for taking the pic – are we spies?!

And then the Sudanese military pounce on us, with camouflaged outfits and guns at the ready. Seems someone saw Bruce taking photographs close to the police station as we were coming through town and has reported us. Things get quite heated and we would have been in big *kak* without Wimpy van der Vyver's Arabic letter of introduction from the South African Embassy in Khartoum. Foreign journalists have been reporting on the atrocities that have been taking place in Darfur and the authorities are edgy. It results in another black mark on the Landy sun visor. Our South African Department of Foreign Affairs has been incredibly supportive and has got us out of many a scrape. By now we know to smile a lot and shake hands. As always it all ends well, this time with old Mr Mohamed, the curator of the ancient port, endorsing the Madiba Scroll of Peace and Goodwill in Arabic.

Dispatch #195 – It's Better Underneath the Water

Mention the Red Sea and it conjures up romantic tourist-brochure images of bikini beaches, palm trees and aquamarine water. This might be true of some of Egypt's Sinai resorts, but not this part of the Sudanese Red Sea where harsh, dramatic mountains, and in some places mud flats or desert dunes, run down to the water's edge, making our progress extremely difficult. We winch the big 130 Land Rover out of the mud and at sunset find a totally deserted stretch of beach. It's a shame about the litter. I count more than a hundred empty plastic and glass bottles washed up in a 10-metre stretch. God forbid, some of them are empty grog bottles – wish there were a couple of full ones. We've been bloody dry for days – booze is absolutely illegal here. We're a bit disappointed, having expected to find a decent beach for the night. There's no doubt that in many places the beauty of the Red Sea lies beneath its waters and the best way to explore is from a dive boat. Off the coast of Sudan dive sites include the wreck of the Italian cargo ship, *The Umbria*, deliberately scuttled in 1940 to prevent surrendering the 3 000 tonnes of bombs it was carrying from falling into the hands of the British.

We get a small charcoal fire going and Mashozi and Anna cut the chunk of mutton we'd bought that morning at a street-side butchery in Port Sudan into chewable bits for the stew pot. The liver is cooked on the grid for a snack. We eat the stew with rice, spiced up with Nando's sauce, and everybody goes for seconds. 'Ouch!' says Bruce, pushing his fingers into his mouth, 'bloody bone chips. Careful, the carcass has been cut up with an axe.' In the night a howling sandstorm threatens to blow the rooftop tents off the Landies. Sleep is impossible and next morning visibility is almost down to zero. We have sand in the eyes, mouth and nose but fortunately it's blowing in the right direction, pushing the Landies towards Eritrea.

Because of the danger of unexploded landmines and bandits, the authorities demand we enter Eritrea via Kassala. In a change from the desert, the town has fruit trees and mountains – beautiful, bizarre jebels that can be seen from miles away. Mashozi giggles as she reads from the guidebook. 'I'd better cover my chin,' she says. 'Kassala is a favourite destination for honeymoon couples, and apparently it's considered extremely erotic for a woman to show her chin.'

We have paperwork hassles and outside Kassala a roadblock sends us back into town for yet another police clearance, which means more black ticks on the Landy sun visor. Even when one is leaving the country the Sudanese have managed to make things as difficult as possible, but we make it across to the few mud huts that make up the Eritrean border. The friendly Eritreans are hugely surprised; not many foreign travellers come this way and they claim we are the first South Africans. 'Beer?' I ask the officials. 'Oh yes!' they say, 'plenty beer. In Eritrea things are more free and easy.'

THE SUDAN, IT'S A HARD, RUGGED, UNCOMPROMISING COUNTRY —

Eritrea

Day 349, Country 28 on the Edge

The dangerous dash across the Nubian Desert is behind us now, as are most of the North African countries. Only Ross has visited Eritrea before so he has been entertaining us with stories of ice-cold beer, music and Italian food. The beautiful Asmara, free and friendly, will make a change from the suspicion and bureaucracy we've had levelled at us of late. Can't wait! For me, getting to Africa's newest country will be a dream come true.

CONSTANT REMINDERS OF THE TERRIBLE CONFLICT WITH ETHIOPIA —

Dispatch #196 – With a Wink She Pats My Belly

So we're out of no-alcohol, Islamic Sudan and we're dying for a drink. The gravel track takes us across wide, yellow grass plains with scattered, flat-topped acacias. It's like the Serengeti but with far pavilions of dramatic mountains. We reach the town of Tessenei. There are still old Fiat trucks everywhere; you can tell the Italians were here. Looking about, there's just one thing on the mind now – we need to find beer. We park the Landies down a side street and Bruce and I walk into a rough-looking place that says 'Hotel'. Immediately the two somewhat goofed bar girls start touching us up – the chubby one pulls at Bruce's T-shirt and rubs his hair whilst the other tall, Somali-looking one feels my beard, gives me a wink and pats my belly. We point at the fridge. 'Beer?' we ask. 'Yes, beer,' the girls nod and giggle. The fridge is full of large brown bottles with no labels. They point to some plastic chairs. There's no doubt that they want us to stay. 'How much for beer?' we ask. Their English is pretty limited, but they tell us '10 nakfa one bottle'. 'We'll take a case,' says Bruce with sign language and a grin. I'm already imagining the scene tonight somewhere out in this beautiful, wild countryside: Landies, tents up, camp chairs around the fire and, for the first time in ages, we'll have ice-cold beers and the chance to unwind after a strictly dry Sudan.

'Let's try one quickly before we go,' says Bruce, grabbing two glasses off the counter and popping off the cap of a big brown bottle with a quick twist of his wrist bangle. 'Cheers,' he says, pouring the contents into the glasses. Jeez! It's bloody carbonated water – our disappointment is boundless. 'Oh beer,' says one of the friendly bar girls with a lopsided grin. 'Only get beer in Asmara.' Shit! Suddenly a camp in the bush doesn't sound all that exciting anymore, so we push on to Barentu in the dark. There's that wonderful 'out of control' feeling, not knowing what to expect around the next corner and just awaiting the next hand from the Zen of Travel in a new country with new languages, people, food and music. '*Look on the right; seems to be some sort of*

203

ERITREAN KIDS LINE THE STREETS TO WELLCOME US.

ERITREA – NOTES
- LOTS OF SECURITY HASSLES IN A COUNTRY THAT'S REPEATEDLY AT ODDS WITH ITS NEIGHBOUR AND SWORN ENEMY ETHIOPIA
- LOOKING FORWARD TO ASMARA. IT'S A FIRST TIME FOR MASHOZI AND ME – NEED TO GET THE PAPERWORK.
- THEN THE CHALLENGE OF THE DANAKIL, KNOWN AS ONE OF THE HOTTEST PLACES ON EARTH – IT'S A NARROW STRIP OF VOLCANIC DESERT RUNNING ALONG THE 'OUTSIDE EDGE'

hotel,' comes Ross's voice over the radio. We pull over and the next moment find ourselves seated in the garden.

What wonderful friendliness. A mum and two daughters run the place. The girls, between giggles, 'speak little bit Eenglish' and soon unearth a bottle of White Horse Whiskey. Celine Dion love songs play crisp and clear. A table is set for us and out comes the *injera*, a sort of local pancake that tastes like a dishcloth. There's hot and spicy sauce, fried cubes of beef, big plates of spaghetti and more White Horse. In the upstairs room I switch the large ceiling fan on full and sprawl out fully clothed on top of the bed. Sudan is behind us; ahead is the Eritrean capital of Asmara. It's a dream come true, a place I've always wanted to visit. We have to report there to be allowed to continue along the edge, and Thomas Rambau from the South African Embassy is waiting to receive us. There will be the signing of the scroll and the meeting of officials. In the middle of the night there's a power cut, and with no fan it's as hot as hell. I open the windows and doors for a breeze and in come the mozzies – we're back in malaria country.

After breakfast, a group of Eritrean government officials arrive to welcome us; they'd been informed of our impending arrival by Asmara but had waited at a different border post yesterday. What a difference – no black marks needed on the sun visor here. Polite, efficient, friendly and welcoming, they talk of the objectives of their 17-year-old country. They aim for improved infrastructure, education, food production, total self-reliance and more efficiency in fighting malaria. There have been no deaths this year at the local hospital thanks to education on the treatment of malaria and the use of long-lasting, insecticide-treated bed nets and keeping village surroundings free of stagnant water and rubbish. 'And the situation with Ethiopia?' I ask. 'We never sleep,' says a stern-looking, moustached fellow with dark eyes. 'We are always in a state of military preparedness.' As we drive out of Barentu hundreds of schoolchildren line the streets to wish us well. We stop the Landies and the teachers use a loudspeaker to select some students to come forward and endorse the expedition scroll on the bonnet of the Land Rover.

We climb a mountain pass built by the Italians, up through the town of Keren, also built by the Italians, which was the scene of a major battle between the allies and Mussolini's forces in 1941. In the mist we can make out blown-up military equipment, tanks, armoured cars and troop carriers – the horrors of the more recent Eritrean–Ethiopian war. There are also beautiful old Italian-built bridges. Asmara here we come.

Dispatch #197 – There's Captain at the Lion Hotel

The first thing that strikes one about Asmara is the organisation of it all: there's no litter, there are zebra crossings, polite drivers, an almost total lack of hooting and confusion, and clean, neat yellow taxi cabs, and there are plenty of inviting sidewalk cafés and coffee shops, bars and Italian restaurants. A Catholic priest allows us to climb the 300 narrow steps to the top of the 25-metre-high tower of the old 1923 red-bricked, Italian-style cathedral. Little Tristan included, we all squeeze into the belfry between the eight massive bells, each weighing more than a hundred kilograms.

Below lies Asmara – a small city that has somehow survived Africa, where streets are clean and neat. The Italian colony of Eritrea was formally declared in 1890 and Asmara was built as its capital between 1890 and 1940. The foundations of an Eritrean identity were laid through a series of border treaties: one with the British over the northern border with what is now the Sudan, and one in the south with both the French who ruled over present-day Djibouti and the Ethiopians who held the greatest length of frontier.

The Italians built roads, railways, factories and cities, and things went smoothly until 1936 when Mussolini decided to extend his influence over Ethiopia. This was short-lived, however. Following the defeat of the Italians in World War II, Italy was forced to give up its three African possessions of Eritrea, Libya and southern Somalia. Eritrea was administered by the British until 1952, when a UN resolution granted it self-government within a federal union with Ethiopia. This Ethiopian occupation resulted in the beautiful city being neglected, but since her liberation in 1991 she's regained her old charm. Down on the streets it seems wonderfully free and Western; along the wide palm, tree-lined boulevards, the packed sidewalk cafés have a mixed Italian–Eritrean cosmopolitan feel and the art deco architecture creates a sense of a city frozen in time.

Thomas Rambau from the South African Embassy recommends the Lion Hotel. It's cheaper than the others, he says, and it's got good food and a bar. Better yet – they've got Captain Morgan. As we book in we meet a group of Zimbabweans; they're waiting for paperwork and transport to the Ethiopian border where they are lifting landmines. 'Things are tough,' they warn us, 'the war machine has worn the country down. Very few expats are here now and there are virtually no tourists; you need special permission to travel, even to get fuel, and there's still no guarantee. We've been waiting here for days.'

Dispatch #198 – The Tank Cemetery

The people are lovely and everybody is really friendly but please, we must understand, we can't go anywhere without government travel permits, and they have to be checked out by military security. We're told again that few foreigners visit the country these days, let alone follow the Danakil coast, because of the war and the closed borders with their arch-enemy Ethiopia. We need to be patient.

THE TANK GRAVEYARD IN ASMARA.

Today is the funeral of a military war hero and all the government ministers are in attendance. We find them gathered in a big white tent outside the tank graveyard. There are acres upon acres of wrecked military tanks, spent shells, armoured vehicles and other relics of war, either captured by the Eritreans or left behind by the Ethiopian communist military junta, the Dergue, whilst evacuating Eritrea. 'We keep this place as a reminder,' says tall, friendly English-speaking Peter from the Department of Tourism as he walks us through the masses of mostly Russian vehicles and tanks.

In a normal country this place would be a scrap metal merchant's dream, but here in Eritrea, says Peter, it remains as a symbol of pride and victory over Ethiopia. What had happened was that after the 1952 mandate for a federal union with Ethiopia, the big brother neighbour had slowly begun to 'colonise' little Eritrea. A resistance movement was started and hostilities erupted in 1961 when a few Eritreans attacked an Ethiopian police station with two stolen pistols – a flash point that started the longest African war of the 20th century, lasting for over 30 years and costing more than 65 000 lives.

Finally in 1993, with 99.81% of the voters saying 'yes' to independence, Eritrea became one of the youngest countries in Africa. This tiny country of 4,4 million triumphed over Russia and America, countries that had at various times backed Ethiopia, which then had a population of 33 million. The Eritreans, tough like the Israelis and fired up on patriotism, were prepared to die for their country, including the women who fought alongside the men. There was hope, peace and independence at last but in late 1997 the two old rivals started squabbling again, first over Eritrea's rejection of the old Ethiopian birr in favour of its new currency, the nakfa, then over bilateral trade relations. Finally and violently, in May 1998, they fought over a small, useless piece of desert dirt on their common border called the Yirga Triangle.

Fierce pride from both sides seems to be the problem. Eritrea and Ethiopia appeared to welcome back the bad old days by proceeding to kill tens of thousands of each other's soldiers and civilians. At the moment there's a ceasefire but the formal demarcation of the border is still pending, so things are tense. As a first-timer I'm finding Asmara fascinating, but Ross is a bit disappointed. He'd visited Eritrea in early 1994 when he was bringing all the kit back from the Cape to Cairo expedition. 'When I was last here this was a new nation just bubbling with hope and patriotism. Now it's quieter and there's a degree of sadness on the streets. It's not the same,' he says. 'The people and the economy are worn down by ongoing hostilities with Ethiopia.' I think of the miracle of our new South African nation and how fortunate we are.

Dispatch #199 – Red Tape

At the Lion Hotel we eagerly await travel permits. If we succeed they will allow us to follow the Danakil coast to the border. Thomas and his colleague from the Embassy, Cynthia Daniels, have been incredibly helpful. 'We're sorry,' they say, 'there's nothing more we can do – it's up to the military. Just hold thumbs.' We are all on edge; if we don't succeed in getting these permissions, the expedition to track the outside edge of Africa will have failed. Despite a comfortable hotel bed and no flapping of the rooftop tent for a change, I have a sleepless night, worrying like hell. If we get turned back, what then? We can't enter Ethiopia from Eritrea because of the hostilities, so we'll be forced to turn around and go all the way to Khartoum in the Sudan for Ethiopian visas and then go down to Ethiopia and across to Djibouti. It would be a bloody disaster and kill the budget and time schedule, and even after all that we would still have skipped the coast of Eritrea. It's so frustrating; there's just so much political shit in Africa.

Outside the hotel I meet a young English student and his girlfriend, looking longingly at the Land Rovers. We chat. 'Please don't use my name,' he says, looking around, 'but many of us young people are just tired out by war talk and

A typical overnight camp – this time on the Danakil Red Sea

Following the edge never easy, always challenging

however patriotic we may be, we don't want to be drafted into the military to spend the best of our lives in the mountains or in the fierce heat of the Danakil. We want to be like you – free to travel and see the world.'

We're all a bit glum at breakfast. All of us have built ourselves up for the challenge of tracking the wild Danakil coast through to Djibouti. Anna puts up the BGAN satellite dish – the emails are plenty. Malaria warriors Eugene le Roux and William Gwebu have had a new Landy Defender sponsored by Menlyn Land Rover in Pretoria. They've already left in a fanfare to distribute 5 000 mosquito nets as part of a journey to meet us on Africa Malaria Day in Mombasa, Kenya, which, if we make it, will be a year from when we left from the Cape of Good Hope. We send this message back:

Hi Eugene, stuck in Asmara awaiting military permissions to travel the Danakil and on to Djibouti and Horn of Africa. No guarantee – only the Zen of Travel will decide. Safari njema!

The Swiss might have invented the clock but it's Africa that owns time …

Dispatch #200 – Into the Danakil

The Zen of Travel is with us again. Our travel permit is handed over; we are free to journey down to the port of Massawa and then to follow the Danakil. Cynthia organises 20 copies – just in case – as some of the roadblock officials will want to keep copies. There's such jubilation; everyone is happy for us and the staff at the Lion wish us well. We stock up on supplies and Tristan gets an ice cream. Cynthia and Major, the embassy driver, escort us out of Asmara. We hoot and wave goodbye, and then commence the twists and turns that take us down the Italian-built mountain pass to bombed-out Massawa, where a war monument of green camouflaged tanks welcomes us to the dusty Red Sea port.

Eritrea's principal port and second-largest town was virtually destroyed by Ethiopian bombing raids in 1990. There's hardly a building that hasn't been damaged by bombs or grenades. Visible out to sea across the Masawa Channel are some of the islands of the Dahlak Archipelago. '*A fisherman's and diver's paradise,*' says Ross over the radio. '*We launched the Cape to Cairo ducks and went out there in '94 – it was incredible.*' Sadly, on this journey, our request to launch had been turned down but at least we can continue along the edge. We go from roadblock to roadblock – it's all polite and friendly, but without our precious travel permit from the military in Asmara we wouldn't have made 10 kilometres.

I fiddle with the pebble in my pocket. Back on the outside edge the immense feeling of freedom is wonderful. Wild, mountainous and windswept, with occasional villages and camels, this is the famed Danakil. Considered to be one of

AFAR CAMELS CROSSING THE DANAKIL —

the hottest places on earth it's also home to the war-like Afar, who in the past, and as part of their warrior status, used to have the rather bad habit of cutting off their enemies' genitals, drying them in the sun and wearing them around their necks as trophies. The thought makes me clench my loins every time I see one of these tough-looking characters with their camels and curved daggers. 'Are they like Woolly Heads?' asks Tristan with a round mouth and big, inquiring eyes. He's got a loose milk tooth – it's irritating him and we try to get him to pull it out with the promise of what the Tooth Fairy will bring. We camp where we end up on the unspoilt dramatic mountainous Red Sea coastline of Danakil. Lying in the water in the late afternoon, it's hard to believe this is the same Red Sea that's been overtaken by tourists and hotels in Egypt. Here it is wild and totally unspoilt, kept pristine by war.

Dispatch #201 – Djibouti Here We Come

Further down the coast the port of Assab lies idle. There are no ships and the cranes stand like monuments to a time when this port serviced landlocked Ethiopia. Now Ethiopia uses Djibouti, and Eritrea has lost valuable revenue. It's such a waste. The heat is unbearable and we can't get diesel as most of the filling stations stand empty. Shell's got some, but we need a permit from the Department of Foreign Affairs and they are closed until tomorrow. There are a lot of troops around.

We push on into the late afternoon and camp in a dry riverbed. The next morning I climb to the top of a dune – the vastness is beautiful. Afar tribesmen water their camels under a cluster of doum palms. Desert gazelle race through the scrub. Later we find them on the beach near the relic of an old Italian lighthouse standing in the dunes. We get stuck again in the desert, and it takes hours to dig and let air out of the tyres. We camp on the beach. The ghost crabs are beautiful but we are disturbed by the sight of thousands of sharks' heads left behind by the shark fin traders who supply the Chinese. Short on fuel, we grind through twisted, tortured land. Thick, broken, jagged sheets of black lava flow down to the Red Sea but between the turmoil there are small, beautiful white beaches and the clearest water imaginable.

We pass more blown-up military vehicles and tanks and then, in a moment, the Danakil is behind us and it's all over with the bang of a passport stamp, a salute and the raising of a red-and-white-striped boom weighted on one side with a heavy wheel rim. We cross a wide, open plain of no-man's-land. Djibouti here we come.

THE DANAKIL – CONSIDERED TO BE THE HOTTEST PLACE ON EARTH.

Djibouti and Somalia

Day 355, Countries 29 and 30 on the Edge

It may be one of the tiniest, youngest and least-known nations in Africa, but whilst its larger, more powerful neighbours are embroiled in a never-ending border dispute, Djibouti stands out as a haven of stability and neutrality. Whilst it consists of little more than the port of Djibouti and an enclave of semi-desert hinterland, reaching this little country for us is a major stepping-stone. But from here, how will we round the dangerous Horn of Africa?

RÉPUBLIQUE DE DJIBOUTI WE CLEAR CUSTOMS AT OBOCK — SUPER FRIENDLY.

Dispatch #202 – Popcorn and the BBC News

Welcome to Djibouti! A length of tatty rope between two poles is dropped. The blue and green Djibouti flag with its white triangle and a red star flutters from a pole at a military outpost. There's a line of stones that marks the border, and some Afar huts and shot-up military equipment. To the right are the jagged blue mountains of Ethiopia and on the left the continuing outside edge of Africa where the Red Sea narrows through the Straits of Bab el Mandab into the Gulf of Aden. The coastline is beautiful and with Eritrea behind us now we're feeling upbeat. Then comes Ross's voice over the radio, '*Shit, did you hear that?*' There's a roar of sound, and I instantly look at my temperature gauge thinking that we've blown a motor. 'Jeez, we're under attack!' I duck as two French fighter jets roar over the Landies, turn out to sea, have another close look at us and then head back towards the city. They gave us the fright of our lives, especially this close to the Ethiopian–Eritrean conflict. The French have a protection agreement with Djibouti – let's hope that this was just a routine patrol.

We continue on through the dust and the heat through the narrow streets and whitewashed buildings of the frontier town of Obock, where we'd been told to clear customs and immigration. We're invited into the shade of a veranda where we sit on the cool cemented floor. The blades of a ceiling fan wobble overhead whilst a bucket of hot popcorn is passed around together with small cups of strong Ethiopian coffee. BBC News plays from a snowy TV fed by somewhat dubious wiring. 'My friends, here in Djibouti you are safe,' says the immigration chief quite proudly. 'The French have just rescued a yacht from the pirates and although the Ethiopians and Eritreans have been fighting for so many years, with so many crazy people killing each other all

AFAR - WITH THEIR CAMELS

AFRICA OUTSIDE EDGE EXPEDITION
OFFICIAL

DJIBOUTI - NOTES
- *23 000 km² AND JUST 314 1CM OF COASTLINE. DJIBOUTI IS SMALL IN SIZE BUT BIG IN AMBITION*
- *DJIBOUTI WAS THE LAST FRENCH COLONY IN AFRICA TO GAIN ITS INDEPENDENCE - 1977*
- *CONTROLLING ACCESS TO THE RED SEA & POSITIONED IN THE GULF OF ADEN, DJIBOUTI IS OF MAJOR STRATEGIC IMPORTANCE.*
- *FRANCE HAS THOUSANDS OF TROOPS AS WELL AS WARSHIPS, ARMOURED VEHICLES AND AIRCRAFT STATIONED IN DJIBOUTI — AMERICAN FORCES ARE ALSO PRESENT*
- *STILL SOMALI PIRACY IS RAMPANT*

around us, here in Djibouti you are welcome. You can camp on the beach and do as you please. And yes, we can organise you 40 litres of diesel – you are welcome.' Our paperwork and passports are stamped. It's late afternoon and the streets are filled with people chewing khat. It's the finest and friendliest border crossing to date, proving that in Africa life is not all black marks on the sun visor.

We camp on a spit of charcoal-grey volcanic sand. Tristan swims in the warm water, Ross and Anna put up their roof tent and Mashozi peels some dry-looking, wrinkled carrots and potatoes for the goat-stew pot. It takes Bruce and I a lot of huffing and puffing to drag over a long, heavy piece of twisted driftwood. Tonight it will provide our light and a cooking fire. With the help of a raised enamel mug or two it will promote good cheer, laughter and discussion and in the morning its smouldering coals will be raked with a stick and blown into life for the early morning coffee. Life, if you allow it, can be really simple.

Dispatch #203 – Lake Assal, Lowest Point in Africa

We got stuck for hours in a coastal mud flat and the battered Landies are covered in mud and dust, with snatch blocks, recovery straps and rope still tied to the bull bars. The Nando's Fight Malaria campaign have flown in a team of South African journalists, including old friend David O'Sullivan from Radio 702. We gather on the salt-encrusted, moonscape shores of volcanic Lake Assal. At 155 metres below sea level its shores make up the lowest land point on the African continent. The earth's crust is shallow here so the area is a minefield of earthquakes, volcanoes and hydrothermal fields. It's also as hot as hell, with temperatures of more than 40 degrees, and a volcano has recently erupted. The Djiboutians with us point out a huge crack in the earth's crust called the Afar Rift – it's said to be the northernmost point of the Great African Rift Valley. Scientists believe that this rift indicates the birth of a new ocean, whereby the Red Sea will eventually flood over the low hills to the north and fill the rift, effectively cutting off Africa's horn. But that's still about 10 million years away, and we should have reached the Cape of Good Hope by then!

The area is also a traditional place for salt gathering and Afar nomads use camel caravans to carry salt from here through the mountains to Ethiopia. Rugged, wild and windswept, David O'Sullivan and I do a live Radio 702 broadcast home. Using a natural table of salt crystals to balance the scroll on, it gets signed from Africa's lowest point by the visitors who've come all the way from South Africa for this crazy outside edge moment.

Djibouti's port is landlocked Ethiopia's only access to the sea. The road in is a dangerous nightmare of dodging hazardous Ethiopian trucks which are hauling fuel and goods up from the coast. It's dark by the time we limp into Djibouti city, dog tired but jubilant. We have 28 countries behind us, and five still to go before getting back to South Africa. Of late, we have forged our route by means of tracks or the Garmin GPS, using dry, rocky riverbeds as roads and letting the tyres down to 1 bar as we race the desert dunes along the Red Sea coast. It's hell for the Landies, murder for the Cooper tyres and tough on the team, but the deserts and coastlines of Sudan and Eritrea are some of the last frontiers of adventure. These dramatic, unspoilt wildernesses with their coral reefs are in areas seldom, if ever, visited by tourists.

Dispatch #204 – Djibouti City

There's a buzz in Djibouti city on the Gulf of Aden – khaki-coloured Hummers and lots of military in over-tight camouflage with short haircuts. We hear stories of the cruising schooner *Le Ponant* that was recently taken by Somali pirates, the French Navy frigate that freed the hostages and the crack helicopter unit that got back the ransom money. Now it's our turn to brave the pirates around the Horn of Africa.

LOADING THE LANDIES.

BRUCE CHEWING KHAT

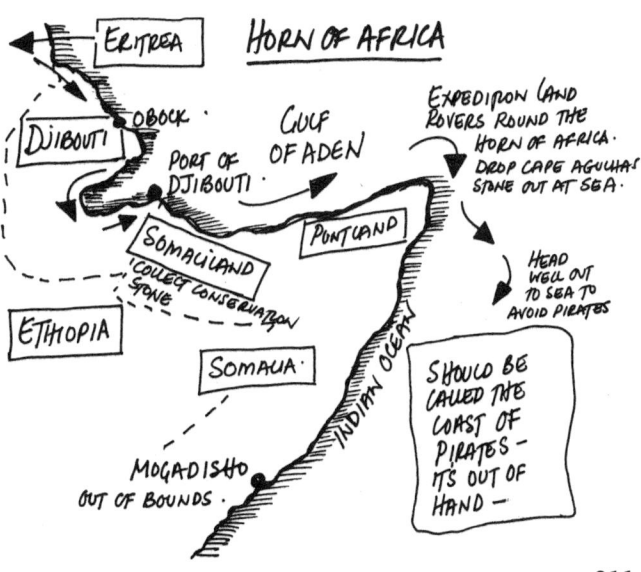

HORN OF AFRICA

Salt-crusted Lake Assal – lowest land point in Africa.

Zim Integrated Shipping Services, friends of our Grindrod sponsors in Durban, come to the rescue. If there's an available ship within the next few weeks they will sponsor the loading of the three Land Rovers and the kit. A conservation stone will be dropped off at the most easterly point of Africa and the calabash, filled more than 350 days ago with Cape Point seawater, will get to round the Horn of Africa.

This morning there's a bit of a panic as Eritrean troops are said to be massing close to the Ethiopian and Djibouti borders. Seems like we made it just in time – will there ever be peace in this troubled area? In the cool of the afternoon there's a buzz on the street corners – the daily plane that carries the bunches of fresh, thin green stems and leaves called khat has arrived from Dire Dawa in Ethiopia. Money changes hands and the traditional chewing of this calming hallucinogenic begins. Then there's the muezzin's evening call to prayer, French soldiers walk in groups and businessmen clutch mobile phones to their ears. Tall, sinuous Somali girls hang around the clubs. Djibouti, protected by the French and American military, is an oasis of peace and prosperity on the troubled Horn of Africa. It's sad for the expedition as we again say goodbye to our mascot. Little Tristan is flying back to South Africa with David O'Sullivan; seems he needs to go back to formal schooling, but with all the Horn of Africa uncertainty around maybe it's a good thing. If all goes well we'll next see him in South Africa. What a privilege: three generations, father, son and grandson getting to adventure together. That's really special.

At the beautiful old French colonial white-painted palace, President Ismail Omar Guelleh endorses the expedition Scroll of Peace and Goodwill in support of malaria prevention. He's really a friendly character; we chat about the expedition and his people invite us out to lunch where we eat big pieces of goat. Their hospitality is great and they say they'll help us in every way possible.

Dispatch #205 – Our Guardian Angel

Gerhard Botha becomes the expedition's guardian angel. He's a *boerseun* from Durban who manages Djibouti's busy container terminal, so busy in fact that they're building another on a piece of reclaimed land out to sea. The survival and success of our journey often depends on the friendly and supportive South Africans we meet along the way, and now it's Gerhard who keeps the Zen of Travel alive. He puts us up in his villa where there's a fridge full of beer, clean sheets and soft beds, TV, air-conditioning and good old South African braais. With Gerhard we talk about Sharks rugby and Durban. After the intense heat of the Danakil it's as if we've stepped into another world. There are even Chinese take-aways from down the road. Gerhard arranges that we meet with the Djibouti press and the Ministry of Health and soon we've put together a malaria- prevention day in the grounds of the local school, aptly named Nelson Mandela College. We distribute nets to mums with babies and the students present us with a picture of Madiba.

A Sprint into Somalia

Dispatch #206 – Dashing to the Most Easterly Point

With Gerhard's driver pulling some strings we manage to get across the border for a dash into Somaliland. Our objective is clear, we need to pick up a 'conservation stone' from the most easterly point of our journey to join the others from the most westerly and northerly points of the continent. That requires a quick trip to Raas Xaafuun, at 51° 27' 52" E. These three replacement stones for the ones we've dropped from Cape Agulhas will be carried back to the southernmost cape where the two oceans meet, as part of our onward dash to Cabo de

A conservation stone from Somaliland –

Boa Esperança. Our arrival at the Cape of Good Hope marks the end point of this crazy outside edge journey, where we will empty the calabash of seawater back into the cold South Atlantic, which if all goes well, and provided we can get the Landies safely around the Horn of Africa, will happen on Madiba's birthday on 18 July.

Back to Djibouti

Dispatch #207 – Somali Pirates

After five days of waiting we suddenly get the green light and race the three expedition Land Rovers down to the port. The 130 Defender Landy has to have the big rolled-up Gemini inflatable boats off-loaded from the roof racks before being reversed into a container. The two Defender station wagons, John Ross and Mary Kingsley, fit snugly one behind the other in the second container. The Landies are tied down to the container floors with cables and turn buckles in case of rough seas. And then we get the news that a Spanish trawler has also just been taken by Somali pirates. 'It's getting out of control, becoming a real danger to shipping,' says Gerhard. Seems that this time they might be operating from a disguised mother ship from which they launch smaller high-speed attack craft.

These pirates are no amateurs. They have sophisticated weaponry and tracking equipment that picks up the radar of passing ships, informers in the port and they even have bank accounts in Dubai through which they channel the ransom money. The golden days of Pirates of the Caribbean, with buccaneer hats, spyglasses, black eye-patches and curved swords might be over but piracy in the Gulf of Aden and around the Horn of Africa is still big business, and right now there seems to be a spate of pirate hijackings.

I get Gerhard to phone Mahen Naidu in Joburg as a practical joke. Mahen is the financial director of Centurus Colleges who've sponsored the Teaching on the Edge Land Rover. Putting on a Somali voice, Gerhard shouts Africa-long-distance style into the phone. 'Mr Naidu … can you hear me? Suleiman Bin Slaaden from Mogadishu. We are Somali … we have your Land Rover and your people. We get your number from the South African man with the big beard – Papa King his name. Very dangerous situation for you, big trouble … they have a secret tank with this Captain Morgan. You want to see them again it's one million … Yes, one million. No don't be an idiot … what's rands?!' shouts Gerhard. 'South African money useless. Dollars one million – we'll also take Euros.'

We all get the giggles. I take the phone: 'All bluff, Mahen, it's me Kingsley phoning you from Djibouti, just to let you know your Landy is on a ship about to round the Horn. Sails on the *Johanna Rus*; leaves about midnight. HOLD THUMBS!' I put the phone down. 'Shouldn't cry wolf,' says Mashozi. 'It would be a shame if our Landies ended up as transport for gun-toting Somali warlords.'

The conservation stone from Cape Agulhas is tossed out to sea off the Horn of Africa.

Kenya

Day 364, Country 31 on the Edge

Kenya, the darling of the West and the centre of the East African Safari Trade, is suffering from a terrible post-election violence hiccup. Things have quietened down now but the country's still in a state of shock. Despite concerns about security and post-election violence, over the years we've fallen in love with East Africa and are delighted to be back. We are also excited to meet up with Eugene and William again, just in time for our one-year expedition birthday.

WE ROLL INTO MOMBASA.

Dispatch #208 – Africa Malaria Day

I can't believe that we've made it to the rendezvous point. Malaria volunteers Eugene le Roux and William Gwebu have travelled 7 000 kilometres through six countries, distributing mosquito nets, spectacles and mobile libraries as they trekked north to join us. It's incredible. Eugene and I had talked about this Africa Malaria Day rendezvous some months before and again on email from Asmara, about how we would meet up from opposing directions. It's amazing to think of all the things that could have gone wrong, but here we are in steamy, sweaty, hot and humid Mombasa, hugging and shaking hands – it's always wonderful when two expeditions meet.

With them they bring fatty biltong and Captain Morgan for the tank, bottles of Nando's sauces and even some vacuum-packed chicken – it brings new energy to our journey. To mark the day we combine our efforts for malaria prevention and education at a local orphanage; the appreciation on the faces of the children receiving life-saving mosquito nets makes it truly worthwhile. British Airways volunteers join us, as do TV and press crews, only too happy to report on humanitarian deeds rather than the suffering of post-election violence. The new mayor of Mombasa endorses the Scroll of Peace and Goodwill in support of malaria prevention.

Dispatch #209 – One Year and Counting!

Exactly one year has passed since we started this crazy trip, today being 27 April 2008. Originally our plan was to have completed the expedition by now, but things are never so cut and dried in Africa and we have been held up with red tape and had to take some time-consuming, roundabout routes to complete our mission. It's amazing to think we have been going at it for a whole year. The expedition objectives remain the same, and we spend our time in Mombasa distributing life-saving mosquito nets to

Africa Malaria Day and we distribute nets to orphanages around Mombasa

Kenya - Notes
- Republic of Kenya - 38.5 million people with an area of 582 646 sq km.
- Our outside edge journey will take us to the Lamu Archipelago, ancient Swahili towns and ruins, Fort Jesus in Mombasa, the Gedi ruins near Malindi
- Africa Malaria Day 25th April / distribution of nets to orphanages / media and sponsors / lots of excitement after post election violence / seems there's hope
- Hot and humid - it's the rainy season

more orphanages around the city. It's the height of the rainy season and malaria is rife.

Dispatch #210 – Backtracking

It's all about remaining true to the outside edge of Africa as our convoy of four Land Rovers – pinpricks of red tail lights in the pouring monsoon rain and overloaded with bales of mosquito nets – backtracks to the Lamu Archipelago against the Somali border. Eugene in the new Defender is driving whilst an armed, camouflage-clad Askari soldier rides shotgun. Even the busses travel with armed military police on the road north from Malindi, which lately has been made more dangerous by the situation in Somalia. In the old town of Lamu donkeys have right of way. There's only one vehicle and it's the district commissioner's Land Rover. This historic place, with its narrow passageways and coral rag buildings, remains the finest example of Swahili architecture on the East African coast. '*Aaaah, habari Captain,*' shouts an old crew member from a voyage of a few years ago when we sailed an old 35-tonne Arab dhow up the coast from northern Mozambique to the Somali border and then back again.

Sailing on the trade winds — Swahili dhows still ply the coast

The Lamu Archipelago is beautiful and the finest way to explore it is barefoot on the creaking decks of a hand-crafted dhow, sleeping on deck under the stars or on a sandy beach. If it's too rough out at sea and you've caught enough fish for the day, you can sail on the landward side of the islands and take the mangrove-fringed channels all the way up to Manda, Manda Toto, Pate, Ndau, Kiwayuu Simambaya and the Somali border. For us, returning to Lamu Island is like coming home as past and present journeys merge into one. We stand at the Friday Mosque in Shela, looking north towards Somalia and the Horn of Africa. The memories of this current expedition flood back; the coast of Sudan, the heat of the Danakil of Eritrea and Lake Assal in Djibouti to name but a few.

In old Lamu town we're back in the same 200-year-old *Jua Paa*, which means 'House of the Rising Sun'. It was our base camp on our African Rainbow dhow expedition. Kahindi, the Giriaman cook and caretaker, greets us warmly. Old carved doors and over 30 steps take us up to the familiar flat rooftop. We're just south of the equator and the Southern Cross hangs over the Indian Ocean. On the opposite side of the continent are Gabon, the Congo and the Gulf of Guinea – so many memories there too.

The sounds of the old 14th-century Muslim stone town rise up to meet us: the clip-clop of the donkeys' hooves, the muezzin's call to prayer, the dragging of slip-slopped feet. They are combined with the smell of jasmine and the teasing 'eyes only' looks from girls with veiled black bui-buis and henna designs on their hands and feet.

Mashozi sprays Tabard under the mozzie net of the high four-poster bed. Bad memories too. She had terrible malaria here, it was her worst ever. Everything in the house is still the same – the old sea chests from Arabia; the well in the courtyard; paintings of a cheetah and the wildebeest migration; an old photograph of two Jahazzi dhows passing each other under full sail; and the old books. The *Rubáiyát of Omar Khayyám* in English lies open on the low Swahili table, and this verse catches my eye:

Waste not your hour, nor in the vain pursuit
Of This and That endeavour and dispute;
Better be jocund with the fruitful Grape
Than sadden after none, or bitter, Fruit.
(1993, Stanza 54)

The Lamu Archipelago will for us always remain a special piece of Outside Edge paradise —

It's the rainy season and the humidity is stifling. We sit on the veranda at Pretleys, which in the old days was the only place licensed to sell alcohol. We order big brown bottles of ice-cold Tuskers all round. The story goes that during Kenya's early days two brothers started a brewery. Sadly, one of them was trampled to death by an elephant, and so one of East Africa's most famous brews became known as 'Tusker' and an elephant was put on the label. A team of donkeys loaded with woven baskets of coral blocks and building sand waddles past. A dhow, heavily loaded with mangrove poles, sails past in the moonlight. Ali the taylor, high on khat, waves from outside and Rama the dhow cook comes over to chat and drink. 'Ah,' he says, 'Papa King, Mama Mashozi, this political violence it was more in Nairobi and in the west near Lake Victoria. It didn't come to Lamu but it was a bad thing for Kenya. And now the tourists they are afraid to visit – we are without work.' I arrange to give him some Kenyan shillings and mosquito nets for his family. We'd sailed together and a special bond had been formed.

We send for fresh samoosas, bite off the crisp corners and squeeze in the juice from small green limes. We could spend weeks here unwinding, but we've got an edge to follow and malaria prevention work to do. The Lamu Archipelago and the north coast of Kenya will for us always remain a special piece of paradise on the outside edge of Africa.

Dispatch #211 – To the Mouth of the Tana

We splash through the mud holes – Kenya's largest river is running red-brown. Tall borassus palms line the banks. 'There are hippos and crocs – lots of *nyama*,' says our informant. 'We've been hunting in the forest. With all the post-election trouble in the slums, the attention of the military and police has turned to the cities and it's been a poacher's dream,' he tells us. Fishing dhows wait for the high tide and a man looks up from gutting a white snapper. The humidity is as thick as Sunday-roast gravy.

At the village of Witu a man points out a mosquito net still hanging over a Swahili bed. 'You gave it to me three years ago. Since then none of my babies have had malaria.' The net is old and dirty, with small holes tied closed with fishing gut. We replace it with a brand-new, long-lasting, insecticide-treated one. It's large and rectangular, big enough to keep a mum and

With Eugene and William we are now 4 Landies – mouth of the Tana River.

William

Eugene

two or three infants safe from the bloodsucking bite of the *Anopheles* mosquito. Crazy when you think of all the children that die, lives that could be saved by a single mosquito net. At the end of the day, however exhausted we are, it always feels good to have saved and improved lives as part of this geographic challenge to track Africa's outside edge. It's what we've come to do.

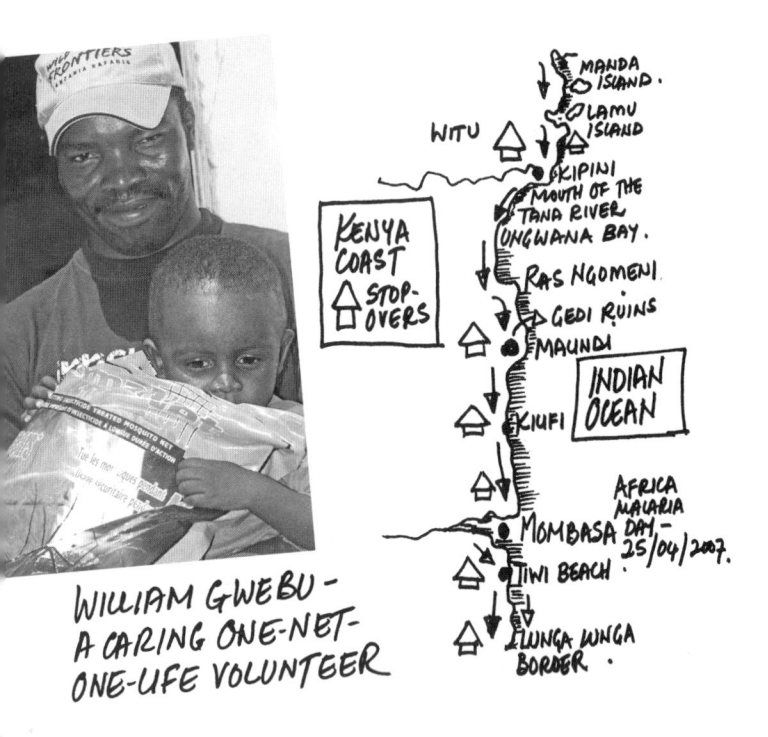

WILLIAM GWEBU – A CARING ONE-NET-ONE-LIFE VOLUNTEER

GEDI RUINS

Dispatch #212 – The Coast of Zinj

It's a short but beautiful coastline. From Lamu we pass Kipini, Witu, Ras Ngomeni and then Malindi, where Vasco da Gama landed in 1498. We stop to photograph and research the ancient Swahili ruins of Gedi, and then it's on to Kilifi Creek, Fort Jesus in Mombasa and on the Likoni ferry to Tiwi Beach and on to Watamu. Conducting One Net One Life malaria prevention work as we travel, our journey down the Kenyan coast is wonderful. The people, as always, are warm and hospitable with a delightful use of English. The Swahili girls flock around William Gwebu, our well-built Zulu malaria warrior. He's having the time of his life and I warn him to take note of a message carved into a big African mask that reads 'Stop Aids before Aids stops you'. We've had the advantage of being amongst the first foreign visitors to have returned to the country after the post-election violence and the bad press that followed. With our malaria prevention story featuring strongly in the local press and TV, we are waved through roadblocks and wished *safari njema*, have a good journey! Not a single black mark on the Landy sun visor for Kenya.

The Swahili coast of East Africa has a warm and wonderful charm to it with a delightful laid-back Afro-Arabic mix. It's mango season and there's bright, yellow fruit everywhere. We reach Shimoni in the rain. It's our last night in Kenya and we stay in the Kenyan Wildlife Service bandas in the forest. Willy's a great cook and is an enormous help to Mashozi. Tonight it's good old Kenyan Farmer's Choice pork sausages with mashed potatoes and veggies. The rainy season humidity is a shocker. A bushbaby makes its way down a baobab trunk for a closer look.

The next morning we park outside an oh-so-British-colonial-looking blue-and-white sign that reads 'Kenya Revenue Authority, Customs Services Department – Lunga Lunga Border'. A customs official sticks his head through the window and in perfect English says, 'I saw you in the newspaper; you were handing out a mosquito net to a little orphan in Likoni. We really appreciate what you are doing to help our people – you are always welcome, sir, in Kenya.' Our passports and carnets are stamped. No problems. Breakfast consists of some hard-boiled eggs from a street vendor. They are 20 bob each and come with a dash of salt in a small torn-off piece of brown paper. Bruce gets a rotten one and he nearly pukes – no refund though. Tanzania here we come.

Tanzania

Day 377, Country 32 on the Edge

Into the United Republic of Tanzania and it's a race against time and potholes to get to the port of Tanga where we need to meet with the mayor and load up more mosquito nets. We'll set up camp there at Kiboko's place, a crazy round little Swiss guy who serves the best and biggest steaks in town and whose nickname aptly means 'hippo' in Swahili.

Dispatch #213 – Goat, Flies and Bees

A sign in English welcomes us to the Horohoro border station. Noisy moneychangers, proud of their literacy, read out each of the 33 outside edge countries listed below the 33 flags that run down the sides of the Landies. Including Tanzania, there are now only two to go and then we'll be back in South Africa. From previous visits, we have great memories of Tanzania; we feel at home here, especially as Ross speaks Swahili. We feel an empathy with the coastal people and a need to help wherever we can in the fight against malaria. We buy a leg of goat and have it cooked choma-style, meaning it is slow-roasted over the coals. We eat in the shade of a massive roadside mango tree. The girls don't eat the goat. They don't like the flies. 'This is nothing,' says Ross, chewing patiently, 'you should have seen the flies where they were cooking it!'

We let the air out of the tyres sponsored by Cooper Tires, which were shipped in and fitted in Mombasa. The road's a shocker, and everybody's tired. We continue to shudder and shake south down the potholed road to Tanga, the largest town along Tanzania's north coast. It's a sleepy frozen-in-time port that briefly served as the capital of German East Africa before this role was usurped by Dar es Salaam. In his book *Bradt Tanzania: With Zanzibar, Pemba and Mafia*, Philip Briggs tell us the following comical story:

> *In late 1914, German Tanga was the setting of a tragically farcical British naval raid. Suffering from seasickness after a long voyage from India, 8 000 Asian recruits were instructed to leap ashore at Tanga, only to become bogged down in the mangroves, then stumble into a swarm of ferocious bees, and finally trigger off German trip-wires. The raid was eventually aborted, but not before 800 British troops lay dead, and a further 500 were wounded. In the confusion, 455 rifles, 16 machine guns and 600 000 rounds of ammunition were left on the shore – a major boon to the Germans. (2002, p. 249)*

THE DENTED, SOOT-BLACKENED CAMP KETTLE –

AFRICA
OUTSIDE EDGE
EXPEDITION
OFFICIAL

THE CHURCH AT BAGAMOYO WHERE DR LIVINGSTONE'S SALT-DRIED CORPSE WAS CARRIED TO —

Tanzania - Notes

- FIRST STOP TANGA AND THEN ON TO BAGAMOYO TO WHERE DR LIVINGSTONE'S BODY WAS CARRIED
- BACK TO ONE OF OUR FAVOURITE COASTLINES, THE SPICE ISLANDS OF PEMBA AND ZANZIBAR, MAFIA ISLAND, KILWA RUINS AND THE MOUTH OF THE RUFIJI —
- AREA: 945 087 SQ KM, POPULATION 41·5 MILLION ENGLISH AND SWAHILI
- LAID BACK & FRIENDLY / BUCKS RUNNING OUT GOT TO KEEP MOVING —

Dressed neatly in longs and a sports jacket, Dr Twaha, a public health specialist, is waiting outside the old market to meet us. A large consignment of long-lasting, insecticide-treated mosquito nets had been dispatched to the doctor in anticipation of our arrival. The logistics of the One Net One Life campaign are always challenging, but with the help of locals such as Dr Twaha we always manage to make it work. We leap straight in.

Dispatch #214 – Kiboko the Swiss Hippo

First we meet with the local health officials, who confirm that the effective use of bed nets, together with correct education, remains the best frontline defence in the malaria war zone. The district commissioner and the mayor sign and stamp the scroll. Everybody's so pleasant and relaxed; it's the Swahili way. 'How is Tanzania getting on,' I ask politely, 'and how do you feel about the political violence in next-door Kenya?' 'Well,' answers the district commissioner, 'unlike our neighbours we do not encourage tribal or ethnic affiliations here in Tanzania; even when we do the census there's no section for tribe. The late president Nyerere encouraged us to be one undivided nation by moving teachers and officials out of their own areas to other districts; officials from Tanga could be sent to Mwanza on Lake Victoria and people from there here to Tanga. Above all, we are proud to be Tanzanians, the economy is picking up and our President Jakaya Kikwete is working hard to stamp out corruption.' We shake hands and pose for photographs – more mementos of lovely people on the outside edge. 'Extra vehicles and trained malaria prevention educationists will be waiting for you in the morning. *Tutaonana kesho* – until tomorrow,' says Dr Twaha.

Down Tanga's wide, tree-lined streets and its old, faded German, British and Asian buildings, dodging bicycles, busses, taxis and pedestrians, we turn right off Ocean Road into our old favourite landmark: Kiboko's Restaurant and Pub. Kiboko welcomes us warmly. He'd come out to Tanzania from Switzerland as a 20 year old to work as an engineer on the sisal plantations. Now, some 25 years later, he's as jolly and as round as ever. The Kilimanjaro Lager is still ice cold and the steaks still so large that he stores our leftovers in his fridge for tomorrow's *padkos*. 'Do you want to buy my place?' asks Kiboko. 'I might have to sell up and move into the mountains, away from the mosquitoes. The bloody malaria is killing me.'

We camp on a piece of lawn amongst trees in Kiboko's well-manicured tropical garden. Up in the roof tent it's like a sauna. The mozzies are thick, Bruce and Eugene are having a snoring competition, the neighbour's dogs bark incessantly and there's the distant boom-boom of nightclub music. I toss and turn with a stomach full of steak and finally doze off in the early hours of the morning, but then seem to be instantly woken by a cacophony of sounds from Tanga's mosques, all of which seem to be competing with each other to get us out of bed to face the hectic day ahead.

Dispatch #215 – The Open Sore of the World

Still rubbing the sleep from our eyes, we're off to the maternity section of the district hospital, bed to bed, mum to mum, One Net One Life, and then down the coastal road to Pangani, where we go from school to school, classroom to classroom and clinic to clinic, distributing nets and providing

'THE BEARD', KIBOKO AND ROSS – IT'S THE BEST FOOD IN TOWN UNLESS YOU WISH TO TRY THE 'ROADKILL CAFE'

221

malaria prevention education. With singing and dancing, curtseys and handshakes, there's wonderful enthusiasm from Dr Twaha, the teachers and the team of Tanzanian health workers. At the old German Governor's headquarters in Pangani, we meet with the district commissioner, a lovely warm-hearted woman. But now, how are we going to cross the Pangani River? The ferry is down.

It's late afternoon and the curious occupants of this old Swahili trading port gather around, but there's no chewing of khat here – it's outlawed in Tanzania. A rubber duck is rolled off the top of the Stomach. It lands with a thud on the banks of the Pangani. Ross and Bruce have got it taped – in go the floorboards; dripping with sweat, we take it in turns to pump the six-metre-long pontoons; the Yamaha outboard is bolted on; and oil is added to the boat fuel tanks. We load up with drinking water, supplies, bedrolls, a tent, first-aid kit and a GPS. It's the only way to remain true to the outside edge. The district commissioner shakes her head in amazement. 'With this balloon boat,' she asks, 'you are going to go all the way down the coast to Bagamoyo?'

Ross and I wave from the boat and the crowd shouts with delight as I open up the throttle. The Landy party hoots and flashes their lights; we chat briefly on the radio and set up two fixed-time satellite phone calls, in case of an emergency, '*See you in Bagamoyo, over and out.*' The land party will have to backtrack, and then take a massive detour inland. Bouncing into the wind, Ross and I hug the coast. We follow thatched villages, tall palm trees and sandy beaches south onto the deserted coastline of the newly proclaimed Saadani Game Reserve. At last light we race the rubber duck up a deserted beach. 'Oh shit. There are bloody sand fleas,' says Ross. The little bastards are jumping a metre high so we take our enamel mugs of Captain and stand in the waves.

The phosphorescence swirls like birthday sparkles between our toes. Dinner is Kiboko leftovers. We roll out our khaki-green canvas bedrolls under the stars and the swaying palms, up on a grassy bank away from the sand fleas, father and son lying on their backs chatting. There's the occasional shooting star, not a human being or light in sight and just the sound of the Kusi trade wind blowing through the palm fronds and the flop of the waves on the beach. 'Mmmm,' mumbles Ross sleepily, 'if one of those coconuts falls on one of our heads it'll be tickets!' 'Shall we move?' I ask. 'Too tired,' comes Ross's mumbled reply, 'let's take our chances. I've set the alarm in time for high tide at 5 a.m. so we won't have to push the boat and can get over the reef.' In the middle of the night the wind stops dead and the mozzies come out for the kill. Ross blunders around putting up a tent and out comes the Tabard spray. I'm too tired to move; I pull the sleeping bag over my head and wake to Ross shaking the bedroll.

The next day, still following the edge, the Kusi picks up into an uncomfortable bone-jarring chop, hour after hour. There are big storm clouds over Pemba Island to the north of Zanzibar – the weather's turning ugly. We're out of shape from sitting too long in the Land Rovers. At midday we pull into the shallows, swallow some Voltaren tablets to ease the lower back pain and share a tin of bully beef. The warm rain hits us in sheets; the sky goes dark and the visibility is poor but at least the wind drops and the sea smoothes out. We reach Bagamoyo at low tide in the rain and are forced to anchor about a kilometre from the shore.

'You better wear strops – sea urchins,' says Ross, 'I'll stay with the boat.' Dripping wet, I walk into Helen and Frank's bar at the Traveller's Lodge. They're old friends from the past. 'Jeez, you look wild,' says Helen, who's from Cape Town. 'Last saw you on your dhow journey, did you make it to Somalia? We heard you were coming.' 'You ugly bastard,' says Frank, 'are you still alive? Have a cold Kili.' He's German and quite a character. Both of them love the East African coast and here at Bagamoyo they have planted an incredible variety of palm trees, their own botanical garden.

The Land Rover party arrives, covered in red mud. Frank gives us one of his Swahili crew to go and relieve Ross and pull in the boat on the high tide. That evening the district commissioner tells us that the word Bagamoyo means 'where you lay down the burden of your heart'. It could be a phrase from a slave's lament, meaning that, although they were to be shipped from the African mainland, their hearts would be left behind in Bagamoyo. Can you imagine how it must have been for the tens of thousands of slaves who were driven here like cattle, yoked and chained, being forced to carry elephant tusks from the interior to be sold, and were then placed on the auction blocks themselves? It is said that only 20% of them survived the death marches to the coast. It was the first time that they'd ever seen the sea; ahead of them lay the slave markets of Zanzibar. The famous Victorian missionary explorer Dr David Livingstone called this trade in human flesh 'the open sore of the world'.

The next day, in a humanist turnabout for the country, we distribute life-saving mosquito nets to mums and babies at the church where Livingstone's sun-dried corpse was carried to before being transported to Zanzibar and then Westminster Abbey. Professor Samahani, the local historian attached to the Catholic mission, looks us up and down through his thick spectacles. He's a delightful old man. The other theory for the meaning of Bagamoyo, he says, was that the phrase 'lay down the burden of your heart' was coined by caravan porters who, on reaching Bagamoyo, finally laid down their burdens at the end of their journey from the interior. 'Yes, many expeditions have come this way,' says Professor Samahani, nodding wisely. 'Burton, Speke, Stanley and Livingstone – they all came here in dhows from Zanzibar and then their overland caravans left from here, but yours is the first one to come from around Africa. *Karibuni*, welcome to Bagamoyo!'

Dispatch #216 – Where You Lay Down Your Heart

It takes us days to get away from Bagamoyo. Alan Turner and a group of friendly expat South Africans have come out to visit us at Frank and Helen's Traveller's Lodge where we've set up our expedition base camp. As always, the support for our expedition is humbling. Gavin Zinn from the Engen garage outside Dar es Salaam offers to fill up all our diesel tanks. The Shoprite team replenish our Land Rover food drawers with everything from beans to bully beef, tinned fruit and cereals. Brad Hansen, his mate Gavin and a Swahili mechanic nicknamed 'Machine' drive all the way down from Arusha in their short-wheel-base Landy to enlist as volunteers. They bring new energy and great humour and will accompany us all the way to the Mozambique border. So here's this bunch of South Africans in a long convoy assisting with the distribution of life-saving mosquito nets to orphanages and clinics in and around Bagamoyo. We're giving a clear message that we care for the women and children of Africa. The response is overwhelmingly humbling. Children sing and dance and there are speeches of appreciation from community leaders and even more messages are written in the scroll.

There's a shady tree, still growing in the town, from where slaves were sold before being transported across the Zanzibar Channel to the island, all crushed in the dank holes of slave ships destined for Arabia, Persia or India. As the major port on the coast during the late 19th century, it was only natural that Bagamoyo was chosen in 1888 as the site for the capital of German East Africa before they moved it north to Tanga.

ROSS OPENS THE LUNCH.

A SMILE OF APPRECIATION

Dispatch #217 – Haven of Peace

It's getting towards the end of the rainy season and heavy clouds gather as our convoy of overworked Land Rovers creaks and groans into Dar es Salaam. In 1866 the Sultan Majid bin Said Al-Busaid of Zanzibar made plans to develop the harbour and build a palace of coral stone, which he later called Dar es Salaam, meaning 'Haven of Peace'. But in 1887 the German colonists shattered the peace, threw out the Arab rulers and firmly established their Teutonic presence, which is still reflected in some of the old administrative buildings. A cathedral was built and a hotel known as the Kaiserhoff opened its doors to a trickle of adventurous travellers and hunters. In 1905 work began on the central railway linking Dar es Salaam with Lake Tanganyika, 1 248 kilometres away to the west. When the British moved in after World War I, they based their administrative and commercial centre in 'Dar' and renamed the Kaiserhoff the 'New Africa Hotel'.

Talking about hotels, we are in luck for a bit of luxury. Protea Hotels, sponsors of our expedition accommodation wherever they have a presence, open their doors to our motley group. It's an opportunity for clothes to be washed and for us to enjoy the treat of great Protea breakfasts and, above all, clean white sheets and air-conditioning. The expedition team emerges washed and scrubbed and even the long line of Landies in the car park gets hosed down. The city is a buzz of clubs, bars, restaurants and traffic. The manager of the Yacht Club, one of Dar's favourite watering holes, endorses our malaria prevention scroll. British Airways arranges for the distribution of mosquito nets to paediatric and maternity wards in a rural hospital. Then they take us out with a merry group of mates to eat at Kevin Stander's Spur Steakhouse.

MUMS WITH BABIES QUEUE FOR MOSQUITO NETS —

The next day, loaded with more bales of life-saving nets, it's across on the ferry out of Dar harbour to the village of Kigamboni in the south. It's wonderful to get out of the city and we camp in the shade of some tall coconut palms on a piece of pristine white sand beach. Brad dispatches his man Machine in the Land Rover shorty to go to the airport with a sign that reads 'Deon' and a handwritten scribble saying: 'Hi Deon, welcome to TZ. Machine will bring you to us.' We'd last seen him when he'd flown out from Port Sudan. Now he's back again, a sucker for punishment. Built like a baobab, he's the only one of the team who can carry a bale of 100 mosquito nets under one arm. He's also a delightful friend and brings biltong and news from home.

Dispatch #218 – South Down the Edge of Africa

The spice islands of Zanzibar, Pemba and Mafia and the Rufiji Delta, along with tropical breezes, white beaches, swaying palm trees, dhow sails, mangrove inlets, beautiful bays, ancient ruins and baobabs, make up the magnificent outside edge of Tanzania. '*Did you see that?*' comes Ross's excited voice over the radio. '*Two SA-registered vehicles have just gone past, flashing their lights and waving at us.*' In our Landy Mashozi's playing a scratched CD which misses a beat with every pothole. Squeezing the 'on' button she puts the mike next to the speaker to give the team a burst of '*Take me home, country roads, to the place where I belong …*'

Following the coast south, we see baobabs, bays and sisal plantations. Mafia Island is out to our left – it's where our old dhow, the *Amina Spirit of Adventure*, had been handcrafted. The coast is wild and beautiful. We cross the Rufiji River, park the Landies and take a symbolic walk over the bridge. We have wonderful memories of a previous journey here in the footsteps of Frederick Courtney Selous. The next significant place on the coast is the historic Arabic ruins of Kilwa, a one-time slave trade terminus that even minted its own coins and traded with gold from Monomotapa. Then it's on to Lindi across the Ngurumbala River and through the thousands of coconut palms to 10 Degrees South, a bar in Mikindani that serves big brown bottles of cold Kilimanjaro with chicken and chips. From there it's south to the port of Mtwara where we do more malaria prevention work and then head south again for Mozambique. South, south, south. South means home. It's a great feeling.

Dispatch #219 – Living on the Edge

The expedition is fired up, the Landies never missing a beat. There's a new sense of urgency the further south we get. The only way to cross from southern Tanzania into Mozambique's northern Cabo Delgado province is by ferry across the Ruvuma River. Rumours are rife. Some say the ferry is not working, others say it's stuck on a sandbank. One traveller tells us that it only runs a few days either side of high spring tide. But all agree that it's buggered and we'll be lucky to cross. So with our hearts in our mouths, we slip and slide out of Tanzania (no black marks) across the mudflats to the ferry point. We've used the ferry in the past and it worked well, especially when it was run by the Catholic Benedictine fathers in Mtwara, so it's sad to hear that it's falling apart. If we can't get across it will be a huge blow for us. A detour will take us all the way to the top of Lake Malawi and then back down again to the coast of Mozambique. It would mean that the expedition would have to split – the Land Rovers going inland and some of us lucky ones travelling by inflatable boats down through the Quirimba Islands to the port of Pemba.

I think back to the other problems we've had on this journey with border crossings. And now, so close to home, probably the last major obstacle to completing the coast is yet another border ferry that might or might not be working – we'll soon find out though. It's called living on the edge.

MALARIA WARRIORS AT MTWARA – SOUTHERN TANZANIA

Mozambique

Day 388, Country 33 on the Edge

First under Arabic rule, the Portuguese then held power for more than four centuries before the local resistance movement FRELIMO was founded in 1962. The war of liberation and the civil war that followed are well and truly over, but Mozambique still suffers from poverty, and malaria is rife. South African volunteers are coming in to help us in our One Net One Life campaign. This beautiful piece of the outside edge promises a great adventure.

Dispatch #220 – Last Country Before Home

Absolute chaos. Two buckets: one red, one green. Sweat pours from their near-naked bodies as Saidi and Gaston bail for their lives – the bilge pump is buggered. Bucket by bucket they're only just managing to keep the ferry afloat; she's leaking like a sieve. Ruvuma water laps around the tyres of the Landies as, in low gear, we keep inching them forward or backward so as to shift the load. Memories of the Congo crossing and many others come flooding back – no pun intended. Abdul Kubanjima, the skipper, and his sidekick old Mohammed ask me if I've got a job for them. I think they've had enough of trying to keep this ferry alive.

To meet us on the river is our old friend from Ballito Bay, Richard Chapman, and a team of malaria warrior volunteers who've driven up from South Africa. With them they brought Babu from Bilene – it's great to see him again. Realising the danger of the leaking ferry, they've launched their rubber duck to escort us across. 'Please take the scroll,' I shout to Richard over the noise of the stuttering, oil-leaking, diesel-blowing, 36-year-old Hatz marine engine that the crew had earlier jump-started from the battery of a lorry with a broken clutch. Richard pulls up alongside and I hand him the khaki-green canvas bag that holds the much-travelled, wood-covered scroll. 'It's a piece of history!' I shout. 'If the Landies go down we need to save it.'

The ferry gets swept downstream; somehow Abdul avoids a sandbank where a few open-mouthed crocs lie sunning themselves. A small pod of hippo snorts and submerges, and slowly we turn diagonally against the current. It takes 45 minutes to do just a few hundred metres but we can't make it to the landing site, so the crew, using spades and shovels, cut the steep riverbank into an angle that allows us to get the Landies off. With difflock, low ratio and the overworked engines roaring, we get them across into Mozambique. We winch through the thick black mud and make our way to the Mozambican customs and immigration. We've made it.

Another iconic point on the 'Outside Edge'. This time it's the mouth of the Zambezi —

Dispatch #221 – Pilgrims of Adventure

'*I've pulled off on the left. It looks good, you'll see my tracks,*' comes Ross's voice over the radio. It's last light and we set up camp in the sand forest just off the road to Palma. There's elephant dung around as well as lion tracks. Villagers tell us that lions are still a problem here and in recent months 24 people have been killed. Richard and his team have brought steak, *boerewors* and news from home. The dented, soot-blackened camp kettle bubbles on the fire. There's the sound of nightjars and the whooping of a distant hyena as I look across the firelight at my fellow key expedition members: Mashozi, Ross, Anna and Bruce. They're looking worn out and all of them have lost weight. This adventure has taken a lot out of them, but they have each handled their respective responsibilities wonderfully.

Although Babu Cossa, our Portuguese interpreter and malaria educator, hasn't been with us the entire time, he has grown enormously in spirit. The young Mozambican whom we met all those years ago in Bilene has become part of the family, often joining us on our travels.

The kettle has boiled; Babu lines up the enamel mugs for *Renosterkoffie* – it's his speciality. Now there are 12 faces around the fire. There's Eugene le Roux and William Gwebu, the two die-hard Nando's Fight Malaria volunteers who joined us in Mombasa. Then there's Richard Chapman, a great adventurer who survived a landmine accident, loves Africa and has travelled all the way from Ballito in KZN with his son Warwick and Tamaryn, Warwick's girlfriend. The

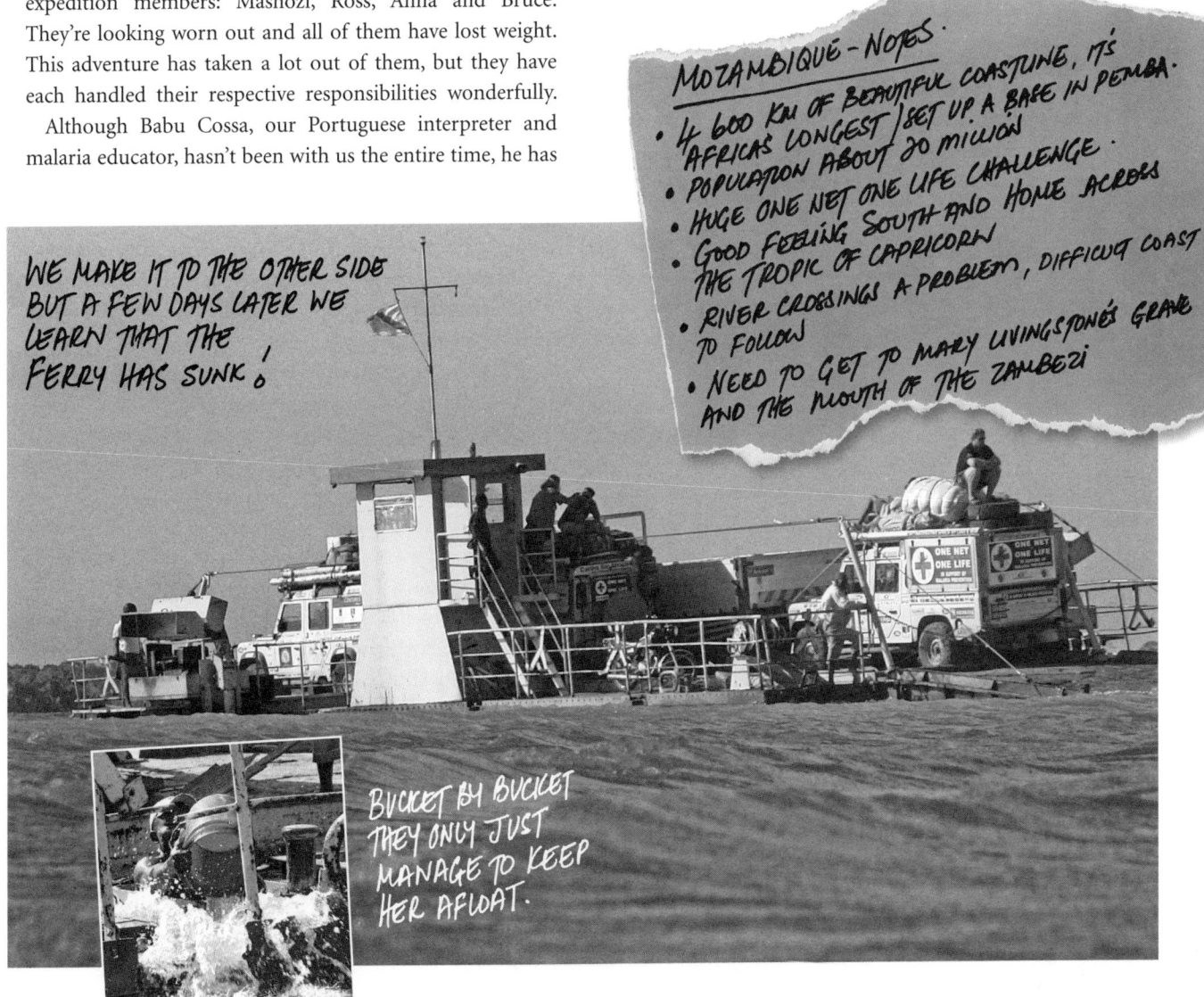

MOZAMBIQUE - NOTES:
- 4 600 KM OF BEAUTIFUL COASTLINE, IT'S AFRICA'S LONGEST / SET UP A BASE IN PEMBA.
- POPULATION ABOUT 20 MILLION
- HUGE ONE NET ONE LIFE CHALLENGE.
- GOOD FEELING SOUTH AND HOME ACROSS THE TROPIC OF CAPRICORN
- RIVER CROSSINGS A PROBLEM, DIFFICULT COAST TO FOLLOW
- NEED TO GET TO MARY LIVINGSTONE'S GRAVE AND THE MOUTH OF THE ZAMBEZI

WE MAKE IT TO THE OTHER SIDE BUT A FEW DAYS LATER WE LEARN THAT THE FERRY HAS SUNK!

BUCKET BY BUCKET THEY ONLY JUST MANAGE TO KEEP HER AFLOAT.

other Ballito vehicle is driven by Big John Wells, who's got a big girth, big beard and big heart. Kindred spirits, they're all a great asset to the expedition. I sip on the *Renoster* and the adrenalin ebbs from my body; the incredibly long and difficult odyssey to track the outside edge of Africa is almost over. The team start to talk about friends, family, pets and the first things they'll get up to when they get back. After all, at the end of the day we're just ordinary people who have an extraordinary passion for Africa and can now smell home.

Dispatch #222 – Music and a Mudbath

Between the beautiful baobabs at Brenda and Rudi's Pemba Dive bush camp we set up a One Net One Life base camp. We've got great memories of this place as it was from here in 2005 that we launched the 35-tonne *Amina Spirit of Adventure* dhow to sail north to the Somali border.

Brenda's a delightful, oddball character, especially around the campfire at night, typically burnt brown by the sun and dressed in her characteristic broad-brimmed straw hat, bikini top that struggles to contain her boobs and old khaki shorts. A few *cervejas* down the hatch and she entertains us with wild attempts at the saxophone and pennywhistle, which get her dogs howling at the moon in protest, whilst Rudi, who was born from German parents in Pemba, cooks up a big pot of his favourite mud-crab curry.

The *50|50* film crew and sponsored teams of volunteers from Grindrod and Captain Morgan arrive to assist. Continuously tracking Africa's outside edge means there's never a dull moment. We do malaria work by dhow and rubber duck, always on the move, with people keen to assist in the fight against the killer disease. Back in camp, Brenda insists that we roll around in the mangrove mud. 'It's my mudbath,' she shouts with glee. 'Come, take off your clobber. Everybody in!'

Rani Resorts, the owners of the beautiful Pemba Beach Hotel, fly our team to Ilha Matemo to assist with their malaria prevention programme and give us a night of luxury at their lodge. Then it's by boat to Ilha do Ibo where João Baptiste, Ibo's oldest resident, endorses the scroll and we hold a malaria prevention event inside the courtyard of the old fort.

Ten days later and all the fly-in volunteers, including Deon, the journalists and film crew, have left. Peace descends on the camp. The team's back down to Mashozi, Ross, Bruce, Anna, Babu, Eugene, William, Richard and his crew and me. Greg

It's Bruce – he's been in Brenda's mudbath!

Rea, Captain Morgan's brand ambassador, is staying on. He's great fun and is always willing to help; he's been a friend of the family for years. 'Follow the heartbeat!' shouts Brenda, raising her straw hat in farewell. Our next challenge is to cross the Rio Lúrio.

Dispatch #223 – Another Blow for the Expedition

On the peninsula of Pemba we go down past the port and the reed huts of Paquitequete. Here, small fishing dhows, blown by the timeless trade winds, fish from Baía de Pemba and even catch huge sailfish on handheld lines. The president has just visited and the town's still swept clean and there are colourful flags and streamers. We continue down past the market, past Pemba Beach Hotel, Wimby Beach and the bar at Russell's Place, the mad Aussie's hostel, where we stop for a final cold *cerveja*. Further south at the village of Mecúfi the street lights are still on at 11 a.m.; seems they forgot to switch them off after the big man left.

A man on a bicycle shows us the way. 'No vehicle has been here for months,' he says. We're trying to get to the mouth of the Rio Lúrio, which separates the provinces of Cabo Delgado and Nampula. '*We'll know if we can cross soon enough*,' says Ross over the radio, '*but it looks safe up to the water's edge.*' We follow his tracks; the tide's going out. Greg is up to his waist searching for a way through. We hire some fishermen to peg out a route with long sticks, but it's at least a kilometre wide. Ross goes first – tyres down to 1 bar, engine screaming. But just five metres and down she goes. I winch him out backwards. It doesn't look good, but now the blood's pumping – I hope we're not being stupidly gung ho.

Babu organises another route to the left that seems shallower. Anna, Greg and Ross take off flat-out into the river, the four-cylinder motor screaming in protest. Sixty metres and down she goes, but really down this time and sinking fast. Rio Lúrio water pours in over the floorboards; the clutch and break pedals are soon submerged and the exhaust is bubbling away deep under the surface. If Ross stalls now it will be a fuck-up. '*I'm sending you man power, 23 guys,*' I shout into the radio. '*One, two, three, go!*' The stuck Landy won't budge, the winch cable snaps. With three vehicles, one behind the other, we put on a snatch strap. It's a race against the incoming tide. '*One, two, three, go!*' Together we drop the clutches and out she comes. It's last light and the tide has turned. Another 15 minutes and we would have lost the vehicle.

We move back off the high-water mark onto a small reed-fringed sand island. The mozzies are thick. Big John's just had a nasty incident. He was filming the goings on when a gang of thugs bumped him and pulled the camera from his hands. Babu is furious and goes off into the night to try and get it back. A group of locals say the thieves are fishermen from Nacala. Three hours later and Babu's still not back. Big John is fed up – it's not only the camera but also all the valuable pics on the memory card. Anna's concerned as some of the computer stuff got drenched in the river, and there'll be no dispatches for a while. Richard's still limping on a bad ankle – he's been that way for eight days now. There's no way we'll get across the mouth. The sand's too soft, the river too high.

It seems there have been some unseasonable rains upstream, and a man on a motorbike says it will take at least a week for the water to drop. We'll have to follow tracks upstream through thick bush to the bridge. It means we won't make our deadline to meet a team that is flying into Nampula. We'll have to tell them we're delayed. We set up the satellite phone and call South Africa, only to get the shocking news of the xenophobia that's erupted there – homes being torched, people being burnt and murdered and a mass exodus of Mozambicans fleeing for their lives. What a shock. Here we're doing our best to show goodwill through our humanitarian efforts whilst at home our countrymen are burning and looting. We're even warned to be careful as there might be reprisals against South Africans in Mozambique. Babu gets back in the early morning – no luck. Everybody's a bit down.

Dispatch #224 – The End of the World
'Use the flesh from green prickly pear leaves. Just bandage it over the wound. It sucks out all the poison – works wonders,' says Arthur Norval, who with lovely Sarah owns a delightful camp and restaurant which overlooks Baía de Fernão Veloso near Nacala, the deepest natural port on the east coast of Africa. It's called Fim do Mundo, which means 'End of the World'. Richard Chapman is going through hell; he's got two tropical ulcers on his ankle and blood poisoning has set in. He's man down and the antibiotics are taking time to work. Poor bloke's got such a high fever that Mashozi is treating him for malaria just in case. First we use peroxide – it bubbles white on contact with the putrefying flesh. Warwick straps on the prickly pear. We fire up the Landies and say cheers. We'll next meet at Ilha de Mozambique.

We continue to inch down the coast. With us is Robbie Brozin, the CEO of Nando's and a man who's personally assisted with the raising of more than a million rand with which to purchase mosquito nets. Four of his close mates, part of his Young President's Organisation forum, have joined him as malaria warriors. It's amazing how the simple things in life still hold true. Robbie and his friends are all highly successful businessmen, champions of commerce and industry who are well able to afford the best in life, but here they are camping under the stars, walking barefoot on the beach, eating simple food cooked on the coals, brushing their teeth in seawater and unselfishly assisting with our humanitarian efforts.

Dispatch #225 – Omuhipiti, Ilha de Mozambique

Beautiful women with the look and feel of the Swahili coast sway to the rhythm of the drums at an event organised by Bita Rodrigues of USAID. More than 500 mums with babies have gathered for a fun-filled malaria prevention day as Robbie and his team assist with the donation of a net to each mum. Ilha de Mozambique, known as Omuhipiti in the Makua language, is a World Heritage Site. It boasts the Chapel of Nossa Senhora de Baluarte, which is the oldest European building in the southern hemisphere. Standing up on the fort battlements and looking out towards Goa Island, the Kas Kazi trade wind pulling at my beard, I can feel the history of the place.

Greg and the Nando's team get a chapa, a local taxi, through to Nampula for a flight home – we've had great fun together. Richard and his team are back with us; fortunately the prickly-pear flesh has pulled out much of the poison but an ugly open wound remains. Then it's Ross's turn to go down. A sharp, burnt stick had gone right through the sole of his shoe and well into his instep. It's gone septic, his groin is swollen and a fever has set in. Anna feeds him antibiotics and soaks his foot in a basin of hot saltwater. These veld sores or tropical ulcers are an unfortunate part of expedition life, and if one looks at old pictures of previous adventures, there will always be one or two people wearing a wide sock of sticky surgical plaster coloured with seeping orange-brown, Betadine ointment. Sometimes these suppurating sores get so bad that we heat up an empty Captain Morgan bottle, place the mouth over the sore then wrap the hot bottle in a cold wet cloth. It causes a suction and pulls out the poison.

Two days later Ross is able to walk and we take the causeway back to the mainland and south down a rutted bush track.

Dispatch #226 – To the Mouth of the Rio Zambezi

We're feeling the pace, running on adrenalin. Getting the Landies across the Melúli and Ligonha rivers is torturous, but we learnt our lesson on the Lúrio. This time we pay a team of about 50 men to wade into the river and stand in two lines marking the shallowest crossing. The instructions to the men are clear. If the vehicles start to flounder, rush in like a rugby scrum and push like hell. It works, and with the Zen of Travel on our side we make it down the coast from Angoch to Pebane, on to Quelimane for more mosquito nets, across the ferry over the Zambezi River and down to Chupanga where Mary Moffat Livingstone, wife of the great Victorian missionary explorer, David Livingstone, lies buried. For us as a family, Chupanga is one of the spiritual places on the river. It is here that one gets a feel for the hardship and dangers that exist for people who travel along the great Zambezi. The inscription on Mary Moffat's gravestone reads:

> *Here repose the mortal remains of Mary Moffat. The beloved wife of Doctor Livingstone. In humble hope of joyful resurrection. Your Saviour Jesus Christ.*

She died in Chupanga House on 27 April 1862, aged 41 years. Although this is our fourth expedition to Mary's grave, we are still overcome by the sadness of the place with its neglected graves and the war-torn mission station. Fortunately the beautiful church has now been restored and the sound of the bell rings out across the banks of the Zambezi. A group of local Sena women join us at the grave, singing softly. Mashozi places a bunch of wild flowers at the foot of the tombstone. Each one of the mums receives a mosquito net. We do not want them or their children to die from the same deadly bite of the *Anopheles* mosquito that killed Mary. Mashozi is a tough and truly remarkable woman but this is an emotional time for her and I find her sitting quietly in the old church, her chin cupped in her little hands. She is touched by Mary's life,

MASHOZI PLACES A SMALL BUNCH OF WILD FLOWERS ON MARY'S GRAVE.

by the incredible hardships she endured, as she too follows her adventurous husband into the wilds of Africa.

At Marromeu, Bruce goes down with bad malaria and Mashozi treats him with Coartem right away. We set up base camp at the old Sena Sugar Mill club grounds, aptly called Sena Grog. We've visited here before and once again they make us incredibly welcome. We feel comfortable leaving Bruce with old friend Pedro Cruz – at least he'll have a soft bed and a fan. Mashozi leaves a note with strict instructions for regular checks, plenty of water and the correct dosage of Coartem. We have to rush off to a bush airstrip to meet a group of journalists and a team from Land Rover Menlyn who have flown in with Lesley Sutton. They confirm the horror of xenophobia, where African immigrants to South Africa are having their homes burnt down in a fit of madness, some being killed. And here we are in the Zambezi Delta, South Africans battling to save and improve lives. Crazy.

At the mouth of the Zambezi we hoist the expedition flag and distribute mosquito nets to an orphanage and the maternity clinic. Three days later, thanks to modern medicine and quick treatment, Bruce is alive and back behind the wheel of the Stomach. We need to get the Land Rover team back to Beira to fly out, and we are pushing to reach the Cape of Good Hope on Madiba's birthday, still sticking to the edge.

Dispatch #227 – Peri-Peri Malaria Warriors

Cesar, Drinnie, Carla, Warren and Gavin, five malaria warriors from Nando's, carry rucksacks, tents, sleeping bags and a large cool box of vacuum-packed chicken – they've flown into Beira and mean business! Off a sand track, north of Beira on the road to Savane, we camp amongst some old, gnarled gum trees filled with the late night cries of screaming bushbabies. Sitting around a roaring fire, Babu gives the new team members a lesson on how to conduct malaria prevention sessions as well as how to capture the correct data regarding the area's location, facilities and malaria risk on the malaria research forms. By the next day we've got a trained and motivated team travelling with us distributing nets. Cesar Dias, who's put the team of volunteers together, speaks perfect Portuguese and is great on the microphone.

As the Nando's Fight Malaria warriors go into the market outside Beira to buy supplies, an angry man comes up to them. 'My brother has just been killed by you South Africans,' he says. 'Why are you killing our people? I have a gun, it would be a pleasure to take you out!' Cesar moves his team out of there in a hurry, back to our remote expedition camp. Two days later we're at the Mango Tree Kids orphanage. Along with the Nando's volunteers, the manager of Tongaat Hulett's mill in Mafambisse has come with his team to assist. We'd been here three years before on the African Rainbow dhow journey and had promised to return. Now children and foster parents get long-lasting mozzie nets and there are soccer balls to go around. We have malaria prevention skits, a dancing competition and a malaria prevention quiz – it's so much fun and the Nando's team are so dedicated. These South Africans have taken the trouble to get away from business and family and are making a difference here in the middle of nowhere out of the goodness of their hearts.

We then head down the Púngoe River, with its massive crocs and mudbanks. A fierce incoming tide, strong winds and the twists and turns of the river make the Púngoe a real challenge, with the rendezvous at Biques taking place in the dark with just a tablespoon of boat fuel left in the tanks. The Nando's volunteers fly out from Beira and we head south – they've lifted our spirits and reinforced the importance of using this outside edge adventure to improve and save lives.

Dispatch #228 – Termite-Mound Cake

The last time we celebrated Anna's birthday we were coming up the Angolan coast. Now it's time to party again. William takes the red spade off the side of the Landy, digs a hole in an old termite mound and makes a fire inside. 'Do we have any eggs?' 'No,' shouts Mashozi from where she's collecting firewood, 'they couldn't take the bouncing so I chucked what was left of them.' William, who doubles up as expedition cook, chuckles as he stokes his ant-heap oven. Ross wipes the orange goo from his hands; he's been busy cleaning big, juicy Buzi River mud prawns. From out of its hiding place in the toolbox, Ross produces a dust-covered bottle of cheap, warm bubbly and theatrically sabres off the top of the bottle with a kitchen knife. The contents bubble into two plastic glasses. '*Feliz dia de anos*! Happy birthday, Anna.' From behind the Land Rovers come the expedition team wearing paper party hats and whistling *Happy Birthday* through those colourful paper whistles that curl out like a chameleon's tongue. Mashozi gives Anna a bunch of pink plastic roses, part of the birthday goodies box bought in Beira. 'Everlastings,' she says. Hot off the grid, the freshwater peri-peri prawns are delicious. William adds to the birthday feast with roast beef, butternut, green beans and salad. Then out from the ant heap comes the egg-free chocolate cake, sprinkled with hundreds and thousands, cut into slices and washed down with *Renosterkoffie*. Who says you can't have fun in the bush?

The next day we cross the ferry over the Buzi and head down the coast to ancient Sofala. Then it's down to Nova Mambone and on to Inhassoro for a night of R&R and a farewell braai to malaria warriors Richard, Big John, Warwick and Tamaryn – we'll meet again back home in South Africa.

Dispatch #229 – Terra da Boa Gente and Beyond

We reached Inhambane in the late afternoon. Dhows and ferryboats move slowly across the bay. In January 1498 the great Portuguese explorer Vasco da Gama anchored in this very bay and was so well received that he called it *Terra da Boa Gente*, meaning 'Land of Good People', and it is still like that. The people of Inhambane province are some of the friendliest and productive in all Mozambique. Their villages of handcrafted reed huts thatched with palm fronds are beautifully maintained. It's *naartjie* season and there are splashes of orange between the tall coconut palms. We load up more bales of mosquito nets to take south. The Land Rover roof racks creak and groan under the weight. We are still doing what we came to do.

The last time we'd crossed 23° 26' 22" S, the Tropic of Capricorn, was with a windstorm blowing in the great sand ocean of the ancient Namib where the cold Atlantic washes against the west coast of Africa in Namibia. Now 420 days and 31 outside edge countries later, we're on the east coast where the warm Indian Ocean washes against the palm-fronded beaches of Mozambique. We pose for a picture.

South of Inharrime, in the area around Quissico Lake, malaria is rife and we move in to help. The days flash by now – no time to waste as we push for the border. We cross the Limpopo River at Xai-Xai and then follow the red-earth track down to the Zongoene lighthouse. It's a beautiful day and long lines of white foaming waves break slowly into the mouth of the Limpopo. Village by village, in the shade of old mango trees, we distribute mosquito nets along the winding sand track through to Praia do Bilene. Here we say goodbye to Babu Cossa – until the next one Babu!

It's a wonderful stretch of coast that takes us on to Bobole, some 50 kilometres north of Maputo, where old friends Paul and Liz Hallows own the famous Blue Anchor Inn. The staff are waiting outside the front entrance, tunefully banging kitchen pots and pans with spoons and ladles and singing a welcome song in Portuguese. Inside, a long wooden table is groaning with the weight of platters piled high with peri-peri flat chicken. What a welcome! With Paul at the bar and Lizzy in the kitchen there's no chance of going short! Their lemon meringue pie is the finest on the east coast of Africa. If ever you want a night of good cheer, great old-fashioned hospitality and a comfortable bed, this is the place to be.

Dispatch #230 – South Africa Here We Come!

With the War of Liberation and the civil war that followed it now in the past, Maputo is slowly reclaiming some of its former glory when it was known as Lourenço Marques. The city is getting a facelift, the port is operating well and hotels and restaurants are full of well-heeled customers. The city's skyline fades behind us as we take the busy Catembe ferry south across Maputo Bay. We stop at Catembe village for the last of the big One Net One Life malaria prevention events. This is a big one, promoted by USAID in Maputo, and members of the press from local TV, radio and print endorse the scroll and scribble in their pads. It's a strange feeling; travelling down the coast, we're beginning to move out of high-risk malaria areas now and this is our last major event.

Late rains have turned the road into a quagmire. We pull into the bush and have one last camp in the wild near the Maputo Elephant Game Reserve. If all goes well we'll cross into South Africa tomorrow. It feels odd, being so close to our own country after more than 420 days of tracking the edge. Tired out from the afternoon's big event there's still time for humour. We sit around the fire, throw some *nyama* on the coals and talk about the journey ahead. It would be so easy to cheat a bit, hit the highway south to the Cape of Good Hope – we could be there in three days. But our outside edge challenge is not like that, and we're still committed.

It's school holidays, and the masses have moved to Ponta Malongane and Ponta do Ouro. There's a Blue Bulls Bar and another for Sharks fans. South Africans are on quad bikes with beers in hand – it all feels so commercial and strange. They ask us to pose for photographs. We're just a few hours from the border. It's unbelievable!

South Africa – The Return

Day 425, and Back to Country 1 on the Edge

So finally we have made it back home to the land of our birth, all of us a bit thinner than when we'd left and running on adrenalin. It's quite emotional and at the Kosi Bay border post we kneel down and kiss the tar. After nearly 14 months of attempting to track the rest of Africa's coastline we now, more than ever, fully appreciate the incredible beauty of our own outside edge paradise.

WE'VE MADE IT BACK HOME TO KZN – NOW IT'S A DASH TO MEET THE DEADLINE OF EMPTYING THE CALABASH ON MADIBA'S BIRTHDAY.

Dispatch #231 – There's No Place Like Home

It's Tuesday 24 June 2008 and Mashozi is playing her scratched *Take me home, country roads* CD again as we cross the southern Mozambican border at Ponta do Ouro into KwaZulu, which means 'place of heaven'. It's a wonderful feeling as the final outside edge border stamp comes down. With tears in our eyes we go down on our knees and kiss the tar – somehow we've made it home.

Chief Tembe and his tribal indunas have come to welcome us. The Tembe Elephant Game Reserve has done an excellent job of conserving wildlife and now its staff add their signatures to those of the more than 5 000 well-wishers from Africa's outside edge who have endorsed the Scroll of Peace and Goodwill. The chief has his own malaria control programme and so to end the expedition's One Net One Life campaign we hand over the last bale of life-saving mosquito nets for his community together with Rite to Sight spectacles for the elderly poor-sighted. A Zulu choir sings a welcome song below a sign that reads 'Kosi Bay Border', above which flutters a South African flag, but our outside edge challenge is far from over. With only 24 days to go to meet the deadline of emptying the calabash back into the cold South Atlantic on Madiba's 90th birthday on 18 July, it's a race against time.

The joy of being back in South Africa is unbelievable. Sure, we know it's not perfect; we've got our own problems but as the Rainbow Nation we have to work through them, especially that of crime. There's no point in comparing us to developed countries like Australia, New Zealand, Canada and the UK, but after some of the countries we've been through, South Africa is an incredible paradise. Sure, people complain about the electricity crisis, crime and the cost of living, but try buying

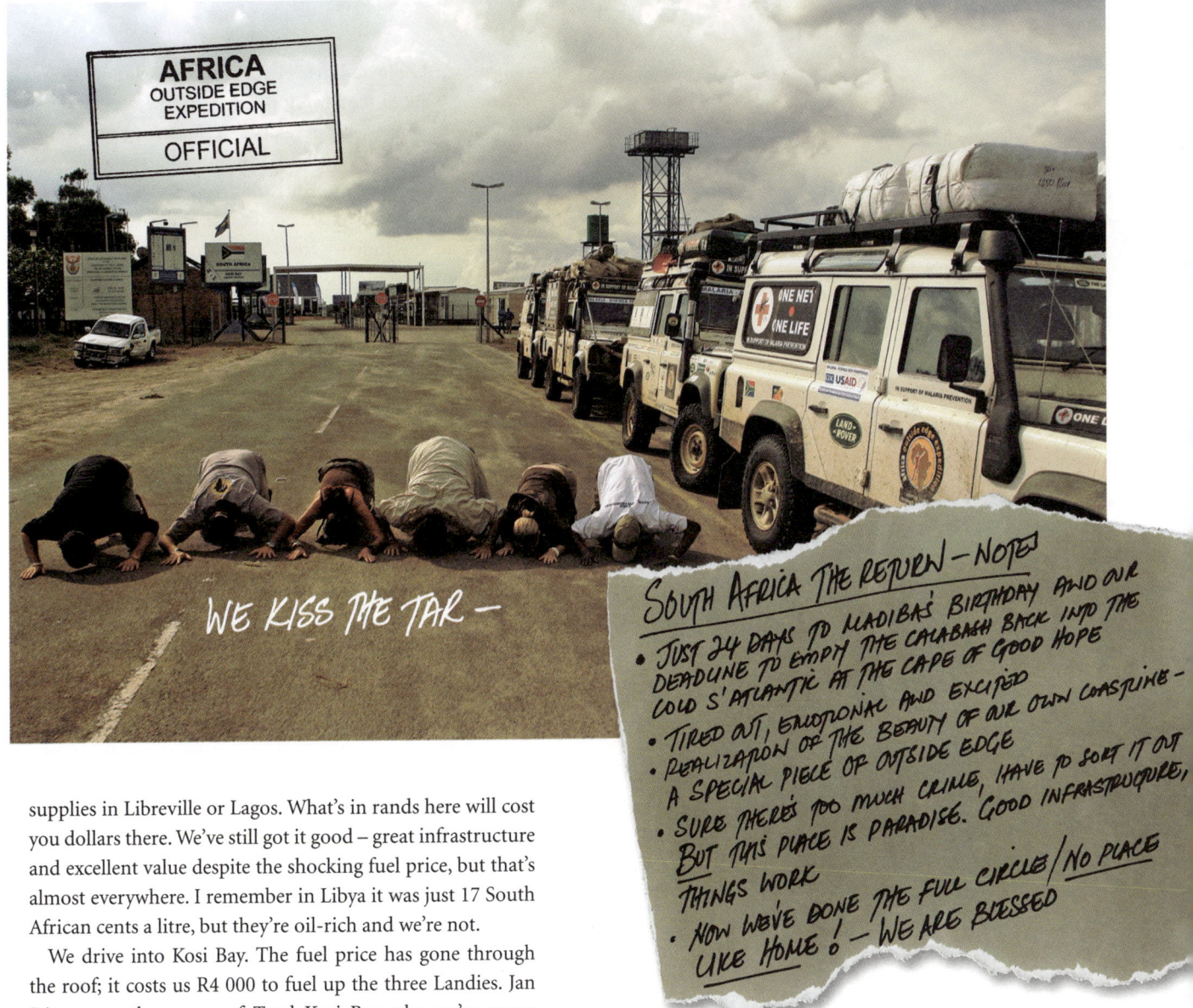

AFRICA OUTSIDE EDGE EXPEDITION OFFICIAL

WE KISS THE TAR –

South Africa The Return – Notes
- Just 24 days to Madiba's birthday and our deadline to empty the calabash back into the cold S'Atlantic at the Cape of Good Hope
- Tired out, emotional and excited
- Realization of the beauty of our own coastline – a special piece of Outside Edge
- Sure there's too much crime, have to sort it out but this place is paradise. Good infrastructure, things work
- Now we've done the full circle / No place like home! – We are blessed

supplies in Libreville or Lagos. What's in rands here will cost you dollars there. We've still got it good – great infrastructure and excellent value despite the shocking fuel price, but that's almost everywhere. I remember in Libya it was just 17 South African cents a litre, but they're oil-rich and we're not.

We drive into Kosi Bay. The fuel price has gone through the roof; it costs us R4 000 to fuel up the three Landies. Jan Dippenaar, the owner of Total Kosi Bay who we've never met before, comes out. 'Not a damn are you okes paying for diesel in my garage,' he says. 'With what you guys have done to help Africa, it's on the house. Welcome home! And there are cheeseburgers and chips all round – you all look like you need a square meal.' Then there's an even greater gift as we get the message that old Zululand mate and humanitarian adventurer Gary Prentice is flying little Tristan into Kosi Bay by helicopter. What an incredible surprise; still in his khaki school uniform he races into his dad's arms. We'd last seen him in Djibouti, and now our mascot is back for the journey down to the Cape of Good Hope. His arrival further lifts our spirits.

Dispatch #232 – Kosi Bay and Beyond
It's good to hear Zulu being spoken again and, oh my goodness, we are overwhelmed by the beauty of our own coast. It's so clean and pristine, especially compared to some parts of Africa's overpopulated coastlines, where the sea is used as a toilet and a dump for stinking litter. By boat, with old family friend Mark Upfold, Ezemvelo KZN Wildlife

Hippos at Kosi Bay

Zulu maidens dance in the dust and we hand over a container library to the Ncemaneni community

The work of a Zulu sand sculptor with Umhlanga Rocks lighthouse in the background.

ranger Nkosi Zulu and marine fundi Scotty Kyle and his son Ewan, we explore the beautiful Kosi Bay lake system where the Tembe-Tsonga have developed an ingenious method of harvesting the fish by way of communal traps intricately woven from indigenous plants and creepers. These are set up in the shallow, sandy channels that wind through the main entrance to the Indian Ocean and through which the fish must pass. We tie the boat to a fish kraal.

Ewan tells us that kraals such as these have been in existence for more than 700 years, handed down from father to son. Nowadays, it's a wonderful example of a community working hand in hand with nature conservation. The other lakes are equally beautiful. There are crocodiles, fish eagles, Egyptian vultures, hippos and raffia palms, the frond stems of which are used to make small rafts that enable the amaTsonga to cross the reed-fringed channels. Down on the beach, close to the mouth, there's a World Heritage Site; a turtle breeding ground of both the leatherback, the world's largest marine turtle, and the smaller loggerhead turtle. It's another piece of outside edge paradise.

Dispatch #233 – Zulu Country

Back in the Landies we head south along some of the highest forested sand dunes in the world, beautiful places with names like Bhanga Nek, Rocktail Bay, Island Rock, Lake Sibaya, Sodwana Bay, Mission Rocks, Cape Vidal and Lake St Lucia. They are all part of the iSimangaliso Wetland Park, rich in bird and wildlife and boasting some of the most spectacular coral diversity in the world. Our humanitarian work continues as, supported by Phinda Resource Reserve's Africa Foundation, we distribute mobile libraries to schools in the area. At rural Ncemaneni School, close to King Shaka Zulu's great military kraal at KwaBulawayo, more than a hundred children with teachers from Centurus Colleges in the Pretoria area arrive for the handing-over ceremony of a 40-foot container library, complete with doors, windows, a veranda and shelves of books. The Zulu children dance in the dust and the Pretoria kids learn about the personal joy of giving.

We're travelling in the land of the Zulu Kingdom, founded by the great King Shaka Zulu. Here the outside edge place names have a romantic ring to them: Mkuze, the Lebombo Mountains, Hluhluwe, Mfolozi, Mtubatuba, Kwa Mbonambi and Empangeni. Then it's on to English-sounding Richards

Bay, at the mouth of the Mhlatuzi River, where the *Zululand Observer* and city fathers endorse the scroll. We push south to beautiful Mtunzini, which in Zulu means 'place of shade', where indigenous trees still shield the residents of this beautiful piece of the outside edge from the hot African sun. There's no stopping us now. On through Gingindlovu, over the Amatikulu River to Mangeti, where the descendants of an early Scottish gunrunner, big game hunter, trader and adventurer by the name of John Dunn still farm sugarcane. John is reputed to have been quite a character. Much loved by the Zulus, he paid the *lobola* bride price for 47 Zulu wives who bore him 117 children.

King Cetshwayo made him a chief, but even John Dunn, the white Zulu, was unable to stop the British from marching on Zululand. On the south bank of the Tugela River, the old border between British Natal and King Cetshwayo's Zululand, and just downstream from Fort Pearson where they say a big croc still hangs out, we stand at the Ultimatum Tree Monument. Here, on 11 December 1878, in the shade of a giant sycamore fig, the British had given the Zulus the unreasonable ultimatum that led to the Anglo-Zulu War. Sitting here I can just imagine the scene: the Tugela swirling past, the British in their red coats, the pomp and ceremony and the Zulu head-ringed elder listening in amazement. Little did the British know at the time that just 42 days later, on 22 January 1879, armed with their characteristic raw-hide shields and short-handled, broad-bladed stabbing spears, the Zulus would use their famous 'horns of the buffalo' attacking formation to annihilate the British at the Battle of Isandlwana. In the words of historian and dear friend David Rattray, from his book *A Soldier-Artist in Zululand: William Whitelocke Lloyd and the Anglo-Zulu War of 1879*:

> *Isandlwana was no British blunder, rather it was a great Zulu victory. Of the total of 1 774 men committed on the British side to battle, no less than 1 329 lay dead. Later that day the British redeemed themselves when the sick and the wounded at the Rorke's Drift hospital held out against an almost impossible attack by 4 000 Zulus, resulting in 11 Victoria Crosses being awarded for valour. Sadly, with more than 2 000 dead at Isandlwana the Zulus had spent themselves in victory and were finally defeated at the Battle of Ulundi. King Cetshwayo was taken into exile, so bringing to an end the Old Zulu Order.* (2007, p. 63)

The Tugela north-bank lighthouse blinks five times into the late afternoon sea mist. We continue around Seula Point where if you're lucky you can still see bushbuck on the beach, and then past Boiling Pots, one of Ross's favourite crayfishing spots. Just a short distance down the beach we reach Zinkwazi, 'place of the fish eagle', where hidden amongst the milkwoods is our Afrika House with its Zanzibar doors, old rugs and carpets, books and carvings – everything is just as we had left it, carefully cared for by Mamthembu and her daughter Phumelele. George our parrot now speaks Zulu; little Edward, the basset cross spaniel, has gone a little grey around the gills, seems he's pined a bit; Lady Baker, the old rottweiler, still has warm intelligent eyes and a ready wag.

Mashozi was right, Abu the Ape from Abidjan with the red fez on his head seems quite relaxed and at home here. His Land Rover journey over, he sits at the foot of the stairs leading up to the Swahili room now decorated with a hand-woven Moroccan carpet from the medieval walled city of Fez. The front door key ring now reads 'Bouctou Hotel, Room 13' – a gift from Timbuktu. Already there are so many memories, but as if on cue I go down with malaria, treat myself instantly and three days later, now even more squeezed for time, we fire up the Landies. Cape of Good Hope, here we come.

Dispatch #234 – Shark Territory
At KwaDukuza, below the monument to King Shaka Zulu at the place where he was murdered by his half-brother Dingaan, who later also murdered Piet Retief and his party of trekkers, Mayor Gumede endorses the much-travelled outside edge scroll in Zulu. At the ceremony are old friends Martin and Debbie Finch, whose family farm is depicted in a painting by George Angus with lions lying down on the beach at the Mvoti River mouth, just a few kilometres downstream from where Nobel Peace Prize laureate Chief Albert Luthuli lies buried. No longer are there lions on the beach; now it's endless sugarcane and smart residential developments that make up this part of the outside edge as, still with the 33 outside edge flag decals and the orange life rings from Gabon attached to the Land Rover bull bars, we rumble on. We witness constructs to a variety of faiths in our diverse

The wild coast of Pondoland – one of the most beautiful sections of Africa's outside edge

Stadium is growing in preparation for the 2010 Football World Cup. Down the Golden Mile beachfront the piers are a wild tangle of fishing rods and Indians – the shad are running. We hoot for a rickshaw and keep moving down the esplanade past the harbour, one of Africa's biggest and busiest ports. On the outside edge is a monument to Dick King, showing him on horseback; it was his epic ride to Grahamstown assisted by his 16-year-old black servant Ndongeni that saved the British garrison in 1842.

Heavy floods have hit the south coast and the bridge at Hibberdene has washed away. We stop to photograph the black-and-white-chequered lighthouse at the mouth of the Mzimkulu at Port Shepstone. It's all so civilised and such a novelty; it makes a change from bully beef sarmies to just grab some fast food as we go, go, go, go. With town names like Margate, Ramsgate and Port Edward, you can tell that the British were here. As we cross the Mtamvuna River into Pondoland there's excited chatter over the Land Rover radios – we are closing in and we can smell victory.

Dispatch #235 – Shipwrecks and Sardines

Down the Pondoland coast some staff from Drifters Adventure Tours help us distribute more mobile libraries to rural schools. The unspoilt beauty of this coast is unbelievable. The old leper colony of Mkambati is now a nature reserve stretching from the mouth of the Mtentu to the mouth of the Msikaba. Nowhere else on the outside edge of Africa have we seen wildebeest, zebra, eland and red hartebeest grazing within sight of passing whales, dolphins and shoals of sardines.

It's tough going and we're feeling the pace. We travel in first gear low ratio, and sometimes on foot and by microlight over difficult terrain to follow the incredibly beautiful Wild Coast. The sardines are running. Millions upon millions of young pilchards are moving east, in shoals of up to 10 kilometres long, and birds flock in their thousands as they congregate to feed off the shoals, as do the dolphins, with pods numbering up to 20 000. It's up there with the Serengeti wildebeest migration as one of the greatest migrations on earth. We've never seen so many whales before and once again we're overwhelmed by the dramatic beauty of our own coast. Drifters lets us use its trail camps along the coast. It's called the Wild Coast for good reason and even old maps warn mariners to be aware of freak killer waves. Shipwrecks are plentiful.

land, from Muslim mosques and Hindu temples, churches of the Methodist, Anglican and Dutch Reformed to white-stoned, open-air circles for the Zionists, and sangomas in the streets. We continue south through Salt Rock, Shaka's Rock, Ballito and past a casino in the shape of Zulu huts (Shaka has surely turned in his grave). There are roadworks en route to the new King Shaka International Airport that is still under construction. We stop at another outside edge icon, the red-and-white-striped lighthouse at Umhlanga Rocks, and then go down to the Old Fort in Durban where the British were besieged by the Boers in 1842.

'Congratulations guys,' comes Bruce's voice over the radio, '*we're back in Durbs – home to the Sharks. Do you see the new stadium?*' And there on the right, close to Durban's outside edge and surrounded by cranes, the massive Moses Mabhida

We stop at the wreck site of the *Grosvenor*, the East Indiaman that went down here in 1782. The wind tugs at my beard. Ross's excited voice comes over his hand-held radio; he's on foot with Anna and Tristan, having left from the Drifters camp at Mkambati that morning. '*I can't believe it*,' he says, '*this must be the best day of the entire outside edge journey. I've never seen so many whales, dolphins, sardines and gannets, and the coast, it's so beautiful. I can see the Landies, keep on coming down the track and you'll see us.*'

Tough Pondo women dive for crayfish and pull octopi and mussels from the rocks. Apparently, of the estimated 125 *Grosvenor* castaways that survived the thundering surf, only six made it to Cape Town. Now the ship has settled under the waves, but treasure hunters still come here in search of bullion. The story goes that some of the *Grosvenor* castaways settled with local tribes and had children and that somewhere in Nelson Mandela's line of forebears there might be a white-skinned castaway. We ride the corrugations through the bright-green tea plantations of the Magwa estate and continue through beautiful indigenous forests down to the mouth where the Mbotyi River Lodge has become the sardine-fever adventure centre. It's a buzz of international film crews, dive boats, 4x4s, helicopters and microlights.

I have a cup of coffee with Nic de Gersigny, a big, friendly bloke who owns SEAL, an adventure diving and safari company. 'This year has been the best ever,' he says. 'Super pods of dolphins, bait balls the size of four rugby fields, thousands of sharks and more Bryde's whales than ever before. Port Edward to Coffee Bay, that's the "hot zone",' he enthuses excitedly. 'Good visibility. It's the highlight of the year for adventure divers worldwide, one of the greatest shows on earth.'

We're back in the Landies. I just wish we had more time; this coast alone deserves six months. Mbotyi is pretty – the forests, waterfalls and beaches. It's no wonder that André Stander, South Africa's most notorious cop-cum-bank robber, hid out in a cottage here whilst on the run from the police. Nine river-mouth shipwrecks lie off the Mzimvuba River at Port St Johns on either side of which, covered in sub-tropical forest, are Mounts Sullivan and Thesiger, which form the famous Gates of St John. Here local historian and author John Costello hosts us at the Outspan Inn. He's a great character and we'd first met him here in 1993 when we'd done our Cape to Cairo in open boats. The next morning, on his motorbike, he leads us out to a film set on the river where they're building a replica of Dr Albert Schweitzer's Lambaréné Mission Hospital. The set builders have never been to the actual site and are using photographic images as reference material. We give them the thumbs up. It's perfect and brings back great memories of our expedition's visit to Lambaréné on the Ogooué River in Gabon. We say cheers to John; he's one of the many keeping the Zen of Travel alive.

We go on past Coffee Bay to make a 5 a.m. call to photograph the Hole in the Wall at sunrise. We're chasing time. Around Mbolompo Point, across the Qhorha and Mbashe rivers, there are delightful old-style Wild Coast country hotels. We continue along the dirt road that takes us past the prophetess Nongqause's kraal. It's quite a story – a sad one that ends with the smell of rotting carcasses, disappointment and outrage

THE HOLE IN THE WALL AT SUNRISE

'SARDINE FEVER'

when the prophesy didn't materialise. It had all started in 1856 when 14-year-old Nongqause gazed into a pool in the Gxara River and saw the faces of her great ancestors, who gave her the message that the Xhosa people should kill all their cattle and destroy their crops.

The result would be that the sun would rise in a blood-red colour, the cattle and crops would be miraculously restored and the ancestors would come back to life with all their warriors to drive the British and other white settlers into the sea. Some 400 000 head of cattle together with grain stores and crops were destroyed. With bated breath the great day dawned but nothing happened and the believers blamed it on those who had refused to kill their cattle. And so the cattle killing continued, leading to 50 000 Xhosa dying from famine and others dragging themselves to the closest white settlement or mission to beg for help from the very people they'd hoped to destroy. The Gcaleka clan had self-destructed and the British banished Nongqause to Robben Island.

The wind blows strongly as we take the small, well-run motorised ferry across the Great Kei River. As I lean on the Landy bonnet, looking out to sea, recollections of so many other outside edge river crossings wash over me. Memories of the long waits and disappointments; the shouting and screaming; the bailing buckets and bribes; oil pissing out from ferry engines and midstream breakdowns; fish traders and touts; dangerous overcrowding and people pushing and shoving; black marks on the sun visor; and vendors selling bananas, groundnuts, mangoes, chickens, boiled eggs and warm beer – I wouldn't have missed it for anything.

Dispatch #236 – Settler Country

We push on to Morgan's Bay, Haga-Haga, Gonubie and the mouth of the Buffalo River where, in 1688, about 20 European castaways were found, survivors of the *Stavenisse* which had gone down on the coast two years before. British settlers arrived 132 years later and on 14 January 1848, during the Seventh Frontier War between the settlers and the Xhosa, Governor Sir Harry Smith annexed the river port and called the settlement East London. However, it wasn't just the 1820 British Settlers who settled here.

As the wind blows cold, we stop the convoy to photograph the beachfront monument to the German settlers, the first of whom had been soldiers in the King's German Legion, had fought for the British and then settled between the white settlers and the Xhosas along the east bank of the Buffalo River. It was a lonely life and to help the German settlers, most of whom were ex-legionnaire bachelors, the British government sent out a shipload of 157 Irish lasses from Dublin. On the Kowie River in Port Alfred we shine the Land Rover lights onto a stone marker that reads: 'In 1820 the British Settlers from Algoa Bay crossed here in their ox-wagons'.

The next day we stand at the Toposcope outside Bathurst. North, south, east and west, through 360 degrees we gaze over Settler Country. Brass plaques, some of which have been recently chipped off and sold to scrap metal merchants, give the direction as well as settlers' names, the ships that they

SHOUTS OF GLEE AT ALGOA BAY AS WE HAND OVER THE CONSERVATION STONES BROUGHT FROM WEST, NORTH AND EAST. THEY'LL REMAIN AT THE ALGOA BAY LIGHTHOUSE.

came out on and the distance from the Toposcope to where they settled. There are good British settler names like Smith, Pigit, Southey, Greathead, Bradshaw, Hayhurst, Wainwright, Ford and Scott. Below us is the small town of Bathurst, chosen by Sir Rufane Donkin as the administrative centre for the 1820 settlers. The St Johns Anglican Church still stands; built by the settlers, it served at times as a fort and refuge in the frontier wars against the amaXhosa. Down at the Pig 'n Whistle, the oldest licensed pub in South Africa, today's jolly locals have coined the phrase 'there's no thirst like Bathurst'.

That night on the Bushmans River we meet the Fowlds family and other descendants of early settler families. Tough, resourceful, hospitable people of the land with a love for the Eastern Cape, they've taken old cattle grazing land and turned it into a pristine wildlife reserve called Amakhala. 'We're part of this country and we're here to stay,' says old friend Grant Fowlds with a good-humoured chuckle. What a jolly evening, with all of us crammed into their cellar pub. Bill, the old man, is a great raconteur and there are also stories from the outside edge – it's a long night.

At Port Elizabeth on the outside edge of Algoa Bay, a convoy of Landies of every conceivable model escorts us into town for a 'Welcome to PE' bash. The next morning up at the Donkin Reserve we photograph the battered Landies in front of the stone pyramid erected by Sir Rufane Donkin in 1820 in memory of his wife Elizabeth. The port city still carries her name and down at the lighthouse at Cape Recife, with the south wind blowing wild white horses across Algoa Bay where the settlers arrived for their first taste of Africa, we tune into the radio to get the last few nail-biting minutes of the Springbok–All Blacks game. *'The New Zealand supporters look like they're at a funeral wake,'* says the commentator. *'It's 30–28 to the Bokke.'* This is the first Springbok side to win at Carisbrook Stadium, aptly nicknamed the House of Pain, since the two countries started playing there in 1921. We leap out of the Landies and dance a jig on the side of the road. We feel well and truly home.

Dispatch #237 – The Garden Route

It's the Billabong Classic at Jeffreys Bay and surfers from all over the world have turned up to ride the perfect Super Tubes. At Chatten farm we meet Anna's family. Through thick and thin Anna has survived her first expedition. She's overjoyed, and her sisters gather round with questions. It's a great homecoming, with *tjops* and steak on the braai. Johan and Estelle, Anna's mom and dad, are full of fun. Johan's grandfather bought the farm from a Scotsman in 1926 and the condition of the sale was that the bar should always remain fully stocked. So after a huge dose of *boeregasvryheid*, Anna's parents escort us on to the white-walled thatched cottages of St Francis Bay and to the historic 1878 Cape St Francis lighthouse. Cheers and *totsiens*, we wave them goodbye.

Then it's on to Oyster Bay – we're feeling burnt out but excited. We go over the Paul Sauer Bridge spanning the Storms River, followed by the Bloukrans Bridge, which at 216 metres has the world's highest commercial bungy jump. Then on through the beautiful Tsitsikamma Forest, Nature's Valley, Keurboomstrand and Plettenberg Bay. No hassles! No black marks on the sun visor here. I feel the pebble in the pocket and have mixed emotions. There's the growing media pressure, calls from radio stations as we drive and journalists meeting us along the route – so many questions. We all should be gung ho, upbeat, bright-eyed and bushy-tailed, but with 444 days into the journey, we're mentally and physically exhausted, somewhat emotional, hanging in on a thread and running only on adrenalin. With just four days to go, it's a countdown to the finish line.

Dispatch #238 – Countdown to the Finish, Day 445

Since Roman times no feast has been complete without oysters and to this day they're still considered a tasty aphrodisiac. It's the last day of the Knysna Oyster Festival, the sun is shining and thousands of South Africans have turned up to sip champagne and slurp oysters. It feels strange to see so many white people. I think we've gone a bit *bossies*. Land Rover sponsor us a night of luxury at the Pezula Golf Estate – we shake off the dust from our clothes, I comb the beard and we photograph the incredible view over the Knysna Heads. Once again we are reminded that we have one of the most varied and beautiful coastlines on Africa's outside edge.

Dispatch #239 – Day 446 and 447

The beauty of the Garden Route unfolds, Sedgefield, the Wilderness, Victoria Bay and over the Groot and Klein Brak rivers. We gaze out to sea from the mouth of Bats' Cave below the Cape St Blaize lighthouse. Below us is historic Mossel

THE WILD COAST OF PONDOLAND

The whale crier at Hermanus – the beauty of our own coast is unbelievable.

Bay, where we have the scroll stamped with the seal from the Post Office Tree. Bartolomeu Dias, unaware that he'd in fact rounded the Cape of Good Hope, sailed into this bay in 1488 on the festival day of St Blaize and stopped for fresh water. As a result they named the bay *Aguada de São Brás,* meaning 'the watering place of St Blaize'. Vasco da Gama stopped here too, before discovering the route to India.

Chasing our deadline, the Landies one behind the other, we follow Fred Orban's Oystercatcher Trail past Boggomsbaai, Vleesbaai, Kanonpunt and the mouth of the Gourits River. Then it's on to Stilbaai and Witsand where we watch the whales breaching behind the waves in St Sebastian Bay before we cross the Breede River at Malgas where the ferry's broken and local farmer Brian Porter and his golden retriever take us across in his tin boat. We arrive at De Hoop Nature Reserve in the cold, where Sonja Chadwick and Sanet Stemmet are there to meet us at the gate. After 447 days on expedition it's luxury in the fynbos. We have great accommodation in Cape Dutch-style cottages and more *boeregasvryheid* along with a full moon. I battle to sleep – it's all happening too fast.

Dispatch #240 – Day 448

Up before sunrise, Bruce's voice crackles over the radio. '*Is this the second to last morning on expedition?*' '*Yes,*' comes my reply. '*Day 448,*' adds Ross. From Koppie Alleen we look out over a bay that stretches from Cape Infanta to just east of Arniston. The view is reflected in Peter Chadwick's sea-specked sunglasses. Peter is with the World Wildlife Fund marine programme and knows this coast like the back of his hand. We look out over the bay, excited to see breaching, tail-slapping Southern Right whales – they are in every direction. 'Up to 40% of the world's population of Southern Rights breed in this bay,' explains Peter. 'It might be just a small piece of the South African coastline but in a world context it's huge and shows the burden of what we as South Africans carry on our shoulders in terms of protecting these special places.' This is one of the greatest places in the world to observe this incredible marine life spectacle. We wave goodbye to Peter Chadwick and his team. Move, move, move – the coast of Africa seems endless.

We follow the sand dunes, white against the green fynbos, through the Overberg missile testing range, past Skipskop to the fishing cottages at Kassiesbaai for more outside edge scroll signings. The bay and town of Arniston are named after an 1815 shipwreck, although the locals refer to this little town as Waenhuiskrans, after a cliff with a massive limestone cave close by which is apparently big enough for a wagon plus oxen. We've got a wicked coastline with an average of one wreck per kilometre. Outside the shipwreck museum in Bredasdorp schoolchildren and teachers line the road to welcome the expedition and sign the outside edge scroll. Eben Human, who has religiously printed our expedition dispatches in *Die Burger* newspaper, is there to welcome us. There's yet more *boeregasvryheid*, and the tables groan with the weight of *koeksisters*, *melktert* and sandwiches (we still can't get over the taste of fresh white bread). Bellies full, it's back along the outside edge keeping out of each other's dust, over cattle grids, past reed-thatched and white-walled Dutch farm cottages, along narrow gravel roads, seeing ostriches and blue cranes in green fields.

With flashing lights and a wailing siren, a red-and-yellow National Sea Rescue Land Rover escorts us into Struisbaai, said to be the largest stretch of uninterrupted sand beach in South Africa. More schoolchildren sing and wave. With TV and press present at Cape Agulhas, where the two oceans meet, we hand over the three 'conservation stones' taken from the most westerly, northerly and easterly tips of Africa to Ettienne Fourie, manager of Agulhas National Park, and Richard Mitchell, the mayor. The stones will be kept in the museum at the Cape Agulhas lighthouse, surely one of the most beautiful on the entire coast of Africa. Completed in December 1848, it is styled on the famous Pharos lighthouse of Alexandria in Egypt. In the early years, oil from the fat-tailed sheep in the area was burned to fuel the light.

Dispatch #241 – Madiba's Birthday, 12 Hours Left

It's early morning on day 449. The Cape Agulhas lighthouse still flashes a warning out to sea as we line the Landies up outside the Tip of Africa Guest House for a farewell ceremony with Derrick and Petra Burger who have hosted us so warmly. Here it's not malaria, bandits, unexploded landmines or the strain of the long journey that threaten to destroy us, it's *boeregasvryheid*! We're slowly being killed with kindness from all these wonderful people. Last night had been a long one over the road at Okkie van Wyk's Zuidste Kaap bar. I told a few stories, which included the one of the King of Voodoo in Benin signing the Scroll of Peace and Goodwill in the sacred forest. Quite unimpressed, a fisherman had mumbled, '*O God, die duiwel het ook die boek geteken.*' ('Oh lord, the devil also signed the book.')

Beautiful coloured schoolchildren at Elim message the scroll with the words: 'Happy birthday Madiba'. The history of this coast is written on their little faces. A mole-hilled track bounces and shakes the overworked Land Rovers through the fynbos down to Quoin Point. 'There are these small abalone poacher's tracks everywhere,' says Alwyn van Wyk, a wonderful character who works with the anti-poaching unit. He spent time with us at the beginning of the expedition and is now helping us at the end. It's a race against the clock. We're still determined to empty the calabash at last light. It must be on Madiba's birthday – we owe it to the great man. We carry on past Buffelsjagsbaai, Shell Point and Kleinbaai to the Danger Point lighthouse where Land Rover owners flash their lights in a greeting – they heard we were coming and have gathered to wish us well. It was off this point that the *Birkenhead*, then the largest iron-clad ship in the Royal Navy, came to her famous end on the night of 25 February 1852. It was a wreck that immortalised the words 'women and children first', as although 445 people died on the *Birkenhead*, every women and child was saved. Alwyn phones ahead for fish and chips at Gansbaai and we eat them as we hug the coast – there's chip fat all over the steering wheel. Gansbaai is famous for great white shark-cage diving, Hermanus for whale-watching, and Onrus, Kleinmond and Betty's Bay are popular holiday resorts. The beauty of this piece of Africa's outside edge is truly remarkable; you have to have gone the full circle to appreciate the splendour of our own coastline. We hug the outside edge past Hangklip, Pringle Bay, Rooiels, Koeëlbaai and on to Gordon's Bay and the Strand where more Land Rovers of well-wishers join the convoy.

Marks on the Landy sun visor, a pebble in the pocket, a Zulu calabash and a Scroll of Peace and Goodwill … we're almost there.

WE EMPTY THE CONTENTS OF THE CALABASH BACK INTO THE COLD SOUTH ATLANTIC – WE'VE MADE IT!

hundreds of campfires and river crossings, buckets of sweat, loads of laughs and thousands of lives saved and improved through this adventure to track Africa's outside edge. It ends in just a few seconds as we all place our hands on the much-travelled calabash of seawater taken from this point 449 days ago. We remove the stopper and shiver with cold as it glugs slowly back into the cold South Atlantic. We hug, kiss and shake hands. Captain Morgan is tapped from the secret tank under my Landy, and we raise our mugs in a salute to Mama Afrika – WE'VE MADE IT!

It's 4 p.m. on day 449. Looking across False Bay we can see the outline of Cape Point – so close yet so far. Already late afternoon clouds are covering the sun, so headlights go on. The wind howls and tugs at the Landies as we race down Baden Powell Drive, the shacks of Khayelitsha on our right. The waves of False Bay break a few metres to our left – we couldn't be closer to Africa's outside edge if we tried. There's a traffic snarl-up in front. A police van has crashed into a car. 'Phone the gate,' I tell Mashozi, 'see if they will stay open.'

Into Muizenberg we rush, past the colourful beach huts, the railway line on the left. Men in yellow reflective jackets wave red flags – bloody roadworks. We speed on through St James and picture-postcard-perfect Kalk Bay. The Cape Point gatehouse phones back. Yes, they'll stay open. Our tyres squeal through the curves. We're through Fish Hoek and historic Simon's Town. A couple of African penguins wobble across the road. 'Slow down,' warns Mashozi as we climb up through the curves with cliffs falling away to our left. The Cape of Good Hope officials urge us through the gates with waves and smiles. There's a long line of Land Rover lights behind us. '*We're all together*,' comes Ross's voice over the radio, '*let's go*.' There's a flash from the Cape Point lighthouse, and with just a few minutes remaining before sunset the convoy turns hard right and drops down to *Cabo da Boa Esperanza*.

Ross shoots ahead and sets up the camera. The team bundles out of the Land Rovers. We slip and slide over the time-washed rocks and long tubes of black-green kelp. We feel humbled: 449 days, 64 327 kilometres, millions of tyre revolutions, tens of thousands of potholes and corrugations,

A SPECIAL THANKS TO ALL THOSE WHO MADE THE OUTSIDE EDGE HAPPEN

The next day, led by a team of traditional dancers, with lights on and hazards flashing, our battered Landies creep through the stone tunnel and into the courtyard of historic Cape Town Castle, where more than 500 well-wishers have gathered to welcome us home. Into the crowd parachutes adventurer Mike Rumble; he'd jumped from a helicopter armed with a symbolic mosquito net and a congratulatory message from Archbishop Desmond Tutu. Carte Blanche TV presenter Derek Watts is the MC. It's a great celebration but our nerves are cracked and we're very emotional.

Later, down at the V&A Waterfront, I fiddle with the pebble in my pocket. Beautiful Table Mountain looms large in the background. In the foreground stand four larger-than-life bronze statues of South African Nobel Peace Prize laureates: Nelson Mandela, FW de Klerk, Archbishop Desmond Tutu and Albert Luthuli. Chiselled into the paving stones below are the words '*UMUNTU NGUMUNTU NGABANTU* – A PERSON IS A PERSON THROUGH OTHER PEOPLE'. Our outside edge journey only succeeded because of all the wonderful people, you know who you are, who pushed the expedition along. *Siyabonga, asante sana, salama* and *kwaheri*. Until the next one.

2008–2009

CHEERS & THANKS AGAIN
Kingsley Holgate
AND THE EXPEDITION TEAM.

South Africa – Tembe-Tsonga fish traps

Glossary

akwaaba – welcome (Ghanaian)
alhumdillah – thank God (Arabic)
asante sana – thanks very much (Swahili)
assalām ʻalaikum – Muslim greeting meaning 'peace be upon you' (Arabic)
auf Wiedersehen – goodbye (German)
baksheesh – a tip/bribe (Persian)
biltong – South African dried salted meat, usually flavoured with coriander seeds
bliksemed – hit (Afrikaans)
boa noite – good night (Portuguese)
boeregasvryheid – Afrikaner hospitality (Afrikaans)
boeremeisie – farm girl (Afrikaans)
boerewors – South African sausage (Afrikaans)
boerseun – farm boy (Afrikaans)
bokkoms – small, dried fish (Afrikaans)
bon courage – 'good courage', meaning 'be strong' (French)
bonne chance – good luck (French)
bossies – South African slang for 'crazy' (Afrikaans)
braai – South African barbecue (Afrikaans)
Bratwurst – Typical German sausage (German)
Carnets de Passage – document to permit vehicular border crossings (French)
cerveja – beer (Portuguese)
Das Südwester Lied – The South West Song, unofficial German anthem for South West Africa, especially Namibia
djellabah – loose, hooded cloak (pronounced galabaya) (Arabic)
dop – slang for alcohol (noun) or the act of drinking alcohol (verb) (Afrikaans)
Eisbein – German dish of pork shank (German)
fynbos – low-lying bush/flowers indigenous to South Africa (Afrikaans)
Guten Tag, wie geht's? – Good day, how's it going? (German)
halala – congratulations (Arabic)
hambani kahle – go well (isiZulu)
howzit – South African greeting (Afrikaans)
inshallah – God willing (Arabic)
ithunga – wooden, milking pail (isiZulu)

Izinthaba zo Khahlamba – meaning 'Barrier of Spears', isiZulu name for the Drakensberg Mountains
Jägermeister – German digestif spirit
Jamahiriya – State of the Masses (Arabic)
jolling – South African slang for 'partying'
kaalvoet – barefoot (Afrikaans)
kak – shit; vulgar South African slang commonly used to mean 'shitty' or 'trouble' or to express distaste
karibuni – welcome (Swahili)
klapped – hit/knocked (Afrikaans)
koeksister – very sweet plaited confectionery, deep-fried and dipped in syrup (Afrikaans)
kwaheri, safari njema – farewell, good journey (Swahili)
lobola – African tradition; groom's payment for his bride
mafuta – fat (Swahili)
mayebabo – an isiZulu phrase that conveys surprise or dismay, like 'alas!'
Médecins Sans Frontières – Doctors without Borders (French)
melktert – South African milk tart (Afrikaans)
merci beaucoup – thanks very much (French)
mgonjwa – sick (Swahili)
mieliemeel – corn flour (Afrikaans)
moskonfyt – grape syrup (Afrikaans)
Nagmaal – communion (Afrikaans)
naartjie – citrus fruit, also called mandarin (Afrikaans)
Nederlander – Dutch national (Dutch)
ngiya khumbula ekhaya – it reminds me of home (isiZulu)
nogal – expression meaning 'at that' or 'rather' (Afrikaans)
nyama – meat, flesh (Swahili)
obrigado – thank you (Portuguese)
oom – uncle (Afrikaans)
padkos – 'road food'; snacks to eat in the car (Afrikaans)
panga – East African broad, heavy knife (Swahili)
pão – Portuguese rolls made with potato
pap – South African maize porridge (Afrikaans)
phutu pap – a crumbly version of *pap*, eaten mainly by the Basotho, Bantu and Afrikaner people (Sothu)
Poste Frontière – border post (French)

potjie – black cooking pot; also the name of the stews cooked in the pot (Afrikaans)
rafiki – friend (Swahili)
Renosterkoffie – Captain Morgan rum and coffee (Afrikaans)
route nacionale – national road (French)
safari kubwa sana – very big journey (Swahili)
safari njema – have a good trip (Swahili)
sangoma – witch doctor (isiZulu)
Sauerkraut – German dish made from fermented cabbage
shukran – thank you (Arabic)
siyabonga – thank you (isiZulu)
sjamboked – hit with a sjambok, which is a traditional heavy leather whip made from rhino or hippo hide (Afrikaans)
stoep – porch (Afrikaans)
Strandlopers – indigenous people of southern Africa who gathered food from the sea; 'beach walkers' (Afrikaans)

strandveld – a type of fynbos found on the western coastal plains of South Africa (Afrikaans)
tannie – auntie (Afrikaans)
taxi-brousse – public bush taxi (French)
terra firma – solid ground (Latin)
tjops – lambchops (Afrikaans)
totsiens – goodbye (Afrikaans)
très difficile – very difficult (French)
tuisgebakte boerebeskuit – homemade rusks (Afrikaans)
tutaonana kesho – see you tomorrow (Swahili)
wa 'alaikum assalām – the response to *assalām 'alaikum*, meaning 'and upon you be peace' (Arabic)
wag-'n-bietjie bushes – 'wait-a-bit' bushes which have inward facing thorns, so you may enter but not escape (Afrikaans)
ware Suid-Afrikaanse braai/regte braai – real South African barbecue (Afrikaans)

Bibliography

Berens, K., R. Blackmore, P. Buckley, D. Clark, K. Densley, M. Dunford, G. Howard, R. Koss, M. Milton, A. Murchie, L. Ratcliffe, A.M. Rogers, A. Rosenberg, F. Sandham, C. Saunders, S. Schafer, A. Shaw, H. Slaton, H. Smith, J. Staines, O. Swift, Y. Takagaki, P. Thomas, A. Turner & C. Wilkinson. 2003. *The Rough Guide to West Africa*. 4th edition. London & New York: Rough Guides Ltd.

Briggs, P. 2002. *Bradt Tanzania: With Zanzibar, Pemba & Mafia Island*. 4th edition. Buckinghamshire: Bradt Travel Guides.

Crowther, G., H. Finlay, G. Cole, D. Else, P. Hämäläinen, A. Jousiffe, L. Logan, J. Murray, A. Newton, D. Simonis, D. Swaney & D. Willett. 1998. *Africa: A Lonely Planet Shoestring Guide*. 7th edition. Hawthorn: Lonely Planet Publications.

Erapi, G. 2007. 'Driving into Mass Graves'. *BusinessDay*. p. 15.

Erasmus, B.J.B. 1996. *On Route in South Africa*. Jeppestown: Jonathan Ball Publishers.

Fraser, S. 2003. *National Geographic African Adventure Atlas*. Witney: Maps International.

Hochschild, A. 1999. *King Leopold's Ghost: A Story of Greed, Terror, and Heroism in Colonial Africa*. Boston: Mariner Books.

Hodd, M. 2002. *Footprint East Africa Handbook*. 7th edition. Bath: Footprint Handbooks.

Kapuściński, R. 2001. *Another Day of Life*. New York: Vintage Books USA.

Khayyám, O. 1997. *Rubáiyát of Omar Khayyám*. Translated by Edward Fitzgerald. San Diego: Wordsworth Editions.

Marsh, J.H. 2006. *Skeleton Coast*. Windhoek: Kuiseb Verlag.

Newton, A. 1994. *Lonely Planet Central Africa, A Travel Survivor Kit*. 2nd edition. Hawthorn: Lonely Planet Publications.

Palin, M. 2002. *Sahara*. London: Weidenfeld & Nicolson.

Rattray, D. 2007. *A Soldier-Artist in Zululand: William Whitelocke Lloyd and the Anglo-Zulu War of 1879*. KwaZulu-Natal: Rattray Publications.

Stannard, D. (ed.) 2007. *Insight Guide to Morocco*. 6th edition. Singapore: APA Publications GmbH & Co Verlag KG.

Velton, R. 2004. *Mali: The Bradt Travel Guide*. 2nd edition. Buckinghamshire: Bradt Travel Guides.

Wayne, S. 1990. *Lonely Planet Egypt & the Sudan: A Travel Survivor Kit*. 2nd edition. Hawthorn: Lonely Planet Publications.

Published by Struik Travel & Heritage
(an imprint of Random House Struik (Pty) Ltd)
Company Reg. No. 1966/003153/07
80 McKenzie Street, Cape Town, 8001
PO Box 1144, Cape Town, 8000, South Africa

First published in 2009, Reprinted in 2009

Copyright © in published edition: Random House Struik 2009
Copyright © in text, maps, sketches: Kingsley Holgate, except map on front cover and p. 4 MapStudio 2009
Copyright © in photographs: Bruce Leslie, except p. 239 (bottom) Andrey Bizyukin, goldenmedia.1@gmail.com 2009

Publisher: Claudia Dos Santos
Managing editor: Roelien Theron
Editor: Leah van Deventer
Designer: Catherine Coetzer
Cover designer: Robin Cox
Project coordinator: Alana Bolligelo
Proofreader: Joy Clack

Reproduction by Hirt & Carter Cape (Pty) Ltd
Printed and bound by CTP Book Printers

ISBN 978 1 77007 504 7
10 9 8 7 6 5 4 3 2

All rights reserved. No part of this publication may be reproduced, stored in a retrieval system or transmitted, in any form or by any means, electronic, mechanical, photocopying, recording or otherwise, without the prior written permission of the publishers and the copyright holder(s).

Every effort has been made to trace copyright holders. The author and publisher would appreciate information in tracing those who have not already been credited, and omissions will be rectified in future editions. Furthermore, while every effort has been made to ensure the information in this book was correct at time of going to press, some details may since have changed. The author and publisher accept no responsibility for any loss, injury, damage or inconvenience sustained by any person using this book.

Please send any comments or updates to:
africaoutsideedge@randomstruik.co.za